THE NEW DELHI REPORT

The New Delhi Report

The Third Assembly of the
World Council of Churches
1961

ASSOCIATION PRESS
New York

Published in the U.S.A. by
ASSOCIATION PRESS
291 Broadway
New York 7, N.Y.

FIRST PUBLISHED 1962
PRINTED IN GREAT BRITAIN

PREFACE

THIS Official Report gives as full an account of the proceedings of the Third Assembly as is possible in the available space. In the chapter entitled 'The New Delhi Story', Dr Samuel McCrea Cavert gives a comprehensive day-by-day narrative of the proceedings of the Assembly.

The Assembly met in three types of session designated 'General Session', 'Business Session' and 'Deliberative Session' (*see* pages 333 and 440-3 below). The proceedings in General Sessions are described in Dr Cavert's narrative account and listed in Appendix 5 (pages 394-5), but are not otherwise reported in this volume.

The chapters on the sections and committees of the Assembly contain the full texts of the official reports and summaries of the discussions on them in plenary session. As a rule the action of the Assembly is printed first in italics; next the text is given in its final form including all amendments accepted by the Assembly; the summaries of the discussions follow, rearranged in most cases for convenience of reference, beginning with general comments and then following the order of the paragraphs of the text finally accepted.

The introductory addresses on the general theme and on the sections and the speeches by Bishop Newbigin and Dr W. A. Visser 't Hooft preceding the act of integration are not included in this volume but have been published in full in *The Ecumenical Review*, vol. xiv, no. 2, for January 1962. Some of the other addresses given in general sessions of the Assembly and the texts of messages received from the Ecumenical Patriarch, the Patriarch of Moscow and the Church of Ethiopia have also been published in *The Ecumenical Review*.

Full records of all that was said in plenary sessions of the Assembly and records of the proceedings of all the committees of the Assembly are available for reference in the archives of the World Council in Geneva.

W. A. VISSER 'T HOOFT
Editor

CONTENTS

I

THE NEW DELHI STORY

By Samuel McCrea Cavert

First Day: Sunday, November 19

Beneath sunny Indian skies, the Third Assembly of the World Council of Churches opened in New Delhi with a great service of worship on Sunday morning, November 19. A congregation of several thousands gathered in the vast Shamiana (tent) erected for the occasion close to the Conference hall known as Vigyan Bhavan (House of Learning) and overflowed into the open spaces beyond. As they came together for prayer and praise and thanksgiving, they felt themselves part of a far greater multitude around the earth who were united on this day in world-wide intercession.

As the procession of more than a thousand official participants moved to their seats at 10.30 o'clock for the opening service of worship of the first assembly to be held on Asian soil, they found themselves in a setting that was distinctively Indian. To meet out-of-doors under a Shamiana was in itself an Indian experience. The hangings of the Shamiana were of beautiful Indian design. A choir provided a prelude in the form of Indian Christian lyrics accompanied by Indian music. No one could fail to realize that something new was happening in the life of the World Council.

If the setting was characteristically Asian, the occasion was manifestly ecumenical. The procession included men and women from every race and every continent. Their colourful national or ecclesiastical costumes, variegated beyond description, bore visual testimony to the fact that never before had there been a Christian gathering representative of so wide a diversity both of historical background and of geographical extent. Among the nearly 200 churches represented were some bodies that were the most ancient in Christian history and others that were fruits of missionary work of the last century.

Opening Worship

The theme of the Assembly, 'Jesus Christ, the Light of the World', was the pervasive note in the opening service of worship. After the hymn 'Praise to the Lord! the Almighty, the King of creation!', Metropolitan Juhanon Mar Thoma (Mar Thoma Syrian Church of Malabar) called the people to prayer in these fitting words:

> We have come together in this place out of many nations because Christ who is the light of the world has shined in our hearts to give the light of the knowledge of the glory of God, and because he has set us as lights in the world and bidden us let our light shine.

In the prayers that followed there was confession that 'we have hidden from men the true light of the world'. The act of thanksgiving, led by Dr Christian G. Baeta (Presbyterian Church of Ghana) included gratitude to God for 'calling us out of darkness into his marvellous light'.

The Old Testament lesson (Isaiah 40.1-11) was read in French by the Rev. Raymond L. Rajoelisolo (Evangelical Church of Madagascar) and a responsive reading of Psalm 122 was led by Bishop Uberto Sante Barbieri (Methodist Church, Argentine). The New Testament lesson (I Peter 2.1-10) was read in German by Bishop Otto Dibelius (Evangelical Church in Germany). The congregation then joined in the hymn, 'Upon thy great Church universal'.

The sermon was preached by the Rev. U Ba Hmyin (Baptist Convention, Burma) after reading the Prologue of St John's Gospel and our Lord's word 'I am the light of the world' (John 8.12). In describing the response of different peoples to the universal Christ, he said:

> When Christian witnesses moved out of the world of Jewish thought and understanding into the wider world of Greek language, thought and life, it was one of the most profound changes and crises of the Church. Greek thought, forms, language, and modes of apprehension were then taken over, and have since become part of the very life of the Church. . . . Now the gospel has taken root in Asia. The question before us is: Is it possible to make the radical break from purely Western ways of thought, to do in Asia what first-century Christians did in the Greek world? . . . This does not mean a disregard of the Christian heritage of the West. It does mean taking it seriously in an Asian setting.

In interpreting the keen concern of Asian churches for unity the preacher said:

> Our divided condition is partly due to the historical ways in which the Gospel has come to us. But our continuance in these divisions, after we have come to see them as a hindrance to the Gospel, can no longer be excused on historical grounds. The ecumenical movement has grown with great force in Asia because Christians have come to see that in Christ they really belong to each other as they belong to him.

The congregation then confessed its faith by uniting in the Nicene Creed, led by Archbishop Iakovos (Ecumenical Patriarchate of Constantinople), in the original Greek. This was followed by an act of intercession, conducted by the Rt. Rev. Henry Knox Sherrill (Episcopal, USA), including prayers for India, for the peoples of the world, for all who work for peace and strive to remove poverty, disease and injustice, for the Church throughout the world and for its renewal and its unity.

After the offering, devoted to needs of refugees in many lands, and the hymn, 'O come, O come, Emmanuel', Metropolitan Juhanon pronounced the benediction. As the procession left the Shamiana the choir again sang Indian Christian lyrics.

Opening Session

In the afternoon the first General Session was convened in the Vigyan Bhavan. At the front of the spacious auditorium was hung a large blue banner inscribed with the single word OIKOUMENE and displaying the symbol of the ship of salvation, with masthead in the form of the cross, upon the sea of life.

Bishop Otto Dibelius, venerable co-president of the Council, was in the chair. After invoking God's blessing he introduced Bishop Lesslie Newbigin, General Secretary of the International Missionary Council, who spoke upon the theme, 'The Missionary Dimension of the Ecumenical Movement'. Bishop Newbigin stressed the fact that the ecumenical movement owes its existence largely to the missionary movement and that the impulse to go into all the world as witnesses to Christ is always essential to the Church. He rejoiced in the prospective integration of the International Missionary Council and the World Council of Churches as a vital contribution both to the missionary life of the Church and to the ecumenical character of the Christian mission. He recalled the prophetic words spoken by J. H. Oldham as long ago as 1920 in outlining possible forms of an International Missionary Council:

> It is becoming less and less possible to discuss missionary matters without representatives of the churches in the mission field, and any organization that may be created will probably have before very long to give way to something that may represent the beginning of a league of churches.

After calling attention to the danger of a false use of the word 'ecumenical' which omits the missionary dimension, he affirmed that mission and unity are 'two sides of the same reality, or rather two ways of describing the same action of the living Lord who wills that all men should be drawn to himself'. He then spoke of characteristic contributions of the foreign missionary movement which should find their place in the life of the integrated Council. The first is the 'continuing and costly concern for individual people and places, expressed in sustained intercessory prayer, sacrificial giving, and personal commitment'. The second is the concern 'to *go* to places where men live without the knowledge of the Gospel, and there to be so identified with these men that they may hear and see, in their own idiom and in the forms of their own life, the grace and power of the Lord Jesus Christ'. In this connection Bishop Newbigin expressed the hope that 'the churchmen of Asia and Africa, having studied the spiritual situation of some of the older churches . . . will be moved to send missionaries to Europe and America to make the Gospel credible to the pagan masses of those continents'. Thirdly, Bishop Newbigin spoke of the changes which integration must involve in both parties:

> For those who have been traditionally related to the IMC, this means a willingness to acknowledge that the particular forms and relationships characteristic of the missionary activity of the past two centuries must be held constantly open to the new insights that God may have to give us in the wider fellowship . . . For the churches which constitute the World Council this means the acknowledgment that the missionary task is no less central to the life of the Church than the pursuit of renewal and unity.

An address was next given on 'The Calling of the World Council of Churches' by Dr W. A. Visser 't Hooft, General Secretary. In a panoramic survey he interpreted the main developments during the seven years since the second assembly in Evanston, called attention to the increasing activities of the Council, indicated major issues to be considered by the Third Assembly, and stressed the call to a deeper unity among all the churches. Describing the World Council as a body 'of considerable fragility' because of its youth, the variety of its membership and its nature as a free association without any constitutional authority over its members, he went on to say:

> The first years of its life have fallen within one of the most troubled periods of history, in which ideological, inter-continental and inter-racial conflicts create acute tensions which have a bearing not only on international relations but also on the relations of churches and therefore on the life of the World Council itself. In spite of all this the World Council continues to live and grow . . . That we are allowed to assemble today as participants in a movement which is very much alive is due to that mysterious Will that constrains us to hold on to each other in spite of all that divides us.

He summarized his presentation in three points: (1) the recognition that 'hitherto has the Lord helped us', (2) the challenge to 'enlarge the place of thy tent', and (3) the call 'with one voice to glorify the God and Father of our Lord Jesus Christ'.

After citing strong statements by Archbishop Söderblom, founder of the Life and Work Movement, and Bishop Brent, at the first Faith and Order Conference in 1927, on the necessary connection between the unity of the Christians and the evangelization of the nations, and referring to John R. Mott's life work, Dr Visser 't Hooft said that integration was the

> natural outcome of a spiritual process which has been going on for a long time and gathering momentum . . . The integrated body will like the World Council before integration be a body rooted in and directed by the churches themselves . . . But there will be a widening of horizons . . . We are today forced to rethink the meaning of the missionary and apostolic calling of the Church in every land.

Dr Visser 't Hooft spoke of 'the importance of the fact that a number of large Eastern Orthodox Churches desire to join our fellowship'.

> In this way a tremendous opportunity is offered to us to ensure that a real spiritual dialogue will take place . . . if we accept this opportunity our ecumenical task will not become easier, but we will surely be greatly enriched.

Speaking of new developments with regard to the Roman Catholic Church, Dr Visser 't Hooft said that since the beginning of the World Council there had been contacts with individual Roman Catholics, but that today

> we have in addition to these contacts the unofficial but most useful relation with the special Secretariat set up by Pope John XXIII to promote the unity of Christendom.

He welcomed the presence at the Assembly of five observers authorized by the Secretariat. It had been possible through the Secretariat to make known the World Council's concern that the question of the Roman Catholic attitude on religious freedom should be clarified by the coming second Vatican Council. With regard to the relation between the Assembly and this Council he recalled Professor Schlink's words:

> It would undoubtedly mean much for Christendom and the world, if it became clear . . . that these councils do not meet against each other and that each does not seek its own advantage, but seeks only to serve the Lord Jesus Christ.

Integration of IMC and WCC

A business session followed—with Archbishop Iakovos, one of the presidents of the Council, presiding—for the purpose of taking the final official steps in the integration of the World Council of Churches and the International Missionary Council. Dr Christian Baeta, chairman of the IMC, reported the action of its Administrative Committee approving the creation of a Commission and a Division of World Mission and Evangelism in the World Council of Churches to carry on in the future the work of the IMC. He further reported the action of formal approval of integration taken by the Assembly of the International Missionary Council, on November 17-18, 1961.

Dr Franklin Clark Fry, as chairman of the Central Committee of the World Council of Churches, presented its recommendations for amendments to the Constitution and Rules of the World Council designed to effect the integration of the International Missionary Council into the World Council (see pages 56-60). Without a dissenting vote the plan as a whole was adopted, and the Archbishop thereupon declared that 'these two Councils are now united in one body with the name of the World Council of Churches'. Dr Henry P. van Dusen, chairman of the Joint Committee which had carried the detailed responsibility for working out the method of integration, led in an act of worship and thanksgiving for the happy consummation of the study and co-operation of many years.

The General Theme

At six o'clock there was the first general session of the integrated body, presided over by Metropolitan Juhanon Mar Thoma. An interpretative address on the assembly theme 'Jesus Christ, the Light of the World', was given by Bishop Gottfried Noth (Evangelical Church in Germany). He said, in part:

> What unites us within the World Council of Churches, and what has brought us together in New Delhi from all over the world, is expressed in the theme: Jesus Christ, the Light of the World . . . If we understand the theme rightly, it will be the determining centre of all our intercession, thought, discussion and action here in New Delhi, even if we do not actually quote it very frequently . . .
>
> The darkness in which the world lives is not an illusion, which one merely has to see through. It is much worse than we usually think: the darkness exercises dominion over us (Col. 1.13) and we are under its sway. Its spell cannot be broken simply by good will. The fellowship between God and man is broken, and this makes the world dark, whether it notices it or not. In the full authority of God's grace, Christ establishes a new fellowship with God, and this makes him the Light of the World. The darkness is driven away, not by a new doctrine of God but by his act of redemption.

Bishop Noth then pointed out some of the ways in which this theme bears on Christian witness, Christian service and Christian unity. In a moving conclusion, especially significant because of its relation to the difficult experience of the Church in East Germany, he said:

> The social revolutions, the technical development, the problem of war and peace, the fear and distress of countless people call for

the love and faith of those who know that God so loved this world that he gave his only begotten Son for it . . . We Christians have not been promised that we shall be the cleverest politicians, scientists, technicians or economists . . . We can rely only on one thing; when Christians face the distress of the world in the name of Christ and in his love, then he sends his light, and the spell of sin—which blinds both the wise and the foolish—is broken. How far the light will penetrate is in God's hand.

In the brief discussion that followed, Bishop A. H. Zulu (Anglican, South Africa) suggested that in the darkness which envelops the relations of nation and races the great question is how to help them see what the light of Christ calls for in local situations.

The evening prayers were led by Principal J. Russell Chandran (Church of South India).

SECOND DAY: MONDAY, NOVEMBER 20

The Rev. Edward Rogers (Methodist Church, Great Britain) conducted the opening worship, including a brief sermon based on St Paul's injunction, 'Bear ye one another's burdens and so fulfil the law of Christ' (Gal. 6.2). He reminded the Assembly that the amazing growth of the Church in the first centuries was not due to eloquence in preaching or to intellectual skill but to the love and mutual helpfulness in the Christian community. He suggested that new strength comes to the Church today as it is coming again to care for people more than for its own position, illustrated, e.g. by interchurch aid and service to refugees.

A mood of high expectation pervaded the Assembly when it convened for a business session on the morning when the applications of twenty-three churches for membership were to be considered. The Rev. Dr Ernest A. Payne, vice-chairman of the Central Committee, was in the chair.

On recommendation of the Central Committee, the Assembly approved the nominations of those who should be asked to serve on the Business Committee, on the Nominations Committee, on the Credentials Committee, and as officers of the sections on 'Witness', 'Service' and 'Unity' (see pages 395 ff.).[1]

[1] In this narrative account names of delegates serving on committees and of delegates who participated in the discussion during business and deliberative sessions are seldom given, as they usually appear in other parts of the volume.

New Members

Great interest was manifested in the applications for membership. They came from twenty-three different churches—the largest number to be received at any one time since the inauguration of the World Council in 1948. Eleven of the applications were from churches in Africa. Two were from churches in the Islands of the Pacific, the first from this region. Two were Pentecostal Churches of South America, the first from the Pentecostal family. Four were Orthodox Churches from Eastern Europe, the Orthodox Church of Russia, the Orthodox Church of Bulgaria, the Orthodox Church of Rumania, and the Orthodox Church of Poland. Notice regarding the application for membership of most of these churches had been sent to the member churches of the Council some months before the Assembly, and all the applications had the considered support of the Central Committee.

In transmitting the proposals of the Central Committee to the Assembly, Dr Visser 't Hooft emphasized the importance of the accession of eleven African churches, many from countries where the World Council had no membership. On the question of relationships with the Orthodox Churches in Eastern Europe, he said that in all the negotiations the Central Committee and its Officers had sought to give absolute priority to the question: How can the cause of Christ, and in particular the cause of Christian unity, be served best? They had been impressed by the desire of the churches in Russia for fellowship with other Christians. The Russian Church leaders had made a thorough study of the work of the Council. The applications from the two Pentecostal Churches had been received 'with deep interest'.

The churches applying for membership in the chronological order of their applications, were as follows:

United Church of Central Africa in Rhodesia
Iglesia Pentecostal de Chile
Moravian Church in the Western Cape Province of South Africa
Eglise Evangélique en Nouvelle-Calédonie et aux Iles Loyauté
Union des Eglises Baptistes du Cameroun
Orthodox Church of Russia
United Presbyterian Church of Pakistan
Church of the Province of Uganda and Ruanda-Urundi (Anglican)

Presbyterian Church in the Cameroons
Presbyterian Church in Trinidad
Finnish Evangelical Lutheran Church of America (Suomi Synod)
Mision Iglesia Pentecostal (Chile)
Bulgarian Orthodox Church
Eglise Evangélique du Gabon
Bantu Congregational Church
Presbyterian Church of Nigeria
Rumanian Orthodox Church
Evangelical Church of North-western Tanganyika
Eglise Evangélique Manianga Matadi (Congo)
Presbyterian Church of the New Hebrides
Usambara-Digo Lutheran Church (Tanganyika)
Orthodox Church of Poland
Congregational Christian Church in Samoa.

The voting on the admission of each of these churches was carried on by written ballots of the delegations. After the ballots had been delivered to the tellers, opportunity was given for any interpretation any church might desire to make concerning its vote. For the Russian Orthodox Church in North America, Archbishop John of San Francisco stated that it had abstained from voting on the application of the Orthodox Church of Russia. Dr H. Alivisatos (Church of Greece) voiced satisfaction in the prospect of Orthodox Churches related to the Moscow Patriarchate coming into the Council. Archbishop Athenagoras of Thyateira recorded the pleasure of the Ecumenical Patriarchate in the decision of the Orthodox Churches in Russia, Bulgaria, Rumania and Poland to seek membership. The Very Rev. Ignatius Hazim (Greek Orthodox Patriarchate of Antioch) expressed a similar view. Bishop Zoltan Beky of the Hungarian Reformed Church in America explained that it had abstained from voting and hoped that the World Council would not be used as a platform for political purposes. Professor Werner Küppers, for the Old Catholic Church in Germany, expressed gratification for enlarged contacts with Orthodoxy.

The result of the balloting, as announced later, showed that each of the twenty-three churches had received far more than the necessary two-thirds majority. For the Church of Russia, for example, there were 142 affirmative votes, 3 negative, and 4 abstentions.

After the report of the tellers had been given, the chairman called the roll of the new bodies, and their designated representatives came to the platform to receive their badges and be seated as official delegates. It was a moving experience to see representatives of so many churches—from all the continents and from eight different historic confessions (Eastern Orthodox, Lutheran, Reformed, Anglican, Moravian, Congregational, Baptist and Pentecostal)—adding their strength to the ecumenical fellowship.

Work of the Central Committee

The chairman of the Central Committee, the Rev. Dr Franklin Clark Fry, made a report of his stewardship for the seven-year period since the assembly of 1954 (see page 334), commenting on and interpreting the extensive account of activities and policies outlined by the Central Committee in the published volume *Evanston to New Delhi*. In addition to a masterly objective summary, he gave intimate glimpses of ways in which the Central Committee had operated. He especially accented the principle that the member churches control the course of the World Council and that the Council's role is to be the churches' servant. On this point he said bluntly: 'The World Council not only disavowed becoming a "super-church" at its beginning at Amsterdam; its total development since then has been the most convincing refutation of the whole notion'. He voiced the judgment that some of the member churches need to make more effective structural arrangements for maintaining contacts with the Council and giving their guidance to it. He added a warm tribute to the faithfulness of the members of the Central Committee and 'the superbly gifted general secretary' and the staff for their effective and sacrificial service.

The Committee on Programme and Finance appointed by the Central Committee in 1956, which had for five years been examining the service of the Council and the provision for supporting it, made a report through the chairman, the Rev. Dr Eugene Carson Blake (see page 342). Underlying the whole report was the conviction that matters of programme and matters of finance must be considered together, not separately, and that 'all financial decisions ought to be made finally in the light of what we believe the World Council of Churches should be and do'. He voiced the judgment of the Committee that the World Council 'must at all cost avoid becoming an institution which just grows' but that 'the fear of bigness must not make us blind to the signs of the times which indicate that we live in an age of world forces' and must act accordingly. He called attention to the specific recommendations for the programme during the next period of the Council's life and for the financial support of that programme. The chairman announced that in order to give full opportunity for scrutiny of the proposals an open hearing would be held on the following day, leading up to later decisions by the Assembly on the proposals.

'*Witness and Service*'

At a general session in the afternoon presided over by Bishop Barbieri, the theme 'Called to Witness' was presented in a thoughtful address by Dr Paul D. Devanandan (Church of South India). He defined the nature of Christian witness as testifying 'to the reality of the New Creation in the Risen Christ as the one determining factor in world history which gives it significance and meaning'. He pictured each Christian congregation as representing the 'community of the New Age', and as therefore having a mission which forbids it to become self-centred or self-contained. The witness of the Church, he added, has to do with all the concerns of secular life and must be borne in the context of man's daily life and secular involvement. He gave special attention to the Christian witness in 'a world of other faiths' and urged that we 'take the dominant philosophical and religious concepts of the non-Christian faiths and make them into instruments of interpretation of the Gospel'.

In the discussion stimulated by Dr Devanandan's presentation delegates from a half-dozen different backgrounds shared, including the Rev. J. Archie Hargraves (United Church of Christ, USA), the Rev. V. D. Sahayam (Church of South India), Bishop H. J. A. Meyer (Evangelical Church of Germany), Professor George Florovsky (Ecumenical Patriarchate of Constantinople), the Rev. B. Probowinoto (Christian Church of Mid-Java) and Professor Herbert H. Trigge (Methodist Church of Australasia). The relation of Christian witness to non-Christian faiths was a focus of special interest. On the one hand it was suggested that a constructive approach to adherents of other religions will recognize that God 'has not left himself without a witness' even in the darkest places. On the other hand, it was insisted that it is not the business of the Christian to pass judgment, whether favourable or unfavourable, on other religions but only to bear witness to Christ as the only Light of the world. Another focus of interest was the idea that in order to be an effective witness a Christian must be knowledgeable not only about the Gospel but also about the secular society in which the witness is to be borne.

At the final session of the day, Bishop Sherrill presiding, Professor Masao Takenaka (United Church, Japan) presented the theme, 'Called to Service', in an address that evoked an unusually wide and alert discussion. He described the ministry of Christian service to the world as no mere adjustment to the times but as an essential sharing in Christ's ministry, as obedience to him, and as an indispensable mark of his Church. This involves 'secular engagement and participation in worldly affairs in the light of the Christian faith'. Christian service, he made clear, is not confined to the narrow limits of what is often called the spiritual side of life but is related to the whole man. He pointed to the danger of limiting Christian service to personal charity, essential as that is, and neglecting the conditions of social justice. The role of the laity in serving the Church through their ordinary secular life was strongly accented and 'the growing reaffirmation of the ministry of the laity in the world' was called 'one of the most gratifying developments' in the Church of today.

In the extended discussion that ensued much appreciation was voiced for the emphasis on Christian service as related to the wholeness of human life, and it was urged that this requires the churches to penetrate into the 'power structures' of today's world in the interest of social justice and a better international order. Another important point brought out in the discussion was the tendency toward governmental and secular monopoly of social services and the consequent importance of the Church's being very clear about the distinguishing characteristics of truly *Christian* service.

Among those who voiced appreciation for Professor Takenaka's analysis, made comments about it or raised questions elicited by it, were Dean Walter G. Muelder (Methodist, USA), Dr Bonar W. Sidjabat (Protestant Christian Batak Church), Father Makary el Souriany (Coptic Church of Egypt), Professor Egbert de Vries (Netherlands Reformed Church), Mr Valentin G. Montes (United Church of Christ in the Philippines), Principal Matthew Wakatama (Methodist, Southern Rhodesia), The Rev. Canon Frank W. Coaldrake (Church of England in Australia), Mr Mikhail Tadros (Coptic

Church of Egypt) and the Rev. Gabriel M. Setiloane (Methodist Church of South Africa).

A day of rich stimulus and inspiration ended with evening prayers conducted by the Rev. Dr Joseph L. Hromadka (Church of the Czech Brethren).

THIRD DAY: TUESDAY, NOVEMBER 21

The Assembly joined in morning worship led by Pastor Jean Kotto (Eglise Evangélique du Cameroun), who gave a meditation based on Romans 14.11-12. It was an illuminating exposition of Paul's attitude towards the 'strong' ones who felt freed from concern about the Jewish Law and the 'weak in the faith' who feared the consequences of freedom. Pastor Kotto used the passage as an illustration of the constant need for mutual charitableness of Christians toward one another's views.

At a brief business session Dr Fry in behalf of the Business Committee presented a proposal of names of those who might be asked to serve on the Committee on Message, with Mrs Kathleen Bliss as Chairman (see pages 70-71). Messages were read to the Assembly from the Ecumenical Patriarch of Constantinople, the Patriarch of Moscow and All Russia, and the Orthodox Church of Ethiopia.

The Ecumenical Patriarch Athenagoras assured the members of the Assembly of his prayers that 'Christians, regardless of their confession, may be illumined by the Christ' and emphasized that 'we are called to rediscover in the life of Christ the way of unity, and to walk in it to the end with cheerfulness, courage and hope'.

Alexis, Patriarch of Moscow, expressed great satisfaction at seeing 'the Russian Orthodox Church a member of the brotherhood of Christian churches and denominations that form the World Council of Churches'. The Russian Church, he wrote, has the 'sacred duty' of witnessing to the faith which 'has found such deep reflection in her services, in the wealth of spiritual experience she has amassed during the ten centuries of her work, and the innumerable manifestations of holiness that have marked that work'. Making this witness does not involve 'proselytizing or other such non-Christian acts', but 'in a spirit of brotherly love and understanding helping other churches to achieve success in their urge towards catholicity'. The Russian Orthodox Church is grateful to God for helping disunited Christendom to realize the sinfulness of division; she is prepared to strengthen the Orthodox witness of her sister-churches in the field of Faith and Order, and to co-operate in the work of all the other parts of the Council. She expects the World Council to display 'an ever-increasing purposefulness' in meeting the 'daily needs of human society' on the basis of the Gospels. In carrying out 'their duty of peace-making' in a 'world full of tension' all Christians must 'resolutely call upon the leaders of states to start negotiations with the aim of achieving at last agreement on universal and complete disarmament, with effective international control'.

In a considerably longer statement on behalf of the Ethiopian Church, which could only be read in part, the Abuna Theophilos commented on a number of issues before the Assembly, including pleas for the rewording of doctrinal formulae where these have given rise to misunderstanding and conflict, for a missionary revival in the Church which will take full account of 'the silent witness of the worshipping community' and avoid 'sheep-stealing', for close co-operation with the state in matters of community development, and for a clear demonstration by all churches in Africa that Christianity is not just a 'white man's religion'.

'Unity'

A general session followed, chaired by Archbishop Iakovos, devoted to the theme, 'Called to Unity'. The Rev. Dr Joseph Sittler (United Lutheran in America) made a thought-provoking address (based on Colossians 1.15-20) which was welcomed with enthusiasm and having as its keynote a 'cosmic Christology', the vision of 'all things' as being redeemed in Christ and finding their centre in him. The whole of nature, as well as of human history, he held, is included in the saving work of Christ and the promise of grace. He said, as a partial summary of the main point:

> A doctrine of redemption is meaningful only when it swings within the larger orbit of a doctrine of creation. For God's creation of earth cannot be redeemed in any intelligible sense of the word apart from a doctrine of the cosmos which is man's home, his definite place, the theatre of his selfhood under God, in co-operation with his neighbour, and in caring-relationship with nature.

Dr Sittler concluded with an eloquent plea for a 'contemporary Christology expanded to the dimensions of the New Testament vision' as a basis for a fuller unity.

In the ensuing discussion there was some difference of view as to whether the 'cosmic approach' would be especially helpful in dealing with unity. Is not the conception too broad, it was asked, to be useful and should not attention be directed to man rather than to the whole world of nature? Will not unity be most likely to be found by drawing together in a confrontation with mankind in need of the Light? The further question was raised by an Eastern Orthodox delegate whether attention ought not to be given to the unseen world, both angelic and demonic, as well as to the visible world.

The participants in the discussion reflected a wide spectrum of both confessional and geographical interest. They included Professor R. R. Hartford (Church of Ireland), Professor Colin W. Williams (Methodist Church of Australasia), Professor Henri d'Espine (Swiss Reformed), the Very Rev. Jerome Kotsonis (Church of Greece), Dr Georg F. Vicedom (Evangelical Church of Germany), the Rev. James T. Crozier (Baptist Union of New Zealand), Archbishop John of San Francisco (Russian Orthodox in America), Father Paul Verghese (Orthodox Syrian Church), Professor Hendrikus Berkhof (Netherlands Reformed) and the Metropolitan of Carthage (Orthodox Patriarchate of Alexandria).

Later in the morning at a hearing attended by all who desired to have more detailed information about the proposals in the Report on Programme and Finance or to raise any questions about it, several items were discussed and explanations made by the Chairman to the general satisfaction of those in attendance.

At five o'clock a reception was given for all participants in the Assembly by the Vice-President of India, Dr Radhakrishnan. It was held at sunset in the beautiful garden of the Rashtrapati Bhavan, residence of the President of India, who was prevented from attendance by illness. It was an occasion of charm and dignity long to be remembered.

In the evening the first session of the three sections were held. These had to do, respectively, with 'Witness', 'Service' and 'Unity', the three major subjects which the Assembly was to consider. The breaking up of the Assembly into these sectional groups, continuing for eight rather lengthy sessions, was designed to provide intensive exploration of the themes and to afford every delegate an ample opportunity to contribute to the discussion and to the formulation of statements to be submitted to the Assembly as a whole.

Fourth Day: Wednesday, November 22

The day began with the first of a series of six periods of Bible study, conducted in three groups co-terminous with the three sections. The leaders were Dr Paul S. Minear (United Church of Christ, USA), Dr Martin Niemöller (Evangelical Church in Germany) and Father Paul Verghese (Orthodox Syrian Church, India). In each of the groups the studies were related to the theme of the Assembly, 'Jesus Christ, the Light of the world'.

Instead of following the conventional pattern of an exposition by a leader, a new method of group study was used which proved highly fruitful. After the leader had read the Biblical passage for the day and had briefly called attention to its basic message and some of the questions it raised, there were some minutes of silence for individual reflection, after which members of the groups had the opportunity to make spontaneous comments of not more than two minutes each. In the last five minutes the leader made a short summary and gathered up the thought of the group in prayer. Many participants in the Assembly found these periods of corporate Bible study to be among the most rewarding hours in the entire programme.

The three sections dealing with 'Witness', 'Service' and 'Unity' continued their work in both morning and afternoon sessions. In order to deal more thoroughly with their responsibilities and to enlist maximum participation by delegates, each of the three sections was divided into sub-sections and assigned specific aspects of the theme for consideration. The patient examination of tasks by sub-sections lacked the popular interest of larger gatherings but secured a more intensive study of problems than would have been possible otherwise.

Representatives of the Orthodox Church in the sub-sections on Unity presented a brief statement[1] as a contribution to the discussion in which they commented particularly on the phrase concerning unity 'with the whole Christian fellowship in all places and all ages' in the proposed statement on 'the unity which is both God's will and his gift to his Church' (see page 116). The Orthodox theologians suggested that this 'new criterion of ecumenical evaluation' was a 'kingly rock', implying 'the hope that unity may be recovered by the

[1] Copies of this 'contribution of the Orthodox delegates to the section on Unity' are available from the Faith and Order Secretariat, 17 route de Malagnou, Geneva.

divided denominations by their *return* to their common past'. 'The Orthodox Church', they concluded, 'is willing to participate in this common work as the witness which has preserved continuously the deposit of apostolic faith and tradition'.

The Laity

In the evening a general session, under the chairmanship of Bishop Dibelius, provided a rich exploration of the subject: 'The Laity: The Church in the World'. In a vigorous protest against the 'protected Sunday Christianity' of the average congregation, Dr Klaus von Bismarck (Evangelical Church in Germany) insisted that the Church can make its rightful impact on society only as it ceases to be preoccupied with a cloistered life of its own and becomes actively concerned with people's working lives in the world. This requires not merely worship and preaching but the witness of those who are actually involved in the non-Christian secularized environment. The professional leadership of the Church, he felt, is doing far too little to help the laity fulfil their responsibility in society. He therefore pleaded for a greater effort of theologians and laity to complement and reinforce each other's roles in the total ministry of the Church to the world.

A perceptive contribution to the thinking of the Assembly on the role of the laity was made by Mr E. V. Mathew (Mar Thoma Syrian Church of Malabar). Speaking out of his own experience in the legal profession, he vividly pictured the dilemma of the Christian layman who has been told by the clergyman that he must not compromise with wrong but who finds that compromise is inevitably involved in the processes of law and politics. He felt that the Church at large has not yet caught up with the new emphasis on the ministry of the laity in society, partly because of the pietistic tradition which makes a separation between a 'sacred' and a 'secular' area of life, partly because of the absorption of the Church, and especially of its clergy, in its own institutional structures. He urged the Church not to be content to proclaim moral absolutes but to help the laity to discover what are the 'legitimate forms of compromise in political life'. He held that the Christian accent should not be on 'keeping oneself pure and undefiled but on how one can most effectively serve the real welfare of the community'. Unless the Church can help its laity in this way, he concluded, it will fail to fulfil its mission in a world of social ferment and social change.

As if in answer to this plea, Miss Mollie Batten (Church of England), described an experiment of William Temple College in examining the role of the Church as seen not from within its own institutional life but from within the concrete situations in which everyday people are living and working. She reported that when the layman who had participated in conferences about their own problems in industry or in education, in political administration or various professions, tried to relate their concerns to a local church they often found it uninterested or unprepared to help. She likened the true function of the local church and its clergy to that of a base for supplying the 'soldiers in the field' with needed resources and proposed that local churches 'minimize the cost of the bases in order to maintain the maximum number of men on operations'.

The key points in the addresses by the three lay speakers were summarized by Dr von Bismarck as follows:

> Our first concern is the recovery of the manifold ministries within the Church and their unity in Christ's ministry of reconciliation for this world.
> Our second concern is the equipment of the laity for their particular ministry.
> The third is the fact that Christ is not imprisoned in our churches. We sometimes have the feeling that you (clergymen) have little understanding for our solidarity with our non-Christian neighbours because your professional concern is so much concentrated on the Church when it is assembled for corporate worship, witness and service.

Fifth Day: Thursday, November 23

The programme of the morning again opened with Bible study in the three groups and continued with the fourth sessions of the sections discussing 'Witness', 'Service' and 'Unity'. In the afternoon there was an important business session, with Bishop Sherrill in the chair, for which the main item on the agenda was action by the Assembly on the report, submitted by the Central Committee, on Programme and Finance (see pages 342-69).

The recommendations of the Business Committee, as presented by Dr Blake, covered approval of the sections of the Report dealing with the scope of the World Council's programme, the organization for carrying it out, and the principles of financial support. In approving these sections record was made of certain explanations, including the comment that since the Report had been prepared before the integration of the International Missionary Council into the World Council an early re-examination of certain questions of organization within the integrated structure will be needed. The section of the Report outlining a proposed budget was referred to the Finance Committee for scrutiny and subsequent report.

Bishop Sherrill made a gratifying report of progress in the effort, which he had headed on behalf of the Central Committee, to secure resources for new headquarters for the World Council in Geneva. In presenting Bishop Sherrill, Dr Fry who had taken the chair, paid high tribute to the Bishop's service as 'far beyond the ordinary call of duty'. Bishop Sherrill first described the collection of converted villas and wooden huts in which the Council's staff is housed and explained the reasons which had made new enlarged headquarters necessary and had led to an undertaking to secure $2,500,000 for this purpose. He presented a detailed record of contributions already made or assured, totalling $2,329,203. He added that rapidly increasing costs of construction required raising the original estimate to $2,750,000 and that further contributions of approximately $400,000 were therefore still needed. If these are not in sight before the end of this year, he explained, the erection of one wing of the building might have to be postponed.

Following the adjournment of the business session, the first meetings of the eighteen committees, to which the members of the Assembly had been assigned for the examination of the many phases of the World Council's activities and policies, were held. The purpose of these committees was to make sure that every part of the World Council's work was scrutinized in considerable detail by a responsible group and that any recommendations resulting from such scrutiny would be brought before the Assembly itself for decision. Each division and each department in the Council's structure was accordingly paralleled by a committee named by the Assembly. In addition there was a larger 'Policy Reference Committee' for considering matters affecting the Council as a whole.

International Affairs

A general session in the evening, held in the Shamiana and open to the public, was devoted to 'International Affairs'. After leading the large audience in prayer the presiding officer, Metropolitan

Juhanon, announced that the pressure of official duties in Nigeria had delayed Sir Francis Ibiam's arrival and that in his unavoidable absence part of his prepared address would be read by Lady Ibiam. The theme was 'What About Africa?'. After paying tribute to the missionaries for what they had done for the African peoples, Sir Francis spoke frankly about the 'stumbling blocks' to the Christian movement in Africa occasioned by discriminatory racial practices. He called attention to concrete cases, including those within the churches as well as those in secular life and some in America and Great Britain as well as in Africa. He emphasized the urgent need for the unity of the Church in Africa and expressed the judgment that the churches which sent missionaries were doing much less than they should to further union. He pointed to the lack of a trained ministry in the African churches and appealed for greater help in removing this handicap. In the recently created All Africa Church Conference he saw a hopeful sign of advance for Christianity in Africa.

The wider international situation was surveyed by Dr O. Frederick Nolde (United Lutheran in America) in an address entitled 'The Future is Now'. As director of the Commission of the Churches on International Affairs he gave an interpretation of its work, stressing particularly its effort to bear a Christian testimony in areas of greatest tension, such as the struggle of dependent peoples for the right to determine their political future, racial segregation, and the cessation of tests of nuclear weapons.

In summary, Dr Nolde outlined seven things which the ecumenical Church should strive to do in the face of today's complex problems: (1) facilitate identification with the whole human family; (2) give impetus and content to the development of an international ethos; (3) fashion a witness which is unaligned with any political or national force but committed to peace with justice and freedom; (4) encourage the building of 'an open society' throughout the world; (5) assist in defining opportunities for peaceful co-operation as a means of living together in a divided world; (6) give prominent place to the claims of social justice for all men everywhere; (7) emphasize world public opinion and moral pressures as a counter-weight to cynicism about effective international action.

SIXTH DAY: FRIDAY, NOVEMBER 24

Following the sessions for Bible study in the three groups, the sections continued their exploration of Christian obedience in 'Witness', 'Unity' and 'Service' throughout the morning. In the afternoon the eighteen committees resumed their task of reviewing the work and policies of the Council. In the evening there was a general session, presided over by Bishop Barbieri, on the concern of the World Council in the realm of Faith and Order.

Faith and Order

The Archbishop of Canterbury (Dr Ramsey) introduced the subject of unity by pointing out that in our Lord's intercession, as recorded in St John 17, the prayer that his followers may 'be one' is combined with the prayer that they may 'be sanctified' and 'be sanctified in truth'. 'Unity, holiness, truth: as the prayer is indivisible, so the fulfilment is indivisible too.' Unity, the Archbishop held, is not something that can be isolated from the other notes of the Church. If our quest of unity is thus isolated, it becomes too superficial to be meaningful. We must recognize both 'a divine urgency' and 'a divine patience' in the matter of unity as well as in the attainment of holiness and in the apprehension of truth. Patience, he advised, is needed 'between those who ask that intercommunion should be immediate and general and those who, with deep conviction and no less concern for unity, think otherwise'.

Dr Nikos Nissiotis (Church of Greece) then interpreted the witness of Eastern Orthodoxy. In Orthodox thinking, he explained, church union is not the result of human agreements but is 'an absolute reality pre-established by God'. Unity among Christians is 'the reflection of the Father's union with Christ by his Spirit realized in the historical Church on the day of Pentecost', and the unbroken continuity of the life of the undivided Church is the ground of its authority. The Orthodox Church does not ask others to 'come back to us' or to deny their own traditions but believes that its witness can help all the other historical churches 'to recover their own true life'. He said that

> this means in practice that Orthodoxy must give up its defensive, confessional-apologetic attitude, and, in the glory of the Holy Spirit, become a mighty river of life, filling the gaps, complementing opposites, overcoming enmities, and driving forward towards reunion. This was how the Church lived in the time of the Fathers, creating new ways for achieving dynamic unity, richer

forms of worship, a really ecumenical theology which regenerated the world through its authentic interpretation of the mission of the Church.

The nature of the unity sought is neither that of 'church discipline under a centralized authoritarian institution' nor one based only on the 'kerygmatic message of the Gospel' but one which is based on and maintained by 'the charismas received from the Holy Spirit by the People of God in the historic Church'.

After acknowledging the theological importance of the considerations voiced by the Archbishop of Canterbury and Professor Nissiotis, the Rev. Philip Potter (Methodist Church, West Indies) spoke from a very different angle, drawing on his experience among youth, especially in the World Student Christian Federation, and among the Younger Churches. He described them both as cherishing 'a dynamic rather than a static conception of the Church'. He warned that we are in danger of 'driving young people into despair of the churches' because local churches are so slow in becoming ecumenical or advancing toward unity. He cited particularly the impatience of youth over the lack of intercommunion. He further voiced the judgment that the Churches of Asia and Africa would have more interest in Faith and Order if its discussions were not so involved in the 'presuppositions of Western Schoolmen'. Finally, he expressed the hope that the World Confessional bodies would have a more positive influence on the movement for union among the Younger Churches.

Seventh Day: Saturday, November 25

Once more the morning was devoted to Bible study and meetings of the sections, and the afternoon to the work of the many committees scrutinizing the programmes of the Council. In the evening the assembly convened in the Shamiana for a united service of preparation for the Holy Communion (see page 332), a large number of Christian people of Delhi joining with the participants in the Assembly.

After a call to worship and invocation by Father Korah Philipos (Mar Thoma Syrian Church of Malabar) the hymns, 'Come, Holy Ghost, our Souls inspire' and 'O sacred head, sore wounded', a Scripture lesson (Isaiah 53.1-6) and the Apostles' Creed, the Rev. Dr Douglas Horton (United Church of Christ, USA) delivered a sermon on 'the Feast of Christ'. Based on the Biblical symbol of the marriage of the Lamb (Rev. 19.6-7), he pointed out that the imagery proclaims that 'true being is the meeting of God and man, of Christ and his people'. For the Christian the 'be-all and end-all of things' is neither the submerging of individuality nor a private heaven of pure contemplation but the *company* of the Redeemer and the redeemed. He interpreted the coming of the Bridegroom as involving both invitation and judgment, and spoke of the appropriate response in terms of witness, unity and service. He then described the Communion Table as the earthly sign of the Messianic Feast and made three suggestions about the spirit of our participation: first, that we be realists, confessing the sad fact of our fragmented approach; second, that Christ, not our interests, must be at the centre; third, that we give ourselves to him to reorient our lives and the life of the Church.

The congregation then joined in confession, in thanksgiving, and in supplication, led by Pastor T. S. Sihombing (Protestant Batak Church), and concluded the service by singing: 'Thine is the glory, risen, conquering Son.'

Eighth Day: Sunday, November 26

Sunday morning was the occasion for a service of the Holy Eucharist celebrated by the Church of India, Pakistan, Burma and Ceylon (Anglican) (see page 332). Two altars had been erected in the great Shamiana for the celebration, which by the announcement of the Church was open to all baptized communicant members of their churches. A congregation, estimated at 4,000, from many races and countries was present, including many Christian people from Delhi as well as participants in the Assembly. It was the first time that an open Anglican service of the Holy Communion had been the main Sunday service at a World Council Assembly. The celebration was arranged by the Cathedral Church of the Redemption in New Delhi and the Bishop of Delhi celebrated in the presence of the Metropolitan of India. Bishops and priests from Anglican provinces all over the world, and from the Philippines Independent Catholic Church and other churches in communion with the Anglican churches, assisted in the administration of the sacrament.

'God is our Refuge and Strength'

In the evening there was a general session devoted to the interpretation of the work of the churches of the World Council in inter-church aid and refugee service. After an urgent word by the presiding officer, Bishop Dibelius, about the continuing need for service to refugees, including refugees from East Germany, followed by an introductory statement by Dr Eugene Carson Blake concerning the spiritual meaning of this service, there was a presentation in five sequences, partly by pictures thrown on a screen, partly by interviews with persons who are actively engaged in the world-wide ministry. Each of the five presentations was related to relevant Scripture and the programme as a whole was described by the title 'God is our Refuge and Strength'.

In the first part the pictures were symbolic, depicting Asian and African conceptions of the Good Shepherd, the Prodigal Son and the Good Samaritan. The second part showed pictures of meeting emergency needs, such as those occasioned by flood, drought and earthquake, accompanied by an interview with the Rev. Kentaro Buma of Japan. In part three the pictures showed the plight of refugees and the ministry to their necessities, with an interview with Mr James Atkinson of Hong Kong. The fourth part portrayed diverse ministries in helping to develop Christian leadership for new nations in Asia and Africa, with comments by Dr Donald M'Timkulu of South Africa and Mr P. C. Joseph of India. The final sequence dealt with the values, both material and spiritual, of the new experience of mutual aid and fellowship, the pictures being supplemented by an interview with the Rev. Alan Brash of New Zealand and Miss A. Fransz of Indonesia. The Anglican Archbishop of the Province of East Africa gave a dramatic description of areas of Kenya stricken first by drought and then by flood.

Ninth Day: Monday, November 27

Before the morning service, Dr Visser 't Hooft announced that it was to have been conducted by General Superintendent Dr Günther Jacob of East Germany. Dr Jacob had prepared the service, but had not received permission to leave his country. In his absence Präses Dr Scharf, chairman of the Evangelical Church in Germany, would read the sermon prepared by Dr Jacob and conduct the service. Dr Visser 't Hooft said that Dr Jacob would be assured that his message had been given to the Assembly. After the service the delegates settled down to patient work throughout the day on their assignments in the committees which were preparing reports and recommendations for plenary session of the Assembly.

In the evening the sections on 'Witness', 'Unity' and 'Service' were engaged in completing reports of sub-sections on particular parts of their work or in acting upon them. A day of undramatic but productive spade-work was concluded with evening prayers conducted by Bishop A. H. Zulu (Church of the Province of South Africa).

TENTH DAY: TUESDAY, NOVEMBER 28

Many delegates arose at an early hour to attend the Holy Qurbana (Eucharist) of St James, at the invitation of the Syrian Orthodox Church of Malabar. The liturgy was celebrated at 7.30 a.m., in the Shamiana, which had been appropriately equipped for the occasion. Copies of the full text of the liturgy, unfamiliar to most delegates from other confessions, were placed in the hands of all so that they could follow the service with appreciative understanding. It included the 'Kiss of Peace', passed with the hands from the clergy to the congregation, and from each member of the congregation to his or her neighbour.

Committee sessions occupied the morning and the final meetings of the sections on 'Witness', 'Unity' and 'Service' were held in the afternoon. The discussions in these sections during the eight long sessions of each were of crucial importance for the results of the Assembly. The thorough examination of main problems, often involving extended debate, made it possible for the Assembly in its deliberative sessions to deal with delicate and difficult issues far more understandingly and constructively.

The Churches and Social Structures

In the evenings there was a general session of the Assembly under the chairmanship of Metropolitan Juhanon, on the theme, 'The Challenge of Social Change to the Churches'. The theme was introduced by the Rev. Emilio Castro (Methodist, Uruguay), who spoke briefly of the study of 'The Christian Responsibility in Areas of Rapid Social Change' carried on by the World Council's Department on the Church and Society during the last six years.

Interpreting major aspects of this study, Dr Egbert de Vries (Netherlands Reformed Church), Rector of the International Institute of Social Studies at the Hague, discussed 'The Churches of the West in a Dynamic Society'. He set the present period of revolutionary social changes in historical perspective and emphasized the way in which these changes now affect Asia and Africa and Latin America as well as the West, creating an 'explosion in expectations'. He called attention to some of the main characteristics of the dynamic society of today and the points at which a challenge to the Christian conscience arises. He held it to be utterly impossible for the churches to remain aloof from these problems, and urged the need both for wrestling with them and also for differentiating between the message of the Gospel and the socio-economic-political structures of Western society or any other particular form of social organization. He suggested that the churches can best help in the search for new social values if they are 'spiritually free of their immediate social environment' while intimately partaking in it. The churches, he further urged, must help people everywhere to understand that their nations 'can only live and prosper in the context of a *world* economy and a *world* community'. He declared that the churches, because of the intrinsic nature of their Gospel, must think in global terms, and that they can provide a firmer foundation for mutual trust and confidence than any secular interest or policy.

'The Challenge to the Churches in the New Nations of Africa and Asia' was the timely topic of Mr M. M. Thomas (Mar Thoma Syrian Church of Malabar), Associate Director of the Institute for the Study of Religion and Society at Bangalore. Reminding his audience of the recent emergence of many independent nations in these continents, he pictured them as struggling not to revive old indigenous traditions but to build a new pattern of society and culture. In this process, although they reject the idea of copying the West, they are absorbing a great deal of its social humanism as well as its science and technology. The churches, partly because of their past identification with Western culture and partly because of a pietistic tradition, have not yet adequately developed 'a positive responsible relation to the people's struggle for a new life'. He pleaded for such a relation, pointing out on the one hand that the Gospel is not to be identified with any one culture or political order and on the other hand that the redemption which Christ offers embraces within its scope 'the world of science and technology, of politics, society and culture, of secular ideologies and religions'. He accordingly stressed the role of Christians in the new nations as that of 'partners in the common struggle for the secular conditions for true human living'.

He also indicated ways in which the Christians in these areas can bear their Christian witness and contribute to responsible nationhood instead of merely building 'segregated Christian communities'.

After this penetrating address, all the more significant because it was an interpretation of the present concrete situation of the Christian community in India, Metropolitan Juhanon concluded the session with evening prayers.

ELEVENTH DAY: WEDNESDAY, NOVEMBER 29

Morning worship was conducted by the Rt. Rev. Chrysostomos, Metropolitan of Myron (Ecumenical Patriarchate) and included a meditation on the text, 'If we love one another, God dwelleth in us' (I John 4.12). The rest of the day was devoted to meetings of the committees and of drafting groups preparing reports for consideration by the Assembly as a whole.

Observers of the Third Assembly who had also been present at Evanston and Amsterdam were impressed by the fact that at New Delhi the delegates were much more ready to concentrate patiently on the give-and-take of discussion of specific points. The greater extent of participation by all delegates, especially those whose native tongue was not English, was also often commented upon. This participation was encouraged by the excellent facilities for interpretation. In the major committee rooms as well as in the hall for plenary sessions there was provision for simultaneous translation into English, French and German and, if needed, into Russian and Spanish.

TWELFTH DAY: THURSDAY, NOVEMBER 30

At the invitation of the Federation of Evangelical Lutheran Churches in India, Lutheran communicants and 'other baptized communicant members of the member churches of the World Council' joined in a service of the Holy Communion, conducted in English according to the use of the Lutheran Churches in India, in the Shamiana at 8 a.m. The celebrant was Bishop Rajah Manikam. Copies of the text of the Liturgy were provided by the church for all participants.

In the morning the final meetings of the Committees, which reviewed the programmes and policies of the divisions and departments of the Council, were held, and the drafts of their reports to the Assembly were completed (see pages 136-315).

Credentials and Elections

In the afternoon a business session of the Assembly was held under the chairmanship of Dr Fry. The report of the Committee on Credentials was presented by its chairman, Pastor F. G. A. Stenström (Church of Sweden), showing the total voting body of the Assembly to be 577. He submitted lists of all delegates and supplementary lists of 105 advisers, 100 youth participants, 59 fraternal delegates, 45 observers, and 120 guests, a total of 1,006 participants (see pages 369-94). He regretfully announced that five delegates from East Germany had not received the permission of their government to leave their country.

As a gratifying item in the list of observers, it was noted that it included five from the Roman Catholic Church, appointed by the Vatican's Secretariat for the promotion of unity. This was the first time that official observers from the Roman Catholic Church had attended an assembly of the World Council of Churches.

A supplementary statement about the financial resources for the new headquarters in Geneva was made by Bishop Sherrill. He gave the happy report that since the beginning of the Assembly further contributions of about $200,000 had been assured, including a substantially increased amount from the German Churches and indications of contributions of money or materials from the Church of Russia and a few others, thus reducing the gap between estimated costs and resources now in sight to about $200,000.

Messages of affectionate greetings were sent to the four living ex-presidents of the World Council: Archbishop Erling Eidem (Church of Sweden), Archbishop Lord Fisher (Church of England), Dr Marc Boegner (Reformed Church of France) and Bishop G. Bromley Oxnam (Methodist Church, USA).

The report of the *Committee on Nominations,* headed by Dr William S. Tindal (Church of Scotland), was then submitted. The first nomination, that of the elder statesman Dr J. H. Oldham, who had been the secretary of the Edinburgh Conference of 1910, as Honorary President, was greeted with prolonged applause. For the presidium six names representing as many different confessions, were presented. They were:

The Most Rev. Arthur Michael Ramsey, Archbishop of Canterbury and Primate of all England.

Sir Francis Ibiam, Governor of East Nigeria, Chairman of the

All Africa Conference, and a Ruling Elder of the Presbyterian Church of Nigeria.

The Most Rev. Archbishop Iakovos, head of the Greek Archdiocese of North and South America.

The Rev. Dr Martin Niemöller, president of the Evangelical Church of Hesse-Nassau, Germany.

The Rev. Dr G. Moses, Chairman of the National Christian Council of India, Principal of Hislop College, and minister of the United Church of North India and Pakistan.

Mr Charles C. Parlin, prominent American Methodist layman and lawyer.

In making the nominations of the six presidents the chairman of the Committee explained that only when they speak collectively as a group are their views to be regarded as representing the World Council of Churches.

A list of nominees for membership in the Central Committee, the governing body in the interim between assemblies, was also presented. It consisted of a hundred names, designed to secure (as far as possible within this limited figure) a fair and adequate representation of the confessional composition of the Council, the geographical distribution of its member churches, and the major interests of the Council. Two additional names were presented from the floor. The balloting resulted in the election of the Honorary President, the six presidents and all members of the Central Committee as proposed by the Committee on Nominations (see pages 399-402).

For the Committee on the Department of Faith and Order Bishop Hanns Lilje (Evangelical Church of Germany) submitted nominations for membership in the *Commission on Faith and Order*. Several questions were raised by delegates who desired to see other geographical areas or other churches represented. Since the number of members is limited to one hundred and twenty, this was not possible without displacing some of the names submitted. Four alternative nominations were made from the floor. The balloting sustained the nominations presented by the Committee (see pages 402-5).

The presentation of the report of the *Policy Reference Committee* was begun at this point (see pages 144-63). The following recommendations, as made by Archbishop Iakovos, chairman of the Committee, were readily adopted:

That the continued aspiration of the Council should be to 'be ahead of the tide of events' instead of being 'pushed into critical situations'.

That the Central Committee be instructed to give special attention to the problem of familiarizing the whole membership of the Council with its work.

That special thanks be extended to the Committee on Programme and Finance for its outstanding work.

That the statements of aims and functions of the Divisions and Departments be approved.

'Why We Must Speak'

At a general session in the evening, held in the Shamiana, Dr Baeta presiding, there was a panel discussion on the topic, 'Why We Must Speak' under the leadership of Dr D. T. Niles (Methodist Church in Ceylon) who posed the questions. The whole presentation was made within the framework of a series of incidents in the life of Jesus, the starting point being the trial of Jesus and the accusations against him. Dr Niles suggested that similar accusations are being made today and that like Peter we are all 'in the courtyard of the judgment hall where Jesus is on trial'.

In response to the question why the Gospel is spreading in Latin America, Dr Emilio Castro (Methodist, Uruguay) said that it is because evangelical Christians have had the personal experience of a new life in Christ which is so meaningful that they want to tell others about it.

To the question how the churches can make the influence of the Gospel felt in public affairs, Mr J. Irwin Miller (Disciples of Christ, USA), as a layman in business, held that they must first realize that the Gospel applies to the whole of human life, and must then speak out of a competent knowledge of social forces and conditions.

Dr Constantijn Patijn (Netherlands Reformed Church), member of Parliament, replying to a question about the Christian witness in politics, declared that although politics often leaves no choice except between unsatisfactory alternatives, Christianity has left its mark on politics in fostering respect for law, a conviction that governmental authority must be used in a responsible way and a sense of concern for the poor and distressed.

A question about the secret of the continuing Christian testimony of the Eastern churches in the face of grave obstacles and oppression was answered by Father Ignatius Hazim (Greek Orthodox

Patriarchate of Antioch) by giving glimpses of Orthodox piety and especially of the significance of the Eucharist in Orthodoxy.

Asked why she had come as a missionary to India, Dr Mary Moore, medical missionary from Scotland, said that it was because of her desire to do what she could to manifest the love of God, as revealed in Christ, to others, and that she remained in India because of her appreciation of the 'spiritual treasures of the Indian Church'.

The final question, addressed to the Rev. Ezekiel Mahabane (Methodist Church of South Africa) had to do with the role of the Christian Gospel in the African revolution. He replied that by its influence in liberating Africans from tribal conflicts and proclaiming oneness in Christ the Gospel had already made a great contribution.

Thirteenth Day: Friday, December 1

The day began at 7.30 in the Shamiana with the Divine Liturgy of St John Chrysostom, which the delegates of the Eastern Orthodox Patriarchates and autocephalous churches invited other participants in the Assembly to attend. The Liturgy was celebrated with great splendour by leaders of Orthodox churches represented at the Assembly in the Greek, Russian, Rumanian and Arabic languages. Members of the Orthodox churches communicated at the service (see page 333).

Reports of Sections

The first of the deliberative sessions for hearing and discussing the reports of the sections on 'Witness', Unity' and 'Service', as these had been hammered out in sectional meetings during preceding days, was held under the chairmanship of Bishop Sherrill. In spite of a crowded agenda all three of these reports received careful attention in the processes of debate in the assembly as a whole. In the case of one report, for example, there were no fewer than thirty-three participants in the plenary discussions and the report was twice remitted back to the drafting committee of the section for reconsideration before final action was taken by the whole Assembly.

Mrs Douglas Horton (United Church of Christ, USA) and Dr Gerhard Brennecke (Evangelical Church in Germany) as co-chairmen of the section on 'Witness' gave an introduction to its report, summarizing the contents under three heads: Jesus Christ, the Saviour of the World; communicating the Gospel; reshaping the Witnessing Community (see pages 77-93). Much of the vigorous discussion that followed was focused on the statements about Christian witness in relation to other faiths. A reference to 'the wisdom, love and power God has given to men of other faiths' was both criticized and defended. The comment was also made that the report should frankly recognize today's wide revolt against the entire Christian message. A reference to baptism was unsatisfactory to a representative of the Salvation Army but was firmly supported by a Russian Orthodox delegate. The suggestions for revision were referred to the drafting committee of the section for study and subsequent report.

The report of the section on 'Service' was presented by Sir Kenneth Grubb (Church of England) who called attention to its main features (see pages 93-115). In the ensuing discussion some of the main points of criticism, which were referred to the drafting committee of the section for consideration, were the following:

There should be a stronger statement about the sin of war and the responsibility of the churches for peace.

The statements about nuclear warfare do not go far enough.

The references to non-violence should make it explicit that this applies to the great powers as much as to Africans struggling for freedom.

There should be a clearer statement that nationalism is as much of a danger in America and Europe as in Asia and Africa.

More specific attention to the sin of racial segregation in the Church is called for.

More attention should be given to the distinguishing characteristics of *Christian* service, especially in view of the increasing service of welfare states.

In the afternoon's deliberative session, under the chairmanship of Dr Payne, Dr David G. Moses (United Church of North India) and Bishop Oliver Tomkins (Church of England) co-chairmen of the section on 'Unity', presented its report (see pages 116-35). Among the questions brought forward in the discussion and referred to the drafting committee, were these:

Would it not strengthen the document to preface it with a statement about the unity of God and the redemption in Christ?

Should there not be an expression of appreciation for the kind of unity which the World Council now makes possible, without any danger of going too far in centralized authority?

Should not the reference to the values of infant baptism be omitted?

Is it not important to lay greater stress on the discovery of unity through obedience to Christ's call to world-wide mission?

The Bible in the Church

In the evening a general session was devoted to the theme 'The Bible and the Churches' Task', Bishop Barbieri presiding. The Archbishop of York (Dr Coggan, Church of England), after stressing the current renewal of interest in biblical studies and citing impressive statistics about the translation and the distribution of the Bible, urged a great advance in both of these responsibilities. He called attention both to the 'population explosion' and to the rapid extension of literacy as intensifying the need for a wide distribution of the Bible and aids to its understanding. He concluded that in the overall strategy of the Church there should be much more emphasis on the provision of Christian literature suitable for many different kinds of readers.

The Rev. E. H. Robertson (Baptist Union of Great Britain and Ireland) who has been conducting a study on the use of the Bible for the United Bible Societies and the World Council of Churches, spoke of evidence of renewal of Bible study in various forms in the Protestant, Roman Catholic and Orthodox churches. There was, he said, evidence of a renewed confidence in the Bible, and of an emerging 'openness' to the Bible. Progress was slow, partly because the relevance of the Bible become much more clearly apparent in times of crisis (such as the Nazi period in Germany) than in quieter times, and partly because the minority who continue to do effective and fruitful Bible study tend to become separated from the majority. Moreover, the Bible 'has many uncomfortable things to say that we do not wish to hear'.

Speaking on 'The Bible in Evangelism', the Rev. Dr A. E. Inbanathan (Church of South India), General Secretary of the Bible Society of India and Ceylon, illustrated his theme by the reminder that some of the most illustrious of Indian Christians, like Pandita Rambai and Sadhu Sunda Singh, had found Christ through the medium of the printed Bible. He pointed out that in Christian history renewed devotion to the Bible had again and again resulted in increased evangelistic activity. He outlined a projected study, to be undertaken under the joint auspices of the United Bible Societies and the World Council of Churches, of the specific ways in which the message of the Bible is being set forth.

In the course of the evening session Dr Moses, as Chairman of the National Christian Council of India, presented to each participant in the Assembly a much appreciated souvenir. It was a desk tray of brass inscribed with the ecumenical symbol of the ship, encircled by the words 'Third Assembly—World Council of Churches—New Delhi, India 1961'.

Fourteenth Day: Saturday, December 2

After a service of worship led by Father Makary El-Souriany (Coptic Orthodox Church of Egypt) in which the prayers and Scripture lessons were selected from the Coptic Orthodox service, the Assembly settled down to another business session, presided over by Dr Fry, for the reception of reports prepared during preceding days.

Reports of Committees

The report of the *Committee on the Division of Studies* was submitted by President James I. McCord (United Presbyterian, USA) (see pages 164-71). It proposed 'The Finality of Christ in an Age of Universal History' as a major subject of study for the next five years. Among comments from the floor were the following:

That the language in which the study is described should be simpler.

That 'finality' sounds too static and does not recognize the creativity of God today.

That the statement about study should have a more evangelical tone and pay more attention to the work of the Holy Spirit.

After Dr McCord had welcomed the suggestions the Assembly voted to approve the general plan and to give the Central Committee authority to decide on the phrasing of the title and the methods of pursuing the study.

Dr McCord then presented a proposal for the future organization and activity of the *Secretariat on Religious Liberty,* which was promptly approved. It outlines two main lines of work: an investigation of the Biblical basis for concern about religious liberty and an historical study of significant thought on the subject.

A third recommendation, which was warmly approved, had to do with *a study of the training of the ministry* in our time, including both sociological and theological aspects on problems of both method and content. The proposal elicited suggestions that co-operation of administrators of theological education be sought, that the study be expanded to take account of confessional and regional studies now under way, and that it include an inquiry as to how emerging new patterns of ministry may be utilized.

The final recommendation asked the Assembly to authorize the Division of Studies to convene a consultation on 'The Christian Witness to Peace', to be attended by both pacifists and non-pacifists. The proposal was well supported and duly endorsed.

The report of the Committee on the *Department of Faith and Order* (see pages 171-5) was presented by Bishop Lilje. Since it left its proposals in the hands of the Central Committee for study and future decision, it was received as information. One of the comments on the report was that the interests of Faith and Order ought not to be separated from other study interests (e.g. those of Church and Society).

The Committee on the *Department on Studies in Evangelism* submitted its report (see pages 188-92) through its chairman, the Rev. Dr Eric W. Baker (Methodist Church of Great Britain). Three recommendations were readily approved:

To authorize a comprehensive study of 'the missionary structure of the congregation' concerned with the evangelistic task of the local church.

To continue the series of publications known as 'surveys in evangelism'.

To approve a joint study with the United Bible Societies on 'the use of the Bible in evangelism'.

Bishop H. Sumitra (Church of South India) brought forward the report of the Committee on the *Department of Missionary Studies* (see pages 192-5). Four recommendations were approved:

To ask the Working Committee of the Department to formulate proposals to the Faith and Order Department and the Department on the Laity for the study of certain common problems.

To invite the directors of the various centres for the study of non-Christian religions to assume responsibility for the next stage of the study.

To continue and extend the studies in 'Growth and Response' of churches in missionary situations.

To approve exploratory consultations on (*a*) factors favouring or retarding Church expansion and (*b*) African Separatist Church movements.

A recommendation concerning relations with the Department of Studies in Evangelism, in connection with its study of 'the missionary structure of the congregation', was referred to the Central Committee.

In the afternoon the flow of committee reports into the Assembly continued at a steady pace. Mr M. M. Thomas (Mar Thoma Syrian Church) presented the report of the Committee on the *Department of Church and Society* (see pages 176-87). Its recommendations were approved as follows:

To authorize studies, as generally outlined in the report, on (*a*) 'Moral Issues in the Change from Traditional to Dynamic Societies'; (*b*) 'The Social, Political and Moral Problems of Modern Industrial Societies'; (*c*) 'Racial and Ethnic Tensions in a Changing World Community'.

Resolution on Race

A resolution on 'Race and Ethnic Relations', proposed by the Committee, was adopted with no dissenting voice. This was designed as a follow-up of the principle enunciated at the Evanston Assembly to the effect that 'any form of segregation based on race, colour or ethnic origin is contrary to the Gospel'. The resolution called attention to mounting tensions, noted with gratitude the effective witness of many Christians in difficult situations, and urged churches everywhere to act more resolutely against 'segregation based on race, colour or ethnic origin' (see pages 187-8).

The Basis

Resuming the report of the *Policy Reference Committee*, Archbishop Iakovos presented a recommendation for the expansion of the 'Basis' of the World Council, of which due notice had already been given to the member churches, by amending section I of the constitution so as to read as follows:

The World Council of Churches is a fellowship of Churches which confess the Lord Jesus Christ as God and Saviour according to the Scriptures and therefore seek to fulfil together their common calling to the glory of the one God, Father, Son and Holy Spirit.

Warm approval was voiced by many, including representatives of Eastern Orthodox, Lutheran, Presbyterian and Old Catholic Churches. Criticisms of the proposed amendment were voiced by delegates from the Seventh Day Baptist General Conference USA, Mennonite and Remonstrant Churches, and the Friends. A written ballot was taken, a two-thirds majority being constitutionally required for adoption. The result of the voting was 383 in favour, 36 against, 7 abstaining. The Chairman declared the amendment adopted and led in prayer for God's blessing on the important action which had been taken.

On behalf of the Policy Reference Committee Archbishop Iakovos submitted a recommendation concerning the *Fourth Assembly* proposing that the number of voting members should be 700, with authority for the Central Committee to increase or decrease the number by not more than 20 per cent. This was quickly adopted.

Approval was also given to a recommendation that the Central Committee, as a general rule, admit no church of less than 10,000 to membership between the third and fourth Assemblies and that a classification of 'associated churches' be set up for churches which meet all criteria for membership except that of size.

Another session for dealing with Committee reports, Dr Fry presiding, was held in the evening when President Nathan M. Pusey (Episcopal, USA) presented the report of the Committee on the *Commission of the Churches on International Affairs* (see pages 262-90). Certain sections occasioned spirited debate. Some felt that the report had gone too far in expressing judgments of a political nature. Others felt that it had not been outspoken enough on some of the issues. An Indian adviser urged the importance of including a non-Western member on the CCIA staff. An Eastern Orthodox delegate was critical of the statement on family planning. A delegate of the Friends wanted the report to include a bolder appeal to the great powers to give up nuclear weapons. At the end of the discussion it was voted to approve the substance on the report and commend it to the churches for study and appropriate action. This was followed by a motion, duly adopted, that a message be sent to the acting Secretary General of the United Nations assuring him of the moral support and the prayers of the Assembly.

An Appeal to Governments

Dr Pusey submitted, on behalf of the Committee, the text of 'An

Appeal to All Governments and Peoples'. Professor Charles A. Coulson (Methodist Church, Great Britain) made a motion, which was carried, to refer it back to the Committee on the grounds of its being too long, including too much that has been said before, and not concentrating on the distinctively spiritual witness of the churches.

When, at a later session (on December 5), the Committee offered a somewhat revised version of the 'Appeal' and President Pusey as chairman explained why a more radical revision had not been made, Professor Coulson moved to substitute a much shorter statement. This dealt less with political complexities and confined itself chiefly to a plea for mutual trust and confidence. Several delegates expressed the conviction that it was important to take account of more factors than were included in Professor Coulson's statement. The proposed substitute was not sustained by the Assembly, and the revised 'Appeal' as submitted by the Committee was adopted, with about a dozen votes in the negative and a few abstentions (see pages 280-4).

Resolution on Angola

Dr Pusey read, on behalf of the Committee, a resolution on the current situation in Angola, strongly criticizing the extreme acts of repression by the Portuguese government and appealing to it to bring to an end promptly the continuing tragedy in that land. This resolution was supported by several who had reliable information about conditions or who felt the Assembly had a duty to protest. Others, including a member of the British Parliament, opposed the resolution, chiefly on the ground that the Assembly ought not to single out a particular nation for attack. A motion to adopt the resolution was carried by such a narrow margin (179 to 177) that by general consent the resolution was sent back to the Committee for reconsideration.

When (on December 5) the Committee reported on its reconsideration, Dr Pusey submitted a new resolution which took account of the earlier debate. It associated the Committee with the statements made by officers of the CCIA and by the Executive Committee of the World Council in June 1961, noted both the deep concern of the Assembly over Angola and its reluctance to take an isolated action against a single nation, and recommended transmitting both the original resolution of the Committee and the debate on it to CCIA 'for further consideration and urgent action'. After a few emendations suggested from the floor, the Assembly voted to adopt this recommendation (see pages 284-90). Evening prayers were led by Bishop Richard C. Raines (Methodist, USA).

Fifteenth Day: Sunday, December 3

In the morning the Assembly held no service of worship, so that delegates could be free to join the Christian people of Delhi in worship in the churches of the community. Many delegates distributed themselves among the twenty-one congregations of the city and others attended the joint communion service conducted in the Shamiana by the Church of South India and the United Church of North India.

At the session in the afternoon, with Dr Payne in the chair, Dr Hans Thimme (Evangelical Church in Germany) as chairman of the Committee on the *Division of Ecumenical Action* presented its report. One of its main points was a proposed enlargement of functions so as to give greater attention to 'relating ecumenical thinking to Christian concern for education in all its aspects', and it was proposed that there be conversations with the World Council of Christian Education and Sunday School Association regarding 'the desirability of closer and more general relationships in the field of Christian education'. The suggestion of an expanded role of the Division in education met a favourable response and general approval was given to the report, leaving its proposals to the Central Committee for such action as might prove practicable (see pages 196-201).

In presenting the first report of the Committee on the *Message of the Assembly to the churches,* the Chairman, Dr Kathleen Bliss (Church of England) said that the members had tried to discern the 'stirrings of the Spirit' in the Assembly and to give voice to them. The Committee conceived the Message not as an address to the world but as a letter to the congregations in the constituency of the World Council. The letter was kept short in order to encourage its being read from pulpits. It reflected what the members of the Committee felt to be three distinctive things about the New Delhi Assembly: that the Asian and African churches have been at the centre of its life; that it has been hopeful, with more clarity and confidence about its Gospel; that along with an emphasis on the uniqueness of Christ there had been more sensitivity to God's working in the world.

The Rev. Robert S. Barbour (Church of Scotland) read the Message as drafted by the Committee (see pages 316-22). It was accompanied by six brief affirmations which could be used as an act of worship by a congregation following the reading of the Message and which would first be used by the Assembly itself at its closing service of worship (see page 54).

In the discussion of the draft Message several suggestions of revision, chiefly of editorial character, were offered, which the Chairman said the Committee would consider. A few suggestions for the insertion of additional content were made, which were declined on the ground that the Committee desired to keep the Message within the limit of a thousand words and to focus it on a few main points. A German Lutheran delegate wanted to see a stronger emphasis on the eschatological hope, especially for the comfort of Christians living in the most difficult situations, but Dr Bliss hesitated to include anything 'which might seem to imply that Christians are not passionately concerned about the present life'. The proposed Message was remitted to the drafting committee for further consideration and subsequent report.

The evening session continued to hear from the committees. The Rev. U Ba Hmyin (Burma Baptist Convention), on behalf of the Committee on the *Youth Department,* introduced its report (see pages 221-8). One of its statements that arrested attention was as follows:

> We believe that the impatience which young people in our churches so often reveal concerning the slow progress towards unity, and towards changing the structures of our churches to make them more free to fulfil the tasks of witness and service, must not be dismissed simply as youthful enthusiasm. Often the activity of youth in pressing for such changes on local and regional levels results from their taking seriously all that has been said in ecumenical gatherings about the fact that the things which bind us together as Christians are more important than the things that divide us.

General approval was given to the report which was referred to the Central Committee for action.

The stream of reports was interrupted to send a message of congratulations to the president of India, Dr Rajendra Prasad, on the occasion of his seventy-seventh birthday, and to express the hope for his speedy return to good health.

Anti-Semitism

Returning to the report of the *Policy Reference Committee,* the Assembly took up a proposed resolution on anti-Semitism (see pages 148-50) which provoked a brisk discussion. In reply to an inquiry why the Assembly singled out only one form of racial injustice when there are so many others, it was urged that there is good reason for special attention to anti-Semitism because the Church has historically been involved in it. In reply to the question whether the resolution ought not to give some attention to the theological aspects of the relations of Christians and Jews, Dr Visser 't Hooft explained that there is a wide division within the Council on the theological issue as had been evident at the Evanston Assembly, and that the Committee desired to limit the resolution at this time to the point on which there was clear agreement. An amendment changed the sentence that Jews are 'not the only ones who reject him', to 'not the only ones who do not yet recognize him'. The resolution as amended was then adopted without a dissenting voice. Among other points it urged that 'the historic events which led to the crucifixion should not be so presented as to fasten upon the Jewish people of today responsibilities which belong to our corporate humanity and not to one race or community.'

In the further behalf of the Policy Reference Committee Dr Robert C. Mackie (Church of Scotland) presented a revised report on *'Christian Witness, Proselytism and Religious Liberty in the Setting of the World Council of Churches'* (see *Evanston to New Delhi,* pages 239-45). The Assembly received the report and commended it to the churches.

The Assembly considered the recommendations of the Policy Reference Committee on *Relations with Non-member Churches* (see page 151), and voted: (1) to reiterate its invitation to churches which accept the basis and purposes of the World Council to apply for membership; (2) to seek contacts with non-member churches with a view to their participation in such activities as may appear to be mutually desirable; (3) to record its pleasure at the presence of observers from several churches, including the Roman Catholic; and (4) to lay upon the hearts of all member churches the importance of constant prayer for Christian brethren in every part of the world.

A fruitful session concluded with evening prayers conducted by Bishop Sherrill (Protestant Episcopal, USA).

Sixteenth Day: Monday, December 4

The Prime Minister's Visit

After a period of Bible study in three groups the Assembly convened in a general session to hear an address by the distinguished Prime Minister of India, Shri Jawaharlal Nehru. Escorted to the platform by the presidents of the World Council and the chairman of the Delhi Committee for the Assembly, Rajkumari Amrit Kaur, he was given a prolonged standing ovation. He was welcomed by Dr Fry, chairman of the Central Committee, who commented that at the first Assembly in Amsterdam the Council had been honoured by the presence of the Princess Regent Juliana and at the second Assembly in Evanston by a visit of President Eisenhower, and was now deeply grateful to the Prime Minister of India for his courtesy. Dr Fry paid tribute to Mr Nehru as one of the truly great personalities of our time and as one universally respected. He voiced the thanks of the Assembly for the privilege of being in India and using the magnificent facilities of the Vigyan Bhavan.

The Prime Minister first expressed his pleasure in the fact that such a widely representative religious body as the World Council of Churches was meeting in India. He was happy also that it was giving so much attention to basic problems affecting the welfare of mankind today. He was glad that the Assembly had not shrunk from facing these problems because of their complexity. He commented that in a democratic society politicians had to perform a difficult role because their personal views were often unacceptable to the masses of the people. Compromise might therefore be necessary but it could be a 'slippery path' if followed too far. One of the things that especially troubled him in today's world was 'the cold war approach', which only aggravated grave problems. One had to be realistic (even though he had found that men who pride themselves on their realism were often hopelessly unrealistic!) but one did not have to make a difficult situation more difficult by being offensive toward opponents. A friendly approach, he concluded, could be counted on to bring a better response, in the case of governments as well as of individuals. Mr Nehru was interrupted several times by hearty applause and as he took his leave was given another standing ovation.

Still More Committees

The report of the Committee on the *Department on the Laity* was submitted by Dr Klaus von Bismarck (Evangelical Church in Germany) (see pages 202-7). The report made it clear that in stressing the role of laymen it is not concerned with their status in the church but is trying to foster 'a deeper understanding and fuller development of the varied gifts and ministries of all members of the Body of Christ'. The report registered appreciation of the fact that in all continents the significance of the ministry of the laity in the world is being more clearly seen. The Assembly voted to receive the report and its suggestions for transmission to the Working Committee of the Department and to adopt the two recommendations: to hold in 1963 an institute of leadership training for the equipment of the laity; and to consider the possibility of holding regional conferences on 'The Laity: The Church in the World'.

As chairman of the Committee on the *Department of Co-operation of Men and Women in Church, Family and Society,* Bishop John W. Sadiq (Church of India, Pakistan, Burma and Ceylon) presented its report (see pages 207-17). Grateful that the principle of co-operation is now widely accepted, the Committee urged that future attention be focused on 'its application both as regards structural changes and the deepening of the spiritual life'. The report pointed out that a number of member churches now permit the ordination of women, that many churches are increasingly using the service of professionally trained women, and that a greater participation of women in policy-making boards of churches needs to be encouraged. Bishop Sadiq emphasized the additional responsibilities of the Department as a result of its now taking on the work on marriage and family life hitherto carried on by the International Missionary Council. The Committee submitted five recommendations to the Assembly:

> That churches which employ ordained women and women professional workers study the ways in which their best contribution can be made.
>
> That churches study needed modifications in their teaching, preaching, pastoral counselling and practical service as a result of social changes affecting the family.

That in countries where state schools provide no religious instruction the churches should help families fulfil their responsibility.

That more specialized attention be given to questions relating to the family and that such matters as sex education, preparation for marriage and responsible parenthood be studied in mixed groups.

That churches be encouraged to act on urgent needs of women and girls, such as the establishment of schools and hostels, as a corrective to the frequent practice of making plans only for men and boys.

In the brisk discussion that ensued representatives of the Church of Scotland urged that the office of elder and similar positions on policy-making boards be opened to women whenever such is not now the case, and an amendment to this effect was voted. A spokesman of the Salvation Army proposed an amendment to 'encourage wider support for the use of women as ordained ministers' but withdrew the amendment after Anglican and Russian Orthodox delegates expressed the judgment that this was a divisive matter on which the Assembly ought not to take sides. There was support for the recommendation of the report that there ought to be a thorough study of the effectiveness of women in the ministry in those churches which have ordained them. The Assembly voted to receive the report and to approve the recommendations, as amended.

The Committee on the *Ecumenical Institute,* which had Dr Victor Hajek (Evangelical Church of Czech Brethren) as its chairman and Miss Edith Mollie Batten (Church of England) as its secretary, presented its report. It interpreted the Institute at Bossey as an instrument for the renewal of the life of the churches through study and worship in an ecumenical setting. It foresaw that the time is near when the budget of the Institute will need to be increased if the academic standing of the graduate school is to be maintained and the concern for lay work developed. The Assembly voted to receive and generally approve the report (see pages 217-21).

Taking up the uncompleted items in the report of the Policy Reference Committee, Archbishop Iakovos presented a statement on *Religious Liberty* (see pages 159-61) for the approval of the Assembly. It went beyond the declaration of this subject adopted at Amsterdam in 1948 by a further analysis of concrete aspects of religious liberty. An Eastern Orthodox delegate desired to add a reference, at least in a footnote, to the statement on proselytism already adopted by this Assembly. Certain editorial changes of a minor character were proposed from the floor and incorporated into the text of the report. It was then voted, with no dissenting voice, to adopt the statement as revised.

At the afternoon session Bishop Richard C. Raines (Methodist, USA) introduced the report of the Committee on the *Department of Information* (see pages 304-15). It called attention to the fact that publications now need to be issued in Russian and Spanish as well as in English, French and German (which are the Council's official languages) if the Council is to serve its constituency adequately. It stressed the growing importance of moving more strongly into broadcasting and television and welcomed the proposed experiment of having the part-time service of a staff member for co-operation with the World Association for Christian Broadcasting. The report reminded the Assembly that the Department of Information serves every area of the World Council's interest and needs larger staff if it is to fulfil what is expected of it. In the discussion it was agreed to take note of the desirability of making Russian and Spanish additional languages of the Council and of several other suggestions mentioned for further consideration. The Assembly gave general approval to the report and transmitted it to the Central Committee.

Finance

The Committee on the *Department of Finance* next presented its report (see pages 291-303) through the chairman, Bishop Alwyn K. Warren (Anglican Church of New Zealand), who made a lucid explanation of the contemplated annual budget for the coming period and the methods of supporting it. He called attention to the gratifying fact that between the second and the third Assemblies expenditures had been kept within available resources. He proposed a 'model general budget' which requires an increase of 47 per cent over present contributions from the churches. He also pointed out that when the additional staff members authorized by this Assembly began their work additional expenditure of about $23,000 would be called for. He expressed the hope that this amount might be provided by contributions from new member churches and increased contributions from churches outside the North American area. Satisfied with these explanations the Assembly voted:

That an annual model general budget of $750,200 (including $23,000 for the two new offices and staff) be approved.
That an increase of at least 47 per cent in contributions from the churches for this budget be approved.
That each member church be requested to re-examine its present giving in relation to its size and economic strength.
That the revenue side of the budget be raised from $727,200 to $750,200 from member churches.

Bishop Warren then explained the supplementary budgets, supported in other ways, for the Division of Interchurch Aid and Service to Refugees, the Commission and Division of World Mission and Evangelism, and the Commission of the Churches on International Affairs. In answer to questions, more detailed information was given by Mr Frank Northam, the treasurer, after which a motion to approve these budgets was adopted. The Assembly voiced special appreciation of the gift of Mrs Thomas J. Watson for the construction of a library at the new headquarters, thanked all contributors to the headquarters fund, paid tribute to Bishop Sherrill for his devoted and faithful service in this connection, and urged churches which had not yet contributed to the headquarters fund to do so. Gratitude was further expressed to Dr Blake for his strong leadership as chairman of the Committee on Programme and Finance during the last five years.

At his final appearance as chairman of the *Policy Reference Committee* Archbishop Iakovos presented a series of recommendations having to do with proposals that had been made for increased budget at various points, and the Assembly voted:

To authorize the appointment of an associate to the executive secretary in the USA and of an additional Assistant General Secretary in Geneva.
To refer to the Central Committee the proposal for additional funds for the Commission of the Churches on International Affairs for service in Asia and Africa.
To transmit to the Central Committee the proposals for financing, outside the general budget, the proposed 'programme projects' of (*a*) a Secretariat for Lay Service Abroad for an experimental period; (*b*) a secretary for a limited period, attached to the Department of Information, for work in broadcasting and television; (*c*) a writer, related to the Youth Department, to prepare ecumen-

ical material for use in the educational programmes of the churches.

Supplementing action having been already taken by the Assembly, it was voted, on a motion from the floor, that the authorized re-examination of the organizational pattern of the World Council be undertaken within the next two years. The Assembly then gave approval to the report of the Policy Reference Committee as a whole.

South African Message

On behalf of the Business Committee Dr Fry then read the draft of 'A Message to Christians in South Africa' (see pages 322-5), prefacing it by a statement that as a result of the 1960 Cottesloe Consultation of member churches in South Africa (a report of which had been mailed to all delegates) three churches had withdrawn from membership in the World Council. The Message declared that during the Assembly 'our convictions concerning the unity of the Church have grown' and it endorsed the Cottesloe statement that 'no one who believes in Jesus Christ may be excluded from any Church on the grounds of his colour or race'. The Message reaffirmed the position of the Evanston Assembly on race and recognized that in the name of Christ many in South Africa are engaged in the struggle for the elimination of racial segregation and discrimination. After several comments of warm approval from the floor, the Message was adopted without a dissenting voice.

Reports of Sections Reviewed

At the deliberative session in the evening Professor Richardson submitted the report of the section on 'Witness' as revised in the light of the earlier discussion. The comments which followed showed that there was still some theological dissent from the view that the Holy Spirit is 'at work among men (of non-Christian faiths) preparing for the coming of the Gospel' and that the light of Christ 'has preceded the bearers of the Good News into the darkest places'. Final action on the report was deferred, awaiting further consideration by the drafting committee.

Dr de Vries then presented a slightly revised draft of the report of the section on 'Service'. There was still some questioning about the paragraph dealing with war, nuclear weapons and disarmament. On the other hand, the judgment was expressed that the statement, as now revised after an open hearing, reflected the most that could be said by the Assembly as a whole. Several proposals for minor revision at other points were accepted, after which the Assembly approved the substance of the report and commended it to the churches for study and action.

Bishop Oliver Tomkins brought forward a slightly revised draft of the report of the section on 'Unity', calling attention to the incorporation of some of the suggestions which had been made from the floor. The Assembly, satisfied with the revision, approved the substance of the report and commended it to the churches for study and action.

Adjournment was taken after evening prayers led by Archbishop Gunnar A. E. Hultgren (Church of Sweden).

Seventeenth Day: Tuesday, December 5

The last of the Assembly's six periods of Bible study was held at 9 o'clock. They had been so helpful that at the end there were spontaneous expressions of appreciation to the leaders.

The report of the Committee on the *Division of World Mission and Evangelism* was introduced by Bishop Rajah Manikam (Evangelical Lutheran, India) at the beginning of the business session under Dr Payne's chairmanship. Bishop Manikam characterized the moment as historic, the first time the new Division had reported. He interpreted the integration of the World Council and the International Missionary Council as meaning that the World Council takes the missionary task into the very heart of its life and that the missionary agencies place their work in clearer ecumenical perspective. Attention was called to a certain measure of overlapping and duplication between the new Division and some of the older Divisions, particularly the Division of Interchurch Aid and Service to Refugees and the Division of Studies, and the importance of an early review of organizational structure was again emphasized (see pages 249-57).

Dr Charles W. Ranson (Methodist Church in Ireland) stressed the need for a simpler organizational pattern for the divisions and departments of the World Council and for more concentration on 'basic priorities' in programmes and budgets. Dr John Coventry Smith (United Presbyterian, USA) moved an amendment, which was adopted, to insert a paragraph which would give stronger accent to the principle that the Division of World Mission and Evangelism is more than a continuation of the interests of the International Missionary Council, and provides a new dimension for the World Council of Churches as a whole, A few other emendations were suggested and accepted. The Assembly voted to receive the report and to commend it to the careful attention of the member Churches and of the Commission on World Mission and Evangelism.

Bishop Manikam presented also, on behalf of the Committee, a recommendation on world-wide evangelism which included a request to the Central Committee to give 'high priority to the task of helping the churches to fulfil their common calling to mission and evangelism'. Dr Alan Walker (Methodist Church of Australasia) felt the Council should go further in direct activity in evangelism and proposed a 'World Christian Mission' under the auspices of the Council, and in the name of the Australian Council of Churches urged the Central Committee to treat this as a matter of urgency. The recommendation of the Committee, as presented by Bishop Manikam, was approved (see page 257).

Sir Francis Ibiam, as chairman of the Committee on the *Division of Interchurch Aid and Service to Refugees,* presented its report, with emphasis on the fact that the Division is not merely an 'ecclesiastical Red Cross' but the churches themselves acting in fellowship. He reminded the Assembly that at Evanston the Division had been given a mandate to develop its work from an emergency and relief service to a permanent programme on a world-wide scale. The report accordingly proposed that in order to provide a more accurate symbol the name of the Division be changed to 'Division of Interchurch Aid, Refugee and World Service' and that its aims, functions and relationships be re-stated along the lines indicated in the report.

A resolution of gratitude to the Division and to all the giving churches mentioning especially what had been done in Algeria, which proved that the service of the Division was not limited to Christians but was as broad as human need, was proposed by a Coptic delegate and adopted.

Four recommendations approving the change of name and the development of organization along the lines indicated, the further working out of relationships with the Division of World Mission and Evangelism, the continuation of service to refugees, and the establishment of a secretariat to deal with problems of migration were approved without debate. The recommendation concerning 'areas of acute human need', which included a request to the Division to intensify its efforts in training leadership in agricultural, industrial, social and educational fields elicited a suggestion accepted by the Committee, that in contemplating projects there should be prior consultation with the Division of World Mission and Evangelism. The final recommendations, dealing with scholarships, especially in Africa, with the Ecumenical Church Loan Fund, and with finance, were then adopted after a few questions from the floor, and the Assembly voted to receive the report as a whole and give it general approval (see pages 229-48).

At a deliberative session in the afternoon, with Dr Fry in the chair, Professor Richardson re-submitted the report of the section on 'Witness', calling attention to three changes made in the light of the previous discussions. The Assembly then voted to approve the substance of the report and to commend it to the churches for study and appropriate action.

Closing Actions

An invitation to hold the Fourth Assembly of the World Council in Addis Ababa was graciously extended by the Abuna Theophilos (Ethiopian Orthodox Church), Metropolitan of Harrar. He referred to the venerable history of the Ethiopian Church and suggested that there are strategic reasons for holding the next Assembly in Africa. Archbishop Frank Woods (Church of England in Australia) expressed the hope that the continent of Australia would be given favourable consideration as the locale for the fourth Assembly and gave assurance of warm co-operation from the Australian churches. Feeling that the decision about an Assembly which is still five or six years in the future ought not to be made at this time, the Assembly referred the matter to the Central Committee.

For the Committee on the Message, Dr Kathleen Bliss presented a revised draft. Three slight changes were made by amendments proposed from the floor: to describe the fellowship in the World Council as being 'as deep as before and wider'; to make reference to progress in defining the nature of the unity we seek; to change 'We must go together also in the way of Christian Unity' to 'We must together seek the fullness of Christian unity'. The Message was then adopted as amended, without a dissenting voice (page 320).

The Archbishop of York (Dr Coggan) moved that a message should be sent to the delegates from East Germany who were refused permission to leave their country, to assure them of the sorrow of the members of the Assembly at their absence, of their prayer for them, and of their joy in the unity in Christ across all barriers.

The final act of the afternoon session was a word of appraisal and gratitude by Dr Fry as chairman of the Business Committee (see pages 326-8). He believed that New Delhi marked one of the great moments in ecumenical history, partly because of the new accession to membership, partly because of the fusion of two movements representing the unity of the Church and the mission of the Church. He was impressed by the increasing breadth of the 'community of faith in which Christ is gathering us'. He regarded the Assembly in New Delhi as having been a bold experiment in holding a wholly democratic gathering, sifting all the work of the Council through committee processes and making room for free debate at every point. In the midst of all this he felt a unity of spirit which had been the great factor in enabling the World Council to come thus far.

Dr Fry then paid a tribute of grateful appreciation to those who had done most to make the Assembly so memorable, including the President, the Vice-President and the Prime Minister of India; the churches of India, the National Christian Council of India, the Indian Committee on Arrangements, the Delhi Committee for the Assembly, the Christian congregations of Delhi; the representatives of the press, the broadcasters; the Commission on the general theme, the officers of sections and committees, the leaders in Bible study and the speakers; the office staff of 297 persons; Jeena and Co. as travel agents; the 'General Secretary non-pareil', the associate general secretaries and the executives of departments. Finally, Dr Fry paid a glowing tribute to members of the Central Committee, especially the 'veterans' who were completing their service, and to the retiring members of the Praesidium, felicitously characterizing each of them.

The presidents-elect, the Archbishop of Canterbury, Archbishop Iakovos, Sir Francis Ibiam, Principal David G. Moses, Pastor Niemöller and Mr Charles Parlin were then invited to take their seats on the rostrum as a symbol of their leadership during the period that lies ahead.

Closing Worship

The Assembly joined in a closing service of worship, with Dr Moses as the leader and Pastor Niemöller as the preacher. There were prayers of confession and of thanksgiving, an Indian lyric by an Indian choir, the recital of the *Te Deum Laudamus* and a Scripture lesson from Ephesians 5. Pastor Niemöller preached on Psalm 119.37, 'Turn away mine eyes from beholding vanity, and quicken thou me in thy way'. Looking forward to the period following the Assembly, he said:

> Our general theme in these days has been 'Jesus Christ the Light of the World'. And we know that actually this light has been present here and willing to show us the right way in the dark problems which we are facing together. There have been, and there are still very oppressive facts and conditions, for which we do not see any solution which we could possibly recommend or promote. We feel nevertheless we are charged with the responsibility to find and show the way how this darkness may be attacked in our Lord's spirit and be overcome by him who has come to be the light of his whole creation. We must not—and this will be our temptation always—abandon and leave it, neither in a sense of despondency nor in an attitude of hope for a world to come, and certainly not if it means that fellow-men have to suffer under its pressure. Nor must we look for any solution which we may find only in our own intelligence, but which will not be in accordance with the spirit of him who is the light, the only light, of the world. We shall patiently have to study, and to work and to wait and to pray for his light, that we may become able to find and to recognize the way on which he will be with us, because it is his way.

Pastor Niemöller's concluding word was a call to self-examination:

> We Christians are not meant to have only the conviction of Christ having absolute and universal superiority; we are meant to be his disciples, his followers, not just his advertising experts and his partisans, who—when they are off duty—live their own life as every man does. Do we deny ourselves or do we still retain our aspirations and selfish claims? Do we take up our cross or are we anxious only to find an opportunity to get rid of it? Do we follow him whom we call our Lord and Saviour, or do we choose and walk our own ways, marked by custom or tradition or fixed by our own autonomous choice? These questions we shall have to answer and we ought not to forget how the Apostle urges the Christians in Philippi: 'Let this mind be in you, which was also in Christ Jesus!'

Dr Moses led in a litany of intercession for all congregations of Christians, for the Church Universal, for the World Council of Churches, for all who are exploited or persecuted, and for a world torn asunder by fear and distrust. Minister and people then joined in the common act of commitment suggested by the Committee on the Message of the Assembly:

We confess Jesus Christ, Saviour of men and the light of the World;
Together we accept his command;
We commit ourselves anew to bear witness to him among men;
We offer ourselves to serve all men in love, that love which he alone imparts;
We accept afresh our calling to make visible our unity in him;
We pray for the gift of the Holy Spirit for our task.

Retrospect

Looking back on the seventeen days of the New Delhi Assembly, no two participants would have quite the same impressions but a few points stand out like mountain peaks that all would recognize. Among these one would feel confident in mentioning the following:

1. The Christian Church, having become world-wide, is now learning how to function as a world community. The entrance of twenty-three additional churches into the ecumenical circle brings its total membership up to 198 national or regional bodies which have in the World Council of Churches an organ through which their basic unity is finding expression in steadily widening common witness and common service.

2. The churches of Asia and Africa are now playing an active and increasing part in the world-wide Christian movement. That the Church of India carried their responsibility as hosts to the Assembly so effectively, and that eleven of the new members of the Council are from Africa, are important testimonies to a new ecumenical situation.

3. The coming of the Orthodox Churches of Russia, Bulgaria, Rumania and Poland into the membership of the World Council affords a lively hope that the Christian community can transcend the political and economic divisions of the world to a greater extent than most people have believed possible. Nothing that has happened in recent time has been so potent a witness that the universal Church

of Christ is not tied to any national culture but can have a corporate life of its own and be a reconciling force.

4. There was fresh evidence that the churches of the world as represented at New Delhi are not content to be self-contained communities, absorbed in their own institutional interests, but have a great concern for the character of the secular life. They were not only determined to stay together (as at Amsterdam) and to grow together (as at Evanston) but to move out together into the world's struggle for social justice and international peace.

5. The uniting of the missionary and the ecumenical concerns through the integration of the International Missionary Council into the World Council of Churches marks a new stage in the Christian world mission. The old distinction between 'sending' and 'receiving' churches begins to break down. All churches are more clearly seen as partners, on a plane of complete mutuality, in the common responsibility of making Christ known, loved and obeyed throughout the world.

6. The New Delhi Assembly was a working body to a much greater degree than its predecessors. The delegates were less like observers of a colourful spectacle and much more like representatives who knew they had hard work to do and were prepared to do it. Far more time was devoted to the patient review of programmes and to the formulation of policies. The New Delhi Assembly made it clear that the World Council is now regarded as the instrument of the churches themselves for great common tasks of world-wide dimension.

II

OPENING ACTIONS OF THE ASSEMBLY

BUSINESS SESSION: Sunday afternoon, November 19, 1961. Archbishop Iakovos, President, presiding.

Agenda: Actions concerning the integration of the International Missionary Council and the World Council of Churches.

1. Archbishop Iakovos called the Assembly to order in Business Session and called on Dr Christian Baeta, Chairman of the International Missionary Council, to report on the action of the IMC concerning the integration with the World Council of Churches.

2. Dr Baeta reported the resolution of the Administrative Committee of the International Missionary Council taken under the authority given to it by the IMC Assembly meeting in Ghana from December 28, 1957, to January 8, 1958:

WHEREAS the Assembly of the International Missionary Council meeting at Accra, Ghana, from December 28, 1957, to January 8, 1958, resolved that:

The Ghana Assembly of the International Missionary Council, having reviewed the steady growth of the relationship of association between the IMC and the WCC, and having considered with care the opinions of delegates, and those of the Christian Councils whose views have been presented, accepts in principle the integration of the two Councils, and desires further steps to be taken towards this goal; and

WHEREAS the Assembly gave general approval to the following process for IMC action, with power to the Administrative Committee to make the necessary adjustments:

(*a*) The draft Plan to be again communicated, as soon as possible, to member organizations, with the following documents: a report on the relevant discussions of the Ghana Assembly, a copy of these Resolutions, full information on the present divisional organization of the WCC and a request . . . for further comment and criticism.

(*b*) Comment from member organizations to be in the hands of the IMC Secretariat by April 30, 1959, and communicated by it to the secretary of the Joint Committee and to the Administrative Committee.

(*c*) The final plan, as prepared by the Joint Committee, to be sent early in 1960 to member organizations, this Plan to take the form of a draft Constitution of the new unified body, with a full explanatory memorandum.

(*d*) The Administrative Committee or an Assembly of the IMC to consider the Plan (Constitution) in 1960 or possibly in the early part of 1961, and, if approved,

(*e*) to send it to member Councils following the provisions of Cap. XII (2) of the IMC Constitution.

(*f*) On the expiry of six months the official action of the IMC is to be signified to the Joint Committee and to the WCC; and

WHEREAS all the member organizations of the International Missionary Council have been fully consulted in accordance with the above paragraphs (*a*), (*b*), and (*c*); and

WHEREAS the Administrative Committee of the International Missionary Council, at its meeting at La Brévière, France, July 20-24, 1959, passed the following resolution in accordance with the instructions of the Ghana Assembly:

> After receiving from Joint Committee following its meeting in 1960 the final and constitutional form of the Plan, Administrative Committee proposes to act upon the authority entrusted to it by the Ghana Assembly. On behalf of the IMC Assembly the Committee will consider this document and, if approved, will resolve that the IMC assents to the proposed integration. This resolution, with the accompanying Plan and Constitution, will be sent to member councils following provisions of Cap. XII (2) of the present IMC Constitution.
>
> For the above purpose the officers are requested to convene a meeting of the Administrative Committee at a convenient date in 1960 and after the meeting of Joint Committee;

NOW THEREFORE the Administrative Committee, acting under the authority given to it by the Assembly

APPROVES the appended Constitution and Rules of the World Council of Churches, and in particular the Constitution of the Commission on World Mission and Evangelism and the Division of World Mission and Evangelism as a suitable constitutional means of securing the integration accepted in principle by the Assembly;

ADOPTS the said Constitution and Rules (subject to the adoption of the same by the World Council of Churches) as replacing the present Constitution and Rules of the IMC from the Date of Integration;

DECLARES that from the Date of Integration the integrated body henceforth to be known as the World Council of Churches, will be in all respects the legal successor of the International Missionary Council; that all assets of the International Missionary Council will, from that date, vest in the integrated World Council of Churches, to be administered by the Commission on World Mission and Evangelism and the Division of World Mission and Evangelism for the purposes set forth in the Constitution of the said Commission on World Mission and Evangelism and in accordance with its Constitution and Rules, and that all liabilities of the International Missionary Council at the Date of Integration will devolve upon this integrated World Council of Churches and in particular upon the said Commission on World Mission and Evangelism;

INSTRUCTS the General Secretary to notify all member organizations of the International Missionary Council of this action; and

INSTRUCTS the Officers that, in the event of the above resolutions not being disapproved in writing within six months after notification by six or more member organizations, they proceed immediately in consultation with the officers of the World Council of Churches to fix the Date of Integration and to make all arrangements for its consummation; and for this purpose to convene an Assembly of the International Missionary Council immediately prior to the Date of Integration.

3. Dr Baeta further informed the Assembly that this resolution had been confirmed by the Assembly of the IMC, at its meeting in New Delhi on November 17, 1961.

4. Archbishop Iakovos called on Dr Franklin Clark Fry, Chairman of the Central Committee of the World Council of Churches. Dr Fry explained that the Assembly had before it a series of amendments to the Constitution of the WCC which were necessary in order to effect integration with the IMC.

5. Dr Fry asked the Chairman whether the following, which had been recommended by the Central Committee, constituted his ruling concerning the amendability of amendments:

The double proviso in Article VIII of the Constitution of the World Council of Churches to the effect that it (the Constitution) may be amended by a two-thirds majority vote of the Assembly

'provided that the proposed amendment shall have been reviewed by the Central Committee, and notice of it sent to the constituent churches not less than six months before the meeting of the Assembly' implies and requires that such proposed amendment must be presented to and acted upon by an Assembly in exactly the form and wording in which it was approved for submission by the Central Committee and circulated to the churches for their consideration. Any modification of it, whether by addition, subtraction or substitution of words, would operate to create a new proposal and so, in obedience to the constitution and in fairness to the member churches, would necessitate repetition of the procedure required by Article VIII and consequent postponement of action until the succeeding Assembly.

The Chairman stated that this was his ruling.

6. Dr Fry presented and moved the resolution of the Central Committee concerning integration with the International Missionary Council:

The Central Committee recommends to the Third Assembly, provided that action to the same effect shall have been taken by the International Missionary Council, the adoption of the following resolution:

> that this Assembly, recalling that in their origins both the World Council of Churches and the International Missionary Council are manifestations and instruments of the same ecumenical movement, and believing that the purposes and functions of the two bodies are inseparable, rejoices that it is now possible to integrate the two Councils in one organization. Therefore, action to the same effect having been taken by the International Missionary Council, the Assembly gives its assent to the integration of the World Council of Churches and International Missionary Council and adopts the amendments to the Constitution and Rules of the World Council of Churches required to give effect to this action as here appended. The Assembly further approves the proposed Constitution of the Commission on World Mission and Evangelism.

Dr Fry corrected a printer's error on page 18 of the printed document which had been distributed to the Assembly so that the final words of Article VI (2) (i) of the Constitution read, in accord with the Workbook: 'Its urgency for world mission and evangelism.'

7. Dr Fry asked the Chairman whether it was the will of the

Assembly that the amendments be read in detail. After taking a vote of the Assembly, the Chairman informed Dr Fry that it would not be necessary to read the amendments. In reply to a query about the Basis, Dr Fry reported that this would be considered as an item of business at a different time.

8. Dr Fry asked the Assembly to note that the resolution of the Central Committee on which the vote was to be taken concerned amendments to the Constitution and Rules of the World Council required to effect integration, and also the proposed Constitution of the Commission and Division of World Mission and Evangelism. It was however planned that the Rules and the Constitution of the Commission and Division of World Mission and Evangelism would be referred to the Policy Reference Committee of the Assembly for consideration. It would be open to that Committee to propose amendments to the Rules and to the Constitution of the Division of World Mission and Evangelism.

9. Archbishop Iakovos asked for discussion on the resolution of the Central Committee. There being none, the *resolution of the Central Committee was put to the vote and carried, nemine contradicente.*

10. Archbishop Iakovos then recognized Dr Fry who announced that by action of the Central Committee, the allocation of delegates' places to the churches in the Assembly had included twenty-five seats for persons specially representing missionary interests of the churches, and that they were already seated.

11. Archbishop Iakovos read the Declaration that the Act of Integration had been accomplished:

> By the authority of the Assemblies of the International Missionary Council and the World Council of Churches, I declare that these two Councils are now united in one body with the name of the World Council of Churches. In the Name of the Father and of the Son and of the Holy Spirit. Amen.

The Chairman called upon Dr Henry P. van Dusen, Chairman of the Joint Committee of the IMC/WCC, to lead an act of worship. Following the worship, Archbishop Iakovos adjourned the Business Session.

Business Session: 9.45 a.m., Monday, November 20, 1961.

Dr Ernest A. Payne, Vice-Chairman of the Central Committee, presided.

Agenda: Actions concerning Assembly Committees and Officers
Procedures concerning Resolutions
Applications for Membership
Report of the Chairman of the Central Committee
Report on Programme and Finance
Seating of delegates from new member churches

12. Dr Payne called the Assembly to order in Business Session and called upon the General Secretary to present the recommendations of the Central Committee concerning Committees of the Assembly.

13. Dr Visser 't Hooft presented the recommendation of the Central Committee that the *Business Committee* of the Assembly be composed of the following:

The Presidents of the WCC
The Members of the Executive Committee
The Chairmen of the Sections on Witness, Service and Unity
The Chairmen of the Assembly Committees on the Division of Studies, the Division of Ecumenical Action, the Division of Inter-church Aid and Service to Refugees, the Division on World Mission and Evangelism, the Commission of the Churches on International Affairs, the Departments of Information and Finance
The Chairman of the Policy Reference Committee
The Chairman of the Nominations Committee
The Chairman of the Worship Committee
The Chairman of the Press Committee
Such limited number of other persons as may be found necessary by the Executive Committee.

The Central Committee also proposed that the Chairman of the Central Committee, Dr Franklin Clark Fry, be the Chairman of the Business Committee, and that Dr Robert S. Bilheimer serve as Secretary. There being no discussion, it was moved and

VOTED to constitute the Business Committee of the Assembly as recommended by the Central Committee.

14. Dr Visser 't Hooft presented the recommendations of the Central Committee that the following persons constitute the *Nominations Committee* of the Assembly:

Dr William S. Tindal, Church of Scotland, U.K., Chairman
Dr H. H. Harms, Evangelical Church of Hamburg, Germany, Secretary
Mr Charles C. Parlin, Methodist Church, USA
Bishop John W. Sadiq, Church of India, Pakistan, Burma and Ceylon, India

Dr Christian Baeta, Evangelical Presbyterian Church of Ghana
The Metropolitan Chrysostomos of Myron, Ecumenical Patriarchate, Turkey
Dr Edwin H. Tuller, American Baptist Convention, USA
Bishop P. L. Simoes, Protestant Episcopal Church, Brazil
The Rev. (Miss) I. E. Merry, Congregational Union of Australia
Bishop A. Wantula, Evangelical Church of the Augsburgian Confession, Poland
Mr V. G. Montes, United Church of Christ in the Philippines

There being no further nominations from the floor, it was moved and

VOTED to constitute the Nominations Committee as recommended by the Central Committee.

15. Dr Visser 't Hooft presented the recommendation of the Central Committee that the following persons constitute the *Credentials Committee* of the Assembly:

The Rev. F. G. A. Stenstrøm, Mission Covenant Church of Sweden, Convener
Dr Norman J. Baugher, Church of the Brethren, USA
Bishop J. A. Do Amaral, Methodist Church of Brazil
Professor Basil Ioannidis, Church of Greece
The Rt Rev. C. M. Kareri, Presbyterian Church of East Africa
Professor A. T. Nikolainen, Evangelical Lutheran Church of Finland
The Rev. Keikichi Shirai, United Church of Christ in Japan.

There being no further nominations from the floor, it was moved and

VOTED to constitute the Credentials Committee as recommended by the Central Committee.

16. Dr Visser 't Hooft then presented the recommendations of the Central Committee regarding the nomination by the Business Committee of the Central Committee of the *Officers of Sections and of Committees* (see Appendix 6).

There being no discussion it was moved and

VOTED that the Business Committee be empowered to confirm the Officers of Sections and Committees as proposed by the Central Committee.

(Note: This action was taken by the Business Committee at its meeting on November 20.)

17. Dr Visser 't Hooft presented the recommendation of the Central Committee that the Business Committee constitute *the membership of the Sections and Committees.* There being no discussion, it was moved and

VOTED that the Business Committee constitute the membership of Sections and Committees.

(Note: This action was taken by the Business Committee at its meeting on November 20.)

18. Dr Visser 't Hooft presented the recommendation of the Central Committee concerning *resolutions* as follows:

Rule number 11 of the Rules of Debate and Procedure in Business Sessions reads as follows:

'If any member desires to propose a *motion not on the agenda,* he shall be permitted to have his motion read. A vote shall be immediately taken as to whether or not his motion shall be included in the agenda.'

For the more logical ordering and better timing of the business of the Assembly, and in order to facilitate the collation of similar resolutions, delegates are urged to give notice to the Business Committee of any resolution they desire to have brought to the Assembly. Ordinarily the presiding officer will not allow the reading of a resolution until it has been examined by the Business Committee, but this will not prevent a delegate from having his resolution read at an appropriate time later.

There being no discussion, it was moved and

VOTED to accept the above recommendation of the Central Committee concerning resolutions.

19. The Chairman called upon the General Secretary to report on the recommendations of the Central Committee concerning *applications for membership.* Dr Visser 't Hooft reported that twenty-three applications for membership had been received since the Central Committee meeting in St Andrews, Scotland. All the churches had indicated by letter that they accepted the Basis of the World Council of Churches. The General Secretary had informed the member churches about the applications from the first nine churches on the list and they had thus had the opportunity to study these applications. The other fourteen applications had arrived since that letter had been written. However, the Central Committee meeting on November 17, having reviewed the list of applications, had decided

nemine contradicente to recommend to the Assembly that all should be admitted to membership.

The General Secretary recalled that he had spoken in his speech at the Opening Session about the significance of the applications from churches in Africa, and referred to the special interest of the first applications from churches in the islands of the Pacific and Latin America and Pentecostal churches. He continued:

> With regard to the Orthodox Church of Russia the Central Committee has already reported in *From Evanston to New Delhi* (page 19) about the action taken to develop relationships of understanding and confidence with that church. The present Central Committee has been concerned with these relationships during the whole period of its existence. In this matter the Committee and its officers have sought to give absolute priority to the question: How can the cause of Christ and in particular the cause of Christian unity be served best? It has become impressed by the desire for fellowship with Christians from other churches which lives in the churches of Russia. It has become convinced that for the sake of the Church of Christ it is important that fellowship should be established between the churches of Russia and the other churches. In this matter we have been encouraged by the fact that the leaders of the Orthodox Church of Russia have made such a thorough study of the work of the Council and have come to know the principles and procedures which govern the life and work of the Council.
>
> More recently three other Orthodox Churches, those of Rumania, Bulgaria and Poland, have also sent in their applications. We remember that these three churches have played an active role in the early period of the ecumenical movement.

The Churches listed in the chronological order of their applications were:

United Church of Central Africa in Rhodesia
Iglesia Pentecostal de Chile
Moravian Church in the Western Cape Province
Eglise Evangélique en Nouvelle-Calédonie et aux Iles Loyauté
Union des Eglises Baptistes du Cameroun
Orthodox Church of Russia
United Presbyterian Church of Pakistan
Church of the Province of Uganda and Ruanda-Urundi
Presbyterian Church in the Cameroons
Presbyterian Church in Trinidad
Finnish Evangelical Lutheran Church of America (Suomi Synod)
Mision Iglesia Pentecostal (Chile)
Bulgarian Orthodox Church

Eglise Evangélique du Gabon
Bantu Congregational Church
Presbyterian Church of Nigeria
Rumanian Orthodox Church
Evangelical Church of North-Western Tanganyika
Eglise Evangélique Manianga Matadi (Congo)
Presbyterian Church of the New Hebrides
Usambara-Digo Lutheran Church (Tanganyika)
Orthodox Church of Poland
Congregational Christian Church in Samoa (Samoan Church LMS)

Dr Visser 't Hooft added that certain smaller churches which had made applications were not on this list. It was thought by the Executive Committee and the Central Committee that it would be advisable to have first a discussion in the Policy Reference Committee to secure a ruling on the size of churches to be admitted.

20. The Chairman recalled the procedure for voting and speaking which had been announced in writing the day before, namely that voting would be by ballot, each member church having one vote, and that statements concerning the vote cast by a church would be in order following the voting. The Chairman asked whether all authorized to vote had a ballot, and proceeded to the vote. As the stewards were collecting the ballot, the Chairman indicated that any authorized by their churches might make statements concerning their vote.

21. The Chairman recognized *Archbishop John of San Francisco* who asked to speak on behalf of the Russian Orthodox Greek Catholic Church of North America. He wished to have recorded an explanation of their vote on the application of the Russian Orthodox Church in the USSR.

> It has become our duty, flowing from deep religious considerations, to abstain by reason of certain circumstances, from voting on the application of the Russian Orthodox Church for membership in the World Council of Churches. But we hope that the causes for those apprehensions which are the reasons for our abstention will vanish in the near future by the providence of God.

22. The Chairman recognized *Professor H. Alivisatos* of the Church of Greece.

> As a representative of the Orthodox Church of Greece and in my capacity as one of the oldest members of the World Council of

Churches who has pled from the very beginning for the full participation of the whole Orthodox Church in the World Council of Churches, I am really happy and with full satisfaction I see the admittance of the Russian Orthodox Church and of the Orthodox Churches of Rumania, Bulgaria and Poland and express my fervent wish and certainty that the Orthodox Church as one Orthodox Unity will have a cordial co-operation with the rest of the sister churches in the World Council of Churches for the glory of Christ.

23. *Archbishop Athenagoras of Thyateira* was recognized by the Chairman.

This Assembly yesterday, by an admirable consent and an overwhelming vote—and by a similar one today—has written a splendid page in the book of the life and work of the World Council of Churches' organization. The vote for the enlargement of its membership is a vote destined to give to this organization more life and strength to continue its upward road, to fight the scandal of the division in our Christian society.

On behalf of the Ecumenical Patriarchate and its Holy Synod, I heartily congratulate the Assembly and convey the blessing of His All-Holiness the Ecumenical Patriarch of Constantinople Athenagoras, to each and every individual member of the World Council of Churches.

It is with great pride that I see today the noble and most Christian-like dream of the Ecumenical Patriarchate materialized and assuming form and proportion. It is well known to every church and individual interested in the most fervently desired idea of the Unity of Christianity, that the Ecumenical Patriarchate first conceived, originated and promoted the idea of such a need.

The General Secretary of this organization, Dr Visser 't Hooft, repeatedly emphasized the fact and truth that in 1920 the Ecumenical Patriarchate issued its famous Encyclical Letter, which henceforth has become the sacred ecumenical document, on which the ecumenical movement of the World Council of Churches is based, and of which it has been justifiably proud.

Having the great privilege to be the Head of the Delegation of both the Ecumenical Patriarchate and of the Patriarchate of Jerusalem to this Assembly, I feel my heart overflowing with joy today over the fact that the vote of this Assembly yesterday and today has significantly increased the World Council of Churches' membership.

During the last decade of the life and work of the World Council of Churches, I have repeatedly had the privilege and honour to represent almost all the Greek Orthodox Patriarchates at her Conferences and at her Central Committee meetings. As one of her five Presidents for four years until the Second Assembly at Evanston, I followed with great admiration and to my heart's content the splendid growth of this organization—her completion, her blooming, and her abundant harvest of beneficial results and fruits. But I am especially glad today that great will be the joy which the Ecumenical Patriarchate of Constantinople will experience over the fact that four more Orthodox Churches are to be henceforth members of the World Council of Churches. Their participation in its work will undoubtedly increase the contribution of Eastern Orthodoxy to the Ecumenical movement, and the message of Orthodoxy will be heard more emphatically throughout the Christian world—its legacy and heritage will be appreciated and shared by all.

Glory be to the Father and to the Son and to the Holy Ghost for this day.

24. Dr Payne recognized the *Rt. Rev. Dr Zoltan Beky,* Bishop of the Hungarian Reformed Church in America, who asked to speak on the admission of the Russian Orthodox Church.

The Hungarian Reformed Church in America feels itself bound in unity of Christian love and fellowship with the great communion of the Russian Orthodox Church. The many thousands of martyrs of modern persecutions bear witness to the glorious Christian faith and loyalty of the clergy and believers of this great Communion. If the official delegates, who present themselves as being designated by that Church will truly represent the membership of their Church, the Hungarian Reformed Church in America will cast its vote in favour of the admission of the Russian Orthodox Church into the fellowship of the World Council of Churches. But if the official representatives of the Russian Orthodox Church will use this platform for political purposes contrary to the true spirit of the Russian Orthodox Church and will try or endeavour to represent the views of their government, based upon the principles of an atheistic materialism and an undemocratic system of one-party dictatorship, then the Hungarian Reformed Church in America wishes to record its objections in the Minutes. At the present time the Hungarian Reformed Church in America will abstain from voting.

25. *Professor Dr Werner Küppers* of the Old Catholic Church in Germany was recognized by the Chairman.

As representative of a Church which has been among the first to seek closer contact with the Eastern Churches in this time and age, I should like to make the following statement regarding the acceptance of the Orthodox Churches of Russia, Rumania, Bulgaria and Poland as members of the World Council of Churches:

1. On the initiative of the Old Catholic Churches, so-called Union Conferences took place as far back as 1874 and 1875 at Bonn. At these conferences, the Church of Russia had particularly strong representation. Wherever possible, these contacts have been continued up to the present time, their ultimate aim being the reunion of the whole of Christendom.
2. The Old Catholic Church has always striven to cultivate and develop these relations with the entire family of Orthodox Churches. For that reason the Pan-Orthodox Conference at Rhodes, as a new starting point of practical Orthodox co-operation, gave us particular joy and satisfaction.
3. We, therefore, regard today's acceptance of these Orthodox Churches into the World Council as an advance in the union between Orthodox Christianity as a whole and the ecumenical movement. We have been in relation with *all* the autocephalous Orthodox Churches in all countries, including the so-called 'churches in exile', and where possible we have fostered those relations. We wish to continue to do so without let or hindrance, and it is our belief that this contact with the entire family of Orthodox Churches will surmount all difficulties and misgivings and will prove a blessing to the ecumenical movement.

26. *Pasteur Jean Kotto* of the Evangelical Church of Cameroun was recognized by the Chairman.

As representative of one of the first churches in so-called 'Black Africa' to join the World Council of Churches, I should like to thank the Assembly which is voting on the question of admitting the Union of Baptist Churches in the Cameroons and the Evangelical Church in Gabon. We are in close contact with the former and are holding negotiations in order to examine not only what still divides us but also what ought to unite us. With the second of these churches we are on good terms, although it is situated in Gabon, a republic geographically adjacent to our own. Both of these churches are inspired by the interest in ecumenism which they received from the Paris Mission to which we express our gratitude. I therefore ask you to support my recommendation and to vote in favour of these two churches becoming members of the World Council.

27. *The Very Rev. Ignatius Hazim,* representing the Greek Orthodox Patriarchate of Antioch, was recognized by the Chairman and expressed his support of the application for membership in the World Council of Churches from the Russian, Polish and Bulgarian Orthodox Churches.

28. The Chairman announced that Dr Hans J. Margull, Dr Ros-

well P. Barnes, and Mr C. I. Itty had been appointed *Tellers* by the Executive Committee.

29. The Chairman called upon Dr Franklin Clark Fry, the Chairman of the Central Committee, to present the *Report of the Chairman of the Central Committee* (see pages 144-5 and Appendix 2) and as he did so expressed deep appreciation for Dr Fry's leadership.

Following the presentation of his report Dr Fry moved that the Report of the Central Committee, *Evanston to New Delhi,* and the report of the International Missionary Council be referred to the Policy Reference Committee. There being no discussion, it was moved and

VOTED to refer the Report of the Central Committee 'Evanston to New Delhi' and the Report of the International Missionary Council to the Policy Reference Committee.

30. Dr Payne recognized *Father Makary El Souriany* of the Coptic Orthodox Church of Egypt who said:

> We appreciate the words of Dr Fry concerning the work of the Central Committee. It gives a real and true picture of what the Central Committee has done during the last seven years since Evanston till now through the wise guidance and leadership of Dr Fry and Dr Payne, the vice-chairman, and the co-operation of the staff and delegates of member Churches. On behalf of the Coptic Orthodox Church of Egypt, I wish to express our deep feelings of gratitude for the work and sympathy of the World Council of Churches, which in our own experience have been felt in every contact with this respected body and instrument of God's grace.

31. The Chairman called on Dr Eugene Carson Blake to present the report of the Central Committee on *Programme and Finance* (see pages 71-5, 145 and 291-300 and Appendix 3).

Following the presentation, Dr Payne asked for discussion but indicated that there would be further opportunity for discussion at the Hearing on the Report on Programme and Finance on Tuesday, November 21, at 11.15 a.m. and at the Business Session of the Assembly on Thursday afternoon, November 23, when action on the Report would be taken. No discussion took place at this time.

32. Dr Payne reported that the detailed *results of the vote on applications for membership* were not yet available but that each of the twenty-three churches had received the necessary two-thirds majority of the member churches present and voting. Dr Payne said that

never, since its formation, has the World Council of Churches had at one time so large and significant accession to its membership. Of these twenty-three churches, some are amongst the most ancient Christian Churches, with a rich history and tradition of many centuries; others are the fruit of missionary work of European and American churches during the past hundred years or so, a striking evidence of the continued spread of the Christian faith.

These twenty-three churches are of varied ecclesiastical tradition, and polity. They include Christian brethren of Orthodox, Lutheran, Anglican, Reformed, Moravian, Congregational, Baptist and Pentecostal persuasion. The two Pentecostal Churches are welcome as the first of their denomination and as coming from Latin America. But every continent is represented, their members are of many nationalities and races, Africa providing on this occasion the largest group.

All have signified their desire to become members of the World Council of Churches, which has recently been described as 'a single community of mutually sustaining fellowship'. We bid them all welcome and, in token thereof, I ask one representative of each of these new member churches to come to the platform to receive their badges as delegates, and no longer simply observers, at this Assembly.

Following the presentation of the delegates' badges, Dr Payne adjourned the Business Session.

BUSINESS SESSION: Tuesday morning, November 21, 1961.

Dr Franklin Clark Fry, Chairman of the Central Committee, presided.

Agenda: Message Committee
Greetings and messages

33. Dr Fry called the Assembly to order in Business Session. As Chairman of the Business Committee, he presented its proposal for the *Committee on the Message,* as follows:

Dr Kathleen Bliss, Chairman, Church of England
Dr R. S. Barbour—Church of Scotland
Mrs Ba Maung Chain—Burma Baptist Convention
Professor Vitaly Borovoy—Church of Russia
The Metropolitan Parthenios of Carthage—Patriarchate of Alexandria
Dr Alford Carleton—United Church of Christ, USA
The Rev. Emilio Castro—The Methodist Church, Uruguay
Dr Paul Devanandan—Church of South India

The Rev. E. E. Mahabane—The Methodist Church, South Africa
Bishop G. Noth—Evangelical Church in Germany
Bishop Bengt Sundkler—Evangelical Church of N.W. Tanganyika
Judge J. M. Tunnell—United Presbyterian Church in the USA
The Rev. Charles Westphal—Reformed Church of France
The Rev. Hendrik van Andel—Dutch Reformed Church (Youth Participant).

There being no discussion, it was moved and

VOTED to accept the proposal of the Business Committee for the Committee on the Message.

34. Dr Fry explained the procedures for the *Hearing on the Report of the Programme and Finance Committee* to be held immediately following the close of the Business Session. All who desired to attend were welcome. Recommendations from the Hearing would be considered by the Business Committee and through it by the Policy Reference Committee or other Assembly Committee.

35. Dr Fry reported that many *messages* had been received by the Assembly. Three of these messages were presented to the Assembly (see page 14). Archbishop Iakovos read the message from His All-Holiness the Ecumenical Patriarch Athenagoras. The message from His Holiness the Patriarch of Moscow and All-Russia was read by Archbishop Nikodim. Extracts were read from the message presented by the Abuna Theophilos on behalf of the Ethiopian Orthodox Church.

Dr Fry adjourned the Business Session.

BUSINESS SESSION, 4.30 p.m., Thursday, November 23, 1961.

Bishop Sherrill, President, presided.

Agenda: Report on Programme and Finance (Appendix 3)
Headquarters Properties Fund

36. Bishop Sherrill called the Assembly to order in Business Session. He called on Dr Eugene Carson Blake to present the recommendations of the Business Committee concerning action by the Assembly on the Report of the Programme and Finance Committee.

Dr Blake on behalf of the Business Committee proposed that the Assembly receive and give general approval to Sections II, III and IV of the Report of the Central Committee on Programme and Finance and presented the following explanatory comments:

(*a*) Section II on 'The Scope of the World Council of Churches

Programme' could not take account of the integration of WCC and IMC, which had not been decided in August 1960, and therefore should be viewed as an account of the history and decisions of the WCC before integration with the IMC;

(*b*) in Section III on the 'Organization of the World Council of Churches', it is explicitly recognized that the organizational pattern there suggested will need early re-examination in the light of further discussion of the WCC and of experience within the newly integrated body. This discussion should take account not only of the material contained in Section II of the Programme and Finance Report, regarding the pre-integration WCC, but also of parallel material regarding the tasks and method of operation of the IMC, including the IMC Report to the Assembly and the material on DWME in the Work Book.

(*c*) the comments under (*b*) apply generally to the whole organizational structure but as specific examples, mention should be made of relationships between the Division of World Mission and Evangelism and the Division of Interchurch Aid and Service to Refugees, of the arrangements concerning the Department of Missionary Studies and the Department on Studies in Evangelism as set out in paragraph 50 of the Report and of the position of the Commission and Department on Faith and Order within the total structure; and

(*d*) general approval by the Assembly at this time of the organizational pattern set out in the Report does not preclude possibility of modifications within that general organizational pattern by decision of later sessions of this Assembly.

Following the discussion recorded below, it was moved and

VOTED to receive and give general approval to Sections II, III and IV of the Report on Programme and Finance, the explanatory comments recorded above being noted.

In discussion the following points were made:

37. *Dr E. H. Johnson,* Presbyterian Church in Canada, made the following comment and proposal in reference to paragraphs (*a*) and (*b*) of Recommendation 1. He stated that these referred to the tasks, methods and history of the World Council of Churches alone. He pointed out that they were quite inadequate as statements of Programme and Organization of the World Council of Churches since integration of the International Missionary Council had taken place. He

felt that if these sections were printed or used in any way there should be a note at the beginning stating that they referred to the situation prior to integration and should be used with parallel materials regarding the work and methods of the IMC with special reference to the IMC Report to the Assembly and the material in the Work Book on the Commission on World Mission and Evangelism. He suggested that the 're-examination and further discussion of certain questions concerning the nature and task of the WCC' called for in paragraph (*b*) take full account of the studies already made of the nature and task of the IMC and of the CWME. To this end he proposed the following sentence be added to paragraph 1 (*b*):

> This discussion should take account not only of the material contained in Section II of the Programme and Finance Report, regarding the pre-integration World Council of Churches, but also of parallel material regarding the tasks and methods of operation of the IMC, including the IMC Report to the Assembly and the material on the Commission on World Mission and Evangelism in the Work Book.

Dr Blake replied that after consultation with the Chairman of the Business Committee he found no objection to the inclusion of this amendment in the Recommendations of the Business Committee on the Report on Programme and Finance.

38. *Dr J. Robert Nelson* of the Methodist Church, USA, spoke to 1(*b*). He asked that the paragraph from page 83 in the Work Book be added:

> With this suggestion we concur at this time, though we believe that the location of Faith and Order within the Study Division is not the best final solution to our problem. Whatever decisions are taken by the Central Committee, now or eventually, we believe that close liaison should be maintained in the realm of study with other departments through the proposed Staff Co-ordinating Committee on Study in which all WCC departments are represented.

Dr Nelson felt that though this was implied, it needed to be stated in a straightforward manner. Dr Blake felt that it was not necessary to refer this request to the Policy Reference Committee since the statement on page 83 of the Work Book is so explicit and has been before the Assembly for some time.

39. Dr Blake proposed on behalf of the Business Committee, and there being no discussion, it was moved and

VOTED to refer Section V of the Report on Programme and Finance to the Committee on Finance.

40. Dr Blake asked the Assembly to note the following passage in paragraph 94 of the Report of the Central Committee on Programme and Finance:

> It is most desirable that proposals for the enlargement of any item of the programme or for additions to the programme should be considered at the time at which the Assembly debates the whole programme and should not be considered piecemeal; any other procedure can lead to distortion of the programme as a result of a desire to perform an adequate task in one particular field of work without due consideration of the claims of other programmes.

To achieve this purpose, Dr Blake proposed on behalf of the Business Committee that the following procedure be adopted:

> The Policy Reference Committee shall appoint a sub-committee for the purpose of dealing with proposals arising from other committees which would involve additions to the General Budget. This sub-committee would:
>
> (*a*) advise the officers of the committee putting forth the proposals concerning the financial position of the WCC in 1962 and the likely position thereafter, and concerning the relation of new proposals to the provisions of the Programme and Finance Report;
>
> (*b*) advise concerning various forms in which proposals could be brought forward, as for instance:
> . . . if funds are available; or
> . . . for the consideration of the Central Committee; or
> . . . to be done immediately, funds to be sought by savings elsewhere; or
> . . . if project funds are available.
>
> (*c*) collect all proposals which are finally made by committees, confer with the Finance Committee concerning them and, if necessary, submit them for general discussion at a meeting of the Committees' Co-ordinating Committee; and
>
> (*d*) thereafter prepare a recommendation to be passed by the Policy Reference Committee to the Finance Committee concerning all proposals, for submission to the Assembly with the report of the Finance Committee.

There being no discussion, it was moved and

VOTED to adopt the procedure outlined above as proposed by the Business Committee.

41. Dr Blake explained in connection with the above procedure that three concerns had been raised at the hearing on the Report on Programme and Finance held on November 21:

1. the need to strengthen the staff of the New York Office;
2. the need to strengthen the General Secretariat with particular reference to relations with Orthodox member churches;
3. and a proposal, with particular reference to the Commission

of the Churches on International Affairs and the Division of Studies, for strengthening the work of the Council directed toward the elimination of war and the establishment of world peace and justice.

Dr Blake stated that in accordance with the procedures now adopted, the first two items would be referred to the Policy Reference Committee and the third item to the committees concerned with this question.

42. Dr Blake proposed that the Assembly adopt the recommendation in the Report on Programme and Finance that the Central Committee be requested to set up the necessary machinery for the re-examination of the organizational pattern as soon as experience indicated this was needed, recognizing that modifications may be made by the Central Committee within the main lines of policy and programme and the general organizational pattern approved by the Assembly.

There being no discussion, it was moved and

VOTED that the Assembly adopt the recommendations described in paragraph 42 above.

43. Dr Fry was then asked to take the chair. He called on Bishop Sherrill to present the Report on the *Headquarters Properties Fund.*

Bishop Sherrill explained that the present facilities of the WCC were very makeshift and inadequate. Visitors to Geneva had been disillusioned by the lack of a chapel and an adequate library. With the generous assistance of the city authorities, a new site in a nearby suburb had been acquired on the outskirts of the 'international area' where headquarters buildings of other bodies would be erected in the near future. The new site would offer sufficient space for adequate buildings and room for future expansion if necessary.

Bishop Sherrill reported that the cost for the essential buildings had been estimated at $2,500,000. Committees had been appointed to help raise this fund. The response was varied—some took the matter seriously and others did not take it seriously. To cite just a few, he mentioned that the Spanish and Pakistan churches had given sacrificially. The Czechoslovakian churches would furnish the glass for the buildings. Campaigns were still going on in the United Kingdom and the Netherlands.

Because of rising costs in building, Bishop Sherrill indicated a rise in cost over the original estimated figure. We still needed

$400,000 to complete the building plan. The present funds would make it possible to build all but one wing. However, Bishop Sherrill reminded the Assembly that it is always more expensive to build such additions later. He reported that the library had been given by the family of the late Mr Thomas J. Watson who had been an elder of the Brick Presbyterian Church in New York and who had become interested in the World Council of Churches through his attendance at the First Assembly in Amsterdam.

Bishop Sherrill expressed the hope that some delegations would endeavour to do something and that others might wish to add to whatever they had already given. He then introduced Mr Frank Northam, the Director of the Department of Finance and Administration of the World Council of Churches. Bishop Sherrill stated that both he and Mr Northam would be available during the remainder of the Assembly to anyone who wished to speak with them about this matter.

Dr Fry adjourned the Business Session.

III

REPORTS OF SECTIONS:

WITNESS

THE report of the Section on Witness was considered in three deliberative sessions of the full Assembly and amended in the light of the debate. The Assembly VOTED *to approve the substance of the Report and commend it to the churches for study and appropriate action.*

THE REPORT

INTRODUCTION

1. We live in critical times, but it is not because of the desperate nature of the problems of our age that the task of witness to the Gospel of Christ is urgent today. The urgency of the Church's evangelistic task arises from the Gospel itself, because it is the Gospel of Jesus Christ. Christ loves the world, which he died to save. He is already the light of the world, of which he is Lord, and his light has preceded the bearers of the good news into the darkest places. The task of Christian witness is to point to him as the true light, which is already shining. In Christ was life, and the life was the light of men, the light that enlightens every man. The work of evangelism is necessary in this and in every age in order that the blind eyes may be opened to the splendour of light.

2. Nevertheless the urgency of the predicament in which our age finds itself should underline for Christians their duty and their opportunity. The whole world has become for the first time in history an interdependent world, in which the peoples of all lands either must solve their problems of living together in peace or must perish together. We live in an age of revolution, in which immense changes are taking place in every sphere of human life. Christians know that God is the Lord of history and that therefore the critical issues of our times have not arisen outside his loving purpose and are not

beyond his control. Hence for them times of crisis will become opportunities for witnessing to the Lord. Conscious of their own impotence in a world of apparently blind and uncontrolled forces, they will nevertheless go forth with joyful confidence, knowing that the Holy Spirit will lead them to where Christ already is, and will enable them to bear their witness in every place to the light shining in the darkness, which the darkness cannot overcome.

3. Today the task of evangelism must be performed in new situations and therefore in new ways. The Church in every land is aware that new situations require new strategies and new methods, an adventuring into new forms of human social relationships with appropriately new ways of approach and understanding, a renewed sympathy with all men in their aspirations and sufferings and a fresh determination to speak to men the truth of the Gospel in the actual situation of their lives.

4. But the Church knows also that the outcome of her mission depends solely upon God and not upon her own cleverness or adaptability in the struggle for co-existence with other ideologies, scientific, technological, nationalistic, political or religious. She knows that she can witness faithfully to the true Light only in penitence and in humble obedience to the voice of the Living God. She knows also, that though the strategies and techniques of evangelism must change from age to age, the Gospel which she proclaims is still the changeless Gospel of God's saving love, in the redemption of the world by our Lord Jesus Christ, made known to us through the power of his Holy Spirit.

5. The considerations which are here offered upon the theme of Witness are not complete in themselves; they must be read in connexion with the other two themes of the New Delhi Assembly. The question of the Church's unity is of vital importance, since the Bible teaches us that the Gospel cannot be authoritatively proclaimed to the world by a disunited Church. The question of the service of Christians to the world in which men suffer is also of essential importance in the matter of Christian witness, for the world will not listen to a Church which professes Christ as Lord but does not do what he has commanded. The three themes of unity, witness and service are in the last resort not three but one.

A · JESUS CHRIST: THE SAVIOUR OF THE WORLD

6. Jesus of Nazareth, the Christ, is the universal Lord and Saviour.

This is our common faith, and it has been confirmed in us by our worship and study together in the Third Assembly of the World Council of Churches. As we have reflected on his Lordship we have realized afresh that the whole world is the continuing concern of the Father's love. It was for the sake of all men that the Son of God became man. The mighty acts of his ministry, death and resurrection and ascension were the out-working of a single purpose, the redemption of the world.

7. We say these words about Christ, not about ourselves. We are not the world's saviour. We are called to witness to him as the Saviour and Lord of all. We cannot bear his name without coming under the searching light of his judgment on all men, beginning with us. This means asking some practical questions in our churches: whether we love men enough to be able to witness to them; whether we are sensitive to the ceaseless work of the Holy Spirit among men; whether we think and act as though Christ died for all men and not just for us. But we acknowledge our blindness and faithlessness and accepting our forgiveness we can testify that Christ never has forsaken his Church; by his spirit its life is sustained and many are brought by him into its faith and fellowship.

I

8. God is his own witness; that is to say, God has been and is at work authenticating his own message to men. When we speak of witness we mean testimony to the whole activity of God in the creation and preservation of the world, but especially in his mighty acts in Israel's history and in the redemption of the world by Jesus Christ. To this testimony the Holy Spirit in the Church bears witness.

9. God continues to bear witness to the Son, as the only Lord and Saviour of all men. In the apostolic witness, coming to us in Scripture in the Spirit-filled Church, God gives us the foundation of all subsequent witness. In the sacraments of baptism and the eucharist, God down the ages of the Church has drawn near to men in Jesus Christ and born witness to his own faithfulness. In the faithful preaching of his Word, God himself bears testimony to the truth. In the very existence of the Church, there is a constant witness—in silence as it were—to the reality of God's dealing with men in Jesus Christ.

10. We stand today in this long tradition of the Church's witness,

having its origin in God himself, repeating itself constantly in the life of the Church. Therefore, we have confidence and enter with joy into the task of witness which has been laid upon us. We can speak as those who know in our own lives that 'he who believes in the Son of God has this testimony in his own heart'. We are convinced that Jesus is the risen, living Lord, victorious over sin and death. Of him and of the restored fellowship with God which he has worked for us and for all men, we would speak to our brothers for whom Christ died.

11. Today men fear death, not so much as formerly because of the sanctions of judgment and hell, as because it brings a total end to their enjoyment of this world, apart from which they know of no other life. The Church in preaching Christ's death proclaims victory over the power of death itself and the reality of a fuller and richer life than this world knows. Baptism signifies passing through the waters of death and entering here and now upon the life of the age to come.

II

12. In Jesus Christ, God has shown man his true nature and destiny. Through faith in Christ men receive power to become the sons of God. Christ has taken our manhood into God and 'our real life is hid with Christ in God'. So we look forward with eager longing to the glorious consummation of all things, when we shall share the fullness of the life of God. Nothing less than this can be the measure of what it means to be human, the fullness of the stature of Christ.

13. Because God in Christ has reconciled the world to himself, we may no longer judge our brother man by ordinarily accepted standards. God has not condemned us: we may not condemn any man. Only the rebellious will of man stands between us men and the realization of our true humanity and our eternal destiny. Joyfully we affirm our solidarity with all men, for our Lord has joined himself to us all by becoming man. Solidarity with all men of every nation, class, colour and faith without distinction in our common manhood is a starting point of the renewal of the life and witness of our churches by the Holy Spirit.

14. In Christ, the promise of God that man should have dominion over the created world is confirmed and demonstrated. The witness of Christ is that the full responsibility for ordering life in this world is with men, and that grace and truth for this task are available to

them in him. He sets men free to know that the uncreated God alone is Lord over men, and that all created things are made to serve man in him. The new knowledge and enhanced power of modern man call aloud for a majestic witness to Christ in the fullness of his Lordship over nature and history, so that man may be able to accept the forgiveness of sins and find peace, wisdom and courage to handle the events of our time.

III

15. The gathering of the Church by Jesus Christ in every age demonstrates the loving purpose of God to draw men out of isolation and sinful separation into a community of brothers with a common Father, God himself. In Christ there is no place for pride in race, language, authority or sex. All are made equal with the humblest that all may share the glory of the Son. By the Spirit the Church is moved to the service of neighbour without distinction or discrimination. Through his Church God witnesses to his purpose to gather all nations, peoples and tongues, all sorts and conditions of men into his city. The story of God's dealing with Israel is the clue for our understanding of God's will for all nations and his present work among them.

16. In a time of rapid social change men find liberation from the constriction of old forms of community, but are demoralized because they do not find true community in their new surroundings. God calls the churches to witness in a life of humble inter-dependence and mutual service so that the will and imagination of men may be made strong to work for new and just relationships between nations, races and classes, and between the generations and the sexes.

17. Above all else, the Spirit stirs up the Church to proclaim Christ as Lord and Saviour to all the nations and in all spheres of life. The Church is sent, knowing that God has not left himself without witness even among men who do not yet know Christ, and knowing also that the reconciliation wrought through Christ embraces all creation and the whole of mankind. We are aware that this great truth has deep implications when we go out to meet men of other faiths. But there are differences of opinion amongst us when we attempt to define the relation and response of such men to the activity of God amongst them. We are glad to note that the study of this question will be a main concern in the continuing study on 'The

Word of God and the Living Faiths of Men'. We would stress the urgency of this study. In the churches, we have but little understanding of the wisdom, love and power which God has given to men of other faiths and of no faith, or of the changes wrought in other faiths by their long encounter with Christianity. We must take up the conversations about Christ with them, knowing that Christ addresses them through us and us through them.

B · COMMUNICATING THE GOSPEL

18. The good news about Christ is relevant to all ages, but, since every age differs from other ages, so must its ways and forms of communicating the Gospel. In every age the Holy Spirit makes possible the communication of the truth, but often the new ways in which he seeks to lead Christ's witnesses seem strange and dangerous to those who are accustomed to traditional methods. Nevertheless, if some kind of a break-through is to be made, the surmounting of obstacles and the seizing of opportunities must be attempted, so that we may confront the real situation of today and thus discover that through the power of the Spirit many apparent impossibilities have become possibilities and that the word of proclamation has still its ancient power. In our discussion we have been concerned chiefly with what seem to us the most important factors in the new situation of our days, which call for a new approach.

I

19. To communicate the Gospel involves the willingness and the ability of the evangelist to identify himself with those whom he addresses. To get alongside our hearer, to sit where he sits, is the essential condition upon which alone we may claim the right to be heard. By such sympathetic identification, in which the love of Christ is reflected, the Christian witness shows that he is not proclaiming his own message or superior gifts, but the truth of Christ; it is as though one beggar is telling another where the bread of life may be obtained.

20. There are certain areas of life today where this kind of sympathetic identification is particularly needful and in which it is especially important that the witness should himself be first of all a listener. Amongst these areas may be mentioned the spheres of youth, the worker and the intellectual. If they are to be won, we must share their concerns, sympathize with their aspirations and

learn their language. Otherwise they will translate our words into their own terms and they will not understand what we are saying. The evangelist must study the milieu in which his message is to be proclaimed. The resurgence of ancient faiths under the stimulus of nationalism is an example of the kind of challenge which demands from us a sympathetic and patient understanding, if we are to convince their adherents that in the Universal Christ is to be found the answer to the desire of all nations. Or again, on the other hand, the view of many intellectuals in our technological society that all religious language, including Christian language, is a using of words that have no meaning at all, is an expression of disillusionment which demands from us a patient study and a sincere attempt to understand its deep causes. Only if we enter the world of our hearers will they be able or willing to listen to us. Instead of dismissing men's negative reactions to our message, we should take upon ourselves the burden of their unbelief.

21. We must search for a common language in which we and our hearers may understand each other. The truth of the Bible can be conveyed in twentieth century words and idioms. This does not imply 'popularizing' the Gospel but rather flexibility in translating our familiar words and images into a new medium. Since we cannot expect men to understand the vocabulary of the Bible until they have learnt its language, we must mould our own speech into the vernacular of everyday language.

II

22. Christian witnesses must be prepared to be tested by the Gospel which they proclaim. Communication involves much more than speaking, and our message will have to be embodied in our life. We must be ready to be judged by the awful standard of the Christ whom we preach. If we are affluent in the midst of poverty or indifferent amidst injustice or suffering, our speaking will avail less than our silence. The Church as manifested by the local congregation will exhibit or obscure the presence of Christ, and onlookers will judge by what they see. The service, unity and common life of the churches are powerful factors in evangelism. Our message has not been truly proclaimed until it has been lived in real life. This sober reflection throws us back upon the mystery that God can and does use us in all our inadequacy to make manifest the truth which our imperfect works conceal. It is Christ, not Christianity, that is to

be proclaimed as the truth, as it is God's power and not ours which brings men to accept it.

III

23. Dialogue is a form of evangelism which is often effective today. Many experiments are being made in this direction. This is not the place to express judgments upon their value, but rather to rejoice in the encouragement which they give to those who see the urgent need for new approaches to the task of evangelism in the twentieth century. There are, for example, the vigorous work of the Evangelical Academies, the leaderless face-to-face exposure of 'group dynamics', the dialogue sermon, the study group, the experiments in corporate Bible study, the 'parish meeting', and so on. They all emphasize the point that the communication of the Gospel today consists in listening first and then in showing how the Gospel meets the need of the times as we have learned to understand it.

24. Small groups have often been found to be a valuable method of encouraging true dialogue. There is much evidence of the way in which church life has been revitalized through the meeting of such groups for study, prayer, action or worship. The less obvious but not less real fellowship of persons who have thus willingly learnt from one another has been a means of rediscovering the meaning of Christian community and of the realization that Christians are not units of an organization but members of the body of Christ. Many who have been drawn into such groups have learnt for the first time the true character of personal life within the Church.

IV

25. We can hardly mention Christian communication in the modern world without raising the question of the so-called mass-media of radio, television and the press. At first sight they may seem to have little to do with personal dialogue, but if we look more closely it will be apparent that in each of these media forms of intimate address take place, which identify and engage the individual listener, viewer or reader. Religious broadcasting and television are still only beginning to explore the possibilities of these new instruments of communication, and it is to be hoped that still more daring and imaginative use will be made of them.

26. It is often said, as we have said, that we are living in revolutionary times; as Christians we believe that God is at work in all the

great changes which are taking place in our age. Christian communication has to be effected within the orbit of these changes. It is not enough to detect the judgment of God upon the *status quo,* which is being destroyed in an age of revolution. Times of revolution are precisely times when, if opportunities are seized, the judgments of God can be made plain and his purpose proclaimed to a world which will be shaken out of its complacency by the events of the day. Though we must resist the temptation to see the hand of God in the particular movements of history of which we personally approve, or to claim his blessing for every cause which seems righteous at the moment, we may nevertheless proclaim in such situations the Lordship of Christ over the whole process which is changing the aspect of our world. But we must firmly reject all those revolutionary movements in all parts of the world which claim a half-religious sanction for a political or nationalistic end, and which pretend to a 'Messianic' significance that justifies even their excesses. No earthly kingdom can set itself up as the Kingdom of God on earth, and no political ambition is wholly conformed to the divine purpose. We must not be blind to the truth that our hope is in God alone, and we must read the signs of the times in the light of his historical dealings with men and with nations as we have learnt about them in the Bible.

27. In all these areas of concern there is both danger and opportunity. We believe that in our present moment of history Christ still stands at the door and knocks. Our communication of the Gospel is, we believe, Christ's own knocking at the door. A door may be a point of entry or of exclusion. We must continue to knock in the name of Jesus at the very doors which are shut against him and against the claims of humanity. To our fellow-Christians we would speak this word of encouragement: the opportunities for witnessing patiently and faithfully to the deed of God in Christ are as many and as great as the difficulties which we face. We must grasp the opportunities, knowing that in them the Holy Spirit of God witnesses with us.

C · RESHAPING THE WITNESSING COMMUNITY

28. The command to witness to Christ is given to every member of his Church. It is a commission given to the whole Church to take the whole Gospel to the whole world. When the Church recognizes that it exists for the world, there arises a passionate concern that the blessings of the Gospel of Christ should be brought to every

land and to every man and woman. These blessings include the alleviation of poverty, disease and hunger, and the creating of a true fellowship that relieves the loneliness of modern mass society. Christian evangelism is therefore a joyful privilege, being sustained by the knowledge that all the world is the object of God's love and is even now under the Lordship of Christ. It is not we who take Christ to men, but Christ himself who gives us to them as the agents of his own work amongst them. The evangelistic task of the Church is to give the whole Gospel to the world, not merely those parts of it which we find congenial; for the unity of the Church itself is bound up with the unity of the Gospel, and neither must be divided into separated or merely partial expressions of the whole. We must be especially careful to note those elements in the Gospel which challenge the bases of the society in which we live and the social configuration of the churches within it, so that under the merciful judgment of God the Church, as the witnessing community, may be continually reshaped to the pattern of the Gospel that is preached.

I

29. To proclaim the whole Gospel must mean to take seriously the secular causes of men's inability to hear or respond to our preaching. Those who are enslaved to the gods of this age, race, wealth, power and privilege, are likely to be deaf to the preaching; and also those who are oppressed by the burdens of poverty and drudgery and racial discrimination will be like the Israelites who 'hearkened not for anguish of soul and cruel bondage'. Witness to the Gospel must therefore be prepared to engage in the struggle for social justice and for peace; it will have to take the form of humble service and of a practical ministry of reconciliation amidst the actual conflicts of our times. The wholeness of the Gospel demands a corporate expression, since it concerns every aspect of men's lives. Healing and the relief of distress, the attack upon social abuses and reconciliation, as well as preaching, Christian fellowship and worship, are all bound together in the message that is proclaimed.

30. Within this whole enterprise of corporate witness, every individual Christian will play his own unique part according to the gifts of the Spirit with which he is endowed. Each stands in his own special place: the missionary in a country that is not his own; the pioneer in new fields of service; the Christian worker in his factory or office or home—each will be conscious that his witness is a part of the

one ministry within the whole mission of the Church and that he is the representative of the whole Church. In the exercise of his vocation he will rely upon the care and prayer of all, and he will acknowledge that he owes to all a reciprocal care and prayer.

31. The Church whose members are thus to be the commissioned witnesses of Christ to the world is made up for much the greatest part of those who earn their living in the various forms of secular employment. In everyday English usage they are called 'laymen', and indeed rightly so, for they are members of the *Laos* or People of God. It is obvious that, if the Christian witness is to penetrate into all those areas where the work of the world is carried on, it must be carried there by laymen. They alone can bring Christian judgment to bear upon all the issues of life in the spheres of industry and commerce, scientific research and social organization, and all the other activities which make up the work-a-day world. Their meeting points in the secular world can become real opportunities for the witness of a living Church in the midst of the busy world's life.

32. To be truly effective, lay testimony must proceed from a thorough understanding of the Gospel, so that it may be clearly and forcefully articulated in language which the hearers can readily comprehend and which they will at once recognize to be relevant to their personal and social conditions. Only laymen can speak to their fellows in terms of their common involvement in the work upon which they are engaged, and can demonstrate that the Gospel of Christ is highly relevant to this actual situation and not merely to some remote 'church' sphere or after-life. The layman who acknowledges his own personal responsibility for evangelism in his daily life will therefore welcome such training as he may be able to get in the matter of the understanding and defence of Christian truth. He will be anxious to clarify his own mind, to remove his own perplexities about the Bible or doctrine or ethics, so that he may the more confidently and convincingly speak to others about his faith. The lay institute in which such preparation for the evangelistic task may be adequately undertaken is needed as much in the churches of Asia and Africa as in those of Europe and America. But for the majority the proper place of training will be the local church. It is possible to set up very helpful courses in lay witness and leadership in many local churches and areas, and many weekend courses have been held with useful practical results. Situations vary widely, and it is not possible here to

specify courses suitable for them all. But the need is urgent and the possibilities are unlimited.

33. The ordained minister can be of great help in the work of preparation for such evangelism. Not only can he assist in such matters as the understanding of the Bible and of doctrine, but he can enter into discussion with laymen and listen to them as they speak of the actual situation in which their witness is to be borne. Together the laymen and the pastors may thus come to a fruitful appreciation of the relevance of the Gospel in the life of the secular world today. The pastor will not attempt to tell the layman how to bear his witness or to do his job, for only the layman can understand its real nature; but there are many ways in which the mutual discussion of the common problem will help to clarify the issues and to stimulate zeal according to knowledge. The pastor and the layman must learn to work as a team, each recognizing that the other has an essential ministry and gift of grace for his own special task in the one Body of Christ. There is an urgent need for all church members to recover the true meaning of certain words; to learn that the laity is really the *Laos*, that is, the whole People of God in the world, including, of course, these who have been ordained; to learn that ministry means any kind of service by which a Christian, exercising his particular skill and gift, however humble, helps his fellow-Christians or his fellow-men in the name of Christ. A far richer fellowship and team-spirit is bound to appear as soon as the whole Church comes to realize its function as the People of God, which God himself has provided with many kinds of ministry, in which one special kind of ministry, that of the ordained clergy, is set apart to strengthen and teach, to encourage and unite all the several witnesses in their various callings whose ministry is set in the heart of the secular world's manifold activity.

II

34. If this penetration of the world by the lay witness is an essential part of God's plan for his Church, we must examine the conventional structures of our churches in order to see whether they assist or hinder the work of evangelism. We must not think of the 'Church' as primarily a building or as an enterprise run by ministers to which people come or are scolded for not coming. We must ask whether we do not too easily fall into the habit of thinking of the Church as the Sunday congregation rather than as the laity scattered abroad in

every department of daily life. We must inquire of ourselves whether our present structures do not preserve our divisions in a fossilized way, instead of enhancing the unity of the witnessing community. The scandal that renders the Gospel insignificant in the eyes of the unbelieving world and turns away genuine enquirers and potential converts is not the true scandal of the Gospel, Christ crucified, but rather the false scandals of our own practices and structures which prevent the message of the Gospel from challenging the world.

35. The situations by which the Church is confronted in different parts of the world today are so varied that it is impossible here to make recommendations which will be equally suitable for all areas. In certain places, especially those in which the Church faces active hostility and organized opposition, it is important to strengthen the local parish, or congregation, in every way possible, to hold it together and tend it as a shepherd gathers and feeds his flock. The pastoral task of the minister and his helpers is quite different in its expression, though not in its spirit and purpose, from its expression in other places, such as, for instance, those in which the local congregation has lost its sense of mission to the world and is happily content to regard its primary function as that of keeping itself alive as a prosperous, going concern. Or again, in many urbanized or industrialized areas in the West, the Church has lost contact with the masses of the people, who do not feel at home in our churches or understand the language that is spoken in them.

36. In such places, it may be that the local church should seek to penetrate into the unevangelized population by the setting up of 'cells' or local Christian community groups: a handful of typists and salesgirls in a big store, a dozen or so workers on the various floors of a factory; eight research workers and their wives in a big chemical plant; a few Christian teachers on the staff of a big school; a little congregation gathered from two or three streets, meeting as a house-church in the home of one of their number. They will try to be the Church, the People of God, in their own particular context. There are obvious difficulties in such attempted new forms of Christian fellowship. There is the obvious danger of fragmentation. But here the ordained ministry may rediscover its function as a travelling apostolate and as a focus of unity. Just because the ordained minister is somewhat detached from secular groupings, he ought to be able to enter into many different milieus. But if his ministry is to be effective in areas such as those where denominations are irrele-

vant, he must be ready to recognize the ministers of other confessions as his fellow-workers and to work with them as a team. What already operates in many universities, schools and hospitals, must be practised in towns and neighbourhoods. Eventually the local church-buildings might function as the centres to which all these groups might come, not destroying their fellowship or their own way of witness, as a 'congregation of congregations', witnessing to the reality of the whole Church to which they all belong and the Lord of all life in whom all human categories and classes are made one.

III

37. Different situations from those which we have taken as examples will undoubtedly demand different patterns of reshaping. The Assembly wishes only to urge that those who know themselves to be called to the responsibility of Christian witness in their own locality should examine afresh the structures of their church life with a view to meeting the challenge and opportunity of a new day. In a spirit of penitence and of willingness to be led by the Spirit of God into new ways of witness, the whole Church must recognize that her divine mission calls for the most dynamic and costly flexibility. We have discussed many situations and the different problems of different areas. We have mentioned only a few examples. We are aware that far-reaching changes are taking place, especially in the traditionally 'missionary' lands of Africa, Asia and Latin America. The way in which the challenge of Christian witness is met in those areas will be an example to us all. The relation of missions to churches is already being greatly modified in some lands, although in some areas progress is slow. Nevertheless in other areas the process is being carried forward courageously and trustfully, so that the churches are carrying increasing responsibility for their own life and witness. In other areas more vigorous action is still awaited. A reappraisal of the patterns of church organization and institutions inherited by the younger churches must be attempted, so that outdated forms which belonged to an era that is rapidly passing away may be replaced by strong and relevant ways of evangelism. This is only one illustration, but an important one, of how the Church may become the Pilgrim Church, which goes forth boldly as Abraham did into the unknown future, not afraid to leave behind the securities of its conventional structures, glad to dwell in the tent of perpetual adaptation, looking to the city whose builder and maker is God.

DISCUSSION OF THE REPORT OF THE SECTION ON WITNESS

First Session, 11.30 a.m., Friday, December 1. Bishop Sherrill presiding.

Mrs Mildred Horton and *Dr Gerhard Brennecke,* co-chairmen, introduced the report.

Dr Albert Outler (Methodist, USA) found the report 'pallid, platitudinous and over-pious' and weak in logic, especially in the confusing use of the word 'witness' and its derivatives.

Professor H. H. Trigge (Methodist, Australasia) thought that some reference to Christ as 'the Son of Man' would be appropriate for today, as it transcended some of the 'Western' influences in contemporary Christianity.

Archbishop Frank Woods (Anglican, Australia) found the report excellent in many respects but missed the note of authority in the section on communication.

Dr J. E. Skoglund (Baptist, USA) thought that the last paragraph of the introduction implied that all past, present and future witness cannot be effective because of the Church's disunity.

Dr. G. O. McCulloh (Methodist, USA) missed in Section A, paragraph 6, the emphasis of Heb. 1.1 ff. on the purpose of Christ in creation and history. *Professor A. Lacocque* (Belgian Christian Missionary Church) agreed, but pointed out that the reference in Heb. 1.1 ff. is to the Old Testament witness. In the whole paragraph he noted a danger of Marcionism leading to Docetism in speaking of the present and the future but not at all of the past.

There was much criticism of paragraph A. III as originally drafted. A proposal by *Bishop Meyer* (Evangelical Church in Germany) for amendments in this paragraph as originally drafted was supported by *President van Dusen* (United Presbyterian, USA) and *Dr C. G. Diehl* (Lutheran, Sweden) and opposed by *Mr M. M. Thomas* (Mar Thoma, India). At the last session the whole paragraph was redrafted.

Professor W. Küppers (Old Catholic, Germany), *Principal Russell Chandran* (Church of South India), *Bishop Barbieri* (Methodist, Argentina), *Commissioner Reginald Woods* (Salvation Army, UK), *Metropolitan Parthenios of Carthage* (Patriarchate of Alexandria, Egypt) and *Bishop Anthony Blum* (Moscow Patriarchate, UK) criticized the drafting of paragraph A. IV of the original draft which was eventually rewritten as paragraph 11 of the final version.

Professor George Florovsky (Ecumenical Patriarchate, USA) found parts B and C over-optimistic. Insufficient stress was laid upon worldwide opposition to the Gospel.

Dr A. D. Fiers (Disciples, USA) seconded a revision of paragraph B. III in a form which did not depreciate the value of preaching. *Dr Sidjabat* obtained the addition of the words 'in all parts of the world' in paragraph 26 after the reference to 'revolutionary movements'.

Dr H. A. Bosley (Methodist, USA) welcomed part C on 'the witnessing community'. *Dr D. G. Moses* (United Church of North India and Pakistan) regretted that this part of the report contained no statement on the relation of the Christian faith to non-Christian religions.

Bishop Emilianos of Meloa (Ecumenical Patriarchate, Switzerland) drew attention to the dangerous inadequacy of the references to the work of the ordained ministry in part C paragraph 33. *Bishop Anthony Blum* (Moscow Patriarchate, UK) supported this criticism.

Second Session, 6.30 p.m., Monday, December 4. Bishop Sherrill presiding.

Professor A. Richardson (Church of England) presented a revised draft taking account of the criticisms voiced at the first session and particularly those directed against Section A, paragraph III, as originally drafted.

The Rev. J. M. Lawson (Methodist, USA) found the report lacking in an emphasis on the humanity of Christ and the call 'Follow me'. There was a shrinking from being too concrete about the world, the context of Christian witness, and an over-emphasis on identification and an under-emphasis on the encounter of the Word of God with men. A stronger emphasis on the Atonement was needed.

Mr N. H. Buchanan (Anglican, New Zealand) explained that in view of the strong emphasis on the work of laymen in parts B and C, the Committee on the Department on the Laity had omitted similar passages from its report.

Professor Roger Mehl (Reformed, France), *Canon I. F. Church* (Anglican, Australia), *Professor H. F. Trigge* (Methodist, Australia) and *Pastor E. Rostan* (Waldensian, Italy) criticized the reference to death in paragraph A. 11 and *Professor Richardson* agreed that the draft required revision.

Professor E. Schlink (Evangelical Church in Germany), speaking to paragraphs 1 and 17, said that it was not yet possible to reach a common statement about God's work amongst men outside the proclamation of the Gospel.

Dr D. J. Beckmann (Evangelical Church in Germany), *Professor A. T. Nikolainen* (Lutheran, Finland) and *Dr Niemöller* (Evangelical Church in Germany) all asked for revision of paragraph 17.

A straw vote having been taken which revealed that opinion in the Assembly was evenly divided on the matter of this paragraph, it was agreed on the motion of *Dr H. P. van Dusen* (United Presbyterian, USA) to defer action on the report so that there could be further consultation on paragraphs 1 and 17.

Third Session, 4.30 p.m., Tuesday, December 5. Dr Fry presiding.

Professor Richardson proposed that the first part of the last sentence of paragraph 1 to which objection had been taken should be replaced by the phrase 'In Christ was life, and the life was the light of men, the light that lightens every man', and that in paragraph 11 the reference to death in the penultimate sentence should be deleted. He proposed an entirely new version of paragraph 17. These proposals were accepted.

The Assembly then proceeded to vote the motion concerning the report.

REPORTS OF SECTIONS:

SERVICE

THE Report of the Section on Service was considered in two deliberative sessions of the full Assembly and amended. The Assembly then VOTED *to approve the substance of the Report and commend it to the churches for study and appropriate action.*

THE REPORT

INTRODUCTION

1. Christian service, as distinct from the world's concept of philanthropy, springs from and is nourished by God's costly love as revealed by Jesus Christ. Any Christian ethic of service must have its roots there. The measure of God's love for men is to be seen in the fact that his Son was willing to die for them.

2. Such is the God we worship and whose creatures we are called to love and serve for Christ's sake. All our service is a response to the God who first loved us. Justice is the expression of this love in the structures of society.

3. In serving him and them, we follow the Christ who deliberately refused the way of force and chose the role of a servant. As the Father sent him, so he sends us to sacrifice ourselves in his service. As Christ took the form of a servant and gave himself for the redemption and reconciliation of the whole man and the whole world, Christians are called to take their part in his suffering and victorious ministry as servants of the Servant-Lord. The power for service is given by the Holy Spirit who uses the Church as his instrument in manifesting the Kingdom of God and Lordship of Jesus Christ in all human relations and all social structures. Service thus is a part of adoration of God and witnesses to his love for us and all men.

4. Reaffirming our common Christian faith, the Third Assembly of the World Council of Churches commends to its member churches

and Christians all around the world the aspirations and needs, the sufferings and hope of all mankind, 'waiting for the manifestation of the Sons of God'. This report draws particular attention to some of the areas of the life of men in society which call for courageous, obedient thought and action today. They include accelerated technological and social changes, racial and ethnic tensions, international relations, armaments and world peace as well as new opportunities for Christian service in our modern world. We are called to participate in service in all these areas of the contemporary world, not because of our human ability or in order to keep up with the ways of the world, but because we accept his call to respond to his redemptive work which is active in every realm of our life. This demands the responsible participation of the whole body of Christ throughout the world in obedience, sacrifice and solidarity with men —the indispensable marks of the servant-church.

RAPID TECHNOLOGICAL AND SOCIAL CHANGE

5. This revolutionary age confronts Christians and churches, indeed all people and nations, with urgent opportunities and challenges to serve. We are all involved and often perplexed by what is happening. The accelerating speed, the intensity, the world-wide sweep, and the complexity of converging social, political and economic revolutions, make a new social phenomenon which evokes differing reactions:

6. (*a*) *fear*, because so much that is treasured seems to be in danger of destruction;
   (*b*) *conservatism* that seeks to preserve and defend as much as possible of the old and familiar structures of society;
   (*c*) *passive acceptance* that deplores change, but accepts it as something inevitable that must be endured;
   (*d*) *positive acceptance* that welcomes change as an opportunity to promote self-interest;
   (*e*) *positive acceptance* that welcomes change as an opportunity to provide a fuller and more satisfying life for mankind.

7. The Christian is not afraid of change, for he knows how heavy are the burdens of poverty and privation carried today by the majority of mankind. He is ready to initiate changes and forward reforms that serve the ends of justice and freedom, that break the chains of poverty; and is willing to co-operate with all who share his concern

for the welfare of mankind. He knows that the gifts of God can be perverted and directed to evil ends, but he knows also that this is God's world. In his time his purpose will prevail, and it will be manifest that he is indeed in control.

8. Hence, the attitude of the Christian should be one of positive but discriminating participation, based on compassion for his fellow-men and on unshakeable confidence in the loving wisdom of God. To those whose sense of security is today so drastically threatened we can speak a word of courage and hope.

The Fact of Change

9. Social change is powerfully motivated by the aspirations of people for a better life. Technological development promises liberation from hunger, disease and misery. Governments accelerate the movements of their national development programmes. The revolutionary changes affect all sectors of society—economic life, social structures, family and community life.

10. The birth of many new nations intensifies this world-wide urge.

11. It has become clear that induced change will increasingly pervade the whole of society, including the attitudes and motivations of man himself. There is danger that men and women will be treated as tools of change and development, rather than as its beneficiaries. If this is so, fundamental human values—dignity and freedom—will suffer. It is true that part of our duty is to strive to provide the opportunity of a fuller life for the generations that will succeed us, but we must not be tempted to justify present suffering by the hope of benefits entirely in the future. We must therefore affirm that the true purpose and justification of change is to serve both the present and future welfare of mankind.

12. In the specific field of economic development, we welcome the vigorous effort to increase production and raise living standards. In much of the world the basic needs of man for food, clothing, shelter, and health remain unmet or are constantly endangered. There are areas of particular frustration remaining static in the midst of surrounding progress. There are countries where economic progress has been slow or erratic, because they depend on the fluctuations of a market outside their control and—to remind us that man does not live by bread alone—there are wealthy societies plagued by anxiety and frustration because the demands of people seem to be endless.

13. Thus a world strategy of development is overdue, and though it

can be undertaken only by concerted inter-governmental action, part of our service—as producers, consumers or taxpayers—lies in our willingness to share with others, and to subordinate our personal, group or national interest to the well-being of all.

14. Undue emphasis on material progress may result in a tragic neglect of basic social and spiritual needs. Economic expansion is essential, but not sufficient in itself. It is the whole man, and not only a part of his personality or body that must be served.

Nature, Science and Technology

15. The character, scope and speed of social changes have been profoundly affected by man's increasing mastery over nature. So spectacular have been the surge of scientific discovery and the effects of the technology based on it, that many men have come to put their faith and hope in science rather than in God.

16. For Christians, who recognize that Christ is Lord of the mind, so that all that has been rightly discovered belongs to us, there cannot conceivably be any kind of choice between science and religious faith. For science is essentially a method of discovering facts about nature and ordering them and interpreting them within a conceptual pattern. Pure science is concerned with the body of knowledge thus acquired; technology with the useful application of this scientific knowledge and technique. The nature that scientists investigate is part of God's creation; the truth they discover is part of God's truth; the abilities they use are God-given. The Christian should welcome scientific discoveries as new steps in man's dominion over nature.

17. We must recognize, however, that many, within and without the Christian Church, are puzzled about the relationships between God, man and nature. There is urgent need for the development of a theology of nature (as part of an inclusive theology) and its statement in language that can be understood by the men in the pew or laboratory.

18. We should not fear scientific discovery, but we should be deeply concerned about its applications. Science and technology are instruments in the hands of man. They can be used for good or evil purposes. The use of nuclear power for war or peace, the abuse or conservation of natural resources, the application of automation, are examples. But a decision about the use to be made of a particular scientific discovery is not a *scientific* decision; it is an *ethical* decision. It will be intelligent only if based on sound scientific and tech-

nological understanding; it will be *good* only if motivated by the will to serve man. Good and intelligent decisions are more likely to be made if the education of scientists helps them to understand the nature of man and God's purpose for him, and if the education of businessmen, administrators and theologians gives them some understanding of science.

19. It is not good that man should be subdued by nature or enslaved by technology. Nor is it good that nature should be mastered by man, if the mastery merely feeds his rebellious pride. But it *is* good that man should increase his knowledge and should use his growing mastery of nature for the benefit of mankind and the glory of God.

Effects of the Technical Society and the Nuclear Arms Race on Human Dignity

20. Large-scale economic organization, mass-media of communication, the call for solidarity in social action, the demand for loyalty to a national way of life—all these exert such pressures as may threaten human freedom and dignity. A climate of opinion in which science is exalted beyond the limits of its proper authority has diminished the sense of moral responsibility and presented an obstacle to Christian belief. This remains an important influence, although it has been weakened by the fact that the success of science in one field now threatens the very existence of mankind.

21. The Christian who seeks to think and speak and act independently in face of such pressures should be able to rely upon both guidance and support of his Church. It must be acknowledged, however, that churches sometimes allow themselves to be the spokesmen of mass opinion making for conformity.

22. A long continued nuclear arms race can be expected to have grave effects on the quality of life within the nations engaged in it. How can feelings for human dignity remain unaffected by years of living with policies based upon the readiness to destroy centres of population in another country? The habit of thinking of persons as potential victims or potential destroyers in nuclear war will surely reduce sensitivity to their worth. Such sensitivity is blunted by callous use of abstract speculation concerning the millions who will die or survive in nuclear war, and by calculations concerning the percentage of all persons in future generations who will suffer from genetic distortions as a result of nuclear tests. Churches should keep reminding nations and governments of the long-term effects upon human

life of pre-occupation with nuclear armaments and the prospects of nuclear war.

The Conflict of Cultures

23. A 'culture' is an integrated whole of ideas, traditions, institutions and customs, the setting of the life of a society, usually integrated around a religious faith. Ours is a world of many cultures. The assumption that Western culture is *the* culture, and that therefore 'Christian culture' is necessarily identified with the customs and traditions of Western civilization, is a hindrance to the spread of the Gospel and a stumbling-block to those of other traditions.

24. No culture has been wholly static but some have changed very slowly. Inner tensions keep them flexible and capable of development, and gradually they change. But, because a culture is an integrated whole, the introduction of alien and unassimilable elements too strong to be resisted leads to its collapse. So, for example, the introduction of labour for wages, or the concept of individuality have sapped the foundations of ancient cultures. Some of the conflicts of culture of our time were unnecessary, brought about by the unconscious, or by the well-intentioned but unthinking, imposition of Western customs and traditions. Others were the inevitable results of scientific and technological developments. The great missionary movement of the Church, however sympathetic and understanding of other cultural values, could not but lead to deep-rooted clashes of loyalty.

25. The cost of cultural conflict is high. We are not concerned with a cold appraisement of sociological trends. We are concerned with men and women, with the shattering of tribal loyalties and community customs, with the dissolution of age-old family patterns, with the aged, lost and bewildered in unfamiliar ways. The price is paid in loneliness and uprootedness. The tragedy is in the conflict between opposing ways of life, each of which is felt to be good.

26. Man cannot live as true man in a rootless world. He needs the structure of a society. Taking the word back to its original meaning: Can a culture be cultivated? The manipulators of public opinion, the advertisers and the politicians, are attempting the task; but the fact is that a culture cannot be imposed. It grows. Nevertheless, when a culture is rapidly disintegrating, one firm and stable sector may become the nucleus around which a new culture crystallizes. Historically, it may be a determined and disciplined political party. Or it

may be a vigorous and vital religious faith. But it may also be that secularism is an essential element of culture in nations which have many religious communities.

27. All the constituents of a culture come within the realm of the dominion and intention of God, and his servants must claim them for him. 'Can the Christian Church be the nucleus around which will crystallize the culture of tomorrow?' is a question about the present response of man's faith, not a question about the ability of God.

28. Because Christ is the Light of the World he is not alien to any culture. A faith that is fixed in him, a company of Christian men and women rooted and grounded in him, serving him, in and through him loving God and neighbour, will be perhaps not so much a crystallizing nucleus—which is a cold and inorganic process—as the leaven in the lump which lives and grows and gives life.

THE RESPONSIBLE SOCIETY—FREEDOM, ORDER AND POWER

The Calling of the Christian as Citizen

29. 'The powers that be are ordained of God.' This classical affirmation of the role of the state in the providence of God has too often been wrongly invoked in justification to *de facto* rulers. Its true meaning is that through government a necessary basic order is given to society. Without some ordering of competing interests, life in society is not possible. The order so created must be directed toward justice. It must provide for the freedom of persons and families and other groups to satisfy their needs and develop their purposes. Recently the state, under different forms, has increasingly been used to promote economic development and in other ways to serve the welfare of its members. And this calls the Christian to new adventures and experiments in Christian service. The weight of state power everywhere increases. The basic attitude of the Christian towards the state must be positive. He is called to be a citizen and in his membership of the state to obey God and love his fellowmen. In the actual situation in which God places him he is called to judge and act as a Christian man.

30. The report of the World Council of Churches Assembly at Evanston (1954) set forth a series of criteria by which Christians should judge political institutions. These criteria called for the protection of human rights, the guarantee of the person's freedom to express

his religious, moral and political convictions, the provision of channels by which the people can change their governments without recourse to violence, respect for forms of association within society having their own foundations and principles independent of the state. These criteria are still valid. At Evanston they reflected the experience of long established constitution states. But since Evanston so many new nations have come into being and are in the early stages of establishing political institutions, that more account must be taken of the difficulties which such nations face. We live in a highly dynamic situation with many quite different national experiments.

31. This situation has been well described in a report of a commission of the East Asia Christian Conference which met in Bangalore in November 1961, in the following passage:

> 32. Abstract judgments of these different systems serve no useful purpose. Each has grown out of political forces and social needs of a particular situation. Moreover, they all have one common aim: to create an independent nation-state serving the urgent social and economic needs of their peoples. While each nation should be free to develop the patterns of political life which suit its genius best and correspond to the stage of political maturity, this freedom cannot be absolute. It should be exercised with understanding of certain basic political and moral requirements of community, both national and international.

33. Some of these systems are more authoritarian than those whose outlook has been moulded by the western tradition of democracy would find acceptable for themselves. Yet the difficulty of maintaining order, of avoiding civil strife, of establishing governments strong enough to deal with the desperate need for economic development, may call for new forms of political life.

34. Recognition of the limitations under which Christians must live and work in many nations does not mean that one form of government is as good as another, that Christians can be indifferent to the nature of political institutions. It is possible for a Christian to live (or die) with integrity under any political system; it is possible for the Church to obey its Lord in all kinds of external circumstances. But some political structures are more favourable than others for the development of responsible citizens. Mature Christians may grow in grace and in courage under oppressive governments. But under such governments, churches may be rigorously limited in their education of the younger generation, in their opportunity for public witness, and in their pastoral service to the community. Love for the

neighbour must move Christians to use whatever opportunities may exist, to work for political institutions which encourage participation by all citizens, and which protect both the person's freedom of conscience and his freedom to express his convictions. No present difficulties justify Christians or churches in acquiescing in either old or new forms of tyranny. Where emergencies may seem to call for temporary authoritarian régimes, let all who support them be warned that power corrupts, and that those who assume it will usually try to keep it. In recent times we have seen on a vast scale the use of methods of terror under many systems on the part of political authorities to preserve their power. There is no greater desecration of the human in men than to intimidate and torture them in order to force them to obey the political authorities against their consciences.

35. Christians can never give the state their ultimate loyalty. The Church must always see both nation and state under the judgment as well as the mercy of God as known in Christ. Churches must be prepared for conflicts with the state in any nation and under any political system. They should hope and pray and work for a political system which, within its own structure, expresses its recognition that man is not the creature of the state, that the state is not the Lord of the conscience.

36. The existence of a church may have great indirect effects on the nation's political life, for the Church is the clearest case of an association within a nation which has its own foundation, independent of the state. If the Church is true to itself it will continually seek to remind all rulers and citizens that the state has essential limitations under God. As the Church struggles to preserve or widen its own freedom to witness, it may open the door for freedom of men as men. Where a church co-operates with a state to force men's conscience or to establish or preserve systems of oppression it is guilty of a great betrayal. Where the Christian may have no political opportunity to work for the changing of social structures, he must work with his fellow Christians to make his Church more responsive to its calling, so that it will support the state as the instrument of a just order, but guard persons against the state when it puts itself in the place of God.

37. We view with great concern the fact that there are still countries which on racial and other grounds, deny a portion of their population a voice in the formation or control of government. However benevolent such a government might appear to be, government with-

out consent of the governed cannot be approved by Christians in our time. It becomes all the more worthy of condemnation if the people so deprived have the education and ability to use such a voice responsibly. In many areas of rapid social change recent revolts and uprisings by the governed have come as a result of this denial of legal means of expression. It is imperative that governments which still deny the suffrage to their people on the ground that they are not ready for it, should hasten the process of education for participation in government. The use of strong measures, involving mass killing by governments to suppress non-violent expression of reasonable grievances by people denied channels of political expression, cannot be condemned too strongly.

38. The Church cannot identify itself with any particular economic, social or political system. However, both because of the opportunities afforded by political action for the improvement of conditions and because of many forms of evil and suffering which result from the misuse of political power, the Church should encourage the individual Christian to be active in the public life of his country. This is a form of loving service to the neighbour in solidarity with the life of the nation.

39. In fulfilling this political service:

(*a*) the Christian must remember always that he is by his action witnessing to Jesus Christ before men;

(*b*) at the same time the Christian must always act in accordance with the particular local or historical situation in which he has been called to serve God and his fellow-men;

(*c*) the Christian must always recognize that *Jesus Christ is the Lord of History and he is at work today in every nation of the world* in spite of, and through, the ambiguous political, economic or social structures and actions in any given country.

THE STRUGGLE FOR RACIAL EQUALITY

40. The principles enunciated at Evanston with regard to 'The Church Amid Racial and Ethnic Tensions' are still valid. Since Evanston much has happened. The problem of race has become even more acute. As peoples have achieved nationhood and as depressed racial groups have achieved new status and dignity, new tensions have been created. The struggle between the old privileged groups

and the new aspiring ones is intensified and extended. The Christian Church is deeply involved and is called to proclaim its principles with clarity and act upon them resolutely.

41. The difficulty is that principles which are clear in the abstract are not always seen to be involved in actual situations. On the race issue the Church usually reflects the pattern dominant in the community. Most church members are apathetic and too many are easily intimidated or manipulated by a vociferous minority of racialists inside and outside the church. We are encouraged by the fact that there are individuals and groups in every society who at great cost have given themselves to the cause of racial justice.

Methods of Action

42. The Church is called to strive actively for racial justice. Christians should not be tied to any one way of action but should make creative use of various means—conciliation, litigation, legislation, mediation, protest, economic sanctions and non-violent action—including co-operation with secular groups working towards the same ends. The Church should seek to ensure that immigration laws are not based on race discrimination.

43. Where oppression, discrimination and segregation exist, the churches should identify themselves with the oppressed race in its struggle to achieve justice. Christians should be ready to lead in this struggle. The revolution is taking place whether we recognize it or not, and without Christian leadership it may be tragically perverted. The churches also have a duty to the oppressor in a ministry of education and reconciliation.

44. Racism and the consequent affronts to human dignity in the modern world often cause oppressed people to resort to violence when they have no other option. We urge all those in power to refrain from the use of violence and to avoid provoking it. Also we must say that the Gospel of Christ specifically urges that hate be met with love, and evil conquered with good. Therefore we call upon all Christians to encourage and support all efforts which seek, through the non-violent way, to combat human indignities and to construct a community permeated by justice and reconciliation.

The Local Congregation

45. The Church has to put its own house in order. It must not be a segregated society. And it is in the local congregation that Chris-

tians meet this problem concretely. No one should be denied the right of worship, membership, service and full participation in the activities of any church because of race. Where language is a barrier, and separate services are therefore required, all groups should still belong to the same parish. The local congregation should reflect the racial composition of all groups within the neighbourhood which it seeks to serve.

46. It is not enough that local congregations should be racially inclusive in the formal sense. Members of minority groups are often hesitant about going into a church dominated by another racial group. There is therefore a further task—the creation of a climate of warm acceptance of minority groups which may have different ways of worship, and other gifts, that will enrich the whole Church.

47. When communities are not involved in direct racial tensions, it is often because they segregate themselves by choice and so evade the problems of 'inter-group living'. Often they contain the very people who by their social position could do most for race relations.

48. The complacency of a secure and homogeneous community may have to be disturbed by a Christian initiative in inviting people of different races into it.

Leadership in the Church

49. Denominations in their own structures must give a lead to ensure that there is no race discrimination in the church. The churches are further called to utilize people of different races in positions of leadership, on the basis of merit only. Pastors should not be assigned only to churches of their own race and Christians should be prepared to accept a minister of another race. Missionary appointments, executive and administrative posts within the churches should be open to qualified persons regardless of race. Churches should give equal opportunity for training to all potential leaders and take special pains to foster the gifts of those less privileged. All Christian institutions should have open policies with respect to housing and employment.

'Separate Development'

50. All races, as indeed all persons, have their own unique contributions to make to the fellowship of human society, but we cannot agree that this is a reason for 'separate development'. On the contrary, it is only in community with others of diverse gifts that per-

sons or communities can give of their best. The expression 'separate but equal' is in concrete actuality a contradiction in terms.

THE CHURCHES' INVOLVEMENT IN WORLD AFFAIRS AND WORLD ORDER

51. The churches are involved with all men in a common historical destiny. As servants of their Servant Lord Jesus Christ they bring to the nations their obedience to Christ who is the Lord of the nations. They form a society that by its nature transcends political and ideological barriers; but through its members it is also deeply rooted in the life of nations with their political and ideological conflicts. In this situation the Church is called to a ministry of reconciliation, prayer and intercession. The nature of its task will vary according to the degree to which a church can influence the policy of the government of the country. In many places only renewal within the church will make constructive involvement in world affairs possible. Only a profound dedication to responsible world order in the heart of all churches and Christians will be adequate.

The Deflation of Suspicion

52. It is not easy for a Christian to find the ways and means of effective influence in our present world situation. The polarization of power between two great blocs creates great danger and tension. The world and its institutions are in the midst of revolutionary change. Monstrous weapons have been developed and tend to paralyze constructive political thought. The sheer complexity of collective relations makes much action appear futile.

53. Years of estrangement and conflict have borne their sad fruit of mutual distrust so that by now nations have false and fixed images of one another. But although deep antagonisms exist, the nations are not necessarily determined to resolve them by war.

54. Do official ideologies really determine national policies? Does any action really live by its textbooks? The Marxist-Leninist view of basic conflict with capitalism does not necessarily mean that global nuclear warfare will inevitably take place. On the other hand the goals of Western society do not necessarily imply an armed crusade. There still remains a suspicion that the other side is out to win completely. The fact cannot be minimized that the USSR has developed a firm confidence that its way of life is superior to the West and must prevail. The West has a similar conviction about its institu-

tions. Yet responsible leaders in both power blocs do appear to entertain the hope that the two great systems can co-exist and even peacefully compete. It has even to be asked whether the two systems are as different in every respect as both sides suppose.

55. Another cause of mistrust is the isolation of large parts of mankind from the community of nations. It develops in the absence of the disciplined intercourse of nations a vicious circle of misinformation, suspicion, fear, distortion and further withdrawal. Reconciliation is impossible in the absence of one of the parties.

56. Often there is distrust between the former colonial powers and the new nations. Younger nations fear that other forms of foreign domination will emerge. On the other hand, former colonial powers fear that the new nations will become enemies of the Western world. Moreover nations are still trying to control the destiny of others, in old and new forms.

Nationalism and New Nations

57. Cohesion of new nations, itself a contribution to international stability, is threatened by the reversion of loyalties to old tribal, linguistic, ethnic and religious groupings. 'Nationalism' can here be understood as the struggle for an inclusive national culture and a wider sense of solidarity and mutuality, a positive factor, indispensable to the life of the new nations. It should not be weakened by other groups in their own interest. The strength of nationalism is in uniting a complex society in constructive nation-building. Its weakness is in its possible perversion into policies of antagonism and exclusiveness against other nations.

58. The new nations and their existing political order depend upon their success in achieving rapid economic progress to match the expectations of their peoples. Therefore, they must seek aid where they can and avoid alignments which would limit the sources of assistance. The powerful nations must respect these proper preoccupations, and should welcome the contributions which non-aligned countries can make in world affairs.

59. The reality of political independence is threatened by economic dependence either upon other countries or upon international industries. Aid from outside is sometimes suspect even when wanted, and is confused by the number of agencies and missions seeking to give it. There is need for more effective use of international agencies to ensure a correlation and simplification of aid programmes and their

adjustment to real needs, and also responsible administration by the receiving countries of the proffered resources. But above all the churches must not cease to champion the cause of making the riches of the developed countries available to those poor in resources.

60. Again, political circumstances of the new states require their own appropriate political solutions rather than patterns established elsewhere. The world knows various forms of government and each is a reflection of basic patterns. The churches' duty is not primarily to favour any one form but to seek the proper protection of human rights and fundamental freedoms for all, political power made responsible by law, government made responsible to the people, and the establishment of those relations between citizens and groups on which alone just societies stand.

61. But it must be said to new nations as to older ones that the evolution of an international order will require of all a measure of surrender of autonomy and sovereignty for the sake of the world community.

International Institutions

62. Peace is dependent not only on goodwill and reconciliation, but in the first place upon the emerging of effective international institutions under the rule of law. Therefore, churches in their desire for peace must recognize the importance of the responsible use and development of international institutions, both in the United Nations and in regional affairs. The aim must be to establish a just system of world order, which provides security through the means to enforce its decisions, but the absence of a commonly agreed interpretation of law and justice, especially among the great powers, challenges the churches to explore such common ground as exists with a view to bringing them together under effective international control.

63. With respect to the policy of new and uncommitted nations in the present world struggles the churches should welcome the constructive possibilities of their mediation in the conflicts of the powers. The dangers of non-alignment may lie in the temptation to refuse responsible choice.

Disarmament

64. The recent violations of the moratorium on nuclear bomb testing have shocked the nations into a new realization of the acute danger and horror of modern warfare. Churches must protest against the

accelerating arms race and the mounting terror which it portends. The First Assembly of the World Council of Churches in 1948 clearly recognized that war is contrary to the will of God. War in its newer forms is understood not only by Christians but by the general conscience of the nations as an offence against both the world of nature and the race of man, threatening annihilation and laying on mankind an unbearable burden of cost and terror. The use of indiscriminate weapons must now be condemned by the churches as an affront to the Creator and a denial of the very purposes of the Creation. Christians must refuse to place their ultimate trust in war and nuclear weapons. In this situation the churches must never cease warning governments of the dangers, and they must repudiate absolutely the growing conviction in some quarters that the use of mass destruction weapons has become inevitable. Christians must press most urgently upon their governments as a first step towards the elimination of nuclear weapons, never to get themselves into a position in which they contemplate the first use of nuclear weapons. Christians must also maintain that the use of nuclear weapons, or other forms of major violence, against centres of population is in no circumstances reconcilable with the demands of the Christian Gospel.

65. Total disarmament is the goal, but it is a complex and long-term process in which the churches must not under-estimate the importance of first steps. There may be possibilities of experimenting with limited geographical areas of controlled and inspected disarmament, of neutralizing certain zones, of devising security against surprise attack which would reduce tension, of controlling the use of outer space. The approach to disarmament needs to be both global and localized. Experts must debate techniques, but the churches should constantly stimulate governments to make real advances.

THE SERVICE OF THE CHURCH IN A DIVIDED WORLD

66. The bond of unity of the Church was vividly experienced as a fact during and after the last world war when political opponents found each other again in the fellowship of Christ. So now the very being of the ecumenical movement is a fact of incalculable value, overarching as it does in a divine fellowship all the bitter international conflicts of today. The entry of the Orthodox Church of Russia into membership of the World Council of Churches is a

dramatic confirmation of our faith that God is holding his family together in spite of our human sin and perplexity and as a sign of hope to the world. The visible unity of the Church would be a service to world peace, certainly not because of any aggrandisement of ecclesiastical power, but as a testimony to mankind that in Christ the barriers are broken down.

67. Already the churches can save brethren estranged by political conflict from the neurosis and false judgments of isolation by seeking every opportunity of renewing their fellowship with them. The churches can commend and encourage further human and cultural encounters across political barriers whereby understanding is increased and the common interests of men recognized. And Christians should strive for a removal of obstacles to communication, the jamming of radio and restrictions on printed matter, which leave men deceived about one another.

68. Where possible the members of the churches should lead public opinion (and should certainly avoid merely reflecting it) in the direction of the objectives of peace and disarmament, and should as local churches and denominations organize themselves to do so effectively. Where the churches do not have power to influence events directly, they can often serve to release a body of opinion in a country, or crystallize it, which would otherwise remain unheard because it believed itself friendless. Everywhere churches should call upon all Christians unceasingly to pray for peace, and to engage in those ministries of reconciliation and mercy which constitute creative peacemaking.

69. To fulfil these functions the churches need to ask seriously whether some of their frustration is not due to past failure to care for the public affairs of the world. There is need of a much deeper understanding of the structural aspect of political life. Christians have to transcend in a new way the ideological positions of the communities in which they live. They are in a unique position to do so.

70. Specifically Christians in all the countries of the world are called by God:

— to hold each other in brotherly concern and prayer,
— to sustain each other in witness under all circumstances,
— to affirm their fellowship with Christians of all races and nationalities through worship, suffering, joy and service 'in the unity of the Spirit',

— to share, as real brothers in Christ, their experience, convictions and all they have learned under any given political, social or economic situation.

In a Changing and Dynamic Society

71. We are forced to re-examine Christian service anew when we face world-wide and rapid social change. Some of our Christian forms of service are so dated as to be unfitted for contemporary society. Some are divided according to confessional and institutional lines. Some are too dependent on external help. Some are deficient in the distinctive Christian meaning of service. With humble repentance, accepting the judgment and the forgiveness of God in Christ, we must obey the Holy Spirit as he leads us to renew or extend our present forms of service, and search for new ways of expressing our obedience as the servant-Church in the contemporary world.

72. It is essential that the Church should help people to think and act responsibly in a changing and dynamic society. This means that the churches must give ample opportunity for their members to be partners in this work. In a real partnership between the clergy and the laity, the laymen must help the theologian to understand the dilemmas of ordinary men and women in a rapidly changing world; and the theologian must help the laymen to see his dilemmas in the light of a cogent Christian faith. It is in this direct partnership that the Church can effectively offer its service and witness.

73. We have already asked that special care should be given to frustrated and lonely men and women, crushed in the crucible of violent change.

74. We press also for a real understanding of what education is, and what it should give children and young people as they prepare themselves for life in a dynamic society. Education is increasingly seen as a tool in economic development, or as a national investment. Moral and spiritual values are taken too little into account. This is a serious challenge to Christian educational planning and action.

75. The ecumenical movement has already helped the churches to find a way of service through action and witness in a time of rapid social change. In the realms of conflict within and between cultures this has not always been deliberately intended. But with the coming together of churches rooted in many national cultures, a dialogue widely and happily extended by the transition in so many areas from 'mission' to 'church', has enabled each member to appreciate and value

unfamiliar cultures. It has also served to deliver them from identifying the Gospel with their own culture. If the opportunity were now clearly seen and deliberately grasped, the ecumenical movement could render immense and vital service as an arena for the cross-fertilization of concepts from different cultures *within one fellowship*.

Forms of Christian Service

76. Christian service or *diakonia* must have forms and structures relevant to present needs and clearly a response to the costly love of God for the whole world.

77. It is rather easy to make an idealistic and abstract appraisal of Christian service. It is not difficult to criticize the limitations of the current forms of service such as hospitals and educational institutions. But our task is to engage in positive participation and concrete involvement in search for the forms of Christian service in the contemporary world which meet real and deep needs. This requires a constant effort to open ourselves to the calling of Christ to serve the world and to commit ourselves to respond humbly yet courageously to his suffering ministry in all realms of life, together with the whole Church of Jesus Christ.

78. In this complex and changing world the forms of Christian service cannot be confined to a single pattern. Each unique situation may require a different form. Also the *diakonia* (service) of the Church is expressed in different ways, through the presence of the individual Christian in the secular world, through the work of Christian service institutions and through the organized life of the churches.

Individual Responsibility and Involvement

79. God gives his gifts in variety to his people. One of the primary callings of the serving Church is to discover and develop these gifts for the sake of the world. The Church's true worship and fellowship express themselves in spontaneous devotion and sheer Christian compassion for service in and to the world. The more we are drawn to Christ, the more we are constrained to serve the world.

80. In a mass society of impersonal relationships, loneliness and frustration and conflict, the individual Christian must surely participate in the ministry of reconciliation. Precisely because government discharges an increasing number of services, we recognize the immense significance of each individual Christian who shares in secular ser-

vice agencies and in government work by turning what might be impersonal service into truly personal service through a consciousness of the saving presence of Christ. Today qualified laymen have many opportunities to participate in the work of intergovernmental, governmental and private agencies in the less developed areas of the world such as malaria eradication and the Freedom from Hunger Campaign. The churches should encourage this. Moreover the churches themselves in such areas have many undertakings requiring technically qualified workers, and the churches should seek wherever possible to use such Christian technicians as are available. Ecumenical work camps for youth have proved their value in awakening a sense of the responsibility of service, and they deserve the support of the churches.

81. All this requires deeper understanding of stewardship in the Church. It should not be narrowly confined but should be seen in the light of total dedication of one's gifts to the glory of God in all spheres of life. More than ever, the churches must help laymen to realize that their responsibility to serve lies in their daily work and to train them accordingly. Signs of renewal can be seen here and there, but there is still much to be done. A Christian does not serve in the world as an isolated individual. He must be supported, guided, and strengthened by the corporate groups.

82. It is clear that in our society many problems can be explored only by Christians as individuals or in groups and not through the official or corporate organizations of the church. Participation in labour unions and management, protests against racial discrimination and practical action, the bringing of honesty and integrity into political life at local and national levels, all these are avenues of *diakonia* (service) open to individual Christians who derive their strength and renewal from the worship and fellowship of the Christian community.

83. Where the Church is in a minority and cannot corporately serve society, the Christian must neverthless identify himself with the servant Christ and the needs of his fellow-men, seeking earnestly for some opportunities of service. And underlying all is the necessity of prayer for the needs and conditions of all men. All Christians can pray, worship and endure patiently even when they can do no more.

Corporate Christian Service

84. Social service has changed considerably in recent years. All over

the world, the state has been taking over responsibilities formerly carried by private agencies. The serving Church must develop strong organs of thinking and action at local, national and world levels to discover concrete needs, and adequate ways to respond to them.

85. Many Christian service institutions have an important role to play. But there is acute need in the fields which government or social programmes have not covered adequately. We recognize again the situation is different according to each country. Educational institutions may be needed in one place and not in another. There are new frontiers of service specially arising out of the rapid development of industrialization and urbanization. Therefore, Christian service agencies must be flexible and ready to transform themselves into mobile tent-dwellers rather than prisoners of institutions.

86. For example, schools may need to be replaced by centres for training adults to participate in their new environment, and Christian hospitals may need to be replaced or supplemented by clinics nearer to the life of the people.

The Ecumenical Service of the Churches

87. Natural and social disasters create acute human needs which should be met immediately by the churches acting together. There are also widespread endemic needs, such as poverty, mental and physical disease, hunger, illiteracy, unemployment and the plight of refugees which demand a maximum response in Christian service. In our time racial discrimination looms large and dangerous, defies the Christian faith, and needs immediate action by all the churches.

88. In these areas ecumenical demonstrations of inter-church aid are needed and they should be shared by all churches regardless of denominational allegiances. The static distinction of 'receiving church' and 'giving church' must go so that all will share spiritual, material and personal gifts in the light of the total economy of the household of God.

89. Projects which increase the ability of people to attain self support are significant. There is a need to assist rural and industrial development by giving technical assistance and by providing for the training of people to share in building a responsible society under the inspiration and guidance of the churches. This requires thorough and comprehensive training and new imagination for a long range service programme.

90. In all this, it must be remembered that the Christian is not a 'phil-

anthropist' and the Church is not a 'benevolent association'. The mark of the serving Church is expressed through joy and suffering in Jesus Christ. The Christian Church is a community in which to rejoice with those who rejoice and weep with those who weep in the solidarity given in Jesus Christ. It is a community which is always open for service in and to the world as a living parable of the Kingdom 'until he come'.

DISCUSSION OF THE REPORT OF THE SECTION ON SERVICE

First Session, 11.30 a.m., Friday, December 1. Bishop Sherrill presiding.

Sir Kenneth Grubb presented the report.

Dr Stuart Peterson (United Presbyterian, USA) said that the use of the formula 'East and West' in the report was ambiguous.

The Rev. P. Mbende (Baptist, Cameroun) and *the Rev. C. Schnyder* (Reformed, Switzerland) asked for the inclusion of material from the Youth Department on Work Camps and longer term lay ecumenical service.

Commander C. A. Herdman (Church of Ireland) and *Dr David G. Moses* (United Church of North India and Pakistan) criticized the theological formulations of the first paragraphs of the original draft.

Professor Roger Mehl (Reformed, France) asked in relation to paragraph 19 whether a theology of nature was possible. Concerning paragraph 39 (*c*) he said that it was only by faith that we know that Christ is at work in history. The devil is at work too.

Mr E. V. Mathew (Mar Thoma, India) criticized the omission from the section on 'The conflict of cultures' (paragraphs 23-28) of a positive reference to the value of a secular culture in a multi-religious society.

The Rev. F. Sillett (Anglican, Northern Rhodesia) contrasted the exclusive emphasis on the use of non-violent means in inter-racial conflicts in the original draft of paragraph 44, with the more ambiguous attitude to the use of nuclear weapons by Western nations in paragraph 64. *Dr J. S. Lawson* (Methodist, USA) supported this criticism and asked for a revision of the reference in the original version of paragraph 64 of the clause in which war 'in its modern form' was described as 'an offence against God'. Examples of non-violence in the racial struggle in the USA and in Asia and Africa were a challenge to the churches to abjure all forms of hate and pride. But *Mr M. M. Thomas* (Mar Thoma, India) thought that 'non-violence' had been over-emphasized by comparison with 'direct action' in an unjustified way. However, the churches could ask the authorities not to provoke the people to violence.

Dr J. Robert Nelson (Methodist, USA) welcomed the reference to the function of local congregations in overcoming race conflict (paragraphs 45-48), but drew attention to the fact that whole congregations and even denominations are set up on a racial basis, so that there is segregation at the top as well as in the locality. The biblical basis for racial unity is the same as that for church unity.

Bishop Swaby (Anglican, Jamaica) preferred 'The Clash of Colour' as the title for the section beginning with paragraph 40. A statement that 'there is but one race of mankind' should be included. The concept of race is un-scientific and un-Christian.

Archdeacon H. de Soysa (Anglican, Ceylon) said that race conflict is sometimes between races of the same colour, e.g. in Ceylon.

The Rev. H. N. Riber (Lutheran, USA) desired paragraphs 61 and 62 to be strengthened because Christians should be ahead of public opinion in requiring the nations to surrender sovereignty in preparation for world government.

Mr S. Levering (Friends, USA), *Mr M. M. Thomas* (Mar Thoma, India), *Dr W. Sykes* (Disciples, USA), *Archbishop John* (Russian Orthodox Church), *Dr Howard Schomer* (United Church of Christ, USA) and *Dr E. K. Ziegler* (Church of the Brethren, USA) all asked for a strengthening of the wording of the paragraphs of the original draft dealing with war and armaments (52-65).

Dr Raymond Wilson (Friends, USA) asked that the WCC as a whole should give priority to questions of war and peace and not leave them to the CCIA.

Pastor A. Appel (Lutheran, France) said in the concluding section (paragraphs 66-end) on Service, the whole range of *diakonia* as the daily work of the layman had been forgotten and that there was insufficient reference in the draft to the pioneer work of Inter Church Aid.

Second Session, 6.30 p.m., Monday, December 4. Bishop Sherrill presiding.

Professor de Vries (Reformed, Netherlands) reported that the drafting committee had met with its critics and had made a number of amendments.

Dr Norman Baugher (Church of the Brethren, USA) and *Dr Heinz Kloppenburg* (Evangelical Church in Germany) desired the omission of the words 'against centres of population' from the penultimate line of paragraph 64, and *Dr Kloppenburg* proposed the deletion of the whole second part of the paragraph on the ground that the subject was covered in the report of the committee of the Assembly on the CCIA. *Professor W. G. Muelder* (Methodist, USA) replied that the drafting committee had held a careful hearing and that the combination of propositions in paragraph 64 represented the best possible balance for a common ecumenical position now.

Professor John Bennett (United Church of Christ, USA) and *Dr John Marsh* (Congregational Union of England and Wales) proposed editorial changes which were accepted by *Dr de Vries*.

REPORTS OF SECTIONS:

UNITY

THE report of the Section on Unity was considered in two deliberative sessions of the full Assembly and amended in the light of the debate. The Assembly then VOTED *to approve the substance of the Report and commend it to the churches for study and appropriate action.*

THE REPORT

I · THE CHURCH'S UNITY

1. The love of the Father and the Son in the unity of the Holy Spirit is the source and goal of the unity which the Triune God wills for all men and creation. We believe that we share in this unity in the Church of Jesus Christ, who is before all things and in whom all things hold together. In him alone, given by the Father to be Head of the Body, the Church has its true unity. The reality of this unity was manifest at Pentecost in the gift of the Holy Spirit, through whom we know in this present age the first fruits of that perfect union of the Son with his Father, which will be known in its fullness only when all things are consummated by Christ in his glory. The Lord who is bringing all things into full unity at the last is he who constrains us to seek the unity which he wills for his Church on earth here and now.

2. We believe that the unity which is both God's will and his gift to his Church is being made visible as all in each place who are baptized into Jesus Christ and confess him as Lord and Saviour are brought by the Holy Spirit into one fully committed fellowship, holding the one apostolic faith, preaching the one Gospel, breaking the one bread, joining in common prayer, and having a corporate life reaching out in witness and service to all and who at the same time are united with the whole Christian fellowship in all places and all ages in such wise that ministry and members are accepted by all, and that all can act and speak together as occasion requires for the tasks to which God calls his people.

It is for such unity that we believe we must pray and work.

3. This brief description of our objective leaves many questions unanswered. We are not yet of a common mind on the interpretation and the means of achieving the goal we have described. We are clear that unity does not imply simple uniformity of organization, rite or expression. We all confess that sinful self-will operates to keep us separated and that in our human ignorance we cannot discern clearly the lines of God's design for the future. But it is our firm hope that through the Holy Spirit God's will as it is witnessed to in Holy Scripture will be more and more disclosed to us and in us. The achievement of unity will involve nothing less than a death and rebirth of many forms of church life as we have known them. We believe that nothing less costly can finally suffice.

A Commentary upon this Picture of Unity

4. The foregoing paragraph must be understood as a brief description of the sort of unity which would correspond to God's gift and our task. It is not intended as a definition of the Church and it does not presuppose any one particular doctrine of the Church. It is based upon a statement worked out by the Commission on Faith and Order, accepted by the Central Committee at St Andrews in 1960 and sent to the member churches for consideration and comment. The 'Toronto Statement'[1] was a landmark in the World Council's thinking about itself and its relation to work for unity. Here we seek to carry that thought a stage further, not by dictating to the churches their conception of unity but by suggesting for further study an attempt to express more clearly the nature of our common goal. Christian unity has been the primary concern of the Faith and Order movement from the beginning, and the vision of the one Church has become the inspiration of our ecumenical endeavour. We re-affirm that we must go forward to seek the full implications of this vision. We present this statement in the hope that the churches both inside and outside the World Council of Churches will study it with care, and, should it be found inadequate, will formulate alternative statements, which more fully comprehend 'both God's will and his gift'.

In him alone . . . the Church has its true unity

5. It is in Jesus Christ, God's Son and our only Mediator, that we have union with God. It is he who has given this gift to us through

[1] *The Church, the Churches and the World Council of Churches,* statement received by the Central Committee at Toronto, 1950.

his coming into our world. Unity is not of our making, but as we receive the grace of Jesus Christ we are one in him. We are called to bear witness to the gift of unity through offering our lives as sacrifices to his glory. The fact that we are living in division shows that we have not realized God's gift of unity and we acknowledge our disobedience before him. Our union with God is a mystery which passes our understanding and defeats our efforts to express it adequately. But as Christ has come visibly into this world and has redeemed men of flesh and blood, this union must find visible expression.

6. It is the living Christ who impels us to work and pray for a fuller manifestation among us of 'the one hope which belongs to our calling'. Thus the Faith and Order movement has found the focal point of its study in the person and work of Jesus Christ. Through its Commission on Christ and the Church it has sought to explore the biblical and historical witnesses to Christ, to determine what unity in the one Lord actually means. The unity which is given is the unity of the one Triune God from whom and through whom and to whom are all things. It is the unity which he gives to his people through his decision to dwell among them and to be their God. It is the unity which he gives to his people through the gift of his Son, who by his death and resurrection binds us together in him in his Sonship to the one Father. It is the unity given to his people through his Spirit, and through all the gifts of the Spirit which enliven, edify and empower the new humanity in Christ.

All in each place

7. This statement uses the word 'place' both in its primary sense of local neighbourhood and also, under modern conditions, of other areas in which Christians need to express unity in Christ. Thus being one in Christ means that unity among Christians must be found in each school where they study, in each factory or office where they work and in each congregation where they worship, as well as between congregations. 'Place' may further imply not only local communities but also wider geographical areas such as states, provinces or nations, and certainly refers to all Christian people in each place regardless of race and class.

Who are baptized into Christ

8. The mutual recognition of baptism, in one sense or another, has

been a foundation stone in the ecumenical discussions of the present century. However, closer examination of the assumptions and implications of this fact invariably brings to light deep and wide divergences in theory and practice amongst the churches of the World Council of Churches. Much progress has already been made through the studies of Faith and Order in the understanding of the one baptism.[1] We would urge that these studies be widely circulated among the churches and that the churches in each place study the meaning of baptism together, and in the light of such studies seek to come to a deeper understanding of the baptism by which all have been sealed into the one Lord through their one faith and the gift of the Holy Spirit.

By the Holy Spirit

9. The Church exists in time and place by the power of the Holy Spirit, who effects in her life all the elements that belong to her unity, witness and service. He is the gift of the Father in the name of Jesus Christ to build up the Church, to lead her into the freedom and fellowship which belong to her peace and joy. For any achievement of a fuller unity than that now manifest, we are wholly dependent upon the Spirit's presence and governance.

Fully committed fellowship

10. The word 'fellowship' (*koinonia*) has been chosen because it describes what the Church truly is. 'Fellowship' clearly implies that the Church is not merely an institution or organization. It is a fellowship of those who are called together by the Holy Spirit and in baptism confess Christ as Lord and Saviour. They are thus 'fully committed' to him and to one another. Such a fellowship means for those who participate in it nothing less than a renewed mind and spirit, a full participation in common praise and prayer, the shared realities of penitence and forgiveness, mutuality in suffering and joy, listening together to the same Gospel, responding in faith, obedience and service, joining in the one mission of Christ in the world, a self-forgetting love for all for whom Christ died, and the reconciling grace which breaks down every wall of race, colour, caste, tribe, sex, class and nation. Neither does this 'fellowship' imply a rigid uni-

[1] 'Conference on the Nature of the Unity we Seek' at Oberlin, USA, 1957, and in the Report *One Lord, One Baptism*, SCM Press and Augsburg Publishing House, 1960.

formity of structure, organization or government. A lively variety marks corporate life in the one Body of one Spirit.

The one apostolic faith

11. The Holy Scriptures of the Old and New Testaments witness to the apostolic faith. This is nothing else than those events which constitute God's call of a people to be his people. The heart of the Gospel (*kerygma*) is Jesus Christ himself, his life and teaching, his death, resurrection, coming (*parousia*) and the justification and sanctification which he brings and offers to all men. The Creeds of the Church witness to this apostolic faith. There are important studies now being undertaken of the relationship between Scripture and Tradition (which is Christian confession down the ages), and attention is drawn to the work of Faith and Order's Theological Commission on Tradition and Traditions.[1]

Preaching the one Gospel

12. Preaching proclaims anew to men in each generation the Gospel of our Lord Jesus Christ. In the faithful preaching of the Word the living Christ is present as our contemporary in every age; he grants us his grace, he comforts us and calls us to a renewed decision for him. In the human words of the preacher every new generation is confronted by the Christ as one who speaks to them where they actually are.

Breaking the one bread

13. Nowhere are the divisions of our churches more clearly evident and painful than at the Lord's Table. But the Lord's Table is one, not many. In humility the churches must seek that one Table. We would urge the Commission on Faith and Order to continue study and consultation to help us identify and remove those barriers which now keep us from partaking together of the one bread and sharing the one cup.

Joining in common prayer

14. God is to be praised in every tongue and in the setting of every culture and age in an inexhaustible diversity of expression. Yet there are certain common factors in Christian worship such as adoration

[1] *The Old and the New in the Church*, SCM Press and Augsburg Publishing House, 1961.

penitence, intercession, petition and thanksgiving which are grounded inevitably in the unique acts of God in Christ, discernible still in our divided traditions. As we learn more of each other, we shall more clearly discern this common heritage and express it more fully.

A corporate life reaching out

15. Mission and service belong to the whole Church. God calls the Church to go out into the world to witness and serve in word and deed to the one Lord Jesus Christ, who loved the world and gave himself for the world. In the fulfilment of our missionary obedience the call to unity is seen to be imperative, the vision of one Church proclaiming one Gospel to the whole world becomes more vivid and the experience and expression of our given unity more real. There is an inescapable relation between the fulfilment of the Church's missionary obligation and the recovery of her visible unity.

Ministry and members accepted by all

16. All agree that the whole Body is a royal priesthood. Yet one of the most serious barriers to unity is our diverse understanding of the nature of the ministry within the corporate priesthood. All who have been engaged in church union negotiations testify to this fact. There are those, for example, who affirm the necessity of an episcopally ordained ministry in the apostolic succession while others deny that it is essential for the true Church. How can two such divergent positions on so important a matter be settled? In this, as in all matters relating to Christ's Church, it is upon the Holy Spirit we must rely. He will, if we faithfully search, reveal to us the ways in which we can have a ministry accepted by all. Here biblical, theological and historical studies must be continued to seek to lay before the churches that which is necessary to have a true ministry according to God's Word. The mutual acceptance of members though not so formidable an obstacle as mutual recognition of ministries, still raises problems for some communions. The achievement of a ministry accepted by all would largely resolve the issues involved in the mutual recognition of members.

In all places and all ages

17. Every church and every Christian belongs to Christ. Because we

belong to him we are bound through him to the Church and the Christians in all places and all ages. Those who are united in each place are at the same time one with believers in all places. As members of the one Body they share both in each other's joys and sufferings. The Church as a universal fellowship means also that we are part of the People of God of all ages, and as such are one with Abraham, Isaac and Jacob, and all their descendants in the faith until the end of the age. Work for unity in Christ is continually attacked by all the evil forces which fear the light of truth and holiness and obscure our own vision also. We now see our unity only darkly, but we know that then we shall see it clearly when we see him face to face. But it is also our hope which gives us courage to expose our differences and our divisions and call upon God to reveal to us even now that which has hitherto been hidden from our eyes. We pray, with the praying Christ, that *all* may be one. To this end we must work while it is day.

II · SOME IMPLICATIONS TO CONSIDER

18. If we accept this picture of the unity for which we must pray and work, it has implications for the life of our churches as lived at the local level, as confessions and as we meet each other in ecumenical fellowship. If we shirk these implications, we come under judgment for turning away from the light that God has given us. So we ask our churches to consider seriously what those implications may be.

A. Implications for Local Church Life

19. The place where the development of the common life in Christ is most clearly tested is in the local situation, where believers live and work. There the achievements and the frustrations are most deeply felt: but there too the challenge is most often avoided. It is where we live and work together daily that our Lord's own test is most clearly imposed, 'by this shall all men know that ye are my disciples, if ye have love one to another'. Before and beneath all outward expression is the commandment to love one another as he has loved us. As soon as we begin to obey this command, we can ignore each other no longer and we shall actively seek the means of giving expression to that love. The Lund Conference on Faith and Order in 1952 put out this challenge in the form of suggesting that Christians ought always to seek to do together everything which conscience did

not compel them to do separately. Loyalty to conscience takes different forms in different traditions. In some churches, the rules of corporate discipline make very clear the limits of corporate action; in others there is a far greater area of free manoeuvre. But all of us must confess that, in the life of our churches at the local level, we are still far from being together in all those ways in which, with a good conscience, we might be. It will be through daily obedience in the paths that are already open to us that our eyes will be enlightened to the fuller vision of our life together. The disclosure of the goal is inseparable from the faithful walking in the way in which he leads us.

20. (*a*) There is need for an increase in opportunities of growing together as local churches; through common worship, Bible study groups, prayer cells, joint visitation, common witness in our communities. Locally as in the whole ecumenical movement we should be especially ready in Christian love to seek out and to establish fellowship with those traditions and minorities to which we are not now related. Even where we are compelled to remain separate at present in central aspects of the life of our congregations there is considerable freedom for developing areas of common worship, witness and service in homes and communities.

21. (*b*) Ordinary social life already brings men together into various associations—academic, professional, industrial, political, etc. Within these forms of unity there is need for a Christian unity of those who may learn from each other how to bear their witness in those settings. Ecumenical thought in the calling of the laity needs to be shared in groups of this kind and it has its own bearing on church unity, for denominational divisions are often found to be quite irrelevant on this frontier. What is the bearing of that discovery upon our inherited divisions?

22. (*c*) Sometimes Christians will find themselves in associations of this kind in situations where their witness will involve sharp conflict, and they may reach a point where they have to break with the association. Wherever such conflicts arise, Christians are called to give their witness to a true expression of unity.

23. (*d*) Since much of this lay witness cuts across denominational lines, it clearly calls for united planning and execution as men and women seek in a common discipline under Christ to express his Lordship over all life, drawing their local churches together in the process.

24. Our division at the Lord's Table may be most acutely felt at the local level, especially if Christians of separated church traditions are truly meeting each other in common obedience to Christ. Where they are content virtually to ignore each other as Christians, or where the ecclesiastical traditions raise no difficulty, the problem may not be felt. But this 'scandal' of eucharistic division appears at every one of the three levels we are considering. Since it is at the local level that it comes home most persistently, if it is seen at all, this is the point at which briefly to consider what the problem is, for there is no point at which we more completely fail to understand each other.

25. For some Christians, the Lord's own command 'Do this' is an imperative which over-rides all our divisions. If Holy Communion is the sovereign means of grace for the forgiveness and conquest of sin, then that is true of the sin of division as well. Thus it is intolerable and incomprehensible that a common love of God should not be expressed and deepened by common participation in the Holy Communion which he offers.

26. For some Christians, the essence of the Christian life is incorporation into the Body of Christ realized as fellowship in an organic and transcendent unity of faith, life and love made visible in a pattern of ministry and sacraments which is indivisible. Then it is intolerable and incomprehensible that those who do not share the organic life should expect to share in its eucharistic expression.

27. For neither view can there be any final peace so long as others who are known to be in Christ are not with us at the Holy Communion. But there are serious and deeply felt differences about how we should behave in our present recognition that God wills a unity which we do not manifest.

28. Although the problem may be most acutely felt at the local level, it is not at this level that it can find any general solution. Local churches may rightly ask, however, that confessional convictions be made clear amongst them if they are to be saved from uncomprehending suffering. In certain places groups of Christians have entered into intercommunion with full knowledge of the gravity of the issues involved. In these instances there has been, if not ecclesiastical approval, at least the withholding of disapproval. None of us can ignore the issues which such action raises. The Table is the Lord's gift before it is our blessing. We must therefore ask whether there are situations, e.g. during unity negotiations, when intercommunion

is possible even before full union is achieved, and all must feel with renewed intensity the agony of broken communion at the one Table of the Lord.

29. In the WCC we commit ourselves, in our local churches also, to an abiding concern for each other. In staying together we have discovered more and more that Christ is present among those to whom we cannot, on the grounds of our differing convictions, grant the full meaning of the word 'church'. If Christ is present with them, is he not calling us in ways we cannot yet clearly discern, to move out towards him in order that we may receive our full unity with him and with his people? When the real Christian encounter takes place locally we are forced to face these vital questions. This self-examination is always difficult; for we cannot and must not surrender those truths and ways of church life which we believe are God's will for his Church, and which the others do not yet accept. At the same time, we cannot and should not refuse to move out to Christ whose presence we recognize in the life of the others.

30. In this situation are we not constrained by the love of God to exert pressure on the limits of our own inherited traditions, recognizing the theological necessity of what we may call 'responsible risk'? We emphasize the word *responsible*; for such actions must be taken with sincere respect for our confessional position and with the full attempt to explore with the Christian communion to which we belong the meaning of what we are doing. Clearly also, the responsible risk will be different according to our different convictions. Nevertheless, unless there is this preparedness to seek for responsible ways of breaking through to fresh understandings, we cannot hope to be shown the way to that growing unity which we know to be God's will for us. Responsible use of local situations to explore such possibilities is a challenge in every place.

B. Implications for the Life of our Confessions

31. When we turn to consider the implications of a commonly accepted picture of our goal for our life as confessions or 'denominations', the first point to be made is the diversity in our understanding of what is meant by confession or denomination. Obviously, such understanding is related to our conception of the Church itself. For some, as for the Orthodox, there can be no simple distinction between 'Church' and 'Confession' for the Church itself is under-

stood as essentially undivided.[1] Others would speak more readily in terms of 'interior schism' or 'divisions' *within* the Church. But for the practical purposes of what follows, we agree that when we speak of confessions and denominations, we simply acknowledge the fact that we recognize the same Christ through a variety of corporate traditions, of long or short history and more or less clearly defined, but within each of them certain crucial elements are always preserved. Gospel and faith, baptism, eucharist and doxology, witness and service in our common life in the Body of Christ are all involved. We concentrate on the problems of (1) a doctrinal basis of unity, (2) baptism and unity, (3) eucharistic fellowship, or lack of it, (4) common action in witness and service, as this affects or is affected by our divided state. It is all too plain that our present answers are not fully adequate—yet no more adequate answers can be given until the churches themselves become more generally and vividly concerned with providing them.

1. *Doctrinal agreement*

32. In our consideration of next steps towards an agreed doctrinal basis for the unity we seek, two useful distinctions may be made—that intellectual formulations of faith are not to be identified with faith itself, and that *koinonia* in Christ is more nearly the precondition of 'sound doctrine' than vice versa. The primary basis of this *kiononia* is the apostolic testimony in the Holy Scriptures and 'the hearing of faith'. Yet this primary biblical revelation was given to and through the apostolic church and has continued to be witnessed to by our common historic Creeds, specifically the Apostles' Creed and the Nicaeo-Constantinopolitan Creed.[2] There is, as it were, an 'ecumenicity in time' which may be realized by serious attention both to the ancient witnesses and also to the gifts of light and truth given by the Spirit in various ages and traditions in the history of the people of God. 'The one apostolic faith', referred to in Part One of this report, is, first and last, faith in Christ as Lord and Saviour to the glory of God the Father. An obvious practical corollary of this understanding is the recommendation that a next step towards

[1] Cf. the contribution from the Orthodox members in the minutes of the Unity Section, obtainable from Faith and Order, WCC, 17 route de Malagnou, Geneva.

[2] Cf. the agreement on doctrinal unity in the Report of the First World Conference on Faith and Order (Lausanne, 1927), the doctrinal basis of the Church of South India and 'Agreed Statements' from the C.S.I.-Lutheran Theological Conversations, 1948–1959 (Madras, 1960).

unity, at the denominational level, would be a fresh consideration of our various doctrinal bases, in the light of the primacy of Scripture and its safeguarding in the Church by the Holy Spirit.

2. *Baptism and unity*

33. Our ecumenical fellowship is essentially based upon the fact that we all want to be obedient to God's commandment in being baptized 'into the body' (I Cor. 12.13). Our failure to share in the one Table of the Lord, to live and act as one visible and united body, is an obvious contradiction to the baptismal gift that we all claim to possess. This contradiction can be explained in some cases by unjustified rationalizations and must therefore be overcome. In other cases, it reflects an obvious lack of agreement as to the true nature of the fellowship into which baptism introduces us.

34. Mutual recognition of baptism (although it goes far) is not in itself a direct means to unity forthwith. This means that we must place our conceptions of baptism in a dynamic, forward-looking perspective and ask ourselves: Where does our baptism lead us? We all agree that baptism is both God's gift and human commitment, and that it supposes a growth into the 'measure of the stature of the fullness of Christ' (Eph. 4.13). By this growth the baptized believers can even now visibly manifest to the world the new race of a redeemed mankind. Common witness to our churches, to the world, to those who have not yet heard the Gospel and to those who refuse it, is our common responsibility here and now. Fellowship in witness and service may help us to discover the meaning of God's gift to all the members of his people.

35. Much fruitful thought is being given, especially in Faith and Order studies, to the deeper meanings of baptism into Christ.[1] Every such examination sheds some new light on a tangled issue. It is important that disagreement as to the meanings and modes of baptism does not now entail outright denial or non-recognition of non-approved baptism. Even more important is the wide agreement that the initiative in baptism is from God by his Holy Spirit and that the baptized person's appropriate response must be expressed in the entirety of the life of faith. Such an understanding of baptism would suggest to those churches which practise infant baptism that this entails a more serious enterprise of Christian nurture than is often the

[1] Cf. *One Lord, One Baptism*, and Faith and Order Commission Minutes, Faith and Order Paper No. 31, 1960.

case—and, to those churches that practise 'believers' baptism', that they should reconsider the place of infants and children in the household of faith. Baptism recognizes God's claim on us as his children. It marks out a person's 'place' in the Family so that even if that person does not 'take his place' it is there for him, awaiting his response to be faithful soldier of Christ in the Church militant.

3. *Eucharistic unity and division*

36. We have already spoken of the deeply felt differences which centre round the word 'intercommunion'. A main responsibility for deepening understanding rests with those who are called to work and speak on behalf of their confessions as such. The present impasse presses the churches to re-examine all possible next steps that might be discovered, at any and all levels of their denominational life. Wherever existing convictions allow for more direct progress towards intercommunion between churches, it should be made without waiting for consensus and common action in the ecumenical movement as a whole. Moreover, if we reversed the usual order of discussion and focused on eucharistic action—what God does and calls us to do at the Lord's Table—rather than (first of all) on eucharistic administration—i.e. the problem of a valid ministry—we might find a clearer way to the heart of an adequate sacramental doctrine. As the matter stands at present, we have a major problem of interpreting to our people the ground (biblical, traditional, etc.) of our widely various practices—some of which seem to make intercommunion 'too easy' and others 'too hard'. There is value in divided Christians experiencing the agony of non-communicating Eucharists—but there is an equal need to re-assure the excluded that the agony is as great for the excluding. We must meet, in a responsible fashion, the rising tide of impatience amongst many young people, and indeed among many others, for more prompt and certain progress, toward mutual understanding in this most central and vital experience of Christian worship and witness. The urgency of finding a way to break through the present impasse on the question of intercommunion makes it imperative that denominations and confessions undertake a new examination of their eucharistic doctrines and liturgies in the light of all these new factors introduced by the ecumenical situation.

4. *Common action*

37. We have said that one outcome of such unity as we have envis-

aged would be the enabling of Christians to 'speak and act together as occasion requires in the tasks to which God calls the Church'. We see two spheres of Christian action which call for unity for their best effect and which promote unity by their very undertaking. The first is in the area of Christian ethics and discipline—especially in the face of the demoralization of modern culture and the increasing importance of divided churches uniting in effective action. The second is in the varied field of Christian education—including the enlistment as well as the training of ordinands with proper gifts and graces. There is, of course, a sense in which this is a peculiar prerogative of each autonomous church. Yet surely the magnitude and scope of the problem as it now faces us, calls for effective, ecumenical action. Such action would itself be a means toward greater unity.

C. Implications for the Ecumenical Movement

38. As we have participated in intensified efforts to clarify the nature of the unity which we seek to manifest, four questions have commanded our attention regarding our fellowship together, especially in the ecumenical movement, and, more particularly, in our mutual commitment in the World Council of Churches.

1. *What are the proper functions and limits of the WCC in regard to unity among its member churches?*

39. (*a*) Our deepest responsibility in the ecumenical movement is faithful prayer for the unity of Christ's Church as and when he wills it. Faith and Order has long sought to encourage such prayer as it is focused in the Week of Prayer for Christian Unity. We give thanks to God that recent years have witnessed a steadily widening observance of this Week throughout the world. But there is also need to think more deeply about the nature of the unity for which we pray, including the part which the ecumenical movement itself can play in developing a common understanding.

40. (*b*) It is agreed that theWCC must not attempt to violate the autonomy of any member church. Neither may the Council make official pronouncements on unity which contravene the recognized doctrines of member churches, nor attempt to impose any one conception of unity.

41. (*c*) In faithfulness to its constitutional function of proclaiming the oneness of the Church, the Council should do all within the

limits of its competence to enable the churches to perceive the meaning of unity and to realize it more fully. All the work of the Council has general relevance to this purpose. But the present and projected programme of the Committee on Faith and Order[1] is of particular importance. We mention only a few of these plans and suggest some others.

42. (*d*) The educative function of the Council is indispensable and needs extension. Most members of churches know little of the beliefs and practices of churches other than those of their own communion or tradition. All kinds of ecumenical conferences thus have value. There is still need for good literature to further ecumenical education. Many helpful publications are issued by the World Council from its headquarters, but in themselves they can only be capable of a very limited circulation in comparison with the size of our constituency as a whole. The general membership of the churches can only be reached if every member church uses its own organs of communication to the full.

43. (*e*) A certain kind of *consultative* assistance can be given by the Council to churches which are engaged in unity conversations. The Commission on Faith and Order has already begun to render such service, though only, of course, upon the request of churches concerned, by sending persons of exceptional knowledge and experience to meet the church members who are responsible for negotiating union.

44. (*f*) The Council's Faith and Order Commission has also convened several consultations on church union with representatives from nearly all countries and churches where union negotiations are in progress. And it has been publishing regularly a survey of such developments, as well as distributing the relevant documents. We trust that this will continue.

45. (*g*) Perhaps the time has now come for the Council to undertake a new service. Although church union negotiations are continuing to arise at a rapid pace in various lands, and we rejoice that this is so, it is not always immediately clear how each of these has important implications for many churches within the Council's fellowship. For example, if churches of two or more communions in a certain country make progress towards union, this has relevance for

[1] As set forth in the Report on the Future of Faith and Order (see Minutes of the Faith and Order Commission, St Andrews, 1960, pp. 113-20).

churches of those same communions in other lands. Now, the Council is alrerady accustomed to sending general statements on unity to the churches for their study and consideration. But could it not also address direct questions to particular churches, asking them on behalf of all the Council's churches to state what reactions they have to specific union negotiations in which their own communions are involved? This would both stimulate the interest of these churches in the obligation to manifest the unity of Christ's Church, and also provide useful information for the good of all. It would not infringe upon any church's inherent autonomy, but serve as a reminder that here too we are all 'members one of another'. We also raise the question as to whether, with due regard for freedom of faith and conscience, the good offices of the Council should be used to help in breaking deadlocks which sometimes arise as a result of church union negotiations and lead to the possibility of further schism.

46. (*h*) In pursuing its studies in the realm of faith and order, the council may now be ready to make penetrating enquiries into the way in which the very structures of the many churches tend to impede efforts by those churches to manifest greater unity. This has been initiated already through the important study on 'Institutionalism',[1] the result of which we expect to see soon. But still more remains to be done in this field of studies on unity.

47. (*i*) Finally, we are persuaded that the time is ripe for a fresh general study, among the member churches, of the conciliar process in the Church of the early centuries. This would be an extension and application of the significant inquiry already begun by the Theological Commission on Tradition and Traditions.[1] This would call attention not only to the results in doctrine, discipline and liturgy, but also to the processes by which they were achieved.

2. *How does current thinking on unity affect our understanding of the nature of the World Council of Churches itself?*

48. Having stood the test of a decade of discussion and criticism, the Toronto Statement still best expresses our understanding of the Council's nature. It could also be fruitfully studied as illuminating the nature of national and regional councils. However, the probing

[1] See *The Old and the New in the Church,* SCM Press and Augsburg Press, 1961.

studies and the prompting developments of these ten years keep driving us to seek further clarification. Mere insistence upon deeper study will not guarantee fresh insight. We are learning what the Council is by *living* together within it; and so it shall be. Nevertheless, the need for careful reflection on the theological meaning of our new life in the Council continues to be unfulfilled.

49. At least we are able to say that the World Council is not something wholly other than the member churches. It is the churches in continuing council. It is not over or apart from the churches but next to them at all times. We should speak of the Council as 'we' rather than 'it' or 'they'. Furthermore, many Christians are now aware that the Council is in some new and unprecedented sense an instrument of the Holy Spirit for the effecting of God's will for the whole Church, and through the Church for the world. What bearing has this upon our conception of the Church's unity?

3. *How may world confessional bodies contribute to the ecumenical movement and the unity of the churches?*

50. Most of these organizations existed many years before the founding of the World Council. Their purpose is not only to clarify and strengthen confessional understanding and loyalty but to serve responsibly in the wider ecumenical movement. Their contributions to the whole movement are well known and much appreciated. Their leaders are, for the most part, leaders in the World Council of Churches also. But opinion today is divided over the effects of their existence and work upon the participation of their churches in the movement for unity and upon the course which they ought to take in the future.

51. Some hold that a deepening understanding of the doctrines and traditions of the various confessions will in the long run enhance the possibilities of unity in the truth, even though for the present it may seem to restrain the churches from joining into full fellowship with one another. It is possible that unity could be further advanced by more frequent conversation between leaders of the confessions at the level of world organization. Already there are theological conversations in process between the Presbyterians and, respectively, the Lutherans and Congregationalists.

52. A contrary view is held by those who see the world confessional bodies as a threat to wider unity in particular areas, a view which some Asian and African Christians have often expressed with vigour.

53. Probably the critical question is whether or not the leaders of confessional bodies agree with the emphasis we have already made upon the centrality of unity of all Christians *in each place,* which must, of course, always seek to be a 'unity in the truth'. If they agree, they will not consider the union of one of their churches as a loss, but as a gain for the whole Church. And a service can be rendered to such churches if the confessional bodies assist them in the responsible study of all issues which are involved in a proposed union.

4. *Is the World Council now able to find new light on the problem of intercommunion?*

54. We call the attention of the churches to the reports of the Youth Assembly of Lausanne, 1960, the Bossey Consultation of March 1961, and the Pre-Assembly Youth Conference at New Delhi.[1] In all of these the tones of anguish and urgency are dominant, and the proposals for the adjustment of church policies on intercommunion are specific. The problem of Holy Communion at ecumenical conferences received particular study in these reports. But the following points may be noted:

55. (*a*) This is not a division between generations but *between and within the churches.* There are numerous older Christians whose sense of anguish and urgency is not exceeded by the younger. It is a problem for all churches and their members, and no one has excuse for apathy or resignation towards it as we meet in ecumenical gatherings.

56. (*b*) Surely a reconsideration of the policy laid down at Lund 1952 is now needed. But it is not yet clear that the proposals made at Bossey in 1961 provide a better agreement. Time for more reflection upon this might well be available before the Fourth World Conference on Faith and Order in 1963, when we hope that further consideration of this question will be undertaken.

57. In this concern for unity at every level of church life, we are mindful that the unity we seek is not for its own sake nor even for our sake. It is for our Lord's sake and for that of the world which he died to save. Unity is inseparable from renewal in holiness and truth, to God's glory. We offer this report to the churches in the

[1] *Youth* No. 2, October 1960, pages 79 ff. (Findings, Lausanne Youth Assembly); *Ecumenical Review,* vol. XIII no. 3, April 1961 (report of Bossey Consultation); both published by the WCC, 17, route de Malagnou, Geneva.

prayer that it may contribute to deeper unity in our witness and service in the name of Jesus Christ, the Light of the World.

DISCUSSION OF THE REPORT OF THE SECTION ON UNITY

First Session, 4.00 p.m., Friday, December 1. Dr Ernest Payne presided.

Dr D. G. Moses and *Bishop Oliver Tomkins* presented the draft report.

Canon R. R. Hartford (Church of Ireland) thought that the report was fair and objective. The work of the Commission on Faith and Order had become even more important since the entry of the Russian Orthodox Church into membership of the WCC.

Dr W. R. Cannon (Methodist, USA) missed the note of Christian unity and witness as expressed in the lives of believers. We are 'called to be saints' and this is a prerequisite of any further measure of unity. We should be thankful for what the Holy Spirit is already doing in our midst. The document should include a call to Christian love.

Mr C. P. Wakiro (Anglican, Uganda) thought that the report was not a success. Co-operation is not enough. Fear had inhibited some members of the section from stating their full mind. The Assembly should enunciate principles of unity according to apostolic faith and practice, and a committee of *lay* theologians from various denominations should be asked to give a clearer definition of unity.

Metropolitan Parthenios of Carthage (Patriarchate of Alexandria) asked for a continuation of dialogue with the Orthodox. To what the report says about the catholic and apostolic nature of unity, something should be added about holiness.

Mr V. G. Montes (United, Philippines) questioned the accuracy of the use of the term 'ministry' in the report as meaning exclusively 'the ordained ministry'.

Professor E. Schlink (Evangelical Church in Germany) was of the opinion that the statement constituted a genuine step forward towards overcoming ecclesiological docetism. This docetism was a real danger, when in many ecumenical statements stress was laid on the unity in Christ of the divided churches, but without laying equal stress on the need for visible unity. In his view the statement was still too formalistic, because while mentioning the Creed, the Gospel, the Sacraments, the Ministry, etc., it did not sufficiently explain the substance of these terms and what is understood by them. It was of crucial importance for the unification of the churches to work out a consensus on their substance and meaning.

Metropolitan Athenagoras (Ecumenical Patriarchate, Canada) said that we must approach the question of unity in terms of love. In the words of the Liturgy 'Let us love one another that we may confess the faith'. According to the Ecumenical Patriarch's statement union is the crown of 'unity' in the sense of brotherliness.

The Rev. S. B. Coles (Presbyterian Church in Canada) urged that paragraph 1 should be prefaced by an affirmation concerning the unity of the Holy Trinity and disunities throughout creation which grieve him. He suggested a form of words. It is nowhere mentioned that unity is purchased at the price of the Cross. *Dr R. M. Clark* (United Church of Canada) and the *Rev. Harry Dorman* (United Presbyterian, USA) supported *Mr Coles.*

Dr J. Norgaard (Baptist, Denmark) thought that the description of unity in paragraph 2 went too far. The quest for uniformity will always create division. The promise of Jesus to Peter (Matt. 16; cf. Eph. 2, 1 Pet. 2) proclaims our existing unity.

Professor J. A. Oosterbaan (Mennonite, Netherlands) asked for the deletion of the reference to infant baptism in paragraph 8.

Professor W. F. A. Küppers (Old Catholic, Germany) wished to add in paragraph 5 'our efforts for unity are thwarted again and again', and in paragraph 17 'both in judgment and in grace' to avoid all idea of self-satisfaction.

Dr Eugene Smith (Methodist, USA) asked for a clearer expression of the relation between mission and unity in paragraph 15, and expressed the concern for deeper unity in fellowship and witness with members of Pentecostal and Fundamentalist groups.

Professor B. Ioannides (Church of Greece) asked for the addition of a footnote to paragraph 31 referring to the statement by the Orthodox members of the section which is to be included in the minutes of the section.

Colonel A. B. Cook (Salvation Army, New Zealand) wished an explicit reference to baptism of the Holy Spirit to be added to paragraph 35.

Archbishop W. L. Wright (Anglican, Canada) asked that a prayer for unity should be included in the text of paragraph 37.

Bishop Rajah Manikam (Lutheran, India) praised paragraphs 42-44 and asked that questions should be addressed to missionary bodies and World Confessional bodies on these subjects.

Curé Léon Gauthier (Old Catholic, Switzerland) and *Commander C. A. Herdman* (Church of Ireland) suggested amendments in details.

Second Session, 6.30 p.m., Monday, December 4. Bishop Sherrill presiding.

Bishop Oliver Tomkins presented the revised report in which most of the suggestions made in the previous session had been incorporated.

The Rev. S. B. Coles (Presbyterian, Canada) moved the addition of two further sentences to paragraph 1. After *Bishop Oliver Tomkins* and *Dr Outler* had spoken against making any further addition, Mr Coles' motion was defeated.

IV

REPORTS OF COMMITTEES:

1 · REPORT OF THE CREDENTIALS COMMITTEE

The following Report of the Credentials Committee was adopted by the Assembly in Business Session:

The rules of the World Council of Churches (both prior to and after integration with the International Missionary Council) state that 'full membership of the Assembly is confined to delegates appointed by the constituent churches to represent them'. In approving integration, the Assembly seated additional delegates representing the interests of the International Missionary Council, who had been appointed by the churches concerned.

The Credentials Committee assumes that its responsibility is limited to an examination of the credentials of voting delegates and does not embrace an examination of credentials of Advisers, Fraternal Delegates, Observers, Guests, Youth Delegates and others not privileged to vote. The Committee has examined the credentials of all delegates and reports that it finds these all in order in accordance with the Constitution and rules of the Council, as in force both prior to and after integration with the International Missionary Council.

The delegate body for the Third Assembly numbers:

583 appointed by the member churches
21 appointed by the member churches to represent the missionary interests of the churches
4 members of the presidium not counted elsewhere

making a total delegate body of 608.

However, 30 delegates appointed by churches and 1 appointee representing the missionary interests of the churches were unable to attend. The total voting body of the Assembly is 577.

We must unfortunately call attention to the fact that the following delegates, advisers, youth delegates, and guests from East Germany have not received the necessary permission from their government to leave the country and are therefore not present in New Delhi. The Assembly will want to remember them especially in prayers.

Delegates:

Mrs Ingeborg Becker
Dr K. A. Gunter Jacob
Bishop E. E. W. Hornig
The Rev. Dr August Kimme
President Reimer Mager

Advisers:

Professor Erich Hoffmann
The Rev. Otto Mosig
The Rev. Bruno Schottstaedt

Guest:

Dr A. Moeller

Youth Delegate:

The Rev. G. Steinacker

Problems which appear to persist from Assembly to Assembly have to do with late substitutions of a delegate for another, occasional lack of official approval of a delegate until on the grounds of the Assembly, and failure to use the regular credentials forms supplied to the churches by the Council. These irregularities create unnecessary complexities for the office, staff and Committee. Member churches are urged to give more precise attention to the comparatively minor mechanical procedures for submitting delegates' names on the approved forms with proper official approval. Anything which the churches can do to name delegates early and also to avoid late substitutions will be a service to future Assemblies.

2 · REPORT OF THE COMMITTEE ON NOMINATIONS

The Report of the Committee on Nominations was dealt with by the Assembly in Business Session:

I. Actions on Procedures

The Chairman read Rule IV concerning the Nominations Committee of the Assembly, and called on Dr Payne to present on behalf of the Business Committee the following interpretation of Rule IV (4) (see page 431):

> If an additional nomination, other than those presented by the Nominations Committee, is put forward in writing by six members of the Assembly acting together, for either the Praesidium or the Central Committee, those presenting such nomination shall indicate in connection therewith the name in the Report of the Nominations Committee for which such additional nomination is to be substituted.

Dr Payne explained that this rule of procedure had been proposed in order that all nominations should conform to the principles as set forth in Rule IV (3). In the event of there being additional nominations, the first ballot would be on the substitution called for by the additional nomination. The final ballot would be taken on the total list of nominations for the Praesidium and the Central Committee with each voter either indicating his approval of the complete list of nominations as it would then stand or voting individually on the several names on the ballot.

Following these explanations, it was moved and

VOTED to approve the interpretation of Rule IV (4) *as proposed by the Business Committee. The Assembly also, by specific action, agreed that this interpretation should apply to the nominations for the Commission on Faith and Order.*

The Chairman explained that on the basis of the action that had just been taken, there were two ways for nominations to be presented:

1. By the Nominations Committee
2. As put forward in writing by six members of the Assembly, acting together, and indicating the name in the Report of the

Nominations Committee for which such additional nomination is to be substituted.

II. Election of Honorary President, Praesidium and Central Committee

The written Report of the Nominations Committee was distributed when the above action had been taken.

At a subsequent Business Session the Chairman, Dr Fry, called on Professor W. S. Tindal of the Church of Scotland, Chairman of the Nominations Committee, to present the Report of the Nominations Committee. Professor Tindal stated that the Nominations Committee had been entrusted by the Assembly with the work of proposing nominations for a new Praesidium and Central Committee. The maximum number of presidents is six, and presidents who are elected by the previous Assembly are ineligible for immediate re-election. He reminded the Assembly that the Central Committee is composed of the presidents, together with not more than 100 members elected by the Assembly from among the fully accredited delegates of the member churches, of which there were almost 600. In making nominations, the Nominations Committee took into consideration the principles as stated in Rule IV (3)—to secure adequate representation of lay persons—both men and women—so far as the composition of the Assembly makes this possible. The Committee also satisfied itself as to the general acceptability of the nominations to the churches to which the nominees belong. This year a further consideration was the fact of the integration of the World Council of Churches and the International Missionary Council and the Committee had endeavoured to act as the Nominations Committee of the integrated body.

Professor Tindal reported that the Nominations Committee proposed *Dr J. H. Oldham,* the Secretary of the Edinburgh Conference of 1910, as *Honorary President*. It seemed particularly fitting for the new integrated body in its first year to send a message of recognition and gratitude to Dr Oldham and elect him as Honorary President.

The Nominations Committee proposed for the *Praesidium*:

The Most Rev. A. M. Ramsey, Archbishop of Canterbury. Dr Ramsey had taken part in the life of the World Council of Churches since its foundation, and especially in the work of Faith and Order.

Sir Francis Ibiam, Chairman of the All Africa Church Conference, a medical missionary for many years and presently Gov-ernor of Eastern Nigeria.

The Most Rev. Iakovos, Archbishop of the Greek Orthodox Church in the Americas, and member of the Praesidium since the meeting of the Central Committee in Rhodes in 1959.

The Rev. Dr David G. Moses, Vice-Chairman of the former International Missionary Council, Chairman of the National Christian Council of India and Principal of Hislop College, Nagpur.

The Rev. Dr Martin Niemöller, President of the Evangelical Church of Hesse, and member of the Executive Committee of the World Council of Churches since Amsterdam.

Mr Charles Parlin, lawyer, layman of the Methodist Church in the USA, Chairman of the Press and Public Relations Committee at Evanston, Vice-Chairman of the same Committee at New Delhi, member of the Finance Committee.

Professor Tindal said that in making these nominations, it was in the mind of the Nominations Committee that, of the many public utterances of these distinguished men, only those spoken by them collectively as the Praesidium could be taken to represent the mind of the World Council of Churches.

Professor Tindal explained that the size of the *Central Committee* was set forth by the New Constitution and Rules adopted at the opening plenary session of the Assembly on November 19. One change enlarged the Central Committee from 90 to 100 members to provide for representation of the missionary interests of the churches. In making the nominations, the Committee endeavoured to take brotherly counsel with each other and to keep in mind confessional and geographical representation. Of the 100 names on the slate, 16 were laymen (9 men, 5 women, 2 lay professors of theology), 32 were members of the old Central Committee, and 21 were from churches not represented on the old Committee.

Professor Tindal asked that the following sentence be added at the end of the list:

> One of the representatives of the Ecumenical Patriarchate will be also the representative of the Greek Orthodox Patriarchate of Jerusalem.

He also asked that the name of Mrs Ba Maung Chain of the Burma Baptist Convention be deleted and the name of the Rev. S'Aye Mya Kyaw of the same church be substituted.

Professor Tindal then presented the proposals of the Nominations Committee for Honorary President, the Praesidium and the Central Committee to the Assembly.

Dr Fry said that two alternate substitutions had been proposed:

The Rev. Mario Sbaffi of the Evangelical Methodist Church of Italy for the *Rev. Paul Mbende* of the Union des Eglises Baptistes du Cameroun; and

Bishop A. Wantula of the Evangelical Church of the Augsburgian Confession of Poland for *Dr H. Binder* of the Protestant Evangelical Church of the Augsburgian Confession of Rumania.

Dr Fry recognized *Dr Helen Kim* (Korean Methodist Church). She stated that in looking over the nominations list, the following analysis might be made: United Kingdom, 9; United States, 21; Russian Orthodox, 5; India, 6; Far East (Japan), 1.

Dr Kim stated that she had difficulty in understanding that these nominations were just and fair from the point of view of geographical representation. She raised the question whether from areas where more than one name had been submitted, a substitution could be made for Korea. She did not want any names dropped. Therefore, she could not make the substitution for a name on the list.

The Chairman reported that twelve members of staff had been appointed as tellers. He again cautioned the Assembly that only delegates in delegates' seats could vote. After giving instructions on the ballot for the substitutions, the Chairman declared the vote closed and instructed the stewards to collect the ballots. Receiving the report of the tellers, the Chairman reported that neither substitution replaced the original names on the Nominations Committee proposal.

The Chairman again stated the two ways in which nominations could be made, and indicated that each voter might indicate his approval of the complete list of nominations as it then stood or vote individually on the names on the ballot. He then called for the vote, and asked the stewards to collect the ballots.

The Chairman subsequently reported that although not all the ballots had been counted for the Honorary President, the Praesidium and the Central Committee it was evident that all had received the necessary votes to be elected. A detailed count of the voting was later submitted, and those nominated were declared elected. (The list of those elected appears as Appendix 7, pages 399-402.)

III. Commission on Faith and Order

The Chairman, Dr Fry, called on *Bishop Lilje* (Evangelical Church in Germany) to present the report on nominations for the Commission on Faith and Order. Bishop Lilje submitted the list of 120 nominations on behalf of the Nominations Committee. He explained that approval had been received from the churches on all but seven and acceptances had been received on all but ten.

In discussion, the following points were made:

Bishop Howells (Church of the Province of West Africa) asked for an explanation for the deletion of Bishop Nku of the Apostolic Faith Missions and the substitution of 'a person from the Independent African Churches'. Bishop Lilje replied that this had been the request from the churches in the area concerned.

Professor Rodolfo Obermüller (Evangelical German Synod of Rio de la Plata) asked why Spain, Italy and Portugal were not represented. He felt that representatives from these Roman Catholic countries might make a very real contribution to the Faith and Order Commission in view of the coming Ecumenical Council. Bishop Lilje replied that no names had been submitted from churches in these countries.

The Rev. Showky Howly (Evangelical Synod of Syria and Lebanon) inquired why the Evangelical Church of Syria and Lebanon was not recognized.

The Rev. Timothy Chow (Methodist Church, Hong Kong) requested the Committee to reconsider the representation from Asia, especially from Malaya and Hong Kong.

A motion to refer the Report back to the Committee was put to the vote and lost.

Bishop M. Evangelista (United Church of Christ in the Philippines) asked whether the fact of no representation on the list from the Philippines was a matter of omission or neglect.

Dr Paul Minear, Director of the Faith and Order Commission, stated that the initiative for making nominations lay in the Faith and Order Commission. Effort had been made to increase the representation from Asia and Africa and representatives from nineteen new countries had been added to the list. It was impossible to include someone from every country.

The Chairman announced that four substitutions had been proposed and took *a vote by ballot, as a result of which, and taking into account withdrawals of their names by the persons concerned, the following were nominated:*

The Rev. V. C. Samuel (Syrian Orthodox, India)
Dr William Stewart (Church of South India)
The Rev. S. Nomenyo (Presbyterian, Togo).

The Chairman called on Dr Minear, who stated that since there had been some misunderstanding and confusion, the Business Committee had requested him to clarify the procedures leading to these nominations. According to the Constitution of the Faith and Order Commission, the Commission shall consist of 100 members appointed by the Assembly of the World Council, with power to nominate additional members up to the number of twenty for appointment by the Central Committee. Recommendations are made by the Commission for appointment by the Assembly. Since the Faith and Order Commission which met in St Andrews in 1960 did not make nominations, the Working Committee exercised its constitutional rights to make nominations for appointment by the Assembly. The 1961 Working Committee adopted a resolution that consideration should be given to the following points in making nominations:

1. members from non-member churches
2. larger proportion of members from Asia, Africa, Latin America
3. theologians rather than administrators
4. fair balance confessionally and geographically
5. initiative for making nominations in hands of Faith and Order Commission.

The Working Committee decided that these objectives could not be met by restricting the list to 100 members and that it would be undesirable to postpone until 1963 the requested expansion of membership. Therefore, the Working Committee decided to ask the Assembly to choose the full complement of 120 in order that the Commission might be at full strength for the studies leading to the Fourth World Conference on Faith and Order.

The Chairman indicated that there were two ways to vote: either for full slate or individually for the names on the list, declared the vote closed and asked the stewards to collect the ballots.

The Chairman subsequently reported that on 422 ballots cast for the Faith and Order Commission members, every person on the nomination list had received at least 419 votes. (The list of those elected is given in Appendix 7, pages 402-5.)

3 · REPORT OF THE POLICY REFERENCE COMMITTEE

The Report of the Policy Reference Committee contained:

i. Recommendations to the Assembly, set out below with a summary of accompanying discussions.

ii. Recommendations to the Central Committee, to be transmitted directly to the Central Committee, without Assembly action, on the following matters:

The Report of the Central Committee
The Report on Programme and Finance
The Fourth Assembly
The Church, the Churches and the World Council o
Churches (Toronto Statement 1950)
The Report on 'Christian Witness, Proselytism and Re
ligious Liberty'
Relations with World Confessional Bodies
Regional Developments.

iii. Recommendations to the Committee on Relationships witl Christian Councils.

The Chairman in Business Session stated that it was understoo that committees of the Assembly had the right to pass directly t the Central Committee and to other committees matters which nee not have the attention of the Assembly. The committees to whic such matters were referred disposed of them at their own discretior The Chairman ruled that delegates had the right to question an such reference of matters to committees.

The following actions arising out of the Report of the Policy Re ference Committee were taken in Business Session.

A. Report of the Chairman of the Central Committee (see pages 334-42)

On the recommendation of the Policy Reference Committee, was VOTED to adopt the following statement:

The Committee appreciates the statement that the World Counc 'sees itself called not only into the tide of events but to be ahea of them', and recommends that this should be the continue aspiration of the Council. It feels that the Council should give its member churches spiritual and practical guidance in a Christian approach to the actual questions and problems of our day, such as materialism, secularism, peace and war, social justice, etc. The WCC should certainly not wait to be pushed into critical situations, but should always take the lead and initiative in asking 'What is the command of our Lord in the present time?' At the same time, the churches themselves should be encouraged to bring their requests in this regard before the WCC. While it is universally recognized that the Council is a Council of *Churches,* and can only do what its member churches authorize it to do, we feel that the Council, as the ecumenical conscience of the churches, should be constantly vigilant for occasions where ecumenical action is particularly desirable, and where it may call upon its members to consider such action.

The Report states, 'The ecumenical movement no longer is, if it ever was, the affair of a coterie of specialists'. While agreeing with the substance of this statement, the Committee feels that perhaps the gravest problem facing the Council is that of familiarizing the general membership of our churches with the details and significance of its work. Many delegates to this Assembly are themselves hearing of much of this work for the first time; while the majority of our church membership is either totally ignorant thereof or is indifferent or occasionally hostile towards it. To help the member churches to follow the Lund advice that churches should habitually all be doing everything together that they are not bound to do separately, the Committee recommends that the Assembly instruct the Central Committee to make this problem one of its major concerns during the next inter-Assembly period. Every possible effort should be made to popularize the Council's activities by promoting distribution of its publications through National Councils as well as through member churches.

B. Report of the Committee on Programme and Finance

On recommendation of the Policy Reference Committee, the Assembly passed with applause a warm *vote of thanks to the members of the Committee on Programme and Finance* for their outstanding work (see also pages 291-9).

C. Aims and Functions of Divisions and Departments

On recommendation of the Policy Reference Committee, it was *VOTED that the Assembly approve the Aims and Functions of the Divisions and Departments as they are stated in the Work Book, and empower the Central Committee to make any adjustmen which may prove desirable before the Fourth Assembly.*

D. The Fourth Assembly

The Policy Reference Committee reported two observations a follows:

(1) The Assembly has two aspects: first, and more essentially, is the legislative organ of the WCC; secondarily, it is massive act of witness. Decisions as to size ought to be relate primarily to the first function, but here two consideratior tend to pull against one another. On the one hand, th Assembly ought to be large enough to give adequate repre sentation to all the member churches, having regard to th range of committee work to be covered. On the other hand, is clear from the New Delhi experience that the Assembly already so large that the problem of organizing its work effec tively within the limits of the time available has becom almost insoluble. Perhaps it would be realistic to recogniz bearing in mind the increases in size and range of functior already referred to, that the extent to which the Assembly ca in fact function as the legislature of the WCC is limited b the nature of the Assembly and by the fact that it meets a long intervals and then only for a brief period. This mear that the democratic and representative character of the WC can be maintained only by an attempt to transact as muc business as possible by correspondence between the Centra Committee and the member churches, as far as possible re serving issues of major importance for Assemblies. In thi connection attention is drawn to what has already been sai about the need for the member churches to face the fact th the effectiveness of their participation in WCC affairs will bea a direct relationship to their capacity to deal expeditious with matters referred to them by the Central Committee.

(2) The Committee notes the action taken at the first session c the Assembly to instruct the Central Committee to make prc vision at the Fourth Assembly for the appointment by membe churches of 25 extra delegates to the Assembly, being person of special competence in the field of World Mission, the name to be proposed to the member churches by the Central Con mittee from a list prepared by the Committee of the Divisio of World Mission and Evangelism.

Upon recommendation of the Policy Reference Committee, *it wa*

VOTED that the number of full members of the Fourth Assembl shall be 700 (*including* 25 *delegates to the Assembly, being pe sons of special competence in the field of World Mission, the names to be proposed to the member churches by the Central Committee from a list prepared by the Committee of the Division of World Mission and Evangelism) and that the Assembly empower the Central Committee, if it thinks fit, to increase or to diminish the said number by not more than* 20 *per cent.*

The Policy Reference Committee attached the following comment to this recommendation: 'Because of increases in the member churches there will probably be heavy pressure on the upper limit, but the committee strongly holds that the Assembly is already so large that efficient transaction of business has become difficult.'

On the motion of the *Rev. Maurice Sweeting* (Lutheran Church in France), it was *VOTED to ask the Central Committee to study the role and method of working of the Assembly and to bring a report to the Fourth Assembly.*

E. Criteria for Membership of the World Council

Upon recommendation of the Policy Reference Committee *it was VOTED to instruct the Central Committee in the following terms:*

Having regard to the criteria mentioned in the Rules (*I*, 3) *and especially to paragraph* (c), *'The question of size must be taken into consideration', and considering that the acceptance of many smaller churches as members of the Council would make the problem of fair allocation of places in the Assembly exceedingly difficult, but wishing to respond to the desire of small churches for fellowship with the other churches in the Council, particularly where this is vitally necessary for them in the fulfilment of their mission, the Committee recommends that the Assembly instruct the Central Committee:*

(1) *to examine the problems involved in the admission of large numbers of very small churches and to report its findings to the Fourth Assembly;*

(2) *to interpret the criterion concerning size in such a way that, as a rule, no church with an inclusive membership of less than ten thousand be admitted to membership during the period between the Third and Fourth Assemblies;*

(3) *without prejudice to any action which may be taken by the Fourth Assembly, to set up a classification of 'associated churches', which will include such churches as, according to the judgment of the Central Committee, fulfil all the criteria of membership except the criterion concerning size. It is under-*

stood that such churches will be kept informed about t activities of the Council, will receive staff visits, and will invited to participate in conferences and courses. They w not have voting representation in the Assembly or Centr Committee, but will have first claim upon 'observer' places the Assembly.

F. Resolution on Anti-Semitism

Upon recommendation of the Policy Reference Committee, a after amendment from the floor, it was *VOTED to adopt the follo ing resolution:*

The Third Assembly recalls the following words which we addressed to the churches by the First Assembly of the World Cou cil of Churches in 1948:

'We call upon all the churches we represent to denounce anti-se itism, no matter what its origin, as absolutely irreconcilable wi the profession and practice of the Christian faith. Anti-semitis is sin against God and man. Only as we give convincing eviden to our Jewish neighbours that we seek for them the comm rights and dignities which God wills for his children, can we co to such a meeting with them as would make it possible to sha with them the best which God has given us in Christ.'

The Assembly renews this plea in view of the fact that situatio continue to exist in which Jews are subject to discrimination a even persecution. The Assembly urges its member churches to do in their power to resist every form of anti-semitism. In Christi teaching the historic events which led to the Crucifixion should n be so presented as to fasten upon the Jewish people of today r sponsibilities which belong to our corporate humanity and not one race or community. Jews were the first to accept Jesus and Je are not the only ones who do not yet recognize him.

In discussion of this resolution, the following points were made

Principal J. Russell Chandran (Church of South India) said he f that this proposal would give a distorted picture of the World Counci social concerns since anti-semitism was only one form of social i justice, and had no peculiar significance. He asked the Assembly not adopt the resolution in view of the fact that other actions of t Assembly had dealt with various forms of social and racial discrimin tion.

Bishop E. G. Gulin (Evangelical Lutheran Church of Finland) su ported the resolution but proposed that the original wording of the la sentence, which read 'Jews are not the only ones to reject him', should amended to read: 'Jews were the first to accept Jesus and Jews are not he only ones who do not yet recognize him.' Bishop Gulin urged that his formulation would prove to be more eirenic and would facilitate he right approach to the Jews.

Bishop Gulin's amendment was seconded.

The Rev. Charles Westphal (Eglise Réformée de France) said he had had it in mind to propose that the word 'refuse' be substituted for the word 'reject'. He would, however, be glad to support Bishop Gulin's proposal. Mr Westphal expressed surprise at the statement made by Principal Russell Chandran. 'Have we forgotten', he asked, 'the irrevocable promises of God to the people of the promise? Discrimination against the Jews does have a peculiar theological significance.'

Dr Robert Mackie, who had presented the Report in the absence of he Chairman, Archbishop Iakovos, pointed out that the Policy Reference Committee had spent much time on the sentence under discussion. He thought that in the form as proposed by the Committee it was serviceable and acceptable. 'The opposite of "accept" is "reject" To change the term is to weaken it. The sentence is not addressed to the ews but is a reminder to us all that anti-semitism is a form of rejection of Jesus.'

The amendment was put to the vote. The Chairman declared that the how of hands indicated the necessity for a count. The count having been taken the result was declared to be: For the amendment 194; against 130.

Sir Francis Ibiam (Presbyterian Church of Nigeria) supported the esolution and especially welcomed the reference to the 'responsibilities which belong to our corporate humanity'. 'The Jew harbours no ill-will against any nation nor does he overthrow any other nation.' Any statement on anti-semitism should include reference to all governments which practise uncharitable acts. On this ground he would like to see a resolution which was addressed to the USA, Great Britain, Russia, China, the Central Africa Federation, South Africa, Ghana, France, etc.

Mr Carl G. Boëthius (Church of Sweden) said that while it was true hat anti-semitism had common features with other forms of racial discrimination there was nevertheless a special reason for speaking about the Jews. The Church had for centuries taken part in discrimination against Jews and was under a special obligation to them, 'as chosen people which represent mankind both in receiving and rejecting Jesus'.

The Rev. Ermanno Rostan (Waldensian Church, Italy) supported the esolution and expressed the wish that it should be expanded by taking nto account all that Scripture, especially the Epistle to the Romans, ays about the eventual restoration of the people of God.

The Rev. Christoph Schnyder (Swiss Protestant Church Federation) proposed that the last but one sentence of the draft Resolution should be ended at the words 'corporate humanity' and this new sentence inserted o follow: 'On the contrary, the Jews remain God's chosen people (cf. Rom. 9-11), for even their rejection for a time must contribute to the world's salvation.'

Dr Visser 't Hooft said that those who had worked on this resolution had been very much aware of the previous discussions within the WCC, especially at the Evanston Assembly. The basic theological problem referred to by previous speakers was one on which there was as yet no consensus of opinion. An attempt to speak on this aspect of the matter could only result in the kind of divided counsels which were so much in evidence at Evanston. On the other hand if the Assembly would content itself with a simple statement directed to the practical issue of anti-semitism it would be possible to reach complete agreement.

The Chairman asked Mr Schnyder whether in the light of what they had just heard, he desired to press his proposal. *Mr Schnyder* said that as he and other members of his delegation had been instructed to bring this proposal before the Assembly he felt he must press it to a vote. The Chairman asked Dr Mackie if the Policy Reference Committee had discussed the theological questions raised by Dr Schnyder's proposal. *Dr Mackie* answered that it had not done so.

Fr Makary el Souriany (Coptic Orthodox Church, Egypt) said he supported the resolution as being concerned with a racial issue, not a political one. 'We agreed in Evanston and St Andrews that any theological study concerning ancient Israel in its biblical meaning must not have any bearing on the existence of Israel as a political entity. So I reject any mention of Israel in this statement.'

Professor John C. Bennett (United Church of Christ, USA) said he feared lest the discussion should result in an uncertain voice on anti-semitism, a result which would be disastrous. 'There is a mid-way position between the view of anti-semitism as merely a racial issue and that which regards it as being based on theological factors. . . . Anti-semitism is in part a result of the misuse of Christian teaching and Christian symbols. Religious feeling is an essential factor in its development. . . . We are dealing with the deposit of centuries of religious hostility, a kind of cultural memory of the West. . . . It is an indication of the problem that Pope John XXIII has deleted some words from the Good Friday Liturgy because they help to perpetuate religious hostility towards the Jews. Similarly, in the United States there has been a review of Christian educational curricula with the same intention.' He hoped that members of the Assembly who came from parts of the world where this 'inherited guilt' was not felt would refrain from causing the voice of this Assembly to be indecisive on the subject.

The Chairman asked Mr Schnyder whether he still pressed his proposal. *Mr Schnyder:* 'I withdraw, but ask that it shall be referred to in the minutes of the Assembly.' *Dr Payne:* 'I give you that assurance.'

Dr H. Berkhof (Dutch Reformed Church, Netherlands), who spoke also for Dr De Vries who was absent, proposed that the phrase 'fasten upon the Jewish people' should be amended to read 'fasten upon Jewish people'. *Dr Mackie* expressed the view that this proposed change was undesirable. Dr Berkhof's amendment was put to the vote by a show of hands and lost.

A motion to conclude the debate in accordance with rule 17 was carried. Bishop Gulin's amendment was put to the vote and carried. The Assembly then proceeded to vote on the resolution as amended.

G. The Report on 'Christian Witness, Proselytism and Religious Liberty'

Upon recommendation of the Policy Reference Committee, it was *VOTED to receive the document on Christian Witness, Proselytism and Religious Liberty in the setting of the World Council of Churches* ('*Evanston to New Delhi*', 239-45) *and to commend it to the churches.*

H. Relations with Non-Member Churches

Upon recommendation of the Policy Reference Committee, *it was VOTED*

1. *That the Assembly reiterate its invitation to churches not in membership, which are willing to accept the Basis and purposes of the WCC, to apply for membership.*
2. *That the Assembly urge the Geneva Secretariat, the Faith and Order Commission, and the National Councils in various countries to seek to make contact with non-member churches with a view to mutual acquaintance and understanding, the dispelling of any misunderstandings there may be regarding the Ecumenical Movement, and also with a view to serious discussion of theological issues concerning Christian mission and unity, and to participation in such activities as may appear to be mutually desirable.*

   That the Assembly draw attention to the valuable paper by Dr Norman Goodall on 'Relations with non-member churches (Protestant)'[1] *and welcome the closer contacts which have recently been established with certain Roman Catholic theologians and other Roman Catholic churchmen specifically concerned with Christian unity and express the hope that these will develop fruitfully in the future.*
3. *That the Assembly record its pleasure at the presence of observers from a number of churches, including the Roman Catholic Church, at its meeting, and lay upon the hearts and consciences of all the member churches the importance of constant prayer for their Christian brethren in every part of the world.*

[1] Available from WCC headquarters, 17 route de Malagnou, Geneva.

I. The Basis

Upon recommendation of the Policy Reference Committee, it was *VOTED that the Assembly resolve that Section I of the Constitution of the World Council of Churches read as follows:*

I. *Basis*

The World Council of Churches is a fellowship of churches which confess the Lord Jesus Christ as God and Saviour according to the Scriptures and therefore seek to fulfil together their common calling to the glory of the one God, Father, Son and Holy Spirit. It is constituted for the functions set out below.

Before the vote was taken the Policy Committee had reported as follows:

THE BASIS OF THE WORLD COUNCIL OF CHURCHES

(1) The Committee carefully considered the Report on the Basis. It received from the General Secretary information that all churches had already received a copy of the Minutes of the Central Committee for 1960, in which that report appeared.

(2) Some churches had written to express their judgment concerning the Basis. Many others had discussed the matter without informing the General Secretariat of the result of their deliberations.

(3) The following churches had informed Geneva that they were in favour of accepting the expanded Basis:

23 Landeskirchen in Germany
The Church of the Province of New Zealand
The Reformed Church of France
The Lutheran Church in Poland
The Evangelical Lutheran Church, Holland
The Netherlands Reformed Church
The Belgian Christian Missionary Church

Oral reports had come concerning the views of other churches and organizations.

(4) Some of the churches, which had written, added special remarks to their answer:

The *Netherlands Reformed Church* says in its decision taken by the General Synod (February 6, 1961):

> . . . This does not mean that it does not regret that some objections against the former wording are not removed, such as a too strong accent on the confession of Jesus Christ as God, without adding a sentence about the importance of his also being human, and the lack of reference to Jesus as the Messiah of Israel.

That on the other hand it is of opinion that as the new wording principally must be seen as an extension and not as an improvement of the old formulation, it would not attach too much importance to the new wording, and this is why it recommends to the World Council of Churches to do everything in its power to avoid that the new wording would get to be a sensational point of difference in the Assembly, and therefore only to accept the new basic formula if a very great majority agrees.

The *Belgian Christian Missionary Church:*

. . . Our church accepts in the hope that those Christian Churches which would not be able to accept or are not yet members of the WCC will not be disregarded or suspected for this reason. Contacts should be maintained or established to the left as well as to the right, since—if we understand rightly—the ecumenical movement does not want to be a new universal church but aims rather at creating a new conscience at the heart of this church which already exists, though broken.

(5) One church has written to express its dissatisfaction with the new proposal. This is the *Remonstrant Brotherhood* (*Arminian Church*) *of the Netherlands*. Its action is as follows:

We highly appreciate the fact that the discussion about the Basis is being continued. We consider that such discussion will continue to be necessary in the future. (Cf. letter from the Executive Council of the Remonstrant Brotherhood to the Central Committee of the WCC, October 8, 1949.)

We are however disappointed with the alterations now proposed, seeing that the phrase 'God and Saviour' has been retained. In this wording we are unable to recognize either the heart of the New Testament witness or the 'specific source and dynamic' of the World Council itself. (Cf. statement made by the Brotherhood at Evanston, August 1954.)

We should prefer to see the relation between our belief in Christ and our common calling to witness, service and fellowship expressed more clearly in the Basis-formula. This would, in our opinion, also help the non-Christian world the better to understand the objectives of the World Council of Churches.

With regard to the other alterations now proposed, we declare that in the substitution of 'confess' for 'accept' we recognize a more positive emphasis, provided that it does not imply submission to an authoritative credal statement.

We are able to accept the addition of 'according to the Scriptures' if this is meant to imply that every confession of Jesus Christ should point men back to the inexhaustible richness of the biblical witness.

We are able to agree to the final words of the proposed Basis if they are to be regarded as doxology, but we trust that the dogma of the Trinity may never become the touchstone of the admittance of churches into the World Council.

Conclusion: The General Assembly doubts whether the propose alteration would be in the interest of the work of the World Counc of Churches.

It was understood that the *Mennonite Church of Holland* is als opposed to the change in the Basis.

(6) *The International Missionary Council* considered the proposal i its meeting just before the Assembly and expressed its approval.

(7) *The International Association for Liberal Christianity and Re ligious Freedom* adopted at its meeting in Davos in 1961 a resolutio which reads as follows:

The General Assembly of the International Association for Liber Christianity and Religious Freedom, meeting in Davos, August 1 1961, and including in its membership churches and groups who a members of the World Council of Churches and others who are no on account of objections against the present formulation of its bas of membership, places on record its considered regret that the pr posed further change in the basis of membership will create problen for a still greater number of churches and groups who would othe wise wholeheartedly support the work of the Council. The Assemb deplores this action of the WCC which retards the advancement religious co-operation throughout the world.

(8) The sub-committee received verbal communications from:
(*a*) Professor d'Espine on behalf of the *Fédération des Eglises Prote tantes de la Suisse*, stating that it had been decided to give its individu delegates freedom to vote according to their own judgment, and that t Fédération desired to reaffirm its declaration of 1940 in regard to th present Basis.
(*b*) Dr George G. Beazley, Jr, on behalf of the *Christian Church* (Disciples of Christ) *in the USA* stating that they welcomed the ne form of the Basis and would vote for it, but that they would look wi concern and even disfavour on any tendency to proliferate statemen which would exclude from the WCC fellow-Christians who confe Jesus Christ as Lord and seek to render obedience to him in faith an love.
(*c*) Dr Westphal stating that the *Synod National de l'Eglise Réform de France* would accept the new Basis as an attempt to express th mystery of the divine revelation which does not intend to impose upc the member churches any particular theology.
(*d*) Professor Konidaris of the *Church of Greece*, a member of th committee, who in expressing his approval of the revised Basis observe that his church would interpret it in the light of the Nicaean-Co stantinopolitan Creed.

The following points were made in the discussion:

The Rev. Professor Henri d'Espine (Swiss Reformed) said:

The delegation of the Swiss Protestant Churches has received a ma date from their General Assembly to draw attention, at the time of the discussion on the Basis of the WCC, to the conditions on which they decided to join in 1940. The statement they made at that time would still remain valid if the new formulation of the Basis were to be adopted. This statement reads as follows:

Decisions of the Assembly of the Federation of Protestant Churches of Switzerland concerning the new formulation of the Basis of the World Council of Churches

After consulting the Churches belonging to the Federation, the Assembly of delegates, at their meeting on June 26, 1961, took the following decisions concerning the new formulation of the Basis of the World Council of Churches.

It left its delegates to the Assembly at New Delhi free to vote, each in accordance with his conviction. On the other hand, it instructed its delegation to draw attention to the conditions on which the Federation of Protestant Churches of Switzerland decided in 1940 to join the World Council of Churches, and to state that its position remains the same with regard to the new formulation, if it is adopted, as with regard to the old formulation.

These conditions are as follows:

'The Protestant Churches of Switzerland expressly affirm that their adherence to the Basis proposed in the Statutes (at that time provisional) of the World Council of Churches does not modify the doctrinal position which they hold, and they loudly declare that they remain firmly attached to the principles of the Reformed Churches in confessing (in accordance with the Holy Scriptures) their faith in Jesus Christ, our Lord and Saviour, their sole, supreme Head.'

Professor H. Alivisatos spoke on behalf of the delegates of the Orthodox Church of Greece. He said that the proposal was gladly accepted 'as the minimum of a right declaration of the Christian faith'. 'The Church of Greece, although aware of the Trinitarian implication of the formulation of the previous Basis, has since the Amsterdam Assembly insisted that the Basis ought to have been formulated in a positive Trinitarian way. . . . The Orthodox Church of Greece therefore gladly accepts and votes for the proposed new formulation in the sense that it is in full agreement with the Trinitarian doctrine as formulated by the two first ecumenical synods of the old and undivided Church and in the so-called Nicaean-Constantinopolitan Creed.'

Dr P. O. Bersell (Augustana Evangelical Lutheran Church, USA) spoke of this 'momentous action' 'as one of the senior members'. 'For years', he said, 'the Central Committee has battled with this question of making more explicit the evangelical and scriptural scope of the Basis, and at long last has succeeded. . . . Particularly do we remember the beloved Bishop Berggrav; all honour to him and his Norwegian brothers for their insistence as the spear-head of the movement to enlarge the Basis.'

Professor J. A. Oosterbaarn (General Mennonite Society, Netherlands), speaking for the Mennonite Brotherhood in Holland, said that the Brotherhood could not vote for the proposed alteration. Their reason was not of a dogmatic nature but out of concern to maintain 'the first function of the Basis, namely, that of indicating the nature of the World Council'. 'It seems to us that such a definition should be as short as possible, mentioning only the essential Christological criterion for membership. . . . By expanding the formula and by making explicit some implications thereof the World Council would leave this excellent foundation. We fear that this would mean a first step in the direction of confessionalism. . . . We should deplore it if the Basis should become an obstacle for certain undoubtedly Christian churches to join the Council and if it should exclude those non-confessional groups whose members accept Jesus Christ as Lord without explicitly formulating the dogmatic implications thereof.'

The Rev. Clifford W. P. Hansen (Seventh Day Baptist General Conference, USA) said that the Seventh Day Baptists 'are strongly committed to the principle of ecumenical fellowship in general and to the WCC in particular'. The addition of the phrase 'according to the Scriptures' would 'win the preference of many of my constituents'; yet 'a significant number of them, with whom I associate myself, object to the proposal'. Mr Hansen enumerated five reasons for this: (i) The proposal fails to preserve the Scriptural differentiation between God and Jesus. (ii) The proposal 'tends to remove Jesus from the life of man and make him ineffective in human behaviour'. (iii) The proposal 'demands too much in the way of interpretation'. (iv) The proposal 'asserts a non-biblical premise which may well lead to adding confusion and division between member churches over the question of Jesus' relationship to his mother, thus doing the opposite of what the Basis was intended to do'. (v) The proposal 'might tend to exclude some conscientious Christians whom Jesus himself would welcome, and thus be contrary to the ecumenical spirit'. 'I therefore hope that this Assembly will oppose the motion in anticipation of some more acceptable proposal in the future.'

Mr E. Raymond Wilson (Friends' General Conference, USA) expressed 'appreciation for the spirit of tolerance and fellowship which the members of the World Council have shown towards the Society of Friends. . . . While the proposed changes are improvements in several ways, they still present several difficulties to some Friends.' Mr Wilson recalled that in 1951 the Philadelphia Yearly Meeting of Friends expressed the desire that the phrase 'fellowship of churches which accept our Lord Jesus Christ as God and Saviour' should be changed to read '. . . *Lord* and Saviour'. 'If our constitution goes further to define the nature of Christ it becomes divisive. All definitions of his nature have resulted in controversy because he is infinitely beyond definition. The phrase "Jesus is Lord" is in accord with New Testament usage.' Dr Wilson also expressed the fear that the proposal would mean that in the basis of membership the major emphasis would tend to be 'on belief in Christ rather than on living in the light of Christ'. 'What we seek as a World Council is unity among diversity, liberty of thought in a common discipleship under Christ, and a humanity redeemed by God and reconciled to him and to each other.' Mr Wilson indicated that 'in deference to the feelings held by many Friends' he would abstain from voting on the proposal.

Dr G. J. Hoenderdaal (Arminian Church—Remonstrant Brotherhood—Netherlands) drew attention to the statement already submitted by the Remonstrant Brotherhood and included in the document before the Assembly (page 153). He again expressed the anxiety of the Remonstrant Brotherhood lest 'further expansion may lead us on the way to a credal statement which can be the work of a church but not of a council of churches'. Dr Hoenderdaal added 'I want to declare that whatever decision be taken in this matter, the Remonstrant Brotherhood wants to stay within the fellowship of the WCC'.

Dr Franklin Clark Fry (United Lutheran Church in America) said it might be useful if someone who had been intimately involved in the six-year period during which this matter had been under discussion underlined the precise significance of the proposed changes. These included (i) the substitution of the verb 'confess' for 'accept'; (ii) the removal of the word 'our' from the phrase 'our Lord Jesus Christ' since 'our' could be regarded as being restrictive; (iii) the setting of the phrase 'God and Saviour' within a Trinitarian reference—a change which he believed should meet some of the difficulties felt in regard to the existing Basis; (iv) the explicit reference to the Scriptures, as proposed by the Church of Norway and desired by many other churches. 'With great respect to those who have felt bound to dissent from the proposed changes, I believe they constitute a clarification which results in a fuller and truer statement of our faith than is provided by the existing Basis.'

The Rev. Albert Gaillard (Eglise Réformée de France) recalled that when the Reformed Church of France assumed its present form as a union of four churches it affirmed its acceptance of the historic ecumenical symbols and of the confessions of the Reformation, 'without being bound by the letter of them, since language can never provide a total representation of the divine mysteries. The Reformed Church accepts the new proposal in the same sense.'

Präses Dr Joachim Beckmann (Evangelical Church in Germany) said that the Evangelical Churches in Germany felt great joy in the proposed reference to Scripture and they also greatly welcomed the reference to 'our common calling'.

Archpriest Vitaly Borovoy (Russian Orthodox Church) expressed in the name of the Russian Orthodox Church whole-hearted support of all that Professor Alivisatos had said. 'The expected acceptance of the new Trinitarian Basis played a very important role in the decision we made to join the WCC and made our task much easier. . . . It is no attempt at confessionalism but a short and scriptural statement of the basic truth of the Christian faith.'

Dr Leroy D. McBain (American Baptist Convention) spoke as representing a 'non-credal denomination which prefers a minimal doctrinal statement'. He feared that any expansion of the present Basis could become a precedent for still further additions until the Basis became 'a burdensome doctrinal statement'.

Dr Eugene C. Blake (United Presbyterian Church in the USA) spoke 'as a representative of a Church which has looked with great hesitation on any expansion of the formulation of the Basis'. He would support the resolution, however, 'in order to make clear to some churches outside our fellowship that it is not "mere togetherness" which is the foundation of the ecumenical movement but an authentic Christian confession based upon the Scriptures'. He would resist any attempt to make the new proposal a precedent for any further expansion of the Basis and hoped that the proposal would be supported by an overwhelming vote of the Assembly.

Archbishop Nikodim of Jaroslav and Rostov (Russian Orthodox Church) said 'All of us assembled here, representing a variety of churches, are Christians. We all believe in the Lord Jesus Christ on the basis of Holy Scripture and we all strive to attain to unity so that there shall be for us one Lord and one baptism. In his holy Gospel the Lord Jesus Christ clearly commands his disciples to preach the Gospel to all creatures and to baptize those who will believe in the Name of the Father, the Son and the Holy Ghost. The Trinitarian wording of the Basis is therefore grounded in nothing less than the Holy Gospel and the Gospel is the corner-stone of the faith that has brought us together.'

Dr C. G. Baeta (Presbyterian Church of Ghana) drew the Assembly's attention to the fact that when the proposed expansion of the Basis was circulated to member councils of the International Missionary Council the response indicated 'widespread and in part enthusiastic support for the proposed change. . . . The accent on the Scriptures and on fulfilling the Church's calling to the glory of the Triune God' were regarded as new emphases in the right direction.

Dr E. H. Tuller (American Baptist Convention) drew attention to the fact that many of the objections so far voiced in discussion had to do not with the new phrases but with the original words 'God and Saviour'. The present Assembly could not amend this phrase. It could only indicate to the Central Committee that some of the churches desired that it should be amended.

The Rev. Leon E. Gauthier (Old Catholic Church) said he would like to assure those who could not accept the new Basis that it did not constitute a new dogma but only an affirmation of the essential message of revelation according to the Gospel and the experience of the Church.

Dr H. Berkhof (Netherlands Reformed Church) said that though he represented a Church which had recorded its acceptance of the proposed changes, he wanted to speak 'for those who do not like the one-sided monophysite character of the original Basis'. He regretted the fact that acceptance of the proposed expansion by the present Assembly would inevitably block the way to any re-writing of the whole Basis at some future date.

Dr Edwin H. Tuller asked whether the text under consideration could be amended during this Assembly.

The Chairman answered in the negative because of the previous action of the Assembly concerning the amendability of amendments (see pages 58-9).

The Assembly voted to conduct the vote on the Basis by written ballot. The vote was taken and the Chairman announced the result of the ballot as follows:

383 in favour
36 against
7 abstentions

The Chairman observed that the Basis in its old form had played a great part in bringing together 198 churches in the World Council. It had first been suggested in 1937 for the World Council and had been used in the earlier history of the ecumenical movement. It had always been recognized that it had limitations and that it might be wise to amplify it. The Policy Reference Committee urged that what the Second Assembly had said about the purpose and function of the Basis (*Work Book*, page 32) should be kept in mind. The adoption of the new form was a historic moment and the Chairman hoped that the new statement might prove to be even more effective than the original.

The Assembly engaged in prayer, asking God's blessing on the step that had been taken.

J. Statement on Religious Liberty

On the recommendation of the Policy Reference Committee, and after amendment on the floor, *it was VOTED to adopt the following Statement on Religious Liberty:*

1. Mankind is threatened by many forces which curtail or deny freedom. There is accordingly urgent need to reinvigorate efforts to ensure that every person has opportunity for the responsible exercise of religious freedom.
2. Christians see religious liberty as a consequence of God's creative work, of his redemption of man in Christ and his calling of men into his service. God's redemptive dealing with men is not coercive. Accordingly human attempts by legal enactment or by pressure of social custom to coerce or to eliminate faith are violations of the fundamental ways of God with men. The freedom which God has given in Christ implies a free response to God's love, and the responsibility to serve fellow-men at the point of deepest need.

3. Holding a distinctive Christian basis for religious liberty, we regard this right as fundamental for men everywhere.

4. We reaffirm the Declaration on Religious Liberty adopted by the World Council of Churches and the International Missionary Council in August-September 1948, and hold to its provisions. We recognize the Universal Declaration of Human Rights, proclaimed by the United Nations in December 1948, as an important instrument in promoting respect for and observance of human rights and fundamental freedoms.

5. Although freedoms of every kind are inter-related, religious liberty may be considered as a distinctive human right, which all men may exercise no matter what their faith. The article on religious freedom in the Universal Declaration is an acceptable standard, always provided that it be given a comprehensive interpretation.

> Everyone has the right to freedom of thought, conscience and religion; this right includes freedom to change his religion or belief, and freedom, either alone or in community with others and in public or private, to manifest his religion or belief in teaching, practice, worship and observance.

6. The recognition of the inherent dignity and of the equal and inalienable rights of all members of the human family requires that the general standard here declared should be given explicit expression in every aspect of society. Without seeking to be inclusive, we illustrate as follows:

7. Freedom of thought, conscience and belief, even considered as inner freedom, requires freedom of access to reliable information.

8. Freedom to manifest one's religion or belief, in public or in private and alone or in community with others, is essential to the expression of inner freedom.

(*a*) It includes freedom to worship according to one's chosen form, in public or in private.

(*b*) It includes freedom to teach, whether by formal or informal instruction as well as preaching with a view to propagating one's faith and persuading others to accept it.

(*c*) It includes freedom to practise religion or belief, whether by performance of acts of mercy or by the expression in word or deed of the implications of belief in social, economic and political matters, both domestic and international.

(*d*) It includes freedom of observance by following religious customs or by participating in religious rites in the family or in public meeting.

9. Religious liberty includes freedom to change one's religion or belief without consequent social, economic and political disabilities. Implicit in this right is the right freely to maintain one's belief or disbelief without external coercion or disability.

10. The exercise of religious liberty involves other human rights. The Universal Declaration proclaims, among others, the right to free-

dom of peaceful assembly and association; the right to freedom of opinion and expression including freedom to seek, receive and impart information and ideas through any media and regardless of frontiers; the prior right of parents to choose the kind of education that shall be given to their children; freedom to participate in choosing the desired form of government and in freely electing officials; freedom from the retroactive application of penal law; and freedom to leave and to return to one's country and to seek asylum elsewhere.

11. The freedom with which Christ has set us free calls forth responsibility for the rights of others. The civil freedom which we claim in the name of Christ must be freely available for all to exercise responsibly. It is the corresponding obligation of governments and of society to ensure the exercise of these civil rights without discrimination. It is for the churches in their own life and witness recognizing their own past failures in this regard to play their indispensable role in promoting the realization of religious liberty for all men.

NOTE.—The religious liberty defined in this Statement should be exercised in accord with the Report on Christian witness, Proselytism and Religious Liberty, received and commended to the churches by the Third Assembly on December 4, 1961.

The following points were made in the discussion:

Professor Berkhof proposed an amendment of paragraph 3 to read as follows: Holding a distinctive Christian basis for religious liberty, we regard this right as fundamental for men everywhere.

The amendment was approved.

The *Metropolitan of Carthage* proposed that the Statement should contain a statement to the effect that religious liberty should be exercised in accord with the report on Christian Witness, Proselytism and Religious Liberty adopted by the Assembly on December 4, 1961. After discussion, *it was voted* to place such a paragraph at the end of the statement, the exact drafting to be left to the officers of the Assembly in consultation with the Metropolitan of Carthage.

The *Metropolitan of Carthage* moved to amend paragraph 10, line 10, to read as follows:

application of penal law; freedom to leave and to return to one's country and to seek asylum elsewhere.

The amendment was seconded and voted.

K. New Staff Appointments

It was reported that the Committee had considered and passed to the Finance Committee proposals concerning the appointment of (*a*) an Associate to the Executive Secretary in the USA, and (*b*) an additional Assistant General Secretary.

Upon recommendation of the Policy Reference Committee, *it was*

VOTED (*a*) *to refer to the Central Committee, without prejudice, an item from the Committee on the CCIA, implying an increase in the General Budget for special services in Asia and Africa, calling for funds additional to the amount of* $5,000 *now included in the budget.*

(*b*) *to transmit to the Central Committee for further consideration the following proposals for activities to be financed outside the General Budget of the WCC under Programme Project procedure:*

(i) that a Secretariat for service abroad be established for an experimental period of three years, related to the General Secretariat, with the understanding that the implementation of this proposal is dependent on the securing of the necessary funds by the Division of World Mission and Evangelism and the Division of Inter-Church Aid, Refugee and World Service. This proposal is supported by a memorandum showing its development from discussions at Willington, 1952, and Davos, 1955, and outlining functions and relationships.

(ii) that a Secretary be appointed for a limited period, who will be attached to the General Secretariat and who will give part time to the Department of Information in the field of broadcasting and television and part time to relationships with those engaged in Christian broadcasting and television who are not directly related to the WCC. It is understood that the implementation of this proposal is dependent on the securing of funds through the Project Fund of the Division of World Mission and Evangelism, and/or other sources.

(iii) that, in relation to the Youth Department, appointment be made of a competent writer to prepare ecumenical materials for those concerned with curricula and with other educational material of the churches. This proposal should be considered in the light of the aims and programme of the Division of Ecumenical Action.

L. Re-examination of the Organizational Pattern of the Council

Canon Coaldrake (Church of England in Australia) called attention to the Policy Reference Committee's recommendation to the Central Committee with regard to the Report of the Committee on Programme and Finance. He moved and *it was*

VOTED that the Assembly endorse the recommendation of the Policy Reference Committee to the Central Committee that the action to set up the necessary machinery for the re-examination of the organizational pattern be taken within two years.

Professor E. de Vries (Dutch Reformed Church) said that he hoped that the Central Committee, in its re-examination of the organizational pattern in connection with the integration of the IMC and the WCC, would take into account the organization of the World Council as a whole.

4 · REPORT OF THE COMMITTEE ON THE DIVISION OF STUDIES

The following Report of the Committee on the Division of Studies was received and the studies proposed therein authorized by the Assembly in Business Session.

The Committee had before it a valuable document, prepared by the Division, on 'Study in the World Council of Churches', and considerable time was spent in reviewing the place of 'study' in the Council's programme. In the document under review, three main functions of ecumenical study are articulated: the first is 'to set forth the advanced issues of world import which affect the life of the churches'; the second is 'to provide a means whereby churches may be led from the stage of understanding one another to the stage of study in depth of their common obedience'; and the third is 'to increase the growth of ecumenical consciousness and conviction'.

How these functions are being performed by the Division and the Departments within the Division may be seen in the fairly full report contained in the volume *'Evanston to New Delhi'*, pages 32-71, and in the several reports of the Departments that will be made to this Assembly. Such reports, we believe, will underscore the wisdom of J. H. Oldham's statement made in 1938: '. . . Study must be undertaken by the Churches *in common,* for the new forces are world forces; they will sooner or later affect the life of every church, and it is therefore essential that on this point the churches should learn from each other and share with each other whatever light God has given to them in their attempt to face new and unprecedented situations.'

It was the function of this Committee to investigate the need for a major study project which would focus for the churches in the next five years an issue of common and far-reaching import, and to make proposals concerning particular studies not already being undertaken but significant enough to warrant action by this Assembly.

A. Major Divisional Study

The greatest part of the Committee's time and energy was given to discussion of this matter. After considerable deliberation, the Committee recommends that the Assembly authorize a major study to be undertaken on *The Finality of Christ in the Age of Universal History*. The proposal is set out as follows:

The Finality of Christ in the Age of Universal History

I. *The motive for such a study*

(1) The situation in which the churches find themselves as they have sought a life of common study and obedience:

again and again, in all the turbulence of our day, in engagement with new knowledge and surrounded by problems and mysteries, Christians have agreed that God is not absent, but have found it extremely difficult to assert how he is present and active in all this.

(2) The situations in which the churches severally, in different parts of the world, have found themselves: e.g.

(*a*) in Asia and Africa (and also in the West) where the religions of mankind would either exclude consideration of the claims of Christ, or would absorb him into a syncretistic relativism;

(*b*) in the West, and increasingly throughout the whole world, wherein the claims of religion of any sort are deemed at best irrelevant and at worst illusory and harmful to man's technical, scientific and moral progress, and where a dominant philosophical assumption frequently treats the language of faith as meaningless.

(3) The situation in which man finds himself:

(*a*) thrown with his fellow-men into the age of universal history, one common stream of events. No longer can any man, any region, any culture, live to itself. Common factors make us all neighbours. Henceforth we, the human race, shall share a common hope, common fears, and a common destiny;

(*b*) with new secrets of nature disclosed to him, and new powers in his hands, with new possibilities for realizing his vocation to have dominion over nature, on the one hand, but on the other with a new temptation to submerge his true humanity under those forces, to become enslaved to the technics of modern civilization and to destroy human life and with it much of the natural order.

II. *The aim of such a study*

To make a contribution towards a theology of Christian witness and action by demonstrating how the good news of Jesus Christ casts light on man's existence, by showing him how God is dealing with him now and will deal with him at the end.

III. *The content of the study*

(1) A re-examination of the biblical witness to the finality of Jesus Christ. This would involve such questions as:

(*a*) the relevance for man's awareness of his existence today of the prophetic and apostolic teaching of the Old and New Testaments including their eschatological and apocalyptic understanding of history;

(*b*) the role of the Holy Spirit in the Church as the means whereby Christ's finality is made apparent in the period between Pentecost and the Parousia; and whereby through the Church's mission Christ is calling all men into the one family of God;

(*c*) in what sense the Bible affords illumination of the conflicts of history as the sphere of God's judging and redeeming acts.

The whole of this is to be undertaken consciously in dialogue with the misinterpretations and partial understandings of the course of history found currently among Christians and non-Christians. Among these may be mentioned messianisms of various sorts, whether overtly Christian or secular.

(2) The relation of this witness to

(*a*) man's religious life

(i) in the East, with the resurgence of ancient religions and the cultural revivals associated with nationalism;

(ii) in the West, with special reference to the religiosity of Church life calling for an elucidation of the phrase 'a religionless Christianity'.

(*b*) man's life with nature, including

(i) an assessment of the scientific enterprise as an expression of man's 'coming of age';

(ii) an investigation of man's new-found oneness with the forces of nature as released through scientific discovery and technological exploitation.

(*c*) man's involvement in the secular order, including specific areas to be delineated by appropriate Departments within the WCC.

IV. *The methods to be followed in such a study*

The Committee asks the Assembly to transmit the following to the Central Committee and the Committee of the Division of Studies, for elaboration of the methods appropriate for the development of this study:

(1) It is highly desirable to have Departments inside and outside the Division of Studies participate to the fullest extent that will serve their purposes. This is no doubt ultimately a matter for the Staff Co-ordinating and Advisory Committee on Studies.

(2) No single method is to be relied upon as a principal method. The Committee suggests that a variety be employed: e.g. carefully organized commissions on various aspects of the study; contributions of individual scholars; regional consultations. The Division will, however, need to watch that the study does not become too dispersed, and that a line of thought emerges which has its own integrity.

(3) The duration of the study should be thought of as the period between the Third and Fourth Assemblies. At appropriate stages the work of the study might be presented in such a way as to catch the imagination and gain the attention of widespread groups within the churches.

B. Proposal for the Future Organization and Activity of the Secretariat on Religious Liberty

The Committee on the Division of Studies recommends that the following be authorized by the Assembly concerning the organization and work of the Secretariat for the Study of Religious Liberty:

1. That in place of the Commission created by the Central Committee, a Committee for the Secretariat for the Study of Religious Liberty be set up to have responsibility for the general supervision of these studies. This Committee would be represented on the Division of Studies Committee by at least two members. It would report to the Divisional Committee, and through it to the Central Committee.
2. That the above Committee and the Secretary should seek competent specialists to pursue further studies concerning the nature of religious liberty as seen by Christians, and of the grounds on which it must be promoted. This study should have two broad aspects:

   (*a*) An investigation of the biblical basis for concern about religious liberty, with close attention to the extent to which the Bible does or does not give guidance in the terms in which the problem is formulated in the twentieth century.

   (*b*) A study of significant thought concerning religious liberty,

Christian and otherwise, which has arisen in various epochs of history.

3. That the Committee and Secretariat arrange for the publication of a brochure or booklet, based principally on studies done by the Commission and Secretary up to this time, for the use of the churches and regional councils. This publication should seek to state clearly the issues that have arisen during the discussions, as well as the points on which significant agreement has been reached. It should include pertinent questions and be suitable for use as the basis of discussion in different parts of the world.
4. That the Committee and Secretariat arrange a series of regional studies on religious liberty which should be launched in an effort to study the widely varying circumstances that arise in different situations: e.g. where a nation is dominated by the ethos of a majority church or national church; where the ideology of political groups is such as to affect the understanding and practice of religious liberty; where cultural factors impede the manifestation of religious liberty; where the emergence of new social patterns, political régimes, peoples and nations places the whole issue of religious liberty in a state of flux; where dominant non-Christian religions play a significant part in the scene.

It is understood that the taking of action on behalf of the WCC in concrete situations is principally the responsibility of the CCIA as heretofore.

C. Theological Education and the Training of the Ministry

The Committee had before it the proposal contained on pages 73-4 of the *Work Book* that the Division of Studies be authorized to hold in co-operation with the Ecumenical Institute a series of consultations under the general heading: 'New horizons in theological education and the training of the ministry.' Such a proposal, we feel, is far too modest. We would call the Assembly's attention to the general authorization given by the Evanston Assembly to the Division of Studies to engage in work having to do with the implications of the ecumenical movement for theological education, and to the fact that the Executive Committee in 1957 authorized a major study of 'Theological education and the training of the ministry'. While such studies could not be pursued due to lack of funds, still the keen interest in this crucial area of the Church's life points to the necessity that such studies be undertaken as soon as possible. After considerable discussion the following conclusions were reached:

1. The Committee considers that there is need for a substantial study concerning the training of the ministry in our time. In many parts of the world the question has appeared: 'How can the work of ministry be performed and new patterns of ministry be recognized and utilized in the new situations in the modern world and what modifications in the traditional academic curricula and methods of practical training are called for in order to meet the challenge of changing times?' A study of this question clearly raises both sociological and theological problems concerning the ministry, and therefore of the method and content of training and education for it.
2. The Committee is aware of concern for this and related matters in other divisions and departments of the World Council of Churches (in particular in the Division of World Mission and Evangelism, the Department on the Laity and the Ecumenical Institute), but there has not been opportunity to develop with them a detailed plan.
3. The Committee therefore recommends that the Assembly authorize a study along the lines indicated in paragraph 1 above, to be developed by the Central Committee through the Division of Studies in collaboration with other Divisions and Departments.
4. The Committee notes that it has made a record of its discussion of this matter, and has transmitted this to the Division of Studies.

D. The Christian's Witness to Peace

The Committee had before it a proposal which arose in the Commission on 'Christians and the prevention of war in an atomic age —a theological discussion' that the World Council of Churches should convene a consultation between pacifists and non-pacifists. The Committee feels that the principal reasons for such a consultation lie on the one hand in the need for Christians with varying convictions on this matter to meet in an ecumenical context, and on the other hand in the fact that the development of atomic weapons has tended to cloud the pacifist/non-pacifist issue. Moreover the new factors in this world situation have tended to set the issue in a different context, namely, raising the question of the Christian's witness to peace.

The Committee therefore recommends that this Assembly authorize the Division of Studies to convene a consultation under the title 'The Christian's witness to peace'. It further recommends that this consultation should be upon the biblical and theological bases for such witness; and that this consultation be of approximately one week's duration.

In discussion the following points were made:

The Rev. A. T. Houghton (Church of England) spoke in favour of the major divisional study indicating that there is much confusion concerning the issues 'uniqueness' and 'finality'.

The Bishop of Pretoria (Church of the Province of South Africa), in reference to the content of the divisional study, desired consideration of the biblical doctrine of creation with special reference to the activity of the second person of the Holy Trinity in creation and its relation to his redeeming work.

Dr William Cannon (Methodist, USA) thought that the statement of the aim of the divisional study equated Christian witness with no more than an analysis of man's present plight. The statement should be evangelical.

Bishop N. S. Booth (Methodist, Congo) indicated concern that the title did not sufficiently express the dynamic adequacy of Christ in this age.

Dr G. O. McCulloh (Methodist, USA) spoke in approval of the proposed study of the training of the ministry.

Dr Henry P. van Dusen (Presbyterian, USA) welcomed the proposal concerning theological education and the training of the ministry, referred to the meetings at New Delhi of theological educators and moved that the Assembly request the Division of Studies to consult with the Continuation Committee of the New Delhi consultation of theological educators.

This motion, which was put forward as an amendment to the proposal of the Committee, was lost.

Dr Eugene Smith (Methodist, USA) indicated the need for careful consultation between the Division of Studies and the Division of World Mission and Evangelism, and moved an amendment which would have referred the implementation of the proposal to the Central Committee. This amendment was lost.

The Rev. John V. Taylor (Church of England) asked that in item C.1 second sentence, the following words be inserted after the word 'performed': 'new patterns of ministry are recognized and utilized'. This proposal was accepted.

Mr Norman Baugher (Church of the Brethren, USA) and *Dr Harold Bosley* (Methodist, USA) spoke in support of the consultation on 'The Christian witness to peace'.

5 · REPORT OF THE COMMITTEE ON FAITH AND ORDER

The following Report of the Committee on Faith and Order was received as information by the Assembly in Business Session.

A. The Committee on Faith and Order of the Third Assembly, after a general commendation of the proposed outline of the preparations for the *Fourth World Conference on Faith and Order* in 1963, makes the following suggestions to the staff for appropriate action:

1. In Australia and New Zealand, because the conditions are similar (e.g. rapid mobility in population and specific moves toward church unions), the issues to be studied should be similar to those obtaining in North America and Great Britain. These studies should make full use of material from previous Australasian Conferences, and should have the greatest possible relevance for those churches that are seeking a way to union.
2. In Europe, including Great Britain, the studies should be such as to invite the churches to grapple with the problems caused by 'the rapid drift towards the various forms of materialistic secularism and sophisticated nihilism'. They face the same need for a radical revision of theological language, and will find a unity in their efforts to adapt traditional ways of speaking about Christ. The central Christian doctrines have become increasingly unintelligible to the contemporary European mind, and their reformulation has become an urgent and inescapable task. This may require the formation of a special commission on theological discourse, which should seek a common, modern conceptual structure, and so help in the diagnosis of those divisions which are due primarily to varying modes of expression. The Committee further requests the Working Committee to establish a study of the theological, biblical and ecclesiological issues involved in the ordination of women.

3. In North America the studies should include an analysis of the general problem of theological discourse, giving attention to the varying and powerful factors in contemporary urban and scientific civilization which make the very intention and substance of Christian affirmations difficult to apprehend. The studies should also be designed to help congregations to understand discussions about baptism, eucharist and ministry, and especially to help congregations to understand the reasons for the positions and policies of those in other traditions.
4. In Asia the studies assigned to *ad hoc* regional groups should include four items:
   - (i) The growing influence and participation of the laity in the life of the churches, and the impossibility of full-time paid ministries in many areas.
   - (ii) The divisive forces which undermine the unity of the congregation, e.g. language, race, culture and caste.
   - (iii) The process of indigenization which presents both opportunity and danger to the churches, and effects changes in the relationship of Asian churches to parent denominations.
   - (iv) The situation of united churches in Asia which experience a tension between a movement to further union with other Asian churches, and a tendency toward increasing self-consciousness, integration, and institutionalism.
5. In Africa, attention should be given to the need for a united Christian witness in face of the missionary successes of Islam; to the disentangling of loyalty to race and culture from loyalty to the Church; to the relationships between the historical churches and the newly emerging sects; and to the need to sanctify both African and European cultures and to bring them both within the one Church.
6. In Latin America, there is great need for Faith and Order consultations in specific areas.
7. In the Near East, study needs to be concerned with the lack of vital contact between Orthodox Churches and between Orthodox and Evangelical Churches; with the battle to reach the secularized educated intellectual; and with the world of Islam.

B. The Committee recommends to the Central Committee that it ask the Division of Studies to establish at an early date a special programme of study on the whole problem of *theological discourse,* including the problem of hermeneutics.

C. The Committee heard reports from various parts of the world about *Faith and Order work in local, national and regional areas.* Some valuable suggestions have been recorded for the use of the Secretariat. The Committee makes the following recommendation:

> There are two tasks to be done: to popularize Faith and Order discussions so that congregations may share in them intelligently, and to achieve wider distribution for all Faith and Order literature. Therefore the Committee, realizing that the following suggestion implies an increase in the General Budget, recommends that it be referred without prejudice for the consideration of the Central Committee. The Committee recommends that resources and personnel be made available for more extensive translation and wider dissemination of Faith and Order studies. The appointment of an editorial secretary to the WCC might serve all the departments in this vital task.

D. The Committee has been gratified to learn of the enlarged Secretariat and greater significance already accorded to the Faith and Order Commission in the World Council of Churches. Yet it has also expressed the strong conviction that the *present position of the Commission and Secretariat of Faith and Order* within the Division of Studies is, as reflected in the Report on the Future of Faith and Order (*Work Book*, page 83), neither satisfactory to the Commission on Faith and Order nor appropriate to the specific nature of its purpose and task. The Committee therefore wishes to inform the Assembly that it is requesting the Central Committee to consider at an early date giving the Commission and Secretariat of Faith and Order the status of a Division within the World Council of Churches as part of its proposed review of the organization of the World Council of Churches (*Work Book*, page 40).

E. The Committee has noted with gratitude the ecumenical interests of the *World Confessional Bodies*, and their co-operation with the World Council of Churches. The Committee hopes that the collaboration will continue and increase, both between the confessional bodies themselves and between them and the World Council of Churches, particularly to avoid duplication of effort, and undue pressure upon the churches' resources of persons and time. The Committee draws the attention of the Working Committee of Faith and Order to the discussion in the section on Unity of the opportunities and the difficulties present in the relationships between the confessional bodies and the World Council of Churches.

F. The Committee welcomes the consideration by the section on Unity of *the statement adopted at St Andrews in* 1960 and the commendation of it, in a slightly revised form, and with a commentary, for study and appropriate action by the member churches. The Committee suggests that the Faith and Order Commission keep the responses of the churches under careful review, and report on them to the Central Committee from time to time. The Committee further recommends that special attention be given to the implications of the Toronto, St Andrews, and New Delhi Statements (page 116) for the theological self-understanding of the World Council of Churches, and suggests that this study should be accompanied by a thorough research into the nature and function of Councils throughout the history of the Church. Further, the Committee requests the Faith and Order Commission to convene a consultation on the significance of seeking unity without uniformity.

G. The Committee wishes to remind the Assembly that the work of the Commission and Secretariat on Faith and Order depends upon a lively intercommunication between these on the one hand, and the regional, national and local Faith and Order Committees on the other. The Committee therefore urges the member churches of the World Council to establish and strengthen Faith and Order work at local, national and regional levels, and asks the Secretariat to supply to all Faith and Order Committees such information and help as may be desired.

H. The Committee requests the Commission on Faith and Order to establish a programme of *joint study of theological problems by Orthodox and non-Orthodox theologians,* and to encourage local, national and regional councils, as well as member churches, to initiate similar work wherever possible.

I. The Committee, conscious of the fact that many *Protestant Churches* and groups do not share in ecumenical conversations, requests the Faith and Order Commission to seek relationships with these bodies in the interests of Christian truth and unity. The Committee recognizes the great diversity of national and regional situations, and urges member churches to take whatever local initiative seems possible.

J. The Committee notes with appreciation the recent growth of conversations, notably those arising out of biblical studies, between theologians of the *Roman Catholic Church* and those of other communions. It welcomes the many new contacts with Roman Catholics in an atmosphere of mutual goodwill, and, in particular, the establishment by the Vatican of the Secretariat for Promoting Christian Unity. The Committee requests the Faith and Order Commission to make special provision for conversations with Roman Catholics, and asks member churches and local councils to take whatever initiative seems possible.

K. The Committee requests the Faith and Order Commission to seek the best means of discussing with Roman Catholic theologians the *fundamental theological issues at stake* between the non-Roman Churches and the Roman Catholic Church, and to consider their implications for policies and practices (e.g. mixed marriages).

L. The Committee notes with deep satisfaction that the observance of the *Week of Prayer for Christian Unity* has steadily increased in many parts of the world, and commends its further observance to member churches as a focus of ecumenical prayer and witness. Recognizing that there are different conceptions of the unity prayed for, the Committee asks the Faith and Order Commission to undertake further study of the nature and implications of such common prayer, and, because of the difficulties concerning dates, it requests the Commission to examine ways by which present difficulties may be overcome.

In discussion, the following points were made:

Dr de Vries (Dutch Reformed) suggested changes in the text replacing the term 'sects' in para A.5 by the term 'separatist churches'. He urged that paragraph D be amended by the addition at the end of the phrase 'taking account of the work of the World Council of Churches as a whole'. He questioned the wisdom of granting divisional status because it would jeopardize the co-operation of the Faith and Order department with the other departments in the Study Division.

Dr George Johnston (United, Canada) asked that the study of the issues involved in the ordination of women should not be limited to Europe and that the study be carried out in close conjunction with the Department on the Co-operation of Men and Women in Church, Family and Society.

After further discussion of various items in the report, *Dr M. Niemöller* moved that the debate be concluded. This motion was carried.

The original motion was then put and carried.

6 · REPORT OF THE COMMITTEE ON THE DEPARTMENT ON CHURCH AND SOCIETY

The Assembly received the following Report of the Committee on the Department on Church and Society in Business Session and authorized the programme of studies as generally outlined in the Report, viz.:

(1) *Moral issues in the change from traditional to dynamic societies* (the continuation and follow-up of the Rapid Social Change study).

(2) *The social, political and moral problems of modern industrial societies.*

(3) *Racial and ethnic tensions in a changing world community.*

Introduction

In reviewing the six years' work of the Department on Church and Society, the Committee noted with great appreciation the progress made in the study of the Common Christian Responsibility toward Areas of Rapid Social Change. This study has dealt with the ethical issues inherent in social, technical and political change in new nations. As a result many churches have been stimulated to consider their responsibility for such changes and they are now in search of a deeper understanding of the moral and spiritual issues underlying them. They are becoming increasingly aware that they must participate in the task of defining the choices before their peoples.

The Committee was also given the task of planning the work of the Department on Church and Society for the coming period. In the light of the reports and the discussion of the living issues facing the churches in different parts of the world the Committee proposes three main areas of study for the Department and the associated Secretariat on Racial and Ethnic Relations.

I. *Moral Issues in the Change from Traditional to Dynamic Societies*

In the coming years the study of rapid social change needs to be followed up and developed through:

—communication of the results of the study to the churches,

especially to those concerned with the teaching ministry and for the policy of the churches and missions;
—assistance to the churches in developing new action projects, experiments and other forms of Christian participation and service in society;
—extension of the study to churches which have urgently asked for it in their countries.

In the light of our experience we also propose a new stage of work focusing on some of the specific issues which have emerged out of the original programme and on which more careful and detailed study is needed. We propose as the general theme of the new study, 'Moral Issues in the Change from Traditional to Dynamic Societies', and that in this the attention of the Department on Church and Society be focused on the following issues:

(1) *The Theological Implications of Social Change.* At various points in our study we have been led to ask the question: What is God in Christ doing in contemporary history with its new techniques, its emphasis on higher standards of living, on new forms of community, changing family structure, the renaissance of traditional religions, and new forms of co-operation in industry? In this situation what is the relation between the mission of the Church and its service in society? Study of these questions is essential for the further development of the Christian understanding of contemporary political and social choices.

(2) *The Changing Combinations of Religion, Nationalism and Secular Ideologies.* In many countries the problem of development is related to the varying combinations of traditional religion, historic culture, nationalism, and some form of socialism. The churches are often bewildered and they are in danger of retreating into isolation. The response of traditional religions and indigenous cultures to social change needs special study in this context. The emergence of new religious cults is also related to the social revolution and needs to be studied. The statement of the Nagpur Consultation on the Word of God and the Living Faiths of Men indicates a point of possible co-operation with the Committee on Missionary Studies.

(3) *Political Dilemmas in the Relation between Individual Liberty, National Unity, and Rapid Economic Development.* In the transition to the dynamic society different forms of nation states are

emerging. This poses difficult choices in defining priorities. How is national planning and state initiative in economic development to be combined with the fostering of individual liberty in state and society? There is also the problem of integrating self-conscious communal groups within the unity of the nation state. The positive task of the Christian is to help define the forms of political life appropriate to these situations and manifest the concern of the Church to develop a responsible society. The forms of individual and corporate participation by Christians in political life at all levels is another problem in which churches in many new nations need guidance.

(4) *The Meaning of Work and Human Relations in Industry.* We have seen in our previous study a great range of problems arising from rapid industrialization and urbanization on which there is need for further study: new conceptions and institutions of work and human relations; the moral problems of the villager turned industrial worker; the relations of management and workers; the effects of the transition from society based on kinship to one based on associations; the conflict between traditional and modern attitudes to work and nature. It is emphasized that there needs to be conversation among Christians of different continents on the scientific techniques and methodology used in social development in different cultures.

(5) *Problems Posed by the Agrarian Revolution.* Change in land tenure, introduction of scientific methods of agricultural production and the emergence of co-operative and collective farming, all raise fundamental questions regarding the relation between the individual, the family, society and the state.

(6) *Life and the Ministries of the Church in Relation to Social Change.* There is need for a study of the patterns of life and the ministries of the Church which are most effective in the Christian witness in changing society. This must include study and evaluation of the actual changes taking place in the church structure. It must also include a study of the proliferation of Christian sects. The relation between the structure of the church and that of society, is another question which must be explored.

II. *The Social, Political and Moral Problems of Modern Industrial Societies*

In the coming period there is also a need to give attention to the dynamic industrial societies, especially in the West. 'The western churches have discovered that "rapid social change" also describes their own situation because they are themselves faced with radical changes in the structure of their economic, political and social life which demand new responses. No doubt the pace of change varies in the different areas and the problems which arise reflect different moments of history. But ecumenical study on social issues has to recognize the world-wide dynamism of society and at the same time be able to grapple with this in its regional and national manifestations' (*Work Book*, page 85).

The importance of this statement is underlined by the fact that the pace of change in industrialized societies is accelerating under the impact of developments in the physical sciences and in technology, and the impact in some areas of political change. Problems of modern industrial society are not confined to Europe and America. The same problems are increasingly real in certain metropolitan areas in other parts of the world. At the Amsterdam Assembly in 1948 it was said that our churches 'have often failed to understand the forces which shaped society around them and so they have been unprepared to deal creatively with the new problems as they have arisen in technical civilization'. The churches must renew the study of society, as an attempt to achieve a prophetic interpretation of contemporary events as the acts of God. The Committee on Church and Society therefore recommends a further major study programme with the title, 'The Social, Political and Moral Problems of Modern Industrial Societies', including six main topics:

(1) *The Nature of Freedom in Relation to Responsibility.* That part of the world comprising West Europe and North America proclaims itself *par excellence* the 'free world'. Personal freedom expressed in its political, economic and cultural institutions is its assumed defining characteristic.

This freedom is questioned by the Communist world, which claims a more really effective freedom, immediately for the proletariat and in the future for all citizens through (i) its classlessness, (ii) its greater economic potential.

The assumptions of both systems demand Christian criticism, if possible, by an ecumenical enquiry using the resources of the respective churches in dialogue with each other. But it must be above all a genuine self-examination on each side.

Questions involved include the following:

(*a*) Economic development is for the sake of freedom (from hunger, from helpless dependence on other men). Where is freedom located in large scale complex economic organization and social planning (socialist or in the various forms it may take under capitalism, and in mixed economies)?

(*b*) Cosmopolitan mass culture destroys traditional relationships and their discipline, and tends to create the anonymous man. It must be recognized that the powerful attraction of the city witnesses to positive values in city life. Aspects of this problem are to be considered in different forms connected with suburban and country communities. Special attention must be paid to the effects on youth, whose freedom may become a problem to themselves and others.

(*c*) How does the cold war affect freedom? Is there a Christian concern to prevent the enforced alignment diplomatically and militarily of uncommitted nations? Is there a value for freedom in such non-alignment? Does fear of subversion or of the appearance of national weakness interfere with freedom of debate on essential moral issues?

(*d*) The ideology of scientism and technologism affects man's understanding of himself. What meanings can freedom have in secular terms? Is there a special place for the arts as an expression of freedom?

(*e*) Freedom and the Church. The biblical and theological understanding of freedom and its social expression. The freedom of the church to be the church in various political orders.

(2) *The Welfare State.* The Welfare State at various stages of development and in various forms is a feature of our times. It has its origin partly in reaction to the failures of earlier capitalism, partly in modern abundance, partly in socialist theory, partly in the Christian tradition of love for the neighbour. What ethos is the Welfare State developing? Is there any danger in too much security? Are there special problems for moral personality arising in the most advanced Welfare States? Does the Welfare State require moral resources not available in actual Welfare States? What is the role of the Church in the Welfare State? What kind of educational provision both popular and at higher levels is required?

What challenge and discipline does it offer to youth? How is the family as an ordinance of God affected by the Welfare State? Through economic aid and other international programmes, are we moving towards a Welfare World?

(3) *The Dynamic Economy.* The Dynamic Economy is controlled by the economic motive and the autonomous energies of science and technology. 'Maximum production and maximum consumption' is its principle. This results in disturbance to the pattern of life in industry, trade and all economic functions and those engaged in them. The stimulation of consumer demand gives rise to intensive mass advertising and salesmanship related to economic interest rather than moral purpose. What are the results in distorting ethical values, imposing artificial burdens on persons and stresses in their relationship? Can debasing of values in the search for mass circulation of the press and TV audiences be avoided? The increase of leisure without corresponding cultural and moral resources poses problems for all. Youth may be special victims, but the ageing also face prolonged leisure in the period of their declining vitality.

The Dynamic Economy is geared also to military aims in the cold war. The resultant economic-military complex of power may have special dangers, especially for freedom, but also for relations between nations and the distortion of values in the giving and receiving of aid.

(4) *The Life of the Church in Modern Industrial Societies.* There is in relation to many countries a strong conviction that the Church is imprisoned in social forms now obsolete. Are churches equipped for any significant role in the dynamic society, e.g. in the functions and training of their ministry, in the pattern of their organization, parochial or otherwise? Are there experiments and innovations in structure or activity that have shown themselves to be relevant? These should be reported upon and their own account of themselves made known to other churches. The care of personality has been largely taken over by the psychologist. A thorough Christian examination of this situation is required. Much of the social service traditionally given by the church is now state-provided. What is the ministry of the Church in relation to depressed groups in modern industrial societies?

(5) *The Church and the Arts.* The Church historically has had close association with the Arts. Much of the greatest architecture,

music, painting, etc. has had an explicitly Christian character. Much great literature has made Christian assumptions about human life. What are the assumptions of modern art, including the socially influential arts of the cinema, the theatre and the novel? Can the Arts help us to interpret human life in modern society? Is there an adequate Christian critique of Art? This field was felt to be of great importance. The existing Department on Church and Society is not equipped to deal with it, but its consideration by churches and national councils of churches would be welcome.

(6) *The Frontiers of Science and Technology*. The frontiers of science and technology are being constantly extended. New developments suddenly offer possibilities of transformation in some area of human life. This is primarily a field for experts. The Committee recommends that a Commission or working group be set up to consider such developments, including the probable effects of automation.

III. *Racial and Ethnic Tensions in a Changing World Community*

The Committee reviewed the report of the special consultation on racial and ethnic relations held in Geneva, April 10-13, 1961, and the following recommendations regarding the programme of the Secretariat of Racial and Ethnic Relations are in substance drawn from it.

The principles enunciated at Evanston with regard to the 'Church amid Racial and Ethnic Tensions' are still valid and are herewith re-affirmed. Since Evanston, however, much has happened. Rapid social change the world over has made the confrontation and interaction among people of the various races and ethnic groups more dynamic than ever before and conflicts more acute. As peoples under colonial rule reach nationhood and as depressed groups achieve new status and dignity, new tensions develop. Along with the just demands of all people for human dignity go the spurious claims of the extremists. There is a recrudescence of the idea of 'white supremacy' and the emergence of non-white racialism in many parts of the world. Anti-semitism in a variety of forms remains a dangerous evil. The Christian Church is deeply involved in these situations and is called upon to proclaim its principles with clarity and to act upon them resolutely.

1. *Areas of Study*

In view of these considerations it is recommended that ecumenical work on racial and ethnic relations be concentrated on the following four major areas:

A. *Analysis of changing race relations from a Christian perspective.*

An analysis of what is happening in our society, and of the causes as well as the consequences of tension, must be made in the light of the Christian belief about the nature of man, the role of society and the purpose of life.

B. *Theological inquiry on the meaning of race.*

An inquiry on the meaning of 'race' from the viewpoint of the Gospel. Among Christians, and even among theologians, there are conflicting views and convictions on this question. What significance can, or should, the Christian attach to the term 'race'? What is the significance of race in terms of the Christian doctrine of creation and of man? What place does race occupy in the doctrine of the salvation of man and the redemption of the world? How should the Church, the Body of Christ or the People of God in history, regard the fact of race? What does it mean for the Church to be a supra-racial community of the faithful? Are the categories of contemporary Christian theology adequate to pursue these questions?

C. *Issues which call for Christian action.*

(1) Racial and ethnic tensions as they affect political life, in particular citizenship rights, church and state relationships, methods of civil action and the role of government in fostering better racial and ethnic relations.

(2) Racial and ethnic tensions affecting economic life, in particular such problems as land and property, employment opportunities and wages and the general economic standard.

(3) Racial and ethnic tensions in relation to social life: education, inter-marriage and the existence of people of different cultural traditions living in the same society.

(4) Racial and ethnic tensions within the life of the church.

The Church must not be a segregated society. Multi-racial or multi-ethnic communities, churches and local congregations, whose membership is limited to people of one racial or ethnic group, must deal with this problem. How can the local congregation be an effective agency of the Christian ministry of reconciliation in a society divided by racial and ethnic tensions?

D. *Study of non-violence in race relations from a Christian perspective.*

This study should consider the theological basis of non-violence and direct action, and also the needs and aims of non-violent action. What is the Christian atttitude towards violence? How does the Gospel deal with the hate, guilt and fear inherent in segregated societies? What have been the specific and general consequences of these movements? Can non-violence produce both moral and structural change in society?

2. *Operative Principles*

It is recommended that the following *basic principles* be employed in the work of the Secretariat as it concentrates upon the issues suggested above:

A. The Secretariat should serve the churches and Christians within the framework of the WCC by stimulating thought and action on matters pertaining to racial and ethnic relations. To this end it should provide the types of service which the churches need and request.

B. The unity of racial and ethnic groups within the churches is of fundamental importance for the churches' effective ministry in the world. The Secretariat should therefore promote this unity both in its work with the churches, and by reminding other divisions and departments of the WCC of their function in relation to it.

C. In dealing with problems of racial and ethnic relations in any specific situation, the Secretariat shall be a servant to the Christian bodies in the country concerned.

D. In dealing with problems on a regional and international level it may be necessary for the WCC and its Secretariat to take a more direct initiative in proposing specific measures and programmes. Such steps should be taken with the full support of the churches concerned.

3. *Lines of Action*

It is recommended that during the years following the third Assembly the Secretariat should:

(1) Undertake ecumenical studies on subjects suggested on pages 183 and 184.
(2) Concentrate much of its attention upon situations of tension in particular countries.
(3) Stimulate the organization of international and regional conferences and consultations to deal with the urgent problems, where this is deemed necessary and useful.
(4) Provide for the exchange of personnel competent to advise churches involved in situations of tension, and the exchange of information including lists of consultants on problems of racial and ethnic relations.
(5) Use existing programmes and facilities to the fullest possible extent, particularly conferences on social problems, institutes, study centres, church committees and departments of national councils of churches.
(6) Co-operate with churches and mission agencies in helping to define the role of missionaries and other personnel in dealing with problems of racial and ethnic tension, in so doing the Secretariat should work particularly closely with the Division of World Mission and Evangelism.
(7) Make itself available to, and co-operate with, other WCC Divisions and Departments, to help them integrate the concerns for racial and ethnic relations into relevant aspects of their programmes.
(8) Establish working relationships according to the accepted procedure of the WCC with other ecumenical, international and non-governmental agencies.

IV. *Techniques and Methods of Ecumenical Study on Social Questions*

Ecumenical study on rapid social change has resulted in a new awareness of the need for study and it has stimulated the search for the methods which will be most effective. Such study involves the combination of the insights of theology, the social sciences, social work and the pastoral ministry. For this reason we have emphasized the method of consultation and study conference. This of course assumes that there is a body of research material available to the churches.

In some areas where universities and governments have not developed research facilities or where Christians have not utilized such facilities, this method has not been effective. We see the need very often for study centres and institutes where Christians can become informed about secular research and where further study and research can be undertaken. More individual research and study by Christian graduate students in the field of theology and the social sciences on the topics of changing society need to be encouraged. Such centres will also help to work out common methods to provide comparable material.

The Committee has noted the active co-operation of national and regional councils of churches in the ecumenical study of rapid social change, and welcomes the establishment of the Committee on Church and Society within the East Asia Christian Conference, as well as the formation of a Commission on Church and Society for Latin America. It hopes that churches in Africa, Asia, Latin America, and the Middle East will develop new agencies to strengthen their work on social questions.

The Committee strongly endorses the increasing emphasis on the inter-relation between 'study' and 'action' and expresses the hope that in the post-New Delhi period this trend will become more widespread.

It is important to involve the laity in all phases of these studies. This will necessitate patience and care in providing for the translation of scientific and theological jargon into the living language of all persons involved.

The study of developments in technology and the physical sciences probably will have to be carried out by specialized and highly trained people; but they must become involved with theologians, politicians and social philosophers in the interpretation of their findings.

In each phase of the study the structure and role of the church will have to be under consideration in order that it may be brought into living contact with persons in the midst of these societies. Only thus can the service of the church be truly a healing and renewing force in that situation.

V. *Co-operation*

Since these studies can be effectively pursued only through participation by Christian churches and groups in different regions and countries, the Assembly should invite the co-operation and support of the regional conferences of churches, and the councils associated with the World Council of Churches and the Commission on World Mission and Evangelism in these programmes of study.

In discussion the following comments were made:

The Rev. Edward Rogers (Methodist Church, UK) recommended that II, Topic 6 'The frontiers of science and technology' be more pinpointed by giving more attention to 'probable effects of automation'. This recommendation was accepted.

Mr Valentin Montes (United Church of Christ in the Philippines) suggested that in the draft of paragraph II (i) c, 'The nature of freedom in relation to responsibility', the phrase 'both sides of the controversy' be changed so as not to give the impression that the WCC is being involved in the East-West controversy. This suggestion was accepted and the Committee was empowered to find an appropriate phrase.

RESOLUTION ON RACIAL AND ETHNIC RELATIONS

The following resolution, proposed by the Committee on Church and Society, was *adopted by the Assembly* in Business Session.

The Third Assembly of the World Council of Churches meeting at New Delhi, having considered the serious and far-reaching implications of racial and ethnic tensions for the mission of the Church in the world, in the light of Christian unity, witness and service:

(1) calls *attention of the member churches to the mounting racial and ethnic tensions which accompany rapid social change and the struggle for social justice in many areas;*

(2) notes *with gratitude:*

(*a*) *the witness of churches and their members in difficult situations, struggling to uphold the unity of the Christian fellowship transcending racial and ethnic divisions;*

(*b*) *the courage and sacrifice of individuals and groups, both Christian and non-Christian, who, in spite of forces urging to violence, are giving leadership in the struggle for human rights in a spirit of forgiveness and non-violence;*

(*c*) *those churches, which, though divided by different approaches to the question of race relations, are willing to meet with each other within the unity of the Christian faith, to talk to each other and to discover together the will of God for their common witness to Christ in society;*

(3) welcomes *the establishment of the WCC Secretariat on Racial and Ethnic Relations and urges the member churches to give support to developing the programme of the Secretariat;*

(4) reminds *all the churches of the declaration by the Evanston Assembly on Intergroup Relations that, 'any form of segregation based on race, colour or ethnic origin is contrary to the Gospel, and is incompatible with the Christian doctrine of man and with the nature of the Church of Christ',* and urges *them to act more resolutely than they have heretofore 'to renounce all forms of segregation or discrimination and to work for their abolition within their own life and within society'.*

The Assembly commends *all those involved to the prayers and moral support of all the churches and Christians within the fellowship of the World Council of Churches.*

7 · REPORT OF THE COMMITTEE ON THE DEPARTMENT ON STUDIES IN EVANGELISM

The following Report on Studies in Evangelism was received and the recommendations for studies contained in it generally approved by the Assembly in Business Session.

The first two meetings of the Committee were held jointly with the Committee on the Department of Missionary Studies. The Joint Committee registered the following judgment:

The Joint Committee of the Departments on Studies in Evangelism and Missionary Studies notes with satisfaction the action of the Assembly in requesting the Central Committee to review the organization of the Council, particularly as it affects the relation between the Departments on Studies in Evangelism and Missionary Studies and the Division of World Mission and Evangelism and requests the Central Committee to take action in this matter at the earliest practicable moment.

The Committee of the Department on Studies in Evangelism found in the Assembly's main theme, 'Jesus Christ—the Light of the World', a starting point for its own deliberations. 'I am the light of the world' (John 8.12), says our Lord. All evangelism centres in him.

But in the further word of our Lord, 'You are the light of the world' (Matt. 5.14), he graciously draws us into his mission to his world. Evangelism is obedient and grateful response to the Commission of our Lord, 'Go, therefore, and make disciples of all nations, baptizing them in the name of the Father and of the Son and of the Holy Spirit' (Matt. 28.19).

Two other passages of Scripture proved to be guiding lights in clarifying our task. The first is a word of assurance that the Church when it is in the act of worship is already a witnessing Church. 'For as often as you eat this bread and drink this cup, you proclaim the Lord's death until he comes' (I Cor. 11.26). Thus, by being in Christ, even before we consciously explore means and methods of evangelism, we are involved in his mission to the world. Witnessing in word and deed inevitably follows: 'You are a chosen race, a royal priesthood, a holy nation, God's own people, that you may declare the wonderful deeds of him who called you out of darkness into his marvellous light' (I Pet. 2.9).

Proposals for Study

(i) *The Missionary Structure of the Congregation*

But *do we* 'declare the wonderful deeds'? This question has to be raised constantly. In view of the urgent need for effective evangelism in these times, as emphasized in the Report of the Assembly Section on Witness, another question, however, has also to be asked and to be answered without delay. Is the congregation which 'proclaims the Lord's death until he comes' so structured that it can communicate the Lord's gift to a world in the vortex of change? The very context of our evangelistic task in a world of renascent religions on the one hand, and gross indifference on the other, underlines the vital importance of this study. The Committee is convinced that one of the main hindrances in the pursuit of the evangelistic calling of the Church lies in the traditional structure of the local congregation. We need to ask to what degree the existing patterns of church life affect its witness. Is there, in fact, need for a revival, renewal or change of church life in certain of its structures to make possible relevant and effective witness to the Gospel? What experiments in revival, renewal or change have been tried and with what effect?

The Committee, therefore, asks the Assembly to authorize the

Department on Studies in Evangelism to carry out in the years between this and the next Assembly a comprehensive study into the problems confronting the congregation in its evangelistic task. The title of this study should be '*The Missionary Structure of the Congregation*'.

In formulating this study the Committee is strongly supported by the finding of this Assembly's Section on Witness, particularly that on the Reshaping of the Witnessing Community (pages 85-90).

A multitude of questions arise when such a study is envisaged. Among the questions raised during the discussion of the Committee are the following: To what degree does the existing structure of our local congregation affect its witness? Does it enable and encourage members of the congregation to go into the world and to live out the Gospel? If not, what changes in structure are needed? What are the areas of economic, political and social life in which members of a Christian congregation meet the world? How deeply should they involve themselves in these? What are the implications of such an encounter with respect to the training of its members, both ministerial and lay, and its life within itself? How shall we think of a local congregation as a people separate from the world and at the same time as a people scattered in the world?

What changes are needed in the structure of the congregation to permit sharing evangelistic opportunities with other local congregations? As these questions are considered, a second series of questions arises: Is the congregation an instrument or an end? In this connection, what is the relevance of 'Woe to you, scribes and Pharisees, hypocrites! for you traverse sea and land to make a single proselyte, and when he becomes a proselyte, you make him twice as much a child of hell as yourselves' (Matt. 23.15), to the life of the churches today? Is there a danger of defining too strictly the difference between those inside and those outside the churches? Which is the congregation's main field of action: service to its own members, or concern and responsibility for the world in which its members live?

As can be seen from the questions, this study inevitably involves a wide range of theological considerations. Of particular importance is the need to clarify the relationship between 'Church' and 'Gospel' and the meaning of 'the Kingdom of God'.

It is recommended that this study should be carried out in several parts of the world by regional working groups, such as Europe,

North America, South America, Asia, Africa, Oceania and Australia. The executive secretary of the Department should be responsible for organizing them. The Committee also recommends that an occasional paper entitled *Concept* be published by the Department. This paper should contain preparatory material for the working groups and such of their findings as are applicable immediately to local congregations. It should also contain significant articles on evangelism and allied subjects. At the completion of the whole study a record of the results should be published in book form.

While considering the subject of this study programme and reflecting on its importance the Committee deeply felt that a possible *theme for the next Assembly* might be 'The Witnessing Church'.

(ii) *Publications*

The Committee notes with satisfaction that the Department has served the ecumenical community by the publication of surveys of evangelism—such as *Evangelism in Latin America, Evangelism in Germany,* and *Evangelism in the United States*—and of a 'Monthly Letter', in which important experiments in evangelism are reported. It recommends that this service be continued.

In view of the call on the Executive Secretary for visits to the field and the need for maintaining at the same time the publication service, the Committee urges that consideration be given to furnishing the Department with additional staff help.

(iii) *The Use of the Bible in Evangelism*

The Committee welcomes the continued relationship of the Department on Studies in Evangelism with the United Bible Societies. It approves the project of a joint study on 'The Use of the Bible in Evangelism' and asks the Assembly to authorize the Department to join in this study. It is understood that it will continue along the lines already explored in two studies which have preceded the present one, namely, the study on 'The Place of the Bible in Evangelism' and the study on 'The Place and Use of the Bible in the Life of the Churches'.

It is recommended that in the study now projected special attention should be given to exploring the biblical background of the doctrine of salvation and how it is understood in various churches and evangelistic movements, and also the importance of the encounter of Christianity with other religions. Such a study should serve as a basis of comprehensive inquiry into the actual use of the Bible in different types of evangelism. The study, it is hoped, will prove helpful in clarifying the relationship between biblical preaching and conversion. It should also aim at a wider use of Bible Weeks, particularly within the churches, and of Bible study between Christians and non-Christians.

The proposal to hold a conference in furtherance of this study is welcomed, this conference to be followed by regional consultations in various areas of the world as opportunity offers.

8 · REPORT OF THE COMMITTEE ON THE DEPARTMENT OF MISSIONARY STUDIES

The following Report was received and the specific proposals and recommendations contained in it authorized by the Assembly in Business Session.

The Committee reviewed with general satisfaction the progress of work on the three major studies undertaken by the Department.

1. With regard to the *Study on the Word of God and the Church's Missionary Obedience*, it noted that Dr J. Blauw's book on the biblical theology of mission was already published in German under the title *Gottes Werk in dieser Welt*, and that an English edition would be published early in 1962, entitled *The Missionary Nature of the Church*. Dr D. T. Niles' book, dealing with the whole range of issues raised for the churches as they discharge their mission in an ecumenical era, would be published in the spring under the title *Upon the Earth*; German and French editions were being negotiated. In addition to these two volumes, commissioned as integral parts of the study, the Commission of theologians which met last summer to consider the draft of Dr Niles' book had produced a statement embodying points of theological agreement on several of the underlying issues. This document is entitled 'Some Basic Considerations regarding the Missionary Task of the Church'. Despite its somewhat academic approach, which it was felt needed more specific illustration and a livelier sense of how mission is seen by those to whom it goes, the statement was considered by the Committee to be of high importance. This document is to be published

as the next WCC Study Bulletin, and it was agreed that the Department should send copies to the responsible authorities of all member churches, and all councils in affiliation with the CWME, as well as to mission boards, theological colleges and missionary training institutions, together with a covering letter recommending study of the document as a basis for continuing discussion.

It is recommended that the Departmental Working Committee be asked to formulate the terms in which to commend to the Faith and Order Department study of certain questions relating to mission and unity which arise from various missionary situations, and to the Department on the Laity the question of suggesting the empirical boundaries which the Church needs to cross today in order to bring the witness of the Gospel to men in the varying groupings in which they actually live.

2. As an interim statement of the stage reached in the *Study of the Word of God and the Living Faiths of Men,* the Committee welcomed the document drawn up by the Consultation held in Nagpur in March '61. It had there been ascertained that several Study Centres would be willing to participate in this on-going study programme, and the Committee agreed to endorse a recommendation made by the Departmental Working Committee, with which the Department on Studies in Evangelism had concurred:

It is therefore proposed to invite the Directors of the various Centres for the Study of Non-Christian Religions to undertake, in the various programmes of their respective centres, responsibility for the next stage of this study. This will lodge the study mainly in the Study Centres for the next few years, this Department taking responsibility for maintaining liaison, stimulating the progress of research, and collating materials produced, so that at a later date the Departmental Working Committee may decide when and how a new stage in the study is to be developed. New material and fresh insights from the work of the Study Centres should stimulate this study to a new advance.

3. Turning to *'Churches in the Missionary Situation—Studies in Growth and Response'*, the Committee learned with pleasure that, in addition to the publication of *'The Growth of the Church in Buganda'*, and *'Christians of the Copperbelt'*, three new studies were now published in cheap editions in India: *'The Church in Delhi'*,

'The Church in the Punjab', and *'The Church among Tamils and Telugus'* (the first being a 'depth study', and the latter two 'aspect' studies). It reviewed the status of six other studies in course of preparation, and two others projected.

It is recommended (1) that to the list of studies already being undertaken there be added one study in some area of Latin America, one in an Islamic territory (preferably in the Near East), and one in the South Pacific;

(2) that the Working Committee's recommendation be endorsed that two further studies be done in the so-called Older Church area, one in Europe and one in North America (several suggestions as to location and personnel have been noted);

(3) that the Department give top priority to this Study for the next five years, it being recognized that it will provide a basis and stimulus for other studies which may be taken up both within and outside of this Department;

(4) that the Departmental Working Committee appoint a panel of three or four persons of high competence, to begin as soon as possible an inductive study of the main issues which emerge from the whole series. In addition to this series of depth and aspect studies, the panel should take into similar consideration a wider circle of books dealing in like manner with local church situations. Theological colleges, teacher training colleges, and institutes of social studies should be encouraged to study in seminars two or three of the books in this series, and to report to the panel on their conclusions. The Executive Secretary of the Department should try to ensure through the appropriate Christian Councils that a follow up programme is carried through in every area in which a situation study has been conducted, and that this programme and its results are fully reported through him to the panel. The panel should decide what form their findings should take and appoint an author to write under their general guidance;

(5) that all studies in the series be published not later than 1964 and that the outcome of the whole process should be completed by the end of 1966, or at the latest before the next Assembly.

4. The Committee gave consideration to certain other suggested

studies. There was strong agreement on the importance of a study on the relation of *Gospel and Law in the actual life of the Churches,* recognizing that the problem of legalism is not confined to any one geographical or cultural field. It was, however, felt that special attention should be paid to this issue in the *Studies of Churches in the Missionary Situation,* and that any further study could best be based on this foundation later.

5. The Committee recommended the holding of two separate exploratory consultations in connection with two further proposals:

(1) One would make possible an exchange of findings and views of methodology between persons engaged on research into factors favouring or retarding *church expansion,* in terms of numerical growth.

(2) The other would be a small meeting concerning *African Separatist Church Movements,* attempting to co-ordinate studies in this important field with a view to offering practical help in reconciliation or prevention of separation, in consultation with and under the guidance of the All Africa Church Conference.

6. Meeting in joint session with the Committee on the Department on Studies in Evangelism, the Committee greatly appreciated the opportunity for exchange of information. It wished to express a keen interest in the study projected by that Department on *the Missionary Structure of the Congregation.*

It is recommended that when the Working Committees of the two Departments meet, ways be devised through which the Department of Missionary Studies will be kept closely in touch with this project and will, if desired, be invited to have some actual participation.

7. The Committee received a report on the present situation and future plans respecting *Publications.* They stressed the importance of maintaining a standard of language which would ensure that books, pamphlets and papers prepared by the Department were found readable generally by interested laymen. Ways were suggested by which the Department's Occasional Papers could be more effectively used to stimulate discussion. Concern was expressed at the comparatively small sales in the USA of the Department's publications.

9 · REPORT OF THE COMMITTEE ON THE DIVISION OF ECUMENICAL ACTION

The following Report of the Committee on the Division of Ecumenical Action was received and generally approved by the Assembly in Business Session, paragraphs 5, 10 *and* 11 *being referred to the Central Committee for further action.*

1. The title 'ecumenical action' is ambiguous. It would be equally appropriate for all other divisions and departments of the World Council of Churches, and gives no clear and distinctive indication as to what is going on in the Division of Ecumenical Action. The Committee on the Division therefore started with the radical question as to whether there was real reason for the further existence of the Division as such, and stressed the importance of the acceptance by the Assembly of the recommendation of the Report on Programme and Finance (paragraph 49), that a general review of the whole structure of the World Council of Churches should be undertaken before the Fourth Assembly. The Committee on the Division took account of the practical and administrative reasons for the creation of the Division in 1954, and found that since Evanston some programme characteristics have emerged which are common to the four departments. These are:

(*a*) concern for the wholeness of the Church
(*b*) outreach to the local congregation
(*c*) foundation in biblical studies
(*d*) concern with the renewal of the churches.

Therefore, the Committee supports for the time being the continuance of the present divisional structure until a better one can be devised.

The Division as a whole is working along three different lines:

2. (i) It co-ordinates and provides common direction for the plans and work of the already existing departments (Laity, Co-operation of Men and Women, Youth) and the Ecumenical Institute. It tries

to help them in their different concerns and to keep a watchful eye on the maintenance of the basic purposes which they have in common. As the Committee at Evanston on the Division clearly stated, it is emphasized again that the departmental committees should be strongly maintained on account of the distinctive and diverse tasks of the four departments, and that they should therefore keep a certain amount of autonomy. On the other hand, the Division is recognized by the departments themselves as a means of mutual spiritual guidance and fruitful exchange of experiences and ideas. The ongoing Divisional Working Committee, of which eight out of eleven members primarily represent the concerns of the particular departments, provides opportunities for common counsel and commitment.

3. (ii) The Division of Ecumenical Action as one of the Divisions of the World Council of Churches reminds them of their common call to 'action'. Although 'action' must not be misunderstood as being merely activistic, and although the other Divisions themselves are always seeking to put into action what they are studying and discussing, the Division of Ecumenical Action stands as a permanent reminder of the need to think and speak and write, not only in theoretical terms, but also in ways which may help the churches to bring their members to a better understanding of their common call to witness and service in the present world. The Division also serves as a channel connecting the work of its different departments with the other Divisions and units of the World Council of Churches.

4. (iii) The Division has a special concern for what will benefit local churches and congregations. It is concerned with helping them as far as possible to promote ecumenical understanding and inter-church relationships particularly with regard to the different concerns of its departments. It is suggested that in this matter there should be closer connection with the Department of Information and with the World Council's publications unit. Relationships should also be developed as much as possible with those agencies in the member churches themselves which have most influence on ecumenical education, such as the institutions where pastors are trained for the congregational ministry, and evangelical academies and other training centres for lay leadership.

5. In this wide context, the Committee on the Division of Ecumenical Action reviewed and re-formulated the aim and functions

of the Division as described in the *Work Book* on pages 104-109. These reformulations will be recommended to the Central Committee as follows:

(*a*) The *aim* of the Division shall be to serve the churches by relating ecumenical knowledge and experience to all aspects of the life of the churches, and by stimulating the growth of ecumenical understanding and commitment through personal contact and other means which may help the churches in process of renewal to fulfil their common calling to witness and service and so to manifest unity.

(*b*) The *functions* of the Division are:

(i) to provide such co-ordination as is desirable for the plans of the existing departments and of any other departments which may be added to the Division;

(ii) to help member churches to promote increasing participation by local congregations in the life of the ecumenical movement, particularly as regards the different concerns of the departments, and to encourage contact and co-operation between groups and movements of renewal within the Church;

(iii) to help the churches to relate ecumenical thinking to Christian concern for education in all its aspects, and to encourage experiments in new methods of ecumenical education;

(iv) to foster co-operation between the World Council of Churches and other world Christian organizations, and to work with other bodies in so far as this will further the aim of the Division.

Some explanation may be added regarding the third function

6. Everywhere in the churches and the world there is a deepening interest in education, and the Committee believes that this matter might become a major part of the future work of the World Council The Committee on the Division of Ecumenical Action thought it would be helpful to start with an explanation of what is meant by 'the Christian concern for education in all its aspects'. It distinguishes between:

(i) '*ecumenical education*', i.e. information about the history and present expressions of the ecumenical movement and education for personal participation in ecumenical responsibilities for witness, service and unity;

(ii) '*Christian education*', i.e. the total work of the churches and congregations in teaching and training adults as well as children and youth to understand the Christian message and its implications for living;

(iii) '*education in general*' as concerned with the basic question of how educational institutions and organizations may help people to become mature persons and to be responsible members of modern society.

7. It is quite obvious that the major educational concern of the Division at present is with *ecumenical education* in the first sense of the word. The Committee on the Division of Ecumenical Action agrees with the Youth Department that the work of ecumenical education among the members of the congregations needs to be strengthened. It is vital for Christian education as a whole that our churches should take seriously the obligation to work out in terms of Sunday School curricula, catechetical instruction and other forms of Christian education, substantial material which enables young people and adults to understand and appreciate the ecumenical movement and prepares them to share in it.

8. But the Division of Ecumenical Action should also be concerned with *Christian education* as a whole. We are well aware of the fact that the structures of Christian education are rather different in the member churches and that not only the doctrinal contents but also the paedogogical methods involved are closely connected with the faith and order of these specific churches; yet it should be a general concern of all churches to come to closer relationships with one another in the field of Christian education, to exchange experiences and new conceptions, and to help each other to reach a better understanding of the biblical meaning of 'teaching the Gospel' (*didaskein*).

9. There is a great hunger for *education in general* in the modern world and especially in the areas of rapid social change. As members of responsible societies who are being asked to contribute on the basis of Christian faith to this common concern to help people to grow to a fuller humanity and to be better equipped for dealing with the challenges of the modern world, Christians and churches are

being requested to take more interest in educational problems generally. While there is the temptation in the world of today to understand education in terms of technology and material progress only, the churches are asked to stress the basic elements of education and to relate Christian insights to educational systems as a whole.

10. Therefore, the Committee on the Division of Ecumenical Action thinks that it is important for the Division to take up 'the Christian concern for education in all its aspects', and to deal with it in appropriate ways. This might involve arranging further conferences in the Ecumenical Institute on questions of Christian education and general education. Beyond this we recommend that the Central Committee consider at the appropriate time the creation of a special unit in the World Council of Churches dealing with educational issues as a whole. (In addition to the interest of the Division of Ecumenical Action, it is recognized that the Commission and Division of World Mission and Evangelism brings a rich heritage of experience of the exercise of Christian responsibility for education in many parts of the world; that the Commission of the Churches on International Affairs has valuable contacts with UNESCO and other inter-governmental organizations concerned with educational issues; and that the Division of Inter-Church Aid is being increasingly involved in educational programmes.)

11. In the meantime it is recommended there should be conversations with the World Council of Christian Education and Sunday School Association regarding the desirability of closer and more general relationships with the World Council of Churches in the field of Christian education. It is also recommended that there should be continuing co-operation with other world Christian bodies concerned with education (e.g. World Alliance of YMCA's, World Student Christian Federation, World YMCA) in order to give more effective Christian service in this realm, which is of the utmost urgency for all our churches and for the needs of all men in the modern world.

In discussion, the following points were made:

Dr Berkhof (Dutch Reformed Church, Netherlands) remarked that the definition of 'ecumenical education' as included in Paragraph 6 (i) is inadequate. Beyond information about the 'machinery of Malagnou', ecumenical education should mean teaching about how to live with other confessions in a local community. Early in life, knowledge that the Church is vaster than a single church, should be given. Dr Berkhof proposed a deeper definition in harmony with the enlarged aim of the Division, which he approved.

Dr Kathleen Bliss (Church of England, UK) welcomed Paragraphs 6-11 of the report, dealing with education. She felt that the new definition of the functions of the Division aided in crystallizing thought about a direction which had been under consideration for some time.

She asked that the Division be given latitude in thinking through the concern of the Church for education, rather than being pinned to the definitions of 'ecumenical education', 'Christian education' and 'education in general' given in the report. She cautioned against any move to try 'to get hold of' the educational organs of the churches for the purposes of ecumenical education. Yet she recognized that men and women and young people are not baptized and confirmed into the ecumenical movement, and that ecumenical education must be part of the churches' total teaching.

She stated that Paragraph 7 was an inadequate description of the work which the Youth Department had been doing about Christian education. Producing materials is only a part of the task. The real heart of the task is to open the eyes of the teacher to a new dimension. Consultation and co-operation can bring a true ecumenical perspective even better than written materials.

Mr James Gray (Churches of Christ in Great Britain and Ireland) welcomed an increased emphasis on education. He suggested that in addition to the work done by the churches as such, there should be co-operation with Christians engaged in Christian education in the schools, e.g. as in Great Britain. These teachers need inspiration from the churches and the churches need to be more keenly aware of the work of these teachers.

Dr Thimme, chairman of the Committee, thanked the speakers for their suggestions. He pointed out to Dr Berkhof that the second half of the definition of 'ecumenical education' reads 'and education for personal participation in ecumenical responsibilities for witness, service and unity'.

Agreeing with Dr Bliss that Christian education is principally a matter to be handled by the respective churches on the basis of their doctrine, he re-emphasized that more exchange is needed between different churches concerning the principles and methods of Christian education.

Dr Thimme felt that Christian concern for the world should include responsibility for education in the world. He would be grateful for the churches' approval of the proposals for the WCC to work on the question of the churches' responsibility for education.

He stated that the Committee on the Division of Ecumenical Action had thought in terms of a *concern* for education rather in terms of *structure*. The Central Committee would be the body charged with considering how more adequate structural provision should be made for dealing with the question.

10 · REPORT OF THE COMMITTEE ON THE DEPARTMENT ON THE LAITY

The following Report of the Committee on the Department on the Laity was received by the Assembly for transmission through the Central Committee to the Working Committee of the Department on the Laity, the recommendations concerning 'The Training of Leaders' and 'Regional Conferences' being adopted.

The Assembly Committee on the Department on the Laity rejoices in the fact that in all continents the churches see more and more the significance of the ministry of the Laity. It is thankful for the place given to this subject in the programme, deliberations and reports of the New Delhi Assembly.

The Committee reviewed the written report of the Department on the Laity contained in *'Evanston to New Delhi'*, pages 76-82. It received the report with gratitude for the inner and outward growth of the work of the Department, and recommended it as a basis for the future work of the Department.

The Committee reaffirms the basic attitude which has guided the work of the Department since its beginning. The Department wants to foster a deeper understanding and fuller development of the varied gifts and ministries of all members of Christ's Body in the world. This, and not a one-sided struggle for status, is our concern.

The Committee wrestled with the question of the right definition of the term 'laity'. Some say that laymen are those Christians who are not ordained; others maintain that baptism is an ordination and that all Christians are therefore ordained for a ministry. Some say that laymen are those who gain their livelihood in a secular occupation; others point to the many church-employed professional 'laymen' and to the specially ordained voluntary clergy. Some say that laymen are those who have not studied theology; others claim that Christians full-time involved in politics, education, etc., need theological discernment no less than pastors or other professional church workers. While acknowledging the fact that there is still no ecumenical consensus about the term laity, most of the committee members emphasized the wholeness of the *laos*, the laity. Wherever in this report and elsewhere any of the above-mentioned distinctions within the *laos* must be made in order to show the complementary character of different relationships within Christ's Body, these must never be considered as divisions but as the development of the varied gifts and ministries within the total ministry of Christ.

The Committee examined the concerns of the Department in the light of the main theme and the discussion in the sections of the Assembly and makes the following statement:

Reflecting the Light

Christ the Light did not remain outside the world to illumine it from above, but entered into human life, conquered the darkness and radiates light from within. This says to us that wherever we are in the world, God is there before us—the light is already there. The responsibility of the laity is to serve as reflecting mirrors or focusing lenses, to beam the light into all parts of the life of the world. Every Christian, carrying out his work as a ministry and using his particular gifts and the opportunities afforded him, can bring the light of God's truth to bear in the world where he is, where dilemmas are faced and difficult decisions made. Clouded or obscured as the light is by the darkness of human sin, 'the darkness has not overcome it'. There is too often a wrong distinction between the 'religious' and the 'secular'. A negative concept of the secular as a place where the light does not shine, could enclose the members of the Church in a ghetto of their own making. It is necessary to affirm, by word and deed, the fact that all of creation is God's, the theatre of his judgment and mercy and glory.

Solidarity with men: We are called as members of Christ's Body to follow him—entering obediently into the structures of the world to witness to the Lord who is already there. We must not do this in an attitude of superiority or inferiority, but in solidarity with our fellow-men. If we hope to re-examine and help to change the structures so that they serve better the true destiny of man, we must be willing to subject ourselves to the conflicts of loyalties which are a necessary part of full participation in our secular work. We face then immediately such questions as: What to do if we can choose only between evils? Where is the frontier between justifiable and unjustifiable compromise? What must be our attitude when our Christian conviction conflicts with a decision of the group we entered because it struggles for a good aim? When, if ever, must the

Christian stand aloof from or actively oppose the structures of society? Is it possible to avoid getting dirty hands?

Worship and work: The worship of God is an end in itself and at the same time serves to strengthen us for our witness and service. In worship we offer to God the work, the concerns and the people of his world, and then return again as his servants into every-day life. In worship we confess our sins and receive forgiveness and courage for the old and new daily tasks. Worship helps us regain our perspective and gives us a certain freedom from the pressures of this world. Are ordained ministers and laymen really aware of this vital link between worship and work? Which changes are needed in the patterns of church life to foster this necessary interdependence? How can the active participation of laymen in worship be strengthened, and where should laymen also help in the conducting of worship services?

Witness: Witness to Jesus Christ is a basic ministry of the people of God. This witness must sometimes be quite outspoken where Christians have to take a stand. But many laymen maintain that more often their Christian obedience demands from them to remain for a long time *incognito* and thus to serve Christ, who 'emptied himself, taking the form of a servant'. As a true man (some would say: as a secular man) in the secular world, not assuming any exclusiveness, a Christian must live and work in such a manner that his fellows begin to ask questions. This affords a vital opportunity for direct witness. This statement raises such questions as: Where is the frontier between the legitimate and the illegitimate *incognito* of the Christian? Is it right to make a parallel between the *incognito* of the Christian and the self-emptying of Christ? Do we always have to await the amazed or irritated questions of our fellow-men before we tell them of our Lord?

Service: Service in and to the world is another aspect of our calling, as a church, as individuals and as groups. Sometimes Christians together must organize a distinctively Christian service. But again more often we are called to serve together with other men within the existing community organizations. Especially in the highly organized societies of our day this involves group action. As the gifts in the Church and the needs of the world are manifold and changing, the patterns of Christian service can never be fixed once for all. Is there a place for specifically Christian service-institutions and groups within the modern Welfare State? How can Christians decide about priorities among the competing calls for service from the family, the neighbourhood, the nation and the Church? Must some churches become less 'possessive' in their demand for service addressed to their members without forsaking the Church's essential task for service?

Wholeness: If we point to Christ's work within the structures of the world we witness to the wholeness which Christ gives. Can we say that his truth is discerned by the scientist, his creativity reflected by the farmer and factory worker, his justice sought by lawyer and judge, his awfulness, beauty and wonder revealed by the artist, his grace and judgments recorded by the historian, his love mediated by all who humbly serve their fellow-men? The light of God is there, but men do not always discern it.

When we bring Church and world together, we serve this same manifestation of wholeness. Laymen must provide a two-way channel of communications between Church and world. If they are not learning to do this or are prevented from doing it, they should be given the training and the fuller freedom to do so. For this is the way in which the dilemmas of the world are brought into the Christian fellowship for study and prayer, the Christian community learns from the rich experience in the institutions of the world, and the world receives reorientation and meaning. This wholeness of all things under Christ is the context of our prayer and work for Church unity. In how far does this broad concept of the unity in Christ help to make a break-through in the manifestation of Church unity in each local place? What is the special role of laymen in this break-through?

Recommendations

Aim and functions: The Assembly Committee examined the proposed new aim and functions of the Department on the Laity as printed in the *Work Book,* and accepts this formulation.

Studies: The Committee instructs the Working Committee to plan the main study work in accordance with the above statement and the questions raised therein. It also instructs the Working Committee to participate fully in the Studies on the Ministry and the Finality of Jesus Christ in History proposed by the Division of Studies, to collaborate with the Youth Department in a study on youth and the choice of vocation, and to continue the Study of Stewardship begun in August in 1961 at the Ecumenical Institute at Bossey.

Sub-committees: The Assembly Committee instructs the Working Committee to establish a sub-committee on studies of the Department on the Laity consisting of two members of the Working Committee and others chosen with a view to the subjects under consideration in order to help the Working Committee and the staff of the Department to fulfil its mandate of study as it is contained in the Aim and Functions of the Department. It also instructs the Working Committee to examine whether besides the sub-committee on studies similar sub-committees for other aspects of the work of the Department on the Laity should be appointed (for instance a sub-committee on publications).

The Training of Leaders: Many member churches of the WCC are at present reconsidering their traditional programmes of lay training and are making plans for developing programmes for equipping the laity for their specific ministry. In answer to the growing number of requests the Committee therefore instructs the Department on the Laity to provide for regional training courses and to hold in 1963 a short-term world institute of leadership training for the equipment of the laity, possibly at the Ecumenical Institute at Bossey. The Committee further hopes that member churches of all continents will delegate to these institutes and courses persons having special responsibilities with regard to lay training.

Regional conferences on 'The Laity: the Church in the World': The Committee thinks it timely to continue the organization of regional conferences on 'The Laity: the Church in the World' similar to the ones for Europe in Bad Boll in 1951 and for North America in Buffalo in 1952. It instructs therefore the Working Committee and the staff of the Department on the Laity to examine the possibility of organizing such conferences in different parts of the world.

Work Relationships: The Assembly Committee examined the criteria for work relationships of the Department on the Laity set out in the *Work Book*. It accepts these criteria and directs the Working Committee to review the existing work relationships of the Department in accordance with the same.

Minutes and Reports of Assembly Sub-Committees: Finally the Committee decided to transmit the minutes of its meeting together with the reports of its sub-committees directly to the Working Committee with the request that the Working Committee and the staff give due consideration to the comments and proposals contained therein.

In discussion, the following points were made:

Professor Rodolfo Obermüller (Evangelical German Synod of Rio de la Plata, Argentina) suggested that a biblical reference (John 10) be added to line 6, paragraph 1, of the statement on *Reflecting the Light,* in order to give a stronger sense of the scattered minority waiting and working in the hope of being gathered in Christ.

Dr Herbert L. Puxley (Anglican Church of Canada) stated that he felt the report was weak and unconvincing, giving little echo of the promise of the preparatory statements. For example, in *Evanston to New Delhi,* there was mention of a widely studied document prepared on the laity by the Central Committee in Hungary, and the *Work Book* outlined interesting points on the contribution of the Department. He felt that the report should not be the only measure of judging the deep interest of the Assembly in the role of the laity.

11 · REPORT OF THE COMMITTEE ON THE DEPARTMENT ON CO-OPERATION OF MEN AND WOMEN IN CHURCH, FAMILY AND SOCIETY

The following Report of the Committee on the Department on Co-operation of Men and Women in Church, Family and Society, including the recommendations to the Churches, was received and generally approved after amendment by the Assembly in Business Session.

Introduction

Up to now, the Department has concentrated its concern on the question of co-operation between men and women in Church and in Society. It did, of course, include family relationships within the scope of its interests, but a new situation has arisen at this Assembly.

The *integration* of the International Missionary Council and the World Council of Churches is now complete. We rejoice in this, as all our colleagues do. For us, this integration has brought with it an extension of our mandate with reference to co-operation in the Family, and has necessitated a change in the title, though not in the fundamental concerns of the Department.

Our discussions have been enriched by the addition at two sessions of representatives from the new Division of World Mission and

Evangelism, who gave a valuable report of the programme of the former IMC in the field of home and family life. They assured the Committee that there is continuing interest among them in this concern and that there will be close co-operation between them and the Department.

We welcome the fact that the missionary outlook and the experience from many different cultural backgrounds are now to enter fruitfully into the programme of the Department under the new mandate. It is already clear that there is an identity of view between those who represent the former IMC Home and Family section and the representatives of the Department.

Because of the new assignment, we are convinced that a *statement* of theological and ethical principles on sex, marriage and family is a necessity. Such a statement would supplement the Department's Davos declaration in 1955 on the complementary nature of men and women.

The Committee is aware of the considerable progress that has been made in the co-operation of men and women among the member churches of the WCC and within the ecumenical movement. While we must be grateful to God for this, we wish also to emphasize the fact that the *acceptance of the principles of co-operation is not enough* and that attention must now be focussed on their practical application both as regards structural changes and the deepening of the spiritual life.

In professional, business and political life, as well as in family life itself, it is the quality of the personal relationships that is of chief importance.

Today, when *social pressures* to conformity are so great, when people live so largely by materialistic standards, Christians need clear guidance and spiritual help from their churches to enable them to make right judgments. They need help to avoid falling a prey to the lust of possessions, power and authority, and to renounce a double standard of morality for men and women and to find ways to witness to the Lordship of Jesus Christ over the life of individuals and societies.

It is our strong belief that in fostering the co-operation of men and women in church, family and society, the Department has a God-given opportunity to demonstrate the redemptive power of Christ and is offered a sphere of service in an area of human relationships often neglected by the churches.

The report is divided into three parts, corresponding to the mandate of the Department.

I. In the Church

There is no doubt that real progress has been made in the co-operation of men and women in the churches. There has been much discussion of the biblical teaching and the doctrines of churches as they bear on the roles of men and women and especially on the status of women in the Church. The *principle* is now widely accepted that women co-operate freely with men as fellow-members of the Body of Christ. This progress is welcomed by the Committee, and its importance must not be minimized.

A certain number of member churches now permit the ordination of women to the *ministry of the Word and Sacraments*. And yet even where women may become ministers in the full sense and are rendering good services which are received with the fullest co-operation of the men clergy and the congregations, there are many other situations in which their services are not always used to the best advantage. They may be expected simply to follow traditional patterns. They may be hindered by a lack of co-operative understanding on the part of male ministers and also of some church members. The contribution which they can bring as women is thus obscured. Women ministers themselves have sometimes failed to seek their own God-given ways of work. To be ordained is not the end alone. Accordingly, it would seem desirable for the churches to collect information about the precise kinds of services performed by women ministers, and their effectiveness.

It is gratifying to note also that other *professionally trained women* are now being used by many churches; nevertheless, there appears to be in certain major areas an acute shortage of qualified women ready to undertake either part-time or full-time professional work. In other areas there is a shortage of jobs for those who are trained and available. Both these situations may be due to the failure of some churches to give women a status commensurate with their talents and education, or to develop the full potential of which they are capable. So it would seem desirable for the churches to collect also the same kind of information as to the precise kinds of services performed by Deaconesses who are doing such important and wide-reaching pastoral work, especially in some new communities, Directors of Religious Education and parish workers, and their effectiveness. Such information should be transmitted to the Department and might perhaps be incorporated in a book on the subject.

In some Communions, women are given recognition and find a sphere of service and prayer in *religious orders*. It would be useful to collect precise information as to the nature of the discipline and service involved.

Turning to the *policy-making boards*, representative church assemblies, convocations, and courts, we have to acknowledge that in many places effective co-operation is neither recognized nor practised. Attention should also be given to the fact that in some churches women are not admitted to the office of eldership nor to similar offices at present open only to men. In trying to improve this situation in practice, churches need to find ways to combine two considerations: (*a*) that women should be chosen not because they are women, but because as individuals they have the required qualifications, and (*b*) that women's groups and interests need to be represented in the interest of co-ordination and unity.

In this respect, it was unanimously agreed by the Committee to draw to the attention of the Assembly the *very small place given to women in the nominations to the new Central Committee and the Commission on Faith and Order.*

When we consider the rapid social changes affecting church, family and society, it becomes clear that the churches ought by their own practice to be giving a lead in shaping the future. It is not enough to propose ameliorative measures or programmes to care for evils that result from the breakdown of community in the contemporary world. At precisely this point genuine Christian co-operation between men and women can be a factor of decisive importance.

Recommendations

1. The Committee suggests that *churches* which employ ordained women and professional women church workers examine the ways in which they are being used and consider how best they may be enabled to make a distinctive and significant contribution, and also give consideration to the contribution of other women including the opening of lay offices and policy-making boards at present open only to men.
2. The Committee expresses appreciation to the *Division of Inter-Church Aid* for the steps already taken, and asks for their consideration of the further expansion of its present scholarship

plans to enable women already employed by the churches in different capacities to supplement their theological and social studies.

3. The Committee recommends to the *Department* that it should extend to the different areas of the world plans for the consultations on the training of women for Church work and the best means of promoting the co-operation of men and women at every level of church life.

II. In the Family

It has become a practice nowadays to speak about countries of rapid social change, but in our Committee we have had to recognize that, as far as the family is concerned, the phenomenon of change extends to all countries, Western or Eastern, the most highly developed ones just as much as the others. The family may have been, in the past, the stable pivot of society, which is often described with complacency. Nowadays, however, we must recognize that the family unit, though by its nature at the centre, is vulnerable, jostled and hit from all directions.

The respective roles of husband and wife, father and mother, are constantly changing along with all the relationships within the family, and between the family and other units of society (factory, school, church, etc.). No general patterns of evolution can as yet be clearly discerned, but some characteristics are apparent.

In some areas, the woman is left alone at the head of the family whether it be for years of migratory labour in the Copperbelt, or for months of seasonal work, as in Italy, or for the daily absence of men from the suburbs of New York.

In other sections of the same societies, the man, with shorter working hours and increased leisure, is becoming more clearly aware of his opportunities and responsibilities as a father, and is more ready to share with his wife (who is herself often gainfully employed and without servants) in the day to day running of the home.

Adults have a diminishing influence and children's personalities are largely shaped by their own contemporaries where homes are emptied of their cultural, educative and economic functions and reduced to mere dormitories. At the same time, changes are taking place in the opposite direction in which there is a re-grouping of the family around common interests including the motor car, radio and television.

The questions facing the Church in these diverse and contradictory situations are, in essence, remarkably similar around the world. The churches have to discover what position and action to take in regard to: sex relations before and after marriage; illegitimacy; in some cultures polygamy or concubinage as a social system sanctioned by law and custom; in some Western cultures short-term marriages, or liaisons, easy divorce; in all parts of the world mixed marriages (inter-faith, inter-confessional and inter-racial) with the diminishing of caste and class systems and of racial prejudice.

Other questions arise as a result of the new educational opportunities open to women and their growing economic independence, which have put an end to their exploitation as cheap labour, but at the same time necessitate new protective measures and new standards of morality to replace the social safeguards of the past (purdah, pre-arranged marriages, etc.).

Finally, the pressing problems raised by the population explosion bring yet other entirely new factors into family life.

All this, and much else, forces the churches to re-examine their teaching, preaching and pastoral care and their witness and service to society. It obliges them, time and again, to turn back to the biblical basis of their faith, in order to re-discover the fundamental elements in the Christian understanding of marriage and family life.

Many requests have come to the World Council of Churches for help in clarifying contemporary problems by means of an authoritative statement. In fact, no generalized statement can define the ethical conclusions to be drawn from individual situations, differing in their cultural or religious settings. Such a statement can only become relevant when matched by studies carried out in each area by the churches of that area, who know the situation at first hand.

In addition to biblical and theological studies, there is constant need to re-state in the light of Christian experience the principles underlying the practice of monogamy, chastity, and marital fidelity and the central place given to self-discipline in all Christian traditions. These elements in the Christian ethic need to receive a quite positive emphasis as the means of receiving God's gifts of joy and fulfilment. Christian teaching is too often reduced to its negative aspects, but the churches are called to bring to the contemporary world the riches of the Christian Gospel and the knowledge of Jesus Christ as Saviour—the only valid answer to human need. They have to make their witness in forms that are constantly new and relevant as they seek to be obedient to the demands of God in an age of change.

Recommendations to the Department

1. That a survey be made of authorized studies and formal statements made or accepted in recent years by churches and other responsible groups of different confessions and cultural background concerning marriage and the family (e.g. the report adopted by the Lambeth Conference of 1958).
2. That a statement of the principles underlying the idea of the Christian family should be prepared as a help to those who study this subject in their own cultural setting. This statement of principles should show clearly the permanence and inherent sanctity of the family without making legalistic judgments or presenting the family as a sufficient end in itself.
3. That a series of detailed studies should be made to show the range of exegetical positions taken by scholars in regard to biblical passages bearing on marriage and family life.
4. That a series of Bible studies related to the family should be prepared for the use of local congregations and groups, so as to help them to face their own situations sustained by the knowledge that the same problems exist in all parts of the world and are a concern common to the member churches of the World Council of Churches.
5. That the Department keep up to date the information already compiled and published on the attitudes of the churches with regard to family planning; that the results of this survey be readily available to any church which may ask for them and similarly that data be made available on request about practical programmes successfully carried out in certain countries by the churches, on their own or in association with governments, private organizations or specialized agencies.
6. That a study be made of the situations arising from mixed marriages (inter-faith, inter-confessional, and inter-racial) and the positions taken by the different churches in regard to them.
7. That the training programme formerly carried by the IMC should be continued by giving help to National Councils in organizing institutes or seminars on marriage guidance and other aspects of family life, by sending specialists to churches asking for them and by promoting the production of literature.

The Department should also continue to provide the technical assistance of specialized teams as has already been done in West Africa with the help of the Division of Inter-church Aid

Recommendations through the Assembly to the Churches

1. That they should study the social changes taking place in their own environments, with special regard to the effect on the family and the consequent modifications needed in their teaching, preaching, pastoral counselling and programme of practical service within the Christian community.
2. That they recognize the special responsibilities placed on families in countries where state schools provide no religiou instruction and give all possible help to such families in the discharge of their responsibilities.
3. That in their efforts to promote a Christian way of life among their people they should give particular consideration to the following possibilities:
   (*a*) that certain ministers or laymen with the necessary experience be designated for specialized work on questions relating to the family;
   (*b*) that a more adequate treatment of these subjects be included in the curricula of theological colleges and faculties;
   (*c*) that, where the study of questions relating to sex education preparation for marriage, responsible parenthood has been traditionally left to women's groups, such study should be promoted in mixed groups.

III. In Society

Christians are involved with their fellow-men in all the affairs of the world. The two great commandments of the Law, interpreted in the context of Christ's love for mankind, oblige Christians and church institutions to act positively for social improvement and to be militant against evil. It can never be enough to seek the redress of injustice, or oppression, or the suppression of fundamental personal freedoms. Christians must try to set new standards and to lead the way in putting into practice the compassion and care inspired in them by the Spirit of God.

The Committee stresses that the Department, like the churches and the WCC in general, must seek to serve men and women i every social context as witnesses to divine love and agents of reconciliation. Its particular concern is with the ways in which men and women may best complement and support each other, and with the discrimination which prevents women from playing their rightful part. Where the needs are so vast and our resources limited, the Department has to select carefully the work which it will undertake. Part of its duty is to help the churches and the WCC to remain sensitive at the points where women and girls may be denied adequate protection by legislation (e.g. in matters like marriage covenants, divorce, inheritance of property) or in adequate economic opportunities, vocational training, hostels, etc.

Certain social problems affecting the co-operation of men and women are extremely complicated, and the solutions are not clear. For example, a great many married women now work part-time or full-time, even while their children are quite small. This happens for a variety of personal reasons, some good, some not so good, and also in response to definite need for their services. Professional women often feel a vocation to continue their work after marriage. We are very much aware that careful studies must be made of this subject and of the effects on home life, and the Department has already made a start. Here too it is never sufficient to protest or criticize adversely. At the same time there is need to dignify women who remain at home to provide for husbands, children, and guests, and who are able to maintain their interest in the affairs of the Church and of society at large.

Recommendations

1. That the *churches* be encouraged to act on their own, or with governmental and other agencies, on urgent needs like the establishment of vocational schools and hostels for women and girls, and other provisions for women in places where the planning has usually been done for boys and men.
2. That the work done by the *Department* (under the auspices of the Commission of the Churches on International Affairs) with the UN Commission on the Status of Women and non-governmental organizations related to it should be intensified in order to provide and receive more information to and from the member churches.
3. That the Department expand its study on part-time work for married women, and that it enlist the help of the East Asia

Christian Conference, the All Africa Church Conference and other groups, to ensure a world-wide viewpoint in the production of findings and material that may be sent to the churches for their information.

Conclusion

The Report, the Committee hopes, gives some indication of the lines along which the Department and its Working Committee can proceed in the period until the next Assembly. The Committee is conscious of the inadequacy of its work but thankful to God for the deep fellowship afforded to its members, men and women in good proportion, to work together in a field which springs from God's own creation of man and woman, and in an area which can make a fruitful contribution to the unity which the churches seek.

In discussion, the following points were made:

Mrs. Grace Hay (Church of Scotland) thought that in section I, *In the Church*, paragraph 2, more stress should be laid on other offices such as eldership and similar offices in various denominations. In addition, more emphasis should be laid on the work of the deaconesses and their pastoral work.

The Rev. Isabelle Merry (Congregational Union of Australia) suggested that in section I, *In the Church*, paragraph 2, it would be useful to mention the fine support that some male ministers have given to qualified women ministers.

Mr Karl G. Boëthius (Church of Sweden) suggested mentioning the contribution women have already made to the Church.

Miss Dorothy M. Young (United Church of Canada) felt that the studies on the types of services mentioned in Recommendation I.1 would be more revealing if there could be some evaluation of the effectiveness of the various types of service.

Miss Elizabeth A. C. Walls (Church of Scotland) made a motion that the following amendment be added to Recommendation 1:

'And that consideration be given to the contribution of other women, including the opening of lay offices and policy boards at present open only to men.'

The amendment was seconded and approved.

Professor Aimo Nikolainen (Evangelical Lutheran Church of Finland) said that although a study undertaken by the Church of Finland might throw great light on the theological problems involved in the ordination of women, it would be important for the Department to analyse the services of women ministers and to circulate information on this subject to member churches of the WCC.

Commissioner Norman Marshall (Salvation Army, USA) proposed an amendment to the effect that the following phrase be placed at the beginning of Recommendation 1:

'The Assembly encourage a wider opportunity for the use of women as ordained ministers.'

The Committee Secretary, *Dr George Johnston*, said that the Com-nittee would be in agreement with such an amendment.

The Most Rev. Frank Woods, Archbishop of Melbourne (Church of England in Australia and Tasmania), opposing the amendment, said that such encouragement lay outside the mandate of the World Council of Churches.

Because of divergent views on the ordination of women, *Miss R. Christian Howard* (Church of England) said that the Department should continue to remain unaligned with a particular point of view.

Archimandrite Pitirim (Patriarchate of Moscow) considered that the ordination of women is a question of principle not to be debated by the Assembly. For the Orthodox, the sacramental notion of the priesthood excludes women. More careful consideration should be given to the theological factors involved.

Commissioner Marshall then withdrew his proposed amendment.

12 · REPORT OF THE COMMITTEE ON THE ECUMENICAL INSTITUTE

The following Report of the Committee on the Ecumenical Institute was received and generally approved by the Assembly in Business Session.

I. Bossey and the Churches

The Committee reviewed the activities of the Institute during the last seven years. It rejoiced in and was grateful for the strong development of Bossey in the service of the churches during these early years of its life.

First of all it was noted that the chief aim of the Institute is to contribute to the renewal of the life of the churches not only through study and discussion but also through the whole development of community life including worship. The intention is that those who have attended the Graduate School, courses and conferences at Bossey, should return to their countries to share their ecumenical experience of community life, worship and study. If this aim is to be achieved, much depends upon the co-operation of the churches in sending to Bossey mature and open-minded men and women, who are capable of benefiting from and contributing to this ecumenical experience, and who are also competent to bring others into lively ecumenical thought and activity.

Hitherto, not all parts of the world have been equally well repre sented at the conferences taking place at Bossey. The Committee appeals to all the churches and their national councils to take ever possible step to ensure that their churches and countries are ade quately represented in the future activities of the Institute. The Com mittee expressed its hope that the churches would keep contact with those participants and students who had gained new experience a Bossey and use them to full advantage on their return.

Since so many people today are looking for a new understandin of the Christian faith in relation to their daily life, although the are not associated with ordinary church life, and others have be come estranged from Christianity and involved in an anti-Christia secularism, it is highly desirable for them to have the experienc provided by Bossey, and that ways and means should be found t make this possible. In view of this the Committee proposed revisio of the statement of the aims and functions of the Institute (*Wor Book,* page 124, ii), namely, to arrange for consultations of repre sentatives both of the same and various professions or occupation *including in them also those who are outside the churches.*

II. Programme

In considering the Programme, it was generally agreed that it i reasonably balanced having regard to the Aim and Functions.

With the coming of a new member of the staff from Africa, ce tain subjects have recently received greater emphasis than befor from the point of view of that continent.

The Committee suggested that in future programmes special em phasis should also be given to issues arising particularly from As and South America. Besides this the following subjects should b considered for appropriate study: syncretism in its specific form in East and West; international studies of family life; the role the churches in changing rural areas.

It was urged that in all conferences dealing with service, speci attention should be given to encouraging young people to take a active part both at home and overseas in the new tasks to which th churches are called.

The Committee gave some attention to the suggestions made du ing the Assembly that fundamental changes are needed in loc church structure to encourage greater participation by the laity, particularly the 'fringe laity'. Bossey, therefore, must consider whether it is in a position to offer the kind of fundamental training which such laymen need in order to understand better the nature of the church and what it means *to be* the church in the world today.

The Committee expressed concern that the efforts of the Institute to establish contacts with non-member churches and non-participating groups in member churches, should be continued and increased. In this way more objective information about the WCC may be given to them and a better understanding of those churches and groups may be evinced for the benefit of all the churches.

In this connection, in the years to come, Bossey should explore the meaning for the whole ecumenical movement of the Pentecostal groups within the life of the whole Church, and their relation to what one may call the Catholic and Protestant streams of Christianity. On the other hand, it was also held that in view of the Orthodox participation in the WCC, it is imperative for Bossey to interpret the characteristics of church life and categories of theological thought of the Orthodox communion to other communions and vice versa. In this way, Bossey can provide a special contribution in making meaningful the participation of such diverse churches and groups within the living fellowship of the WCC.

With regard to the Graduate School, the recommendation of the former Board was endorsed that the term of four and a half months should be followed by a three months' period of practical experience in different kinds of church activity in carefully selected places. In this way the students would be able to gain a better understanding of the real life situation in various parts of the world and the task of the churches within them. The staff of the Institute will have to ensure that this practical work is well-planned and guided in each locality, and that this practical experience is soundly related to the whole work of the Graduate School in a final period of two weeks at Bossey. Thus, the Graduate School would provide an integrated whole of ecumenical education.

III. Relations with Similar Institutes

It was agreed to recommend the extension of the services of Bossey to facilitate research in the Ecumenical Movement and to provide means for the interchange of study and experience among similar lay academies and ecumenical institutes. The fulfilment of such a function would certainly require additional library personnel and this must be studied in relationship to other budgetary needs, but the development of new institutes throughout the world emphasizes the urgent need for mutual help. In the growth of library resources, careful thought must be given to a more effective co-ordination of the two libraries at present maintained by WCC Headquarters and the Institute at Bossey.

The churches now agree that Lay Institutes are a very valuable means of the renewal of the churches. Bossey, out of its established and unique character, should continue, whenever and wherever possible, to assist Lay Institutes in existence or in process of formation. In some situations it is important that such Institutes, while founded within the life of the churches, should stand at some 'distance' from the organizations of the churches in order to reach out to laymen and women in different walks of life. Nevertheless, the purpose of such Lay Institutes, as of Bossey itself, is to renew the life of the churches and therefore continual watch must be kept so that no Institute becomes simply a Conference Centre, on the one hand, or a 'substitute church', on the other. These Lay Institutes in all their activities provide great opportunities for the expression of ecumenical concern. This aspect of their work would be furthered if the members of the staff of each Institute were representative of different Christian traditions. Bossey could help to prepare them for their tasks.

IV. Staff and Setting

The Committee accepted the present staff situation, noting the addition of Mr Makulu as Fourth Staff Member according to the decision taken at Evanston but not implemented until August 1961. In view, however, of the growing work of the Institute, and the heavy demands upon it, the Committee therefore recommends that the staffing situation be kept under review. They envisage that before long it will be necessary to increase the staff if the academic standard of the Graduate School is to be maintained and the emphasis on lay work, particularly in the summer programme and ecumenical research, are to develop in response to the needs of the churches and the circumstances. This would involve a reconsideration of the budget for Bossey by the Central Committee.

In view of the urgent need for expanded physical facilities at Bossey, the Committee strongly endorses the decision of the Central

Committee to go forward with the construction of a library and an auditorium at the earliest possible moment.

13 · REPORT OF THE COMMITTEE ON THE YOUTH DEPARTMENT

The following Report of the Committee on the Youth Department was received, generally approved and referred to the Central Committee for further action by the Assembly in Business Session.

1. Believing that the *Aim* and *Functions* of the Youth Department, as set out on pages 117-19 of the *Work Book,* represent the task that the Department should fulfil, we recommend their adoption.

2. We believe that the impatience which young people in our churches so often reveal concerning the slow progress towards unity, and towards changing the structures of our churches to make them more free to fulfil the tasks of witness and service, must not be dismissed simply as youthful enthusiasm. Often the activity of youth in pressing for such changes on local and regional levels results from their taking seriously all that has been said in ecumenical gatherings about the fact that the things which bind us together as Christians are more important than the things that divide us. It is clear from history that movements for renewal can and have been frustrated by indifference and disobedience. The 'pressure' sometimes felt to be coming from Christian youth and students, is first of all an expression of their prayerful determination that what God has revealed to us (in the ecumenical movement) as his will, shall not be obstructed by our lethargy or fear of change.

3. A major task of the Youth Department lies in the area of *ecumenical education.* In the fulfilment of this task it is necessary to discover the best avenues into the life of the member churches, and to find methods for meeting the different needs of the various regions. For example:

(*a*) Where traditional catechetical material is used, ways should be found to draw out the manner in which the traditional material is illumined by the growing ecumenical understanding. Thus when baptism is interpreted to young people, the meaning of the recognition given to the baptism of other churches needs to be explored.

(*b*) Where notes for catechisms, new catechisms, or syllabi are being prepared, ways should be found of making relevant to young people the significance of what the churches are now saying and doing together in order that they may be brought into active partnership in the process of ecumenical growth.

(*c*) On the study of the Bible, where scholars are reaching an increasing level of understanding across confessional lines, ways need to be found for enabling the young people of our churches to share in this growing ecumenical discussion.

(*d*) In preparing young people for responsible participation in society it is vital not only that they be brought together across confessional lines but that ways be found to enable them to meet one another across national and regional lines on these questions.

4. The Youth Department must take the initiative in helping member churches in the fulfilment of these aims by

(*a*) making and keeping contacts with those responsible for Christian education in the member churches, in order to broaden and deepen the consideration of how the churches can attain these goals.

(*b*) sharing ideas among the churches through publications and personal contacts.

(*c*) serving as a channel through which help can be given from one church to another and by one region to another.

(*d*) calling consultations (where possible, in co-operation with other bodies such as the WCCESSA, WSCF, YMCA YMCA): e.g. theologians and pastors of churches still relying on catechetical instruction in the training of their young people; or a regional meeting in French-speaking Africa to discuss ways of using the wider resources of the churches to the best advantage in their new and distinctive situation.

5. The Youth Department should secure the services of a writer to interpret the growing ecumenical literature to those who prepare the educational materials of their churches. A proposal for this has gone to the Policy Reference Committee and will be presented in their report.

6. Strengthened WCC-WCCESSA relations are essential to the effective working of the Youth Department. The Committee on the Division of Ecumenical Action has mentioned this concern in its report, thus placing the matter in its larger setting. The resolution of the Committee on the Youth Department is included as an Appendix to this report, and is referred to the Central Committee.

7. Ecumenical progress depends upon the development of organs at the regional and national level. We urge the member churches to further this growth and ask the Youth Department to stimulate these developments. We suggest the following points for their consideration in so doing:

National Ecumenical Youth Councils

(1) To serve the needs of youth within the National Council.
(2) To stimulate ecumenical activities of young people at the local level, and enable them to work together for the renewal of the Church and in service to the world.
(3) To create an awareness of the ecumenical dimension of Christian education.
(4) To give young people ecumenical experience through participation in ecumenical youth service, conferences, study, etc.
(5) Members outside the National or World Council of Churches may be received, provided such members are nominated by their responsible bodies.
(6) To act as correspondents with the WCC Youth Department and as the channel for informing their constituencies of Youth Department programmes.
(7) To encourage constituent members to work together to the fullest extent possible in ecumenical education and action.

Regional Ecumenical Youth Councils or Conferences

(1) To serve the needs of youth with the Regional Council or Conference.
(2) To deal with specific regional needs, and to provide channels for mutual witness and service between the member churches and nations within the region.
(3) To maintain contact with the WCC Youth Department.
(4) To further the growth of ecumenical youth councils on the national level.

8. *Confessional Youth Movements.* Confessional movements are asked to take care that any future development of confessional youth bodies should not endanger ecumenical encounter on regional and world levels. We would ask whether the limited opportunities for young people to meet on these levels are not best utilized by ecumenical meetings; and would ask the churches to do their utmost to provide opportunities for their young people to participate in the widest range of ecumenical activities.

9. *Ecumenical work camps.* Ecumenical work camps have proved to be one of the best ways of involving young people in the ecumenical movement. In the fifteen years of camps since 1947, over 11,000 youth have participated in 436 camps in fifty-two countries.

Experience has shown that the peculiar genius of Ecumenical Work Camps lies in the fact that such an international and interconfessional community of work, worship, Bible study, discussions and life together provides

an opportunity for ecumenical encounter and education within the context of a manual service project;

a confrontation with the social and political issues which face the world and the Church today; and

a common life in the Body of Christ where youth become aware of their responsibility to work for the unity and renewal of their churches.

We recommend that this programme be expanded and developed. The Youth Department should

continue co-operating with national ecumenical youth councils in organizing camps, and we look forward to these councils assuming more responsibility for these camps;

encourage the initiation of ecumenical youth service projects on the international and national levels; and

develop pilot projects (such as camps in industrial situations, community service development and long-term work camps) with the aim of evolving the programme to include new forms of ecumenical youth service which move beyond the traditional pattern of work camps.

10. *Proposed Secretariat for Service abroad.* The Youth Department Committee welcomes the proposal of the Central Committee

for the establishment within the World Council of Churches of a Secretariat to deal with the service of lay Christians abroad. We recommend that this Secretariat begin operation as soon as possible, that the Secretary come from Asia or Africa, that the Secretariat concern itself with the service of both adults and young people abroad. We assume that the opening of this Secretariat in the WCC will stimulate the co-ordination at the national level of all church-related agencies involved in this area.

11. *World Youth Projects*. We welcome the proposed improvements in the administrative procedures for World Youth Projects whereby this programme may be more closely related to the DICASR and through it with corresponding agencies within the member churches; at the same time we remain convinced of the need for this kind of ecumenical programme (sponsored with WCCE) through which young people may assist one another in building up youth work around the world.

12. *East-West Relations*. We welcome the increasing opportunities for the meeting of Christian youth across all political barriers. We desire the Youth Department to assist in arranging wherever possible for suitable young people from our churches to attend meetings in which this kind of encounter is possible. The Prague All Christian Peace Assembly seeks to be such a point of meeting, and we believe that there should be more such meetings.

13. *Mission and Vocation*. The aim of the Youth Department as proposed includes 'to serve the churches in their responsibility of evangelization among youth . . .'. A critical review of the work of the Youth Department in the past seven years leads us to think that this basic purpose has not been given sufficient emphasis. It is possible that this lack of emphasis on evangelism is a reflection of the present mood of Christian youth and the demands of the member churches. The churches throughout the world appear to emphasize more the Christian nurture of youth within the Church than Christian witness among youth outside. The Youth Department should take such steps as will help churches and youth movements to recover a sense of mission among youth outside the Church. There are certain factors of the present time which underline the urgency of this task.

(*a*) The present-day population explosion has made our world a world largely populated by youth.

(*b*) The missionary experiences in the past period make us believe that evangelism is more effective among youth than adults. We should be aware, however, that the youth of today are more under pressure than other sections of society to resist the claims of the Christian faith.

(*c*) In this period of rapid social change, youth play a strategic role in the affairs of their nations.

Integration of the IMC with the WCC makes it all the more necessary that the Youth Department should engage in a more thoroughgoing way in the participation of youth in world mission and evangelism.

(*a*) The Youth Department should help the churches in realizing the urgency and the strategic importance of evangelism among youth.

(*b*) The Youth Department should make known to the churches and church youth movements the new concepts of mission developed in recent ecumenical thinking and the new patterns of mission which are emerging.

(*c*) In the present-day world we are witnessing a new phenomenon called 'youth culture'. Evangelism among young people cannot be effective unless the Gospel is addressed as Good News to those who live in this culture. We also stress the need to find ways of bridging the gap between the generations. The Youth Department is asked to stimulate studies of this problem on national and regional levels.

(*d*) Modern youth appears to be more interested in questions about man than about God. They care more about life than about faith. They often fear that the acceptance of the Christian faith will obstruct them in their aspirations to be human. The consequences of this for evangelism among youth need exploration.

(*e*) Here and there churches are making pioneering efforts and experiments to convey the message of the Gospel to the youth outside the Church. We suggest that the Youth Department make known such experiments to stimulate the thinking and imagination of the churches to venture into similar experiments.

(*f*) The rediscovery of the role of the laity and the effectiveness of Christian witness by laity leads us to the conviction that

Christian youth should be trained for these ministries to the world within their secular vocations, at a quite new pitch of intensity.

(*g*) Often the churches speak of youth as 'future' members of the Church. Because they are full members by virtue of their baptism, we urge the churches to offer opportunities for young people to participate fully in every aspect of the churches' life.

(*h*) Young people should be helped to understand that service opportunities in the secular realm should be regarded as a means of effective witness to the message of the Gospel. Particularly young people who go abroad to serve should be enabled to realize the evangelistic possibilities in their venture.

APPENDIX

Memorandum for the Central Committee on WCC-WCCESSA Relationships

1. We agree with the Youth Department that the work of ecumenical education among the members of our congregations needs to be strengthened, and concur with the judgment that nothing is more urgent for the advancement of the whole ecumenical movement. It is now vital for Christian education as a whole that our churches should take seriously the obligation to work out in terms of Sunday School materials, catechetical instruction and other forms of Christian education of young people the implications of our common conviction that God has called into existence through his Son one people to manifest in witness and service his reconciling love for the world. There is no doubt in our minds but that the Youth Department in the next period should take up this matter with the responsible persons and agencies in the member churches. Membership in the WCC implies the determination to take seriously both the task of leading the membership toward a unity in Jesus Christ, and the task of preparing members for and exposing them to ecumenical encounter.

2. The life and work of the WCC as a whole is seriously handicapped without any direct or continuing contact with the Christian education departments of the member churches. It seems logical to us that this lack is best corrected through an enlargement of the mandate to the DEA to include a concern for the function of Christian education. This raises the question of relation to the WCCESSA which presently performs certain functions in this area which the churches in time may wish to commit to the DEA or other units of the WCC. The earlier

development of the WCCESSA as a separate body concentrating on the particular concern of Christian education in contrast to the WCC which is concerned with the total life of the churches means that the drawing together of these functions cannot be affected by a simple integration of the two bodies. Bringing the work of the WCCESSA into the WCC would require a thorough rethinking of the structure, programme and relationship between the two bodies and a thorough review of the place and function of Christian education in the light of the wider nature and task of the WCC.

3. We think that negotiations with the WCCESSA on the basis of the understanding in paragraph 2 should be entered into to see whether it is desirable and possible for these functions to be brought into the WCC. For the moment, however, the Youth Department is placed in an extremely difficult position while it stands in the relation to the Youth Department of the WCCESSA as the sole bridge between two agencies of very different history, character and method of operation. We are told that the Board of Managers of the WCCESSA desires to explore and improve co-operative procedures with the WCC, and has authorized its staff to begin and continue conversations on purpose, structure and work of both agencies. We receive this news with satisfaction and request that representatives of the WCC be authorized to confer with representatives of the WCCESSA to explore the further relationship between the two bodies.

(See also report of the Committee on the Division of Ecumenical Action, paragraphs 6 to 11.)

In discussion, the following points were made:

Dr A. D. Fiers (Disciples of Christ, USA) welcomed the proposals for co-operation between the WCC and the WCCESSA. He felt that it was important to recognize that the WCCESSA is the specialized international organ for Christian education. He hoped that before the World Council entered into the field of Christian education and the Central Committee proposed structural changes, there should be careful planning and consultation between the two organizations to insure good timing in the development of international ecumenical action in Christian education.

Pastor Jean Kotto (Evangelical Church of the Cameroons) felt that the word *étranger* in the French translation of paragraph 10 of the report was badly chosen. *Dr Visser 't Hooft* explained that *étranger* meant in a country other than one's own. He said that many Asians wish to serve in another country, and he agreed that perhaps another French phrase might be found as equivalent of the English 'abroad'.

14 · REPORT OF THE COMMITTEE ON THE DIVISION OF INTER-CHURCH AID, REFUGEE AND WORLD SERVICE

The following Report of the Committee on the Division of Inter-church Aid, Refugee and World Service was received, and resolutions I-VIII adopted by the Assembly in Business Session.

I. Introduction

The facts of human need are so evident today that everywhere people in positions of responsibility are aware of the necessity to confront them. Governments have created, both within their boundaries and beyond them, instruments through which the obligation to work for the elimination of poverty, disease, and human degradation is accepted. Many voluntary agencies are working for the same end.

As Christians we acknowledge with gratitude this demonstration of service. It is a fresh reminder of our calling to be present in places of need and, by our daily professions and corporate actions, to minister in the name of Christ. The calling and constraint to serve are clearly set forth in the Bible and especially in the example and commands of Jesus Christ and in apostolic injunction.

We are reminded especially at this time to be vigilant so that no area where the churches together are called to minister is left unmanned. In time of emergency the churches created their common agent for such tasks—the Division of Inter-Church Aid and Service to Refugees. They have used it in a variety of ways, as the report of the Central Committee (*Evanston to New Delhi,* chapter IV) and the reports which follow clearly show.

While the churches' service is inadequate in view of the resources at their disposal and in face of the world's desperate need, they have nevertheless demonstrated to themselves and to the world the way in which Christians can be present with their Lord where suffering is widespread and acute, and where patience and hope far surpassing human understanding are called for.

The Second Assembly of the World Council of Churches found that this Division is an indispensable expression of the life and fellowship of churches who intend to stay and grow together. It is hoped that this Assembly will find the churches ready to use the Division and its experience to explore many new ways of serving with Jesus Christ. This report is an indication of the ways in which the Division has been of service and how it may be used in the future.

The churches may adapt these means and others in their actions. What is laid upon us is that we should find our brother, and be with him even as Christ found and visited us, and that we be ever ready to undertake together whatever Christians are called upon to do.

II. Inter-Church Aid as an Instrument of Service

The churches, in obedience to the Lord's command and in their common concern for service to mankind, have found in the programme of Inter-Church Aid, as developed by the Division, an effective and acceptable instrument of corporate action, diakonia, and witness in response to the world's urgent need. As Christ's ministry is to the whole man and his compassion world-embracing, his Church is called to a ministry of love in every area of human distress. In answering this call the member churches of the World Council of Churches have been renewed spiritually and have been helped in their search for unity within the one body of the serving and suffering Lord.

Inter-Church Aid covers three major areas of service:

1. Through the Division the churches, according to their ability, take corporate action in dealing with people in need, whoever they are, wherever they are, and whatever their need may be. Such action includes refugee service, relief work, the meeting of emergencies through natural, political or social disasters, and aid in finding a lasting solution to the problems of poverty, disease, hunger, underemployment and unemployment. The Division also seeks to help in the rebuilding of social structures where these have been destroyed. Methods employed are a specific centralized organization working for all churches, or individual, national, or corporate action, co-ordinated in a common strategy and carried out under an accepted plan.

2. Through the Division, the churches make resources available to other churches, either for the strengthening of the life of those churches or for the purpose of enabling them to minister to those in need within their own areas.

3. Through the Division the churches enter into direct relationship with each other within or across confessional borders, and experience mutual strengthening and fellowship.

III. The Continuing Function of Inter-Church Aid

In the light of experience of past years, the Assembly re-affirms the aims, principles, and methods of Inter-Church Aid as a necessary and permanent task of the ecumenical movement within the World Council of Churches. It recognizes the following considerations as pertinent to this aspect of the work of the Division, and renews the mandate in these terms:

1. The churches which have covenanted together to manifest their underlying unity in Christ must seek to do this in every part of their life, and this includes the sharing of their resources both in personnel and materials.

2. Part of the responsibility of an ecumenical body is to help the churches to fulfil in all aspects the commission received from Jesus Christ. The 'ministry to the saints' and the care of the needy are an essential factor in that commission.

3. The churches, in seeking deeper unity, must take every opportunity to further this purpose. An important means to this end is the stretching out of helping hands to one another across national and confessional boundaries. Churches engaged in this experience are led to a greater appreciation and understanding of one another.

4. Churches desiring the renewal of their life must open themselves to the forces which make for renewal. Churches possessing resources do in fact find new life and vision as they share their resources with others. Churches which are weak and struggling against great difficulties are encouraged and helped by the aid received, and more particularly by the knowledge that they are remembered in their need by fellow-Christians.

5. The churches, which experience a world-wide fellowship

within the World Council of Churches, are confronted with need on a world scale and recognize both an opportunity and an obligation for a world-wide mobilization of the churches' resources to meet such need.

6. Churches, bound together in an ecumenical movement, have an opportunity of framing together a world-strategy of inter-church aid and of developing or adapting this strategy to meet new forms of need as they emerge. They are obliged to help individual churches to fulfil their ministry each to other in mutual service under the guidance of such a strategy.

7. The churches joined together in a world fellowship have the opportunity of providing men and women with training and competence so as to help them fulfil their ministries and realize their obligation so to do.

IV. Organization and Structure for the Extended Service of Inter-Church Aid

The responsibilities of Inter-Church Aid have grown and developed within two very obvious realities. The first has been the world situation itself with its vast areas of human need never before known or experienced in history. The second was the new awareness of the churches within the fellowship of the World Council of Churches of the necessity of an ecumenical approach to meet the emergent Christian responsibility in ministry to the needs of men.

A. *Mandate*

At Amsterdam the Division was given a mandate to develop the work of Inter-Church Aid from an emergency and relief service to a permanent, positive, and continuing work of the life of the World Council of Churches. At Evanston the Division was given a mandate to develop these ministries on a world-wide scale. In accordance with these authorizations, and subject to the guidance and decision of the Central Committee, the past years have seen the attempt to carry out this two-fold mandate. The Division has therefore been organized and staffed to help the churches achieve this purpose in such ways as:

(1) the organization and co-ordination of emergency relief and service to people in need;

(2) the strengthening of the churches and of their national and regional co-operative agencies for the maintenance of their life, for their ministries to people in need, and for the undertaking of projects calculated to raise the social and economic standards of the people amongst whom they are working;

(3) the provision of certain centrally organized operations to carry out tasks which can best be accomplished internationally and ecumenically on behalf of all the churches, for example the Service to Refugees, Health and Scholarship Programmes, etc.

(4) to support enterprises of the Division of Inter-Church Aid within the mandate to be carried out by other Divisions and Departments of the World Council of Churches, e.g. the Division of World Mission and Evangelism, the Churches' Commission on International Affairs, the Department on Co-operation of Men and Women in Church and Society, the Youth Department, and the Department on Church and Society.

B. *Methods*

The ways in which the churches have provided for the carrying out of these purposes through the Division are:

(1) by providing themselves with a central staff whose knowledge of the churches and their needs makes possible informed giving and responsible distribution of aid;

(2) by providing themselves with a staff of technically competent people to carry out certain specific operations, for example in the Refugee Service, ecumenical teams, etc.;

(3) by creating an organization through which requests for help may be responsibly presented and responsibly met;

(4) by creating an Ecumenical Church Loan Fund (ECLOF) which with its own administrative body in Switzerland, related to the Division, and a constellation of national committees related to it, makes available low-interest loans on a revolving fund principle for the aid of churches and especially of local congregations. By this method Inter-Church Aid strengthens the will to self-help;

(5) by creating a network of committees and commissions centred upon a Divisional committee and the Annual Consultation of the Division of Inter-Church Aid and Service to Refugees, for dis-

cussion and consultation and for development of broad outlines of a world-wide strategy;

(6) by giving this a recognized functional form as a Division of the World Council of Churches directly related and answerable to the Central Committee and Assembly, thus ensuring that this aspect of the churches' life shall have its place and be seen in the perspective of their total task.

C. *New factors affecting the life and work of the Division*

The new factors both in the life of the churches and of the world which have influenced the development of the World Council of Churches as a whole have had their effect upon the nature and scope of the task of the Division of Inter-Church Aid and Service to Refugees.

1. *New factors in the life of the churches*

(*a*) During recent years many churches, especially in Asia, Afric and Latin America, have emerged into autonomy and independenc and have sought and received membership in the World Council o Churches. This means that as members of the World Council o Churches they may request aid from their sister churches in th Council for the fulfilment of their task.

(*b*) The 'Study of Christian Responsibility toward Areas of Rapi Social Change' has uncovered the need of the churches to engage i such ministries and to undertake such projects as will serve to ex press their Christian social responsibility. The study has provide an illuminating critique and appraisal of the ministries of Inter Church Aid, and has pointed the way towards the carrying out o enterprises which make for the establishing of social and economi justice and the building of a responsible society. This task calls fo the service of experts who can be at the disposal of the churches an of national councils and regional councils to help in the formulatio of such projects as well as assist in working out their practical im plications.

(*c*) *Integration*

The granting to the Division of Inter-Church Aid and Service t Refugees by the Second Assembly at Evanston of a world-wide ma date meant that the ministries of the churches through the Divisio were extended into the lands where mission boards and societies ha been long at work. In the years following the Second Assembly much care was taken in the establishing of relationships between the Division and the International Missionary Council, and this has led to an increasing understanding and collaboration between the Division and the IMC and the missionary societies in their several tasks. The integration of the International Missionary Council and the World Council of Churches means that there will be opportunity for day-to-day co-operation of the Division of World Mission and Evangelism and the Division of Inter-Church Aid and Service to Refugees, and steps have already been taken through cross-representation on the Divisional committees and in the outline of procedures for collaboration between the two Divisions (Document E, *Work Book*, page 141) to ensure the acceptance of this opportunity. The possibilities of changes in the structures and procedures of the Divisions and Departments of the World Council as a whole are provided for in the Programme and Finance Committee Report (see page 351, paragraph 49). It is already clear that there will be a broad 'everyman's' land in which joint action of the Division of World Mission and Evangelism and the Division of Inter-Church Aid and Service to Refugees will both be possible and necessary, and that the closest consultation between the staff and committees of the two Divisions will be required. Some reinforcement of the missionary work of the Church may be possible because the Division of Inter-Church Aid and Service to Refugees is able and will continue to serve in ways and places not usually open to the traditional missionary agencies, to draw upon resources given by an increasing number of supporters who accept the necessity for Christian and humanitarian service, and to enlist workers who may not find their vocation in traditional missionary work but who are prepared and equipped to serve side by side with the men and women who are commissioned by the missionary agencies.

2. *New Factors in the world*

(*a*) The work of the Division of Inter-Church Aid and Service to Refugees, as of the World Council of Churches as a whole, is affected by the political factors which are shaping our contemporary world. In Europe, Asia, Africa and Latin America, the winds of change are blowing. Almost every political crisis creates new groups of refugees or migrants. New nations often come to birth in the travail of the multitudes who are affected by political, social and economic change, which is the preliminary to or the consequence of the achievement of political independence. Opposing ideologies create new barriers between peoples of the world. It is the task of the Division of Inter-Church Aid and Service to Refugees to continue to seek resources from the churches and to co-ordinate the service of the churches to men and women in need, whatever the cause of their need and whatever their national or ideological allegiance. The Division is encouraged to take every possible action within its mandate to summon the churches to the work of relief and rehabilitation of the victims of such political upheavals, and to prepare the churches for such situations and to strengthen them in such times of crisis.

(*b*) Recent years have witnessed the development by governments and inter-governmental agencies of large-scale plans for social and economic aid for under-developed countries and under-privileged peoples. The task of the Division in informing the churches of the opportunities which these programmes present in rendering Christian service and of calling them to take such opportunities and where appropriate to help them to do so, is one which should be continued and enlarged, especially where such plans and programmes are calculated to serve the hungry and the homeless.

(*c*) In spite of everything that has been attempted and achieved in the under-developed areas, it is apparent that there are many areas of acute human need. Some of these are as yet untouched by governmental and inter-governmental plans for rehabilitation. In others, the situation continues to deteriorate in spite of all endeavours to bring aid to them. To these areas the churches should give special attention in encouraging governments to assume their proper obligations in anticipating and supplementing such governmental services, and in developing the churches' own long-range programmes in the light of government-supported programmes. The role of the Division in making a survey and study of these areas with a view to informing the churches of the nature of the needs to be met and of helping the churches to meet these needs, must be continued and supported.

V. New Organizational Structure of the Division and Proposals for an Extended Service

As the Division has sought to respond to needs and opportunities for service in a growing ecumenical fellowship, it has grown in a particular way and developed certain patterns of organization and methods of functioning.

In preparing for the next period between the Third and Fourth Assemblies, arrangements must be made both for the continuing and developing of the present services of the Division and for its equipment to deal with anticipated new needs and opportunities. The period between the Third and Fourth Assemblies should see the Division becoming better equipped for its world-wide service. This means a recognition that methods and procedures of inter-church aid and service appropriate to the particular problems and needs of national situations in Asia, Africa and Latin America must be established.

To achieve these purposes it is recommended that the name of the Division be changed, that there be a revision of the aims of the Division and that the functions of the Division be re-stated. (The details of these proposed changes are to be found under Section B, 'Proposed Future Structure of the Division of Inter-Church Aid and Service to Refugees', pages 133-5 of the *Work Book.*)

In order that the structure of the new organization of the Division may be able to express its world-wide ministry and its unifying purpose there will be:

(*a*) The central administration.
(*b*) The area secretariat.

The basic approach of the Division to the churches and peoples will be on the basis of areas. Area secretaries will have primary responsibility for the relations of the Division with churches and councils in their areas and for relationships with such ecumenical regional organizations as are or may be established. The area responsibility will be divided into five principal areas: Asia, Africa, Latin America, Europe, Orthodox Churches and countries and the Middle East and Old Catholic Churches.

(*c*) The functional secretariat.

The functional secretaries will be expected to provide the specific competences for inter-church services rendered in certain definite fields of action. These secretaries will be responsible for such functions as Refugees, Material Aid, Scholarships, Fraternal Workers, Health, ECLOF, Migration, and Areas of Acute Human Need.

The Division in its services to the churches works mainly through their co-operating agencies, such as national Christian councils or the departments and commissions of councils that are organized to gather resources for inter-church aid, relief and refugee work. Requests from the churches in need of help are normally accepted only after clearance and approval are given to them by the national council or the appropriate ecumenical body in the country concerned, and support for them is sought through the relief, refugee and inter-church aid agencies of the churches in the countries which are in a position to help. These agencies are responsible for presenting the requests to the individual churches and often to the local congregations. It is in this way that through these ministries churches are put into direct touch with each other across national and confessional boundaries. In countries where there are no national councils, churches deal directly with the Division in presenting their requests or in offering their help. In this mutual support of the churches of one another, and in their common task of meeting human need, the distinction between giving and receiving churches and countries ceases to have validity. All are engaged together in the task of inter-church aid as an expression of their fellowship within the World Council of Churches.

While the Assembly notes that no widening of the Division's mandate is called for, it welcomes the outline of its understanding of its task as expounded in the document, 'The Nature and Scope of the Task of the Division of Inter-Church Aid and Service to Refugees' (chapter 4a, *Work Book,* pages 127 ff., and chapter 4, document B, of the *Work Book*, page 133) and the proposals for development of the Service to Refugees and of the Scholarship Programme. It authorizes the Division to continue to develop its work along these lines and to build up the structure described in these documents.

VI. New Emphases in Inter-Church Aid

1. As the churches have added to their work of relief and reconstruction and the longer-range tasks of inter-church aid in which all churches both give and receive, they have come more fully to share their spiritual, intellectual, material and personal gifts and have found a deepening fellowship with one another.

2. The ecumenical fellowship within the World Council of Churches calls for the more favoured churches to help other

churches in the fulfilment of their tasks. These ministries fall into three categories:

(i) *Those in which the older and more established churches may help the younger churches to establish themselves.*

(*a*) The newly independent and autonomous churches are still in need of assistance in various fields, and especially through the service of those qualified to help them strengthen their life and train their leadership.

(*b*) An extension of the present scholarship programme is called for in order that provision may be made for the training of theological students at university level and for the giving of opportunity for advanced or specialized training to ordained ministers and laymen. There is need for facilities by which students in need may be given grants-in-aid in order to pursue higher courses of study both in theology and other disciplines.

(*c*) In many parts of the world the maintenance of Christian witness depends upon small groups of Christians. These minority churches need constant assurance of their place in a wider fellowship. Material and spiritual help must be provided for them on a continuing inter-church basis. While it is the responsibility of all churches in all countries to welcome into their fellowship Christians from other lands, and especially students who come for training and those who come to serve so that they may make a Christian witness in the lands where they have their temporary dwelling, many minority churches—notably in Europe—are confronted with special opportunities for such ministries and need the help of their sister churches in order to fulfil them. Supported, therefore, by their sister churches, they are enabled to fulfil the duty of giving hospitality to the strangers in their midst.

(*d*) The well-tried principles and work of the Ecumenical Church Loan Fund (ECLOF) has an increasing value in this kind of inter-church aid. It is hoped that where the Christian community is strong enough to carry its proper share of financial responsibility, the national Christian councils or other appropriate bodies will form ECLOF committees within their own countries.

(ii) *Those which help churches to make their witness through the deepening of their sense of stewardship.*

(*a*) The recognition and acceptance of responsibility for Christian apostolic mission is integral to the life of every church. Inter-church aid has sometimes been used both to awaken and to sustain this sense of responsibility among the churches to witness to the Gospel. Ecumenical centres, leadership training through conferences, and research, give strength and impetus to the churches in fulfilment of their mission, and help is required for the provision of these instruments of evangelism.

(*b*) The churches, especially among new nations, are presented with many opportunities to engage in social and philanthropic work, but in order to accept these opportunities they need to develop projects which are beyond their own means either to initiate or support. While it is recognized that governmental or inter-governmental agencies alone can provide the major resources for meeting the needs of relief, rehabilitation, health and educational programmes, the churches have a role both in encouraging governments to undertake these tasks and also in the provision of help, or for the carrying out of governmental and inter-governmental schemes where they are established, e.g. in the Freedom from Hunger Campaign and the Food and Agricultural Organization of the United Nations. Where governments or other agencies are not covering the field, churches should endeavour to respond in creative ways to situations of acute human need through pilot and demonstration projects. In fulfilment of these purposes there would be great advantage in having at the disposal of the churches through the Division a mobile team of competent men and women who would be able to move swiftly to areas of emergency in order that the churches might be advised of ways of dealing with the practical situation and on the methods of establishing liaison with governmental and inter-governmental agencies both in soliciting and using their assistance.

(*c*) If the churches are to extend their services in these ways, then both in the churches which are giving aid and in those which are receiving it there must be a deepening sense of Christian stewardship. While there is cause for satisfaction in the increasing participation of an ever-growing number of churches in the work of inter-church aid, the tasks to be accomplished will call for the making available of still larger resources. The development of a sense of responsible stewardship within the churches is a pre-requisite of their engagement in the task of helping to build responsible societies.

(iii) *Those which involve the younger churches in work beyond their borders.*

(*a*) All churches are involved in the world situation and all may contribute through the World Council of Churches in seeking solutions for the problems which the situation has created. There is an urgent need to tackle the problems of housing, homelessness, and illiteracy. Refugee situations in many countries remain acute. The continuing world refugee problem is a sickness of our time in which the refugee himself is an involuntary victim of war or of political or social upheaval. Since the churches wish to see an end to such problems they must concern themselves with the question of world order and give thought and effort to the ways and means of eliminating the causes of war and the political and religious strife which creates the refugee problem. To this end the Division of Inter-Church Aid and Service to Refugees should be encouraged to work in ever closer collaboration with the Commission of the Churches on International Affairs so that the practical work of the churches through the Division may be matched by responsible representations of Christian judgments in the areas where political decisions are taken

(*b*) The economic developments in modern society have facilitated the mobility of peoples. The churches have an urgent task to help, both materially and spiritually, an increasing number of migrants. The World Council of Churches is requested, therefore, to provide an appropriate instrument within the Division of Inter-Church Aid and Service to Refugees through which

(i) the concern of the churches regarding discriminatory and unduly restrictive migration laws and policies can be communicated to governments;

(ii) advice can be furnished to the churches regarding the counselling and aiding of migrants in preparation for migration in the areas from which they come as well as in their new areas of settlement;

(iii) a Christian concern can be communicated to governments respecting policies which, for political, religious or racial reasons, compel people to leave their homes or to remain in exile against their will, and which prevent their repatriation.

3. Although the Division of Inter-Church Aid and Service to Refugees has already provided for the dissemination of information to the churches, both concerning the needs to be met and the ways of meeting them, through the appointment of an Information Officer on the staff of the Division and through closer relationships with the Department of Information, the involvement of all the churches

in this ministry to one another and in their service to human need requires a development of such information services, especially through the provision of literature in languages other than the three official languages of the World Council of Churches.

Conclusion

The foregoing review of the task of the Division, both in its record of achievements and the proposals for future development and action, places the purpose and function of Inter-Church Aid and Service to Refugees in the clear perspective of a world-wide *diakonia.* This wide and varied programme, conceived as it is at present, is a proper concern of the churches and of the World Council of Churches.

The concluding emphasis of Professor Masao Takenaka in his address to the Third Assembly 'Called to Service', is a cogent and pertinent reminder to the churches and their members of the continuing responsibility of interpreting service, as Jesus Christ manifested it, to the people of this generation.

What we need today is to accept this decisive service of Christ and to make the decisive change within ourselves. We need a revolutionary renewal, both in ourselves and in the structure of our churches, to respond to the transforming power of God which is going on in our changing world today. In this sense Christian service has an eschatological note as expressed in the preparatory document for this Assembly:

> Our service as individuals, no matter how good it may be, is always inadequate, always limited by our sins and errors. But only in so far as the churches accept Christ's service in repentance and renewal are they able to continue their service in the world until his coming.

RECOMMENDATIONS TO THE ASSEMBLY

I. The Third Assembly gratefully *acknowledges* the increasing service of the churches to one another and to people in need as recorded in the Report to the Central Committee on the Division of Inter-Church Aid and Service to Refugees (see '*Evanston to New Delhi*', chapter IV, page 109) and the Report of the Assembly Committee on Inter-Church Aid.

(1) The Assembly *notes* the developing concept of the Division's

work as outlined in the document 'The Nature and Scope of the Task of the Division of Inter-Church Aid and Service to Refugees' (see *Work Book*, pages 127 ff.), and *authorizes* the Divisional Committee to continue to work out the policy of the Division along the lines indicated in this document. The Assembly also *requests* the Divisional Committee to give special attention to the reports of the Sections of the Assembly, notably that on Service, and particularly to those points which have relevance to the nature and scope of Inter-Church Aid, Refugee and World Service.

(2) The Assembly, *recognizing* the need for the development of administrative organization and financial procedures within the Division in order that it may fulfil its mandate more effectively

(*a*) *approves* the change of the name of the Division from Division of Inter-Church Aid and Service to Refugees, to *Division of Inter-Church Aid, Refugee and World Service;*

(*b*) *requests* the Divisional Committee to continue to build the organization of the Division on the general lines indicated in document B, *Work Book,* chapter IV, page 133.

II. *Relationships between the Division of World Mission and Evangelism and the Division of Inter-Church Aid and Service to Refugees*

The Assembly, *recognizing* that the integration of the International Missionary Council and the World Council of Churches will call for the closest collaboration between the Division of World Mission and Evangelism and the Division of Inter-Church Aid and Service to Refugees,

(*a*) *requests* the Central Committee to give most careful attention to the development of relationships between the two Divisions and, if appropriate, to consider the appointment of a joint committee to give guidance in such developments;

(*b*) *authorizes* the Division of Inter-Church Aid and Service to Refugees to work out its relationships with the Division of World Mission and Evangelism along the lines of the document 'Procedures for collaboration between the Division of World Mission and Evangelism and the Division of Inter-

Church Aid and Service to Refugees' (document E, *Work Book,* page 141).

III. *Refugees*

The Assembly, having received reports concerning the continuing refugee problem,

(1) *calls the attention of churches* to the plight of refugees and homeless and uprooted people everywhere, reminds them that in spite of their efforts and those of governments and inter-governmental organizations in recent years, especially during World Refugee Year, the refugee problem persists not only in areas where it has long existed in Europe, the Middle East and Asia, but in its new manifestations in Africa, Latin America and the Caribbean, and *calls upon* the churches, therefore, not only to continue but to intensify their efforts on behalf of these refugees, counselling and assisting them as may be appropriate in their individual circumstances to re-patriate, to establish themselves where they are, or to resettle elsewhere;

(2) *authorizes* the Division of Inter-Church Aid and Service to Refugees to continue to maintain an appropriate service to refugees along the lines laid down by previous decisions of the World Council of Churches, and to continue its collaboration with the United Nations High Commissioner for Refugees and related bodies in co-operative projects mutually agreed upon in the interests of refugees; and

(3) *authorizes* the Division of Inter-Church Aid and Service to Refugees to exercise an appropriate service of consultation and advice to member churches and councils of churches in rendering their own ministry to refugee groups in their midst; and to present to the member churches for their support projects looking toward solutions of specific refugee problems.

IV. *Migration*

The Assembly, having received a report of the action of Central Committee in calling a World Conference on Migration at Leysin, Switzerland, June 11-16, 1961, and of its recommendations in the light of the findings of the Conference,

(1) *commends* the Conference Report, 'In a Strange Land', for study and action by the churches; and

(2) *authorizes* the Division of Inter-Church Aid and Service to Refugees to

(*r*) undertake further *studies of migration* in specific areas with a view to assisting the churches in their ministry to migrants;

(*b*) provide *counselling services* to churches and their agencies which need practical assistance in making arrangements for migrants, such as pastoral, welfare and reception services, contacts with churches in other countries and with inter-governmental or other agencies;

(*c*) provide *co-ordination* for the exchange of information, views and methods, and clearance of specific matters of concern amongst churches involved in assistance to migrants;

(*d*) provide facilities for *demonstration projects* in specific areas of migration;

(*e*) provide through the Commission of the Churches on International Affairs for the making of *expert representations at the inter-governmental level* in order to bring Christian thought and practice to bear upon migration policies and programmes and assist National Councils and churches to do likewise at the governmental level;

(*f*) in general undertake such *actions* as would keep before the churches the ever-changing conditions in the field of migration; and

(*g*) *establish* within the Division of Inter-Church Aid and Service to Refugees, *a secretariat for migration* in order that its guidance may be made available to the churches.

V. *Areas of Acute Human Need*

1. The Assembly *urges the churches* to give special attention to and show generous concern for the areas of acute human need. whether caused by natural disaster or rapid political, economic, or social change.

2. It *approves* the continuing effort of the Division of Inter-Church Aid and Service to Refugees in encouraging the churches

to meet immediate need through relief work and in long range con structive projects, especially in the newly independent countries.

3. It *calls upon* the Division to intensify its efforts:

(*a*) in strengthening existing agricultural, educational and socia projects;

(*b*) to encourage and support the initiation of other projects i collaboration with the churches in the areas of need, c specific comprehensive and demonstration projects in th agricultural, industrial, social and educational fields de signed to lift economic and social standards and train leader ship and develop the community life of the people in area of need.

Note. Where appropriate, prior consultation should be arrange with the Division of World Mission and Evangelism con cerning such projects and their long-range support.

4. The Assembly *welcomes* the great efforts of governmental an inter-governmental agencies to improve economic and social stan dards in the developing countries, calls upon the churches to col laborate with and support their efforts, and requests the Division t keep the churches informed of possibilities for specific co-operatio in the practical field.

5. The Assembly *authorizes* the Division, in collaboration wit other divisions and departments, and especially with the Divisio of World Mission and Evangelism, to support the churches in recruit ing and equipping men and women for work in these areas and par ticularly through such programmes as voluntary service overseas work camps, ecumenical teams, and specialized social service.

VI. *Scholarships*

The Assembly *requests the Central Committee* to act on an author ization to the Divisional Committee of Inter-Church Aid and Ser vice to Refugees

(1) in close collaboration with the Division of World Missio and Evangelism to *review* further the emergency needs of th churches for scholarships, especially in Africa, and to tak action to assist the churches by this means in training leaders both lay and ministerial;

(2) to *develop* further the services of the Division to the churche especially in helping them to formulate common procedure

and standards for scholarships and a common strategy in meeting new needs in this area.

VII. *ECLOF*

The Assembly *commends* to the attention of the churches the significance of the Ecumenical Church Loan Fund (ECLOF) as a form of inter-church aid and having noted the successful operation of ECLOF in Europe over many years, and having learned of the development of its services in Asia, Africa, Australia and Latin America, *calls upon the churches* to furnish ECLOF with the necessary capital resources in order that its benefits may be made more readily available.

VIII. *Finance*

The Assembly *having received* the report on the finances of the Division of Inter-Church Aid and Service to Refugees

(1) *notes* with gratification the increasing involvement of the churches in the work of inter-church aid, refugee, and relief services, and the growing support of the Division of Inter-Church Aid and Service to Refugees:

(2) *calls the churches* to increased efforts in view of the significance of these ministries and desperate situations of human need in many parts of the world;

(3) *asks the churches* to continue to underwrite the work of the Division, to do everything possible to meet the requests of the churches presented through the Division of Inter-Church Aid and Service to Refugees, and to see that their help to people in need flows through church channels;

(4) *requests* all member churches to take their share in supporting the Division's service programmes;

(5) *encourages* the churches to take such action as may be necessary to ensure that their gifts may be used not only for relief and emergencies but also for longer-term and creative projects, inter-church aid and social and economic rehabilitation in the areas of acute human need.

Following the presentation of the Report, *Father Makary el Souriany* (Coptic Orthodox, Egypt) moved *and it was VOTED to adopt the following resolution:*

The Assembly expresses its gratitude to the Division of Inter-

Church Aid and Service to Refugees, and to the giving churches, for their deep concern for the sufferings of the Algerian people and for their aid to the refugees of this country, which proves that the churches do not discriminate in their services between adherents of different religions. The churches give according to need and not to creed.

The Assembly requests the churches to continue this human service. Prayers of the churches are also required, that God may establish peace in this land.

15 · REPORT OF THE COMMITTEE OF THE ASSEMBLY ON THE COMMISSION AND DIVISION OF WORLD MISSION AND EVANGELISM

The following Report of the Committee of the Assembly on the Commission and Division of World Mission and Evangelism was received and amended, the Resolution adopted, and the Report commended to the churches and the Commission on World Mission and Evangelism by the Assembly in Business Session.

I. INTRODUCTION

The integration of the International Missionary Council and the World Council of Churches brings into being a new instrument of common consultation and action to serve the Churches in their missionary task under the new conditions of the second half of the twentieth century. In it we see the good hand of God leading us into the next phase of the Church's mission. It is at the same time a fitting symbol of the fact that missionary responsibility cannot be separated from any other aspect of the Church's life and teaching. The Christian mission is one throughout the world, for there is but one Gospel of salvation for all men, one Saviour and Lord, who is the light of the world. Today, thanks to the faithful witness of those who went before us in the missionary movement, the Christian mission has a world-wide base. Every Christian congregation is part of that mission, with a responsibility to bear witness to Christ in its own neighbourhood and to share in the bearing of that witness to the ends of the earth.

As we face the new situation, we are at the same time heirs of the spiritual riches of the missionary movement of past centuries. The very existence of a World Council of Churches is a sign of God's blessing upon that movement. At the centre of it there has always been a deep concern expressed in sustained intercession, sacrificial giving and personal commitment. This spiritual heritage must not be dissipated; it must remain, ever renewed in the hidden life of prayer and adoration, at the heart of the World Council of Churches. Without it the ecumenical movement would petrify. Integration must mean that the World Council of Churches takes the missionary task into the very heart of its life, and also that the missionary agencies of the churches place their work in an ecumenical perspective and accept whatever new insights God may give through new relationships.

The missionary task is not finished. It is rather entering upon a new and more challenging phase. All our concerns with one another must not cause us to forget the fact that two-thirds of the human race are without the knowledge of Christ as the light of the world. We owe them that knowledge. We have no better claim to Christ than they have. Nothing else that we can offer them is a discharge of that debt.

The calling of God to his Church today is for a new offering of life. For some, especially among the youth of the churches, it is a call for life-long missionary service abroad. For all of every age, and out of every nation, it is a call to total and unconditional commitment to the mission of God.

The newly integrated World Council of Churches can have no higher privilege than to be the servant of the churches in that mission.

II. Structure and Policy of the Commission and Division of World Mission and Evangelism

The programme of the new Division is not here fully described. It will provide a new frontier, a new dimension of the World Council. We have made a general outline of its task. We cannot now define all its deeper meanings nor the extent of its activities. Only the experience of living and working together can teach us these. Our temptation will be to think of the Division simply as the continuation of the interests of the International Missionary Council with emphasis on Asia, Africa, and South America. We must resist this temptation. This is the Division of World Mission and Evangelism of the World Council of Churches. We are concerned not with three continents but with six. In co-operation with every department of the World Council and with the full resources of the Christian community in every land we must help the churches to confront men and women with the claims of Jesus Christ wherever they live. We now propose to venture forth. We pray that we shall be sensitive to the leading of God's Spirit as he begins to use the structure that has been created.

The Committee has carefully considered the 'Proposals concerning the Policy, Structure and Programme of the Commission and Division of World Mission and Evangelism' contained in the *Work Book* of the Assembly (pages 142-5), approves them as a reasonable interpretation of the statement of the Aim and Functions of the Commission and Division (*Work Book*, page 26), and commends them to the Commission as a sound guide for the next few years. In particular it wishes to stress the following points:

(*a*) *Policy regarding the structure of the Division*

The Committee endorses in particular the emphasis placed upon flexibility, decentralization and minimum involvement in long-term operational responsibilities. If the Division is to help the churches in joint action for mission, it will be necessary to keep the administrative arrangements flexible, and to avoid allowing departmental structures to determine the lines of action. It should be the policy of the Division to make its staff available to help in any situation where joint action for mission seems possible. When need is shown for long-term operations, it should help to bring into existence the necessary instruments for such operations, but it should not itself generally become responsible for them. The effectiveness of its work will not be seen in the activities which bear its name, but in the renewal of missionary action in the churches themselves.

(*b*) *Joint action for mission*

The Committee has carefully considered the proposals entitled 'Joint Action for Mission' as suggested in the *Work Book* and developed in a subsequent document. The Committee welcomes these proposals. It believes that missionary advance in many parts of the world requires a redeployment of the resources available in specific geographical areas. A first necessary step towards this is that churches and related missionary bodies in a given area should together survey the needs and opportunities confronting them and the total resources available to meet them. This process of survey should be followed by a consultation of the churches and mission bodies in that area, aimed at securing real and effective redeployment of resources in the light of the agreed goals. This kind of common action will be impossible unless there is a fresh penitence, reconciliation and commitment on the part of all the bodies concerned. It will also raise in many cases searching issues in the realm of faith and churchmanship. The facing of these issues, both spiritual and confessional, will be a necessary pre-condition of missionary advance. The Committee therefore hopes that the Commission and Division will seek to implement these proposals in consultation with churches, related mission agencies, and national and regional councils, taking due account of the confessional issues which may be involved, and making use of the best material available on questions of missionary strategy.

The Committee recognizes that such development in the direction of joint action for mission will call for profound changes in the thinking of the churches and their people about their missionary responsibilities and in their commitment to the task of mission. It therefore urges that the development of the proposal set forth in paragraph 4, on page 145 of the *Work Book,* regarding education for mission and evangelism should receive early attention from the Commission and the Division.

(*c*) *Helping the churches in evangelism*

The Committee looks forward to the appointment as early as possible of a member of staff in the Division of World Mission and Evangelism whose main responsibility will be evangelism, and believes that this will make possible action to strengthen the evangelistic work of the churches. It asks the Commission, in consultation with the Department on Studies in Evangelism, to develop means for ascertaining what kinds of help the World Council can offer to the churches in their evangelistic work, and to consider the possibility of preparing a statement on the policy and programme of the Commission in this field. This should include procedures by which the Commission can maintain touch with the departments of evangelism of the churches and national councils, and by which they are adequately represented in its counsels. It should be the task of the Commission to keep before councils and churches its declared Aim: 'To further the proclamation to the whole world of the Gospel of Jesus Christ, to the end that all men may believe in him and be saved.' The Committee asks that the relation between 'Mission' and 'Evangelism' in the work of the Division should be a matter of continuing study.

III. Relationships

The Committee rejoices in the achievement of integration, but notes the extent of overlapping and duplication in the divisional programmes of the Council. It welcomes the provision which has been made for an early review of this matter and expresses the hope that the implications of integration will be given full effect in the life and work of the Council as soon as possible.

(*a*) *With the Division of Inter-Church Aid and Service to Refugees*

The Committee recommends that the statement entitled 'Procedures for Collaboration between the Division of World Mission and Evangelism and the Division of Inter-Church Aid and Service to Refugees' (*Work Book,* page 141) be approved as a starting point for developing relationships between the two divisions in the immediately ensuing period. While accepting the definition contained in this statement of the *focus* of the concerns of the division, it draws attention to the very wide *range* of these concerns and to the need for the fullest collaboration and consultation between the two divisions. It urges that the question of relationships between the two divisions be subject to early review in terms of the provisions of paragraph 49 of the Central Committee's Report on Programme and Finance as adopted by the Assembly (see page 351).

(*b*) *With the Division of Studies*

The Committee expresses the judgment that the proposed relationship between the Departments of Missionary Studies and Studies in Evangelism on the one hand and the DWME on the other (*Work Book,* pages 40-41), while accepted as a starting point, will require early review, in order to eliminate any undesirable duplication; such review to be in accordance with the provisions of paragraph 49 of the Central Committee's Report on Programme and Finance as adopted by the Assembly (see page 351).

(*c*) *With the Division of Ecumenical Action*

The Committee re-affirms the long-standing concern of the missionary movement for the development of Christian Home and Family Life programmes, and commends the plans of the Department on the Co-operation of Men and Women in Church, Family and Society to carry forward work in these areas, in consultation with the Division of World Mission and Evangelism.

Specifically, the Committee recommends approval of the statement entitled 'Agreement on the Christian Home and Family Life Programme of the IMC and the Department of Co-operation of Men and Women' (*Work Book*, pages 116-17).

(*d*) *With National Christian Councils*

The Committee has reviewed the relationship of the DWME and the National Christian Councils and is agreed upon the following statement:

> In the past the IMC carried the main responsibility for relationships between many of the National Christian Councils in Asia, Africa and Latin America and the churches of the West. Because these relationships were not exclusively missionary, they are now shared with other divisions of the World Council. None the less, the Division should continue the former practice of the IMC of working through the Christian Councils affiliated to it or co-operating with it, whilst at the same time serving as a clearing-house for those concerns which fall within its responsibilities.

IV. Programme

The Committee has had before it the 'Report of the International Missionary Council' and, while not attempting to review all phases of the programme reported in it, has given some attention to the following matters:

(*a*) *The role of the Christian laymen abroad in the mission of the Church*

The Committee has prepared the appended statement on the above subject and recommends that it be transmitted to churches and Christian Councils for their study and action. The Committee also recommends that the issue continue to receive high priority in the work of the DWME.

The Committee has also considered the proposal regarding a Secretariat for Lay Service Abroad, and approved it with the hope that it may be implemented as soon as possible, and that after an experimental period of three years it be reviewed. It has also prepared some detailed suggestions on this proposal for submission to the Central Committee.

(*b*) *Bible Weeks*

The Committee has heard with enthusiasm of the growth of a new form of Bible Week which was promoted by the United Bible Societies and the WCC, and has been used in many places, to help the renewal of the church. The form of this Bible Week is adaptable to different circumstances. Where it is tried, it should not follow any rigid pattern, but starting from the pattern suggested by the United Bible Societies, should be adapted to local conditions. The Bible study should always be local and related to the existing structures of the Church.

The Committee expresses its profound appreciation to the United Bible Societies for what they have done to develop the Bible Week project and recommends that the project be commended to the member churches and the councils affiliated to the Commission on World Mission and Evangelism, so that it may be given the widest possible effect in local areas; that arrangements be made for the distribution of descriptive materials; that at every stage consultations with the United Bible Societies be secured, and that one theme and relevant Bible passages be selected for a Bible Week project in 1963, to be used wherever it seems suitable.

(*c*) *Broadcasting*

The Committee has discussed the question of the responsibility of the World Council of Churches in general, and of the Division of World Mission and Evangelism in particular, in the field of broadcasting (including television and sound radio). It has had opportunities for conference on the subject with the Committee on the Department of Information. It has noted with appreciation the effort made by that Department with limited resources to fulfil the assignment given to it by the Evanston Assembly. It has also learned of the plans for the formation of a World Association for Christian Broadcasting and expresses the hope that this body may become an effective instrument of the churches in this field.

The Committee recommends:

1. That a person be appointed for a limited period, to be attached to the General Secretariat of the WCC and to give part of his time to the Department of Information and part to liaison and co-operation with the World Association of Christian Broadcasting, in process of formation;

2. That this arrangement be strictly of a provisional nature, the hope being that the WACB will develop to the point where the WCC may advise its constituency that the WACB is able to handle their concerns in this field, other than those relating specifically to ecumenical interpretation and information;
3. That the CWME seek resources through the Projects Fund to finance the above appointment;
4. That the Division continue to give attention to questions of Christian co-operation in the field of radio and television in so far as they relate to the responsibilities of the Division for mission and evangelism, and to contact with the regional Christian councils regarding these questions.

(*d*) *Matters considered by the Committee upon which recommendations have been made to the Commission on World Mission and Evangelism*

1. *Christian Literature.* The Committee recommends procedures for securing a new and better co-ordinated strategy for Christian Literature by means of a series of consultations in the various regions of the world.

2. *Study Centres.* The Committee has reviewed the development during the past seven years of a series of study centres in Asia and Africa, and recommends to the CWME procedures to secure better support especially when new centres are being inaugurated.

3. *Publications.* The Committee has reviewed the IMC's programme of publications and recommends to the CWME procedures to secure their more effective use. It has noted the growing importance of 'World Christian Books' and made recommendations regarding the training of writers.

4. *The Training of the Professional Missionary.* The Committee has heard with satisfaction an interim report on the planning for this study, has noted that it is conceived in terms of a world-wide base of mission, and has commended it to the CWME as a matter of urgency.

5. *The Remuneration of Missionaries.* The Committee has noted a request from the Continuation Committee of the East Asia Christian Conference that the DWME should take up with mission boards and churches the need for fuller mutual consultation regarding terms of service and remuneration of missionaries, and has made recommendations on the subject to the DWME.

6. *'The Pattern of the Ministry in a Missionary Church.'* The Committee has reviewed proposals for a study on the above theme and has made recommendations to the CWME.

Resolution

Mindful *of the greatness of the privilege which is given to all churches in being witnesses to the light of the world;*

remembering *the request of the Lund Conference that the churches should 'act together in all matters except those in which deep differences of conviction compel them to act separately';*

bearing in mind *the statement of the Assembly regarding the unity which we seek as a unity of 'all in each place . . . reaching out in witness and service to all'; and*

having received *and carefully discussed a proposal from the Australian Council of Churches for a 'World Christian Mission';*

The Assembly:

(1) *Urges the churches to seek together in each place the help of the Holy Spirit in order that they may receive power to be together Christ's obedient witnesses to their neighbours and to the nations;*

(2) *Draws the attention of the member churches to the revised basis and functions of the World Council of Churches, consequent upon the integration of the International Missionary Council and the World Council of Churches; and to the fact that all commissions, divisions and departments of the Council have a mandate to promote a missionary and evangelistic spirit in the members of all churches, and to support the churches in their world-wide missionary and evangelistic task; and therefore invites them to make use of the resources of the World Council of Churches in their work of mission and evangelism.*

(3) *Requests the Central Committee that, in its deliberations throughout the period after New Delhi, high priority should be given to the task of helping the churches to fulfil their common calling to mission and evangelism.*

APPENDIX

THE ROLE OF THE CHRISTIAN LAYMAN ABROAD IN THE MISSION OF THE CHURCH

In the years since Willigen much discussion has been given to the matter of the 'non-professional missionary', but it has resulted generally in little action. The very term suggested someone on the fringe of the activity of the professional missionary. In actual fact one of the greatest missionary opportunities confronting the churches today lies in the potential witness of great numbers of Christian laymen criss-crossing the world in the service of business, government and other occupations. At the same time there is a new impulse of disinterested service showing itself in a variety of voluntary schemes. This vast new resource which God has given to the church has been largely unharnessed. In what ways can we liberate this potential for the church's mission? What is the role of the layman in the mission of the church?

(1) *The need and the possibilities of the work of the layman*

Large numbers of laymen already abroad in business, government and other occupations need to be related to the work of church and mission and called into active participation. Those going abroad under various technical assistance programmes with a purpose of service, call for special study because of their parallel concern to serve and the possible complications of their political involvements.

Many countries are urgently recruiting doctors, engineers, university staff, artisans and other technical workers. We should develop procedures for making these needs known to our churches and directing Christian men and women to these strategic posts. It is important that the churches take the initiative in vocational guidance at this point and encourage able Christian laymen to enter important secular work abroad from a Christian missionary motivation. In thinking of the layman we should also bear in mind his family and the potential witness and service of his wife.

(2) *Proposed relationship to the church in the homeland and in the land of service.*

The churches in the homeland should take steps to find out about their people going to serve abroad and to establish an appropriate relationship for them. This should include (*a*) a recognition of their role in the mission of the church, (*b*) guidance and orientation for this service (*c*) fellowship and backing in their work so that they might have an intelligent and informed purpose as Christians in their going abroad.

In the land of service the indigenous church should make provision for receiving the layman into its fellowship and relating him to its life and work. This relationship should provide the man from abroad with the fellowship of belonging to a community, the pastoral care of a church in that country, and the involvement in Christian responsibility. In such a relationship his life and work and home will have the supports they need and may find their full meaning amid the difficulties of a strange environment.

Where Union churches and chaplaincies with foreign language services exist, they should be related as closely as possible to the indigenous church.

(3) *The nature of the missionary contribution of the layman*

The layman's contribution must not be thought of mainly in terms of religious activities in his spare time. This approach might distract him from his main work and make him both a poor amateur missionary and a poor worker in his secular profession.

His primary missionary contribution is as a competent and responsible worker in his own field. For Christ's sake he renders an able and diligent service and witnesses to him by the conduct of his work. In his daily occupation he has a particular opportunity for mission in the contacts he has with his fellow-workers. He also has a special opportunity to contribute in movements of social reconstruction and nation-building. His second contribution and field of witness is in the character of his personal life and of his Christian home. It is here that the wife plays an important role and can render a great service. At the same time the layman abroad and his family will also be loyal and active participants in the life and work of the local congregation.

(4) *The preparation of the layman*

The conditions of life and work abroad demand that adequate orientation be provided. Frustration through inefficiency, loneliness, little pastoral care, problems of food, health and hygiene, unfamiliar customs and ways, all combine to give a rough shock. Such orientation should therefore be long enough to cover such things as culture and customs, problems of health and general adjustment to living conditions, the relation of Christian faith to the religion in the area, some knowledge of the Church and its work in that area, and biblical studies.

In the land of service provision should also be made for an initial period of orientation to the country and its church. Opportunities should be provided periodically for conferences of laymen on the problems and opportunities of their position. It is essential that wives be included as fully as possible in the programme of orientation.

DISCUSSION OF THE REPORT OF THE COMMITTEE

In discussion of the Report as a whole the following points were made:

Dr Charles W. Ranson (Methodist Church in Ireland) expressed joy at the union of the World Council and the International Missionary Council, together with concern (reflected in Section III of the Report) at the extent of duplication and overlapping in the programmes of the Council. He noted the serious congestion of business in the later days of the Assembly due to the multiplicity of reports, and the lack of time to look at the programme as a whole. This abridges the freedom of the Assembly and forces it to delegate crucial tasks to Central Committee. In a growing organism untidiness is inevitable. But structure should be related to function, as is not now the case. If the Council is to realize its possibilities it must be simplified in structure. The Central Committee will approach this task with wisdom. It will need determination also.

Dr John Coventry Smith (United Presbyterian, USA) expressed appreciation of the report for its adequate and constructive handling of details. He pointed out that Bishop Manikam, in presenting it, had set these details in a larger perspective. He desired that the report embody this world perspective, and therefore *moved* that the report be amended by the insertion of a new paragraph. (In consequence of the vote on this motion recorded below, the paragraph appears in the report reproduced above, as paragraph 1 of Section II.

The motion was seconded. *Bishop Manikam* expressed willingness, on behalf of the committee, to accept the insertion if desired by the Assembly. *The motion was put to the vote and was carried, nem. con.*

The *Archbishop of York* (Dr F. D. Coggan, Church of England) requested that references to 'the Bible Societies' in Section IVb be corrected to read 'the United Bible Societies'. This was done.

He further suggested that Section IVd.i be amended to read: 'A new and better co-ordinated strategy' instead of 'a more co-ordinated strategy'. In accepting this revision *Bishop Manikam* pointed out that the sentence in question was intended merely to indicate the subject of a detailed memorandum which would be transmitted to the Commission on World Mission and Evangelism.

Professor L. H. Cragg (United Church of Canada) expressed appreciation for the attention given in the Report and its Appendix to the role of Christian laymen abroad in the Mission of the Church, but objected to the merely cursory reference to wives in the last sentence of the Appendix. He recognized that wives who were unable to adjust to an overseas situation were at times a hindrance and cause of failure. But he thought the document should stress the positive and valuable contribution which wives often made with their husbands, and requested revision in this sense. *Bishop Manikam* gave assurance that the Appendix would be amended to cover this point.

The Rev. Dr John Marsh (Congregational Union of England and Wales) raised a point of order with reference to the amendment of a document subsequent to its passage by the Assembly. *The Chair* ruled that only the Appendix would be amended and that this was not formally part of the report under consideration.

Dr A. Dale Fiers (International Convention of Christian Churches, USA) referred to the ambiguity of paragraph IIc in referring to 'procedures by which the Commission can maintain touch with the departments of evangelism of the churches and national councils, and by which they are adequately represented in its councils'. He suggested that the concluding phrase 'in its councils' be changed to read 'in the Commission' in order to be certain of adequate representation of departments of evangelism in the membership of the Commission. *Bishop Manikam* stated that 'councils' was a typographical error. The text was intended to read 'in its counsels'. This correction was noted.

The Chairman and *Bishop James K. Mathews* (Methodist, USA) made reference to the provision of the Constitution of the Commission on World Mission and Evangelism which provides that 'members appointed by Central Committee shall include persons representative of the field of evangelism'. Dr Fiers declared himself satisfied and withdrew his suggestion.

The Chairman noted that Section IVc on Broadcasting had been dealt with in the actions taken on the Report of the Policy Reference Committee. This gave the Commission a somewhat broader mandate than the present report.

Bishop Manikam moved the adoption of the resolution with which the report concluded.

The Rev. Frank Hambly (Methodist, Australia) expressed satisfaction that the Australian proposal for a Christian World Mission had resulted in this resolution. He regarded it as an important summons to the churches to act together in this important field.

The Rev. Alan Walker (Methodist, Australia) stressed the magnitude of the missionary task confronting the churches during the remainder of the twentieth century in view of the rapidly expanding population of the world, and the possibility that the WCC could lead the churches into more concentrated action together in this field.

The Resolution was put to the vote and adopted.

16 · REPORT OF THE COMMITTEE ON THE COMMISSION OF THE CHURCHES ON INTERNATIONAL AFFAIRS (CCIA)

The Assembly in Deliberative Session approved the substance of the following Report on the Commission of the Churches on International Affairs and commended it to the churches for study and appropriate action.

Introduction

1. We speak of international affairs and the ecumenical witness to the world of nations, for Christians are called to testify to the righteous and merciful will of God, the Sovereign of men and nations. Christians have an obligation to work out and apply urgently their testimony to the problems which vex the relations of states. The churches do not have competence to speak on many technical aspects of these questions, though they must strive to be informed and not ignore the technical factors when they formulate their testimony. Neither they nor their agencies dare to be silent on fundamental issues, if they are to be faithful witnesses to the Ruler of all mankind and to his redeeming Son, Jesus Christ.

2. Knowing that Christ has overcome the world, Christians should approach the dark crises of our times with an invincible hope, a conviction that new and more promising beginnings are possible in the affairs of nations, if they will turn from fear and narrow self-interest to the pursuit of the common weal. This is a time of judgment, when the consequences of wrong decisions may be visited upon many generations. It is also a time of great opportunity, if men will use the good gifts of God to meet the claims of justice and to advance the general welfare. With this understanding and perspective we approach the tasks of the World Council of Churches and its Commission of the Churches on International Affairs.

I. The Organization of the CCIA

3. The aims and basic structure of the Commission of the

Churches on International Affairs, as they were laid down prior to the First Assembly of the WCC and have now been confirmed in the new Constitution of 1961, have proved their worth. They provide sufficient safeguards to assure responsible action, and at the same time allow the Commission to address itself quickly to rapidly changing international situations. The contributions made by the CCIA in prompt and relevant representations at the time and place of international decisions, in the information and advice offered to the churches and national commissions as well as to the World Council of Churches and the International Missionary Council, have constituted a significant form of ecumenical witness and service. The Committee is grateful for the efforts of the staff, for its competence and for the range and quality of its work. The CCIA has earned the confidence it has won.

4. The need to strengthen and undergird the work of the CCIA in a number of ways seems clear. The new importance of Asia and Africa in the ecumenical movement as well as in international relations needs to be given greater expression in the membership of the Commission and of its Executive Committee. The idea of supplementing the members of the Commission through the formal appointment of consultants in order to improve the representative character of CCIA deliberations as well as to command additional technical competence, merits exploration. While budgetary considerations may preclude much expansion of staff, the Committee strongly approves the proposal to appoint, in co-operation with the EACC, a secretary in Asia, and hopes that a similar arrangement may be made at the proper time in Africa in consultation with the All Africa Church Conference and also in Latin America. In addition, more effective relations to inter-government regional organizations are desired and provision should be made for specialized study of international problems.

5. Fuller and better co-operation with the national commissions on international affairs and assistance in the formation of new ones should remain high on the list of priorities. Membership of the youth in our churches in these commissions is much to be desired and should be sought. Correspondence should be supplemented by personal visits. Regional conferences could be of assistance. The provision of educational material adapted to the needs of national commissions, member churches and related councils, merits greater attention. The work of the CCIA would undoubtedly be assisted by

the regular submission of information and judgments by the national commissions. Since the present staff ought not to be asked to carry a much heavier load, the possibility of voluntary help should be explored.

6. If the work of the CCIA is to have any value, however, as it goes about its combined prophetic and highly practical task, a great obligation rests upon the churches in whose name it claims to speak. For, too often in the past, the valuable work done by the CCIA has passed unnoticed in the world—though not by the statesmen of the world—because most Christians have remained completely ignorant of the judgments the CCIA has passed and the proposals it has made. The churches should not merely continue to support the work of the CCIA both materially and with their prayers, but they should see that this work is not wasted by ensuring that their congregations are kept fully informed at every stage.

7. Omitting explicit mention of problems concerning the care and settlement of refugees which are dealt with in the report on the Division of Inter-Church Aid and Service to Refugees, this report considers certain other of the more urgent responsibilities of the ecumenical movement toward the world of nations.

The considerations set forth below assume that in general the work of the Commission will continue to follow the lines laid down in its constitution and the cumulative policy statements of CCIA and of its parent bodies.

II. International Peace and Security

8. Since war is an offence against God, the task of the Christian is to do all in his power to prevent, and even to eliminate, war. Nevertheless, the elimination of war, though especially in the context of nuclear power essential to the future survival of mankind, would not by itself solve all outstanding problems. Nor is it a question only of a possible nuclear war. There are many areas of the world where so-called 'limited' wars have been raging for years. But the evils which they have brought in their train—subversion, terrorism, counter-terrorism, corruption of police and public values, concentration camps, refugees, even genocide—have been no less horrible or evil.

9. Even limited wars are fraught with psychological danger. Men

have been asked by governments to do things they have no right to demand, especially in the field of subversion. Though it is difficult to give the word a precise definition, subversion is to be condemned. Again and again in political discussions words and phrases are used with different meanings in different countries. Subversion is one of them.

10. Spying and espionage are considered part of subversion, but subversion means much more than spying. Subversion in the new twentieth-century form signifies a deliberate attempt by one nation to undermine the economic or political structure or stability of another. This practice builds up barriers of mistrust between nations, which contribute to international tensions. To define the area in which such subversion is carried on is more difficult than simply to state that it is carried on. The churches must pay attention to this task. The task falls especially to the CCIA, a body which is in the position of bringing to bear a reasonably detached judgment on these problems, for it must stand for Christian values which by their nature apply to all sides in controversial disputes. The contribution of the CCIA in matters of this kind becomes all the more significant as the CCIA itself becomes the more representative of all the churches. The churches must not be identified with any ideology; they must be in the world but not of it, for they can only stand for Christ.

A. *Disarmament and nuclear tests*

11. The most serious problem facing the world today is that of disarmament. General and complete disarmament is widely recognized to be the desired goal. But there are different views regarding its meaning and the procedures to achieve it. There are some who feel that the only satisfactory solution is one in which some kind of strong international control ensures that nations are disarmed to such an extent that aggressive war becomes impossible. This would necessarily involve the emergence of some kind of world police force. Others feel that such a goal is at the present unrealistic; the best we can hope for at this stage is a form of disarmament such that at the end of the day there will exist in the world a balance of mutually controlled power at a much lower level than we have now. Steps toward disarmament will necessarily be gradual.

12. As no universally acceptable definition of general and comprehensive disarmament exists, it is suggested that the CCIA should

take this matter under consideration and see if it is not possible for them to reach a definition of the goal towards which all should be striving.

13. An immediate start on disarmament negotiations is urgently needed. All the great powers are committed to some form of general disarmament, even if they are not absolutely clear whether they all mean the same thing by it. There are already before the United Nations at least three separate disarmament proposals from the Union of Soviet Socialist Republics, the United States of America and Great Britain. These plans must of necessity have many points in common. Accordingly, it is recommended that an immediate study be made of all existing governmental plans of disarmament, with a view to analysing them, and extracting from them the points which are common to all, and also seeing what points of controversy still remain. This should provide a useful basis for subsequent negotiation among governments. If, as seems likely, the resources of the CCIA will not cover such study, it may be possible to find some other body to undertake the work on a factual basis, leaving the final evaluation to the CCIA.

14. As this method could be used with profit in fields other than disarmament two general points should be made. First, nations do not always mean the same thing by the same words. To take but one example, the Soviets' and the United States' conceptions of an international force are vastly different, even though precisely the same words are used in each country to describe them. Second, the positions of nations shift and this makes lasting evaluations of their positions extremely difficult. All the same, there is a certain virtue even in pointing out the shift when it comes, and in trying to understand the reasons for it. The churches, in fact, could render an immense service if, through continuing analysis of problems, they were able to point out at any given moment what—or indeed who—is the main obstacle to peace.

15. The first of these problems is the more difficult. The motives of governments in the field of disarmament sometimes remain extremely obscure. The churches will always be in difficulty unless they are able to understand fully the motives behind any given action. At the earliest possible moment there should be a conference between Christians from various countries with specialists present, especially from the Soviet Union and the United States, who in a completely confidential atmosphere would be able to explain their

governments' policies. It is unlikely that ministers or government officials could attend such a conference. However confidential the meeting, it would be almost impossible to expect such people to speak frankly or freely. But in every country there are persons who, while not actually in the employ of the governments, are so close to them that they would be able to give a very clear analysis of the motives and reasons behind a particular action. Such people might be invited to the proposed conference and it is recommended that the CCIA, in the very near future, examine the possibilities of calling such a conference. This idea should also be considered by the Ecumenical Institute at Bossey. Such a conference would supplement and focus the great work for peace already done by the several regional conferences of the churches in various parts of the world and by the Christian Peace Conferences at Prague. Christians may differ sharply on international issues, but they can discuss them in charity.

16. The statements already issued by the officers of the CCIA regretting the nuclear tests by France and the resumption of nuclear tests by the Soviet Union are endorsed. While fully appreciating that the latter development has put the government of the United States in a very difficult position, the fervent hope is expressed that they will not find it necessary to embark on atmospheric tests. The resumption of the Geneva Conference is welcomed and Christians everywhere are urged to join in prayers for its success. The problems have not been made any easier by the events of the past six months, but the situation could be improved if an immediate start were made on general disarmament negotiations.

17. The churches' duty in articulating the Christian conscience is to be in advance of all governments. It must therefore be made plain that the Geneva talks cannot succeed unless there is at least a small measure of confidence on both sides. Such confidence is not likely to exist if one of the powers taking part in the talks is preparing for the resumption of tests while the talks are actually going on. It is realized that pending the conclusion of an agreement regarding inspection and control there is no way of testing this matter. It is therefore imperative that a legally binding treaty be speedily concluded.

18. The attention of all countries which do not possess nuclear weapons is called to the example of the great country in which we are now meeting, whose Prime Minister has declared that India

would within a very few years possess the means of making atomic weapons but does not intend to do so.

19. Great emphasis is to be placed on the advantage which can be obtained from technical co-operation between the great power blocs, not only as an end in itself, but also as a possible means towards political negotiations. The original test-ban talks were initiated by technical discussions to see if such a ban were feasible, and it is noted that considerable progress has been made on such a basis in other fields, for example, the Antarctica Treaty and the International Geophysical Year. Related to this too is the tentative agreement between the United States and the Soviet Union on the principles which should guide the powers when approaching disarmament talks, and this could profitably be followed up by technical discussions on possible forms of enforcing disarmament control. A similar technique might well be applied to the regulation of the use of outer space, a matter which is already beginning to give concern.

20. There is need for an understanding and recognition of the rights of conscientious objectors in the nuclear age. The position of wholly undefended nations should also be further considered. It is desirable that each nation examine its present defence position to see whether there are any steps which can be taken unilaterally without endangering the nation's security. This would help to manifest goodwill and to create a better atmosphere.

B. *Reduction of tension and areas of concern*

21. A number of areas of special concern in the present world can be identified. Among them are Berlin, the Congo, Angola, Algeria, Viet-Nam, Laos, Korea, Cuba and the Dominican Republic. Of these Berlin seems to be the most dangerous, though the potential danger in Viet-Nam is also regarded as very real.

22. In discussing the Berlin issue representatives of churches tend to divide along national and bloc lines. For example, representatives of churches in Eastern Europe maintain that it is not possible to view the Berlin issue in isolation, that one has to consider the whole political position of Germany and Eastern Europe, and indeed the history of these countries during and since the war, as well as the political position inside the Federal Republic itself, While not dissenting from the view that the Berlin question could not stand in isolation, representatives from churches in the West maintain that

the building of a wall across a city, dividing families and churches and driving humble people to desperate acts, is something which no Christian can condone, and that no nation has a right to use the people of another nation as tools for its own interest.

23. It is possible, however, to agree on a set of general principles which might be a guide to nations in situations of this kind:

(*a*) Any attempt to change an unsatisfactory situation by force must be opposed;
(*b*) The churches have a clear duty to issue a solemn warning that any nation which deliberately embarks on a course of action bound to raise tension must be condemned;
(*c*) Settlements should involve equitable concessions from both sides;
(*d*) There should be a readiness to accept provisional settlements when final solutions cannot now be achieved;
(*e*) The world must learn to live patiently with problems for which at the moment no satisfactory solutions are possible.

24. The approach taken in regard to the problem of disarmament is also applicable in the case of Germany with particular reference to the specific question of a limited form of controlled armaments, which could probably ease tension in this very dangerous area. There are in existence at the moment a number of plans for this, for example, the Rapacki Plan, the Eden Plan, the Gaitskell Plan and the like. It is hoped that the CCIA will undertake a study of these plans on the same basis as the study of disarmament plans, to isolate the points of agreement or disagreement.

25. The Churches have a duty at this dangerous moment to warn the nations against any new provocative acts in the Berlin situation. Examples which may be cited are any further attempt to isolate West Berlin from the East or from the West, or the arming of the Bundeswehr with nuclear weapons. Christians must make it plain that, quite apart from the rights or wrongs of any particular case, political actions which split churches or families or divide Christian from Christian are matters they can under no circumstances condone.

C. *The Responsibility of non-aligned Nations*

26. In the present state of world tension, the non-aligned nations have a very positive and important role to play in the work of conciliation. It may even be that these nations are demonstrating a more

Christian spirit than some of the nations which have been the traditional home of Christianity. Their policy has enabled these countries to take the power blocs as realities and to establish positive relations with them, reserving to themselves the freedom to judge all issues as they arise and to take steps on such issues without any prior commitment. It is only right, however, to point out that the non-aligned nations will discharge their role in world affairs only as they act as responsible powers themselves.

27. Big power blocs should not try to draw non-aligned nations to their side. Such actions would be deleterious both to the nations themselves, and to the powers trying to win them over. Such attempts should be deplored.

III. The Changing Structure of the International Community

A. *A Universal Organization of Nations*

28. The structures and institutions of political government and international order offer no lasting security and stability and are subject to the constant flow of historical change. Our time is shaped by fundamental developments in the economic and social conditions of life all over the world, as well as in the forms of government and in the distribution of political power and influence in the international community. A growing number of formerly dependent peoples are entering the society of nations and are sharing the responsibilities of independence in a world that lacks harmony and order. This world is torn by deep antagonisms between political systems and by conflicts of power, and exists under a precarious equilibrium of terrible means of destruction.

29. Because of present divisions and tensions a perfected system of world-wide co-operation cannot be expected in the near future, but human society must move towards those ordered forms of universal political co-operation for the safeguarding of peace and the realization of social justice and the welfare of all nations, which modern technical development and the interdependence of peoples demand and make possible. Christians will recognize in this world of chaotic disorder and deep distrust the evidence of human fallibility. They will not cease to proclaim in a divided humanity the reign of love and justice and to strive for peace and for the fellowship of all men and nations.

30. In the present stage of transition and change the United Nations has fulfilled an indispensable task. Even if its endeavours to secure disarmament have thus far failed and its efforts to prevent international conflicts have not always succeeded, the United Nations has facilitated the integration of newly rising states into the international society, has assisted world-wide co-operation in the economic development of all nations, has ensured talks and negotiations among opposing states in a time of crisis, and has defended the basic standards of justice, law and human dignity in international life.

31. To be equal to its role in international life, the United Nations must have the constant support of all its members. Work for the maintenance of peace and assistance given under the difficult conditions of peoples rising to full independence places heavy responsibilities and financial strains upon the United Nations. The churches should urge governments to discharge their full responsibilities towards the United Nations and to be prepared to increase their efforts for the common cause of peace and orderly progress.

32. By its Charter an organization of universal concern, the United Nations is intended to include all independent nations which are ready to accept the obligations of membership. Its task of co-operation and conciliation is seriously hampered by the absence of representatives of large parts of the world's population from its councils. The isolation and estrangement of the absent nations, and a lack of balance within the organization itself, are the unfortunate outcome of this situation. The outstanding instance is the People's Republic of China. Consideration should also be given to the absence of those nations which have been divided by the political conflicts of our time where solutions have not yet been found.

33. The United Nations is developing from a conference of national delegations into an organization with an authority of its own, empowered to undertake special responsibilities. This step forward requires an impartial and independent status for its administration.

34. Rapid de-colonization has overtaken the provisions of the Charter relating to the administration of dependent territories. Whilst these arrangements continue to function successfully in certain cases, an acute need is felt for institutions within the framework of the Charter which could more generally assist peoples in their

transition to independence and prepare them for the responsibilities of full government either before or after the beginning of their independent status. Christian churches should urge upon governments concerned their obligation to provide for a timely and sufficient preparation of the people for their tasks in a free government.

35. Nations should not use the claim of sovereignty to exclude reasonable discussion of the international implications of their failures to protect human rights in their territories.

36. All nations should refrain from interfering for selfish interests in the full development of new states.

B. *Regional Institutions.*

37. Regional economic and social organizations can be valuable in themselves and also in developing a wider community in the world. Their advantages include the limitation of national sovereignty, the use of methods of peaceful settlement, the devising of new techniques of international co-operation, and the stimulation of economic growth. These organizations must be framed with due regard to the higher interests of the international community so that they do not result in exclusiveness and separation from other nations. Opening wider areas for a free interchange of goods and of services may help the world community in its present stage of growing interdependence and exchange between nations, and thus prepare for a greater unity in the future.

C. *Peaceful change and settlement*

38. At the present time traditional methods of violence for effecting change have ceased to be accepted by international opinion as instruments of national policy. But in an age when all political and social forces of the world are in perpetual flux and the increase of populations and their migrations constantly create new dangers of unrest, the abrogation of war should not be identified with the mere maintenance of the status quo. Otherwise increasing tensions may finally result in violence and bloodshed.

39. The stability of international order and the respect for international law are basic elements of peace. The protection of the existing order, however, should be accompanied by the recognition of legitimate demands for its alteration, in so far as these further the maintenance of peace and serve the common good of the interna-

tional community. That such changes can be brought about by mutual agreement is shown by the peaceful emergence in recent years of many newly independent states.

40. Christians should insist that governments and international organizations use to the full the available means for providing peaceful solutions by agreed change, and develop procedures for prompt international action for peace in emergencies.

41. So far as possible legal disputes between nations should be resolved by arbitration and judicial decisions. Governments should refrain from undermining the legal settlement of differences by making reservations which limit the general competence of international tribunals.

D. *International ethos*

42. A deep foundation of moral values and ethical convictions underlies international order. From this it derives its authority and its basic principles.

43. Diversities of religion, culture and tradition, apparently so great between the main regions of the world, do not exclude the existence of a unified set of values, living and developing in the conscience of mankind. These do not in all cases derive from Christian sources but Christians have a special opportunity and duty to contribute to their articulation and development.

44. A more profound study of the nature and content of these moral foundations of international law and order will help nations of different traditions to understand and accept their common allegiance to basic ethical conceptions.

IV. Problems of New and Developing Countries

A. *Problems of political development*

45. The mid-twentieth century has seen the emergence of many nations from a state of political subjection by alien powers to a status of political independence. We rejoice in this. We note, however, that there are nations and people still under foreign political domination. Such domination, recurring in human history, is not the result exclusively of any one particular political system. Wherever it occurs and under whatever system of political life, and wherever the consent of the governed is spurned and their welfare subordin-

ated to the interests of the ruling power, this is unjust and the Christian conscience condemns it.

46. Both in the interests of human justice and international peace the transfer of political power to those to whom it should belong must be made without self-serving delay. We recognize that problems exist where a people has not been sufficiently prepared to assume the responsibilities of political independence. In such cases the process of necessary preparation must be greatly accelerated. To eliminate ambiguities in the role of ruling powers, and to expedite the achievement of independence, it is desirable that international assistance through agencies of the United Nations be associated with such a process.

47. Where other factors exist, such as the presence of ethnic or racial minorities, sufficient guarantees for the protection of the rights of these minorities should be assured by the people achieving independence. Where history has thrown two or more races or religious groups together in the same country, as the total welfare of all such people can be secured only through the mutual acceptance of each other as citizens of a common country and members of a common nation, it is necessary that no single group seek to perpetuate political advantage for itself at the cost of justice for all. While legitimate fears of minorities need to be allayed, no minority should be vested with such power of veto as to deny the rights of the majority and the welfare of the whole community.

48. Developing nations have to contend with many difficulties. Divisive tendencies arising from traditional patterns of life are a serious difficulty. In such a context, nationalism, cherished and fostered as bringing cohesion in the life of the peoples, has a creative role to play. On the other hand there is the danger that it may act as an impediment to creating a sense of community with neighbouring nations. Furthermore, when, in the general desire to create a sense of national identity, nationalism is confounded with a spurious revival of old customs, the latter becomes an enemy of progress.

49. It must be recognized that in the world of our day the interdependence of nations is a reality. The ideal that the Christian seeks along with all those interested in the promotion of human welfare, is a community of nations wherein each nation can develop its own life only in the context of an active and just international association.

B. Problems of economic development and social interdependence

50. It is a matter of gratification that many of the more advanced nations have sought to aid the progress of the economically less developed countries. Such aid is more than a matter of charity. Human justice demands a more equitable distribution of God-given resources to all the children of men. Human solidarity requires that nations collaborate for the creation of wealth for their common welfare. When economic co-operation is viewed thus, no political advantage can be sought by the donor of aid and the receiver of the aid has the obligation of using it responsibly.

51. To develop economic co-operation along these lines we urge a more adequate strategy for world development. The urgency of the situation in less developed countries and the rising expectations of their people call not only for a quantitative increase in assistance but for a qualitative planning, so that the best results may be secured within a reasonable span of time. Frustrated expectations may lead people to destructive revolt rather than along the path of peaceful revolution.

52. Donor countries should correlate their aid programmes. Unless bilateral aid is preferred by the parties concerned, both financial and technical aid should be channelled through international co-operative agencies like the United Nations. This should avoid waste and fruitless competition, and elicit a response free of suspicion from those receiving the aid. In developing countries, planning for a balanced development is absolutely necessary to avoid creating new problems and the compounding of old ones. All planning for development needs to be related to available and potential resources, including personnel, to execute such plans. The role of social change which is both created by development and aids such development must be taken into consideration.

53. In the long run trade, not aid, is the most effective instrument in furthering development. International co-operation to secure effective markets for the developing countries is necessary. Safeguards against the impact on the economics of these countries of changes in international monetary policies and of fluctuations in prices, both of primary commodities and of machinery for productive purposes, have to be developed. Training for technological and administrative skills, supplemented by education to inculcate a sense of social responsibility, has to be stepped up. Accelerated programmes for

education on a wide scale and the supply and pooling of resources for such plans must engage the continuing attention of both donor countries and receiving countries. Research in the special problems of developing countries is of paramount importance if sound plans are to be devised. A rational and co-operative regional distribution of productive enterprises needs to be encouraged more fully to meet consumer needs. In all these a more rational and correlated approach to development is imperative for all involved.

54. In this context special emphasis is laid on the need to control the growth of population, especially in developing countries. It is an error to think that such control is needed only in densely populated countries. The immediate necessity is to bring population pressures and economic growth into a more balanced relationship. It is known that even in countries where the national income has increased markedly within the last decade, the benefits of such increase have been largely off-set by mounting population pressures. As standards of health improve, mortality rates decrease dramatically, and unless birth rates are brought into balance many countries that have obtained political independence will find the prospects for genuine economic independence remote. While some developing countries have taken steps to promote responsible family planning, more energetic and comprehensive steps are needed even in such countries. The more developed countries should provide technical knowledge and assistance when so requested by developing countries.

55. Aid can never be and should not be a one-way affair. Out of their rich cultural heritage, the developing nations have much to contribute to the enrichment of the life of the people of the world as a whole. Nations should contribute to each other from the wealth of their wisdom, experience and other resources that the life of each may be the richer for it.

V. Human Rights and Religious Liberty

56. The protection of human rights by international instruments has grown in more recent development to be a fundamental concern of international law and order. It has been the constant endeavour of the CCIA to urge governments to implement the standards proclaimed in the Declaration of Human Rights of the United Nations

and to assist in the work, yet to be completed, of elaborating covenants by which all states will undertake to assure civil and political as well as economic, social and cultural rights. International efforts to advance the status of women are also followed with care. The Committee approves this work and asks the CCIA to continue with it.

57. The position of man in society, as defined by declarations and conventions on human rights in international law, can be more effectively secured by the creation of international safeguards for the observance of those rights. This will open for individuals direct access to international institutions against infringements upon these liberties by their own governments. The European Convention on Human Rights and Fundamental Freedoms has created such institutions and these are working well. The CCIA could profitably explore similar developments in other regions, always provided that such international standards as have been recognized shall not be lowered.

58. As all peoples of the world rise to a growing consciousness of the foundations for a just and progressive human society, guided by the moral principles of freedom, justice and equal rights for all, governments still responsible for dependent territories should accept —as some already have—some basic code of human rights as legally binding upon the exercise of power.

59. In the present time the improvement of economic conditions and of means of communication, migration and cultural exchange opens new ways of contact and co-operation between peoples of all continents, creeds and traditions. Freer movement may carry with it a better understanding of peoples and may help to surmount old prejudices. There may arise, however, the danger of new racial tensions, since the evolution of social groups to higher status and greater freedom may arouse fresh opposition by formerly privileged groups. One must hope for the establishment of healthy communication between men from various countries and continents in the spirit of a common human fellowship without distinction of ethnic origin, race, colour, sex or creed. Christians living together in the common brotherhood of the family of God must oppose racial discrimination in all its forms as contrary to Christian doctrine. They must work as individuals and as communities for the abolition of racial privileges and injustice, and thereby bear witness to the Christian faith.

60. The growing together of the peoples of the world, the exchanges and migration between various countries and continents, lead to a new confrontation of religions. In many parts of the earth renascent non-Christian religions exercise a great influence upon the social life of the nations. Christians living in a minority in these countries may be confronted with the resurgence of the concept of an established religion or with endeavours to form the social life of a country after the traditions of a non-Christian religion. This calls for a re-assertion and rethinking of the principles of religious freedom which the World Council of Churches has stated in former declarations (Amsterdam Declaration on Religious Liberty, 1948). The churches will benefit in their future work by actions on religious liberty taken by this Third Assembly, notably the report on 'Christian Witness, Proselytism and Religious Liberty' and the Statement on Religious Liberty (see pages 159-60).

61. The fundamental implications of religious freedom must be respected within every system of government and within every system of relationship between Church and State, in a country with a state religion as well as in a secular state.

62. The CCIA is commended for its work since the Evanston Assembly. It is hoped that the preceding paragraphs will be helpful to it as it goes about its difficult but highly important mission in the next period of the activities of the World Council of Churches.

In discussion, the following points were made:

Professor Hamilcar Alivisatos (Church of Greece) asked the CCIA to arrange for regional conferences to make people familiar with the work and achievements of the CCIA.

Bishop Beste (Evangelical Church in Germany) regretted that the report did not contain anything about the dangerous atmosphere of hatred and false statements which the press created today in some countries.

Mr M. M. Thomas (Mar Thoma, India) wished to refer back the report for a more detailed statement on the future organization of the CCIA. He took exception mainly to paragraph 4. It seemed to him essential that the CCIA should be more representative in its composition. *Dr Pusey* answering drew attention to the budgetary limitations applying to the CCIA.

Colonel A. Bramwell Cook (Salvation Army, New Zealand) approved of the formula used in paragraph 8 that war was an offence against God. That was an improvement on the report of the Service Section which (as originally drafted) made the same point only in regard to modern war.

Mr Samuel R. Levering (Religious Society of Friends, USA) spoke in favour of the report. He suggested that in paragraph 18 mention should be made also of those nations which already possess nuclear weapons. They should give them up, even if that meant a certain infringement upon their sovereignty.

Dr Georg F. Vicedom (Evangelical Church in Germany) expressed the opinion that Christians should not meddle with questions of the policy of the day. The Assembly of the WCC should not deal with politics. He criticized paragraph 24 where specially one-sided plans were recommended in such a way that the report took sides with one party in the political struggle. As to the resolution on Angola, it seemed to him that the CCIA singled out there a question where the Church had nothing to fear from the power criticized whereas in other more dangerous cases the churches remained silent. He regretted that the right of peoples to self-determination was overlooked. The millions of Europeans under foreign domination were forgotten. He recommended the Assembly to reject this report.

Professor Roger Mehl (Reformed Church of Alsace and Lorraine, France) referred to paragraphs 30, 31. He approved the backing given there to the UN. He suggested, however, laying more emphasis on the limitations which stood in the way of the development of UN. In clearly stating these shortcomings the report would be more acceptable to general opinion.

The Rev. T. Sihombing (Protestant Christian Batak, Indonesia) underlined paragraph 40 of the report. The statement there made would be applicable to the negotiations over West Irian.

Professor Egbert de Vries (Reformed, Holland) expressed his satisfaction with the report. Especially the statements in paragraphs 45-55 on the situation of developing countries were a real step forward. He suggested some slight alterations in paragraph 55 to indicate more clearly that both the more and the less developed countries have much to learn from each other.

Bishop Emilianos (Ecumenical Patriarchate of Constantinople) uttered his apprehension about the report's recommendation on family planning (paragraph 54). Many churches had definite views on theological aspects of the question and it would be necessary to make mention of these opinions. He suggested bringing into the report an observation on further study of this question.

Bishop Rajah Manikam (Lutheran, India) said that Section V (paragraphs 56 ff.) of the report missed a golden opportunity to speak out on religious freedom in the Asian and Near Eastern countries. Not only in Asia but also in the Near East the Christian mission stood before obstacles in attitudes which would not allow the propagation of the faith. He suggested that the CCIA should enter into consultation with the EACC and the African Churches in order to study the question further in the next years.

In closing the debate, *Dr Pusey* made special mention of the contribution of the Secretary of the Committee, Dr Scheuner.

II. Telegram of Greeting to the Acting Secretary General of the United Nations

In Business Session, the Assembly voted to send a telegram o greeting to the Acting Secretary General of the United Nations.

III. An Appeal to all Governments and Peoples

The Assembly in Business Session adopted the following Appeal

1. The Third Assembly of the World Council of Churches, a which are gathered Christians from all parts of the world, addresse this Appeal to the government and people of every nation.

2. Today, war itself is a common enemy. War is an offence t the nature of man. The future of many generations and the heritag of ages past hang in the balance. They are now easy to destroy since the actions or miscalculations of a few can bring about a holocaust. They are harder to safeguard and advance, for that require the dedicated action of all. Let there be restraint and self-denial i the things which make for war, patience and persistence in seekin to resolve the things which divide, and boldness and courage i grasping the things which make for peace.

3. To turn back from the road towards war into the paths o peace, all must renounce the threat of force. This calls for an en to the war of nerves, to pressures on small countries, to the rattlin of bombs. It is not possible to follow at the same time policies o menace and of mutual disarmament.

4. To halt the race in arms is imperative. Complete and genera disarmament is the accepted goal, and concrete steps must be take to reach it. Meanwhile, the search for a decisive first step, suc as the verified cessation of nuclear tests, should be pressed forwar despite all obstacles and setbacks.

5. To substitute reason for force and undergird the will to disarm, institutions of peace and orderly methods to effect change an to settle disputes are essential. This imposes a duty to strengthe the United Nations within the framework and spirit of the Charte All countries share this duty, whether aligned with the major powe blocs or independent of them. The non-aligned can contribut

hrough their impartiality; with others they can be champions of he principles of the Charter.

6. To build peace with justice, barriers of mutual distrust must e attacked at every level. Mutual confidence is the most precious esource in the world today: none should be wasted, more must be ound. The fundamentals of an open society are essential that conacts may freely develop, person to person and people to people. 3arriers to communication must go, not least where they divide eoples, churches, even families. Freedom of human contact, infornation, and cultural exchange is essential for the building of eace.

7. To enhance mutual trust, nations should be willing to run easonable risks for peace. For example, an equitable basis for disrmament involves, on the one hand, an acceptance of risks in an nspection and control which cannot be fool-proof, and, on the ther, the danger that inspection may exceed its stated duties. Those who would break through the vicious circle of suspicion nust dare to pioneer.

8. There is a great opportunity for constructive action in the truggle for world development. To share the benefits of civilization vith the whole of humanity is a noble and attainable objective. To ress the war against poverty, disease, exploitation, and ignorance alls for greater sacrifice and for a far greater commitment of scienific, educational, and material resources than hitherto. In this comnon task, let the peoples find a positive programme for peace, a noral equivalent for war.

9. A creative strategy for peace with justice requires universal ecognition of the claims of humanity—of all people, whatever their tatus, race, sex, or creed. Lest man's new powers be used to derade his human freedom and dignity, governments must remember hat they are the servants of their citizens and respect the worth of ach individual human being. The supreme achievement for a overnment is to enhance the dignity of man, and free him for the reative exercise of his higher powers.

10. In making this Appeal to all governments and peoples, we re constrained by obedience to Jesus Christ, the Lord of history, vho demands righteousness and mercy and is a light unto the ations and the hearts of men. For the achievement of peace with ustice, we pledge our unremitting efforts and call upon the Churches for their support in action and in prayer.

Discussion of the Appeal took place in two different sessions. Th points made in the first session were as follows:

Professor C. A. Coulson (Methodist, UK) criticized the first draft a not apt to speak immediately to ordinary people. The document was to long, the language difficult. He made especially four points:

1. There should be mention that people from all countries of th world are gathering here at Delhi and meet each other in trus and love.
2. There should be a clear reaffirmation of the doctrine that war i contrary to the mind of Christ.
3. Governments should be addressed in spiritual ways and admon ished.
4. The pledge given at the end of the Appeal should also comprise th assurance of help to governments which follow the line of th Assembly.

He moved to refer the Appeal back for redrafting.

Dr Pusey pointed out that the message had already been very muc abridged.

Dr Fry put the motion of Professor Coulson to the vote.

The motion to refer the Appeal back to the Committee was accepte

The points made in the second discussion were as follows:

Dr Pusey reported that preparations had been made by soliciting th views of church leaders around the world in case the Assembly shoul desire to issue such an Appeal. It appeared to the Committee at Ne Delhi that there was evidence of such a desire, and it therefore worke carefully on the draft originally presented. After the Assembly ha referred back the new draft, the Committee worked to include as mar as possible of the suggestions made from the floor. This redraft w now before the Assembly and Dr Pusey read it out and moved its ado tion. The motion was seconded.

Professor Coulson believed that the original draft was sent back b cause it was too long, it said the wrong things, and did not say the rig things. The new draft had the same weaknesses; it was still too lon and in particular the paragraphs 2-6 did not reflect the wonderful e perience of New Delhi, and the document went on saying things th have often been said before. In view of this Dr Coulson offered a 1 sentence alternative and read it. He believed it represented the spirit the Assembly.

ALTERNATIVE DRAFT FOR AN APPEAL TO ALL GOVERNMENTS AND PEOPLES

1. In a time of deepening crisis, the Third Assembly of the Wor Council of Churches addresses a special appeal to the governme and people of every nation.

2. We recognize that war is our common enemy, and that an end of the cold war and the growth of peace depend upon mutual faith and trust. The world's greatest problem today is to learn how such confidence may be established.
3. In our Assembly, composed of representatives from nearly every nation, with very different traditions, and with the world's tensions represented among us, we have found it possible to live and work together in friendship, co-operation and mutual trust. This experience justifies us in reminding governments and people that the problems they desire to solve are not merely political, or technological, but are also spiritual.
4. This is most certainly true of the problem of peace, when we wish to reassert our conviction that war is contrary to the mind and teaching of Christ. For this reason we desire to encourage you with the promise, which we have found true in our own experience here in New Delhi and elsewhere, that there are spiritual resources available to those who seek them.
5. These are the resources which alone make possible the growth of mutual trust, and a willingness to run reasonable risks for peace.
6. In the same way such action for peace will be the more effective if our belief is also shown by constructive action to aid those new and developing countries where the war against poverty, disease, hunger, exploitation and ignorance is one in which all the nations can combine. We call for a common crusade to share such skills and resources as we possess.
7. For the furtherance of these ends we pledge our unremitting efforts, and we want all governments to know that whenever any one of them proposes any policies that serve this purpose, all of us everywhere will support them.
8. Finally, we call upon the churches that have sent us to this Third Assembly of the World Council of Churches, to play their part, both with their prayers and by their actions.

The *Chairman* asked if Dr Coulson intended to move his wording as an alternative.

Dr Coulson agreed, and it was moved and seconded:

> that the Assembly does not approve the 'Appeal to all Governments and Peoples' in its present form, but that the following statement be adopted in its place, and sent to the Central Committee with authority to make such small drafting changes as appear desirable, but without any significant change in content.

Sir Kenneth Grubb (Church of England) wished to support the Appeal as presented by Dr Pusey on behalf of the Committee. The Committee had carefully considered a shorter version but chose the longer because today peace is the product of many forces in the world, and this fact was reflected in the longer draft of the Appeal.

Dr Herbert Gezork (American Baptist Convention) supported Sir

Kenneth Grubb and believed Professor Coulson's statement had no teeth in it and was too platitudinous.

Dr Charles Ranson (Methodist Church in Ireland) asked that decision be deferred until Professor Coulson's text could be put before the Assembly in writing and moved accordingly.

Dr Pusey said Professor Coulson's objections to the original draft had been considered and in small part used in the redraft. But the Committee believed that Professor Coulson's formulation left out things that ought to be said. To adopt Professor Coulson's motion without having time for careful verbal scrutiny would be unwise.

Dr Ranson stood by his motion that the discussion be adjourned until Professor Coulson's wording be duplicated and available. *The motion was put to the vote and defeated.*

Archbishop John of San Francisco (Russian Orthodox, USA) believed that the Appeal as presented by Dr Pusey lacked spiritual and religious strength. The name of Christ in whose light we were gathered was not mentioned. He therefore proposed that the words in paragraph 10 'Lord of history' be altered to read 'Christ, light of the world and Lord of history'.

Sir Francis Ibiam (Presbyterian, Nigeria) wished to support Professor Coulson's formulation as being neither too short nor omitting anything of value.

Bishop Chandu Ray (Anglican, Pakistan) moved that the Assembly be asked to express its mind between the two drafts. He thought Professor Coulson's formulation had nothing new in it.

Professor Russell Chandran (Church of South India) believed Professor Coulson's amendment was the weaker of the two and commended the Appeal as presented by Dr Pusey.

Dr Coulson, replying to the debate, believed that people would not spare time to read the Committee's draft, which was so like previous ones.

Dr Coulson's motion was put to the vote and lost.

Dr Pusey, answering Archbishop John, pointed to the phrase 'a light unto the nations' and asked that no change be made.

Archbishop John asked that the name of Jesus Christ be included.

Archbishop John's motion to insert the name of Jesus Christ in paragraph 10, *being put to the vote, was carried. The Appeal as redrafted by the Committee and amended by the Assembly was then adopted.*

IV. Action on Angola

The Assembly in Business Session noted and associated itself with the observations in the first two paragraphs of the following statement and adopted the recommendation framed in the third paragraph.

1. The Committee on the CCIA noted that the Chairman and Director of the CCIA after consultation with officers of the WCC and the IMC issued a statement on the subject of Angola on June 5,

1961; and that the Executive Committee of the WCC also adopted a resolution concerning Angola in June 1961. (Both of these statements are quoted below.) The Committee commends the officers of the CCIA and the Executive Committee for their prompt action in this very serious matter and associates itself with their statements.

2. The Committee recognizes from the debate that the Assembly as a whole has a deep concern regarding the serious situation in Angola. It believes that the debate and the close vote showed both anxiety lest nothing be said by the Assembly on this important matter and reluctance to take an isolated action against a single nation when there are other very serious situations which claim attention.

3. The Committee now recommends that the proposal originally submitted in regard to the situation in Angola and the record of the debate held on December 2, together with a report of the current proceedings on the subject, be transmitted to the CCIA for further consideration and urgent action, and also in so far as the work on relief and rehabilitation continues to be involved, to the Division of Inter-Church Aid, Refugee and World Service.

Appendix to the Action on Angola

A. Statement of the Chairman and Director of the CCIA made concerning Angola, June 5, 1961:

> Many churches and individual Christians are alarmed by the serious conditions which have developed in Angola. The reports of wanton destruction of human life and the accompanying violation of essential human rights have shocked world public opinion. There is indeed danger that the situation will further deteriorate if justice is not wisely served. In these circumstances we as officers of the Commission of the Churches on International Affairs would be failing in our duty if we remained silent. We therefore call attention to certain general statements which have been made on several occasions by the World Council of Churches and our Commission, and we suggest that they are immediately relevant to Angola. We express the hope that action along these lines will be promptly initiated.
>
> In face of any refusal to recognize for the people of Angola the right to determine their own political future, we say: 'the legitimate right of the self-determination of peoples must be recognized. Specific assurance of independence or self-government should be given and administering authorities should take reasonable risks in speeding progress towards this goal.'
>
> In face of every failure to build the competence necessary for independence or self-government, we say: 'When nations are still subject to minority or foreign rule, they must be allowed to move swiftly but

with adequate preparation to a form of government in which persons of whatever racial background have their rightful place.'

In face of reported violence, compounded in its severity by acts of retribution, we say to all involved and especially to those who have been party to terrorism and murder: 'Christian concern for the worth of man involves insistence on respect for the Rule of Law, as essential to a just society. This includes freedom from arbitrary arrest, an independent judiciary and public trial, the right of habeas corpus and all that is involved in equality before the law for all persons and all communities.'

B. Statement of the Executive Committee made in June 1961 concerning Angola:

The Executive Committee of the World Council of Churches is deeply disturbed at the reports it has received regarding the present tragedy in Angola.

It (1) deplores the mounting evidence of a rapidly deteriorating situation as a result of which large numbers of Angolans are being deprived of life and liberty;

(2) appeals to the Government of Portugal in the name of humanity and of the Christian principles so long professed in Portugal, to refrain from deliberate actions involving the death and maiming of thousands of Africans, including women and children, and the attack on those with education and gifts of leadership, as well as the widespread destruction of property;

(3) is concerned that by its present policy the Government will inevitably forfeit the sympathy and respect of other nations concerned for the welfare of Africa and its peoples;

(4) associates itself with the statement issued by the officers of the Commission of the Churches on International Affairs on June 5, 1961, which drew attention to the need to apply in Angola the principles of self-determination and the need for the rapid training of indigenous leadership and the establishment of the Rule of Law;

(5) requests the Commission of the Churches on International Affairs to make representation accordingly to the Portuguese Government and at its discretion to the Commission recently appointed by the United Nations;

(6) notes that already the Division of Inter-Church Aid and Service to Refugees has sent aid to the tens of thousands of Angolan refugees now in the Congo, and requests the Division to continue and extend this operation;

(7) requests its member churches, of whose deep concern it has been made aware, to press upon their governments the urgency of the situation, and to remember constantly in prayer their fellow-Christians in both Portugal and her overseas provinces, and all those involved in the present emergency.

Discussion in connection with action on Angola took place in two sessions. The first discussion centred upon a draft resolution which had been presented by the Committee.

DRAFT RESOLUTION ON ANGOLA

The Third Assembly of the World Council of Churches in session in New Delhi cognizant of the situation in Angola, desires to appeal to the government of Portugal in the name of humanity and of all that the Christian conscience cherishes to bring to an end promptly and without delay the continuing tragedy in that land. We are deeply grieved at the acts of repression by Portuguese authorities over groups and peoples in Angola and at the wide-spread violence in the land. We are further grieved that a nation with a great Christian tradition should have so departed from the pursuit of human values that it stands accused at the bar of world opinion.

Believing that the fate of Angola is of international import, the Assembly urges Portugal to take immediate steps so that the legitimate rights and political aspirations of the indigenous African people of Angola may be met expeditiously.

The Assembly draws the attention of member Churches to the large number of refugees from Angola and urges them to treat the work of relief among these refugees as of urgent priority and to step-up and extend relief measures already undertaken.

The Assembly notes with sorrow that many Angolan pastors and laymen as well as Christian missionaries in Angola have been subjected to great difficulties in their legitimate work of ministry to a people in great distress. The Assembly urges Portugal to restore to missionary bodies working in Angola such facilities as would enable them to continue their vocation in freedom.

The restoration of order so imperative in Angola for a peaceful and constructive settlement of the present conflict, should be achieved by humane methods. The Assembly requests the CCIA to continue its efforts in co-operation with other international agencies to bring a speedy end to the tragedy in Angola.

The main points of the discussion on this draft resolution were as follows:

The Rev. E. G. T. Madge (Baptist, UK) approved the resolution. He gave a detailed analysis of the situation which had developed in Angola and of the methods employed by the Portuguese Government.

Mr Peter M. Kirk, MP (Church of England), spoke against the resolution. He expressed his horror at the deeds of Portugal but asked: How many other countries had to share in the blame? The resolution seemed to him to pick out Portugal as a weak point, condemning a country not represented in this Assembly. Portugal would be judged unheard. Mr Kirk pointed to the fact that Angola was a recent case. Was it really advisable to single out one more recent case and be silent on others?

Mr Bonino (Methodist Church, Argentina) declared himself for the resolution. The situation in Angola justified such an action. He declared himself satisfied with the alteration in paragraph 4 citing pastors of Angola besides missionaries.

The Rev. Professor R. Obermüller (Evangelical German Synod, Argentina) was of the opinion that what was said about Angola could also be said about the situation in Berlin and East Germany. He opposed the resolution.

Mr Oswald H. Clarke (Church of England) opposed the resolution. The Assembly did not, as stated, have full information about the situation in Angola. It would not be advisable to speak of Angola alone and overlook other similar situations. Why not refer also to Algeria and Berlin? The speaker feared that here was an attempt to play to the gallery in an Asian country.

The Rev. T. E. F. Honey (United Church of Canada) moved to refer the resolution back to the Committee.

Dr Pusey spoke against this motion. The CCIA has been fully aware of the facts of the situation and had already taken action as from the CCIA as well as from the Executive Committee. The Committee of the Assembly had voted for the resolution by an overwhelming majority.

The motion of the Rev. T. E. F. Honey was put to the vote and lost.

Bishop do Amaral (Methodist, Brazil): Why not include Russia and Cuba in this resolution?

Commander Herdman (Church of Ireland) opposed the resolution. He emphasized the great difficulties which the Portuguese Government faced in Angola.

Präses E. Schlieper (Lutheran, Brazil) raised the following points against the resolution:

1. It would have an inevitably bad effect on the situation of the small Protestant minority in Portugal.
2. It seemed to him unacceptable that the Assembly single out one country without naming others.

Dr Fry asked the Assembly whether it would like to refer back the resolution. (Voices: No! Vote!)

Bishop N. S. Booth (Methodist Church, Congo) underlined the facts given already on the dangerous situation in Angola.

Sir Kenneth Grubb moved to close the debate.

The motion was accepted.

The resolution was then put to vote and there voted

Yes: 179
No: 177

Dr Fry suggested, following voices from the floor of the Assembly, that in view of the very narrow majority the matter should be referred back to the Committee.

This suggestion was generally approved.

In the *second discussion,* the following points were made:

Dr Pusey introduced the supplementary report and said his Committee, after the previous narrow vote on the motion on Angola, were concerned lest the action suggested that the Assembly was not deeply oncerned about events in Angola, or was not certain of its authority n such matters. The new report was intended to make the position lear. Dr Pusey moved that the Assembly approve the proposed method f proceeding.

The Chairman said that approval would imply associating the ssembly with the previous actions of the officers of CCIA and Executive Committee of WCC concerning the situation in Angola.

Mr. C. P. Mathew (Mar Thoma, India) suggested that the word similar' be omitted from the last line of paragraph 2 of the report. If he Angola situation had many counterparts, why pick it out at all? The peculiar nature of the Angolan situation required that on the fourth ine of paragraph 2 the words 'on this important matter' be replaced by on an issue involving wanton destruction of human life as government olicy'. He so moved.

Mr M. M. Thomas (Mar Thoma, India) supported this amendment.

Dr Pusey believed the point was covered in the motion carried previously, and in the action of the WCC Executive, but would defer to the vish of the Assembly.

Bishop Chandu Ray (Anglican, Pakistan) believed that the new words roposed distorted the whole meaning of the paragraph. The record of he debates on the subject in the Assembly already covered the point.

The amendment being put to the vote was lost.

Mr. C. P. Mathew moved the excision of the word 'similar' from the ast line of paragraph 2.

The amendment being put to the vote was carried, nem. con.

Bishop N. S. Booth (Methodist, Congo) then asked for unanimous upport of the new report as thus amended. He referred to the facts of ersecution and hardship known to all. But in particular he asked the ssembly to realize the importance of its platform for this kind of ction which the Portuguese might heed. He spoke also of the right of he Assembly to be specific in its corporate witness on such matters.

Principal M. Wakatama (Methodist, Southern Rhodesia) said that ince the Portuguese authorities were directing attacks on the Church, he Church had a right and duty to speak, and to speak quickly before t might be too late.

Commissioner R. J. Woods (Salvation Army, UK) proposed different pening words to avoid the suggestion that Portugal was being picked ut. In answer to the chairman, Mr Woods agreed to withdraw his proosal and transmit his views to CCIA along with the other material eferred to in the report.

The Rev. E. Rogers (Methodist, UK) asked if the debate was to be e-opened on the merits of the Angola situation itself.

Dr Pusey said he interpreted the reference to transmitting the record f the previous debate as including the vote.

The Rev. J. W. Roxburgh (Church of England) as a voter against the arlier resolution, welcomed the new draft as no longer isolating Portugal.

Bishop Macario Ga (Philippine Independent Catholic Church) speaking neither for nor against the motion, believed that the position of the

WCC was so well known that it was superfluous and unnecessary to come out publicly in such a delicate matter as Angola.

Dr Pusey concluded by hoping the whole proceedings had in no way suggested that the Assembly had no right or duty to speak on such an issue as Angola.

The motion that the Assembly associate itself with the previous statements of the CCIA and the Executive Committee was put to the vote and adopted.

17 · REPORT OF THE COMMITTEE ON FINANCE

The following Report of the Committee on Finance was received by the Assembly in Business Session.

[Since the Report of the Committee on Finance covers a series of separate questions which were presented item by item to the Assembly, the report is reproduced below section by section and the record of discussion and action follows each section of the report. The text of the Report of the Central Committee on Programme and Finance, to which frequent reference is made, is reproduced on pages 344-368 below.

I. THE BUDGETS OF THE WORLD COUNCIL OF CHURCHES

'1. Section V of the Report of the Central Committee on Programme and Finance, which bears the above title, was referred by the Assembly to the Finance Committee. That chapter covers the most important items considered by the Finance Committee and those items will therefore be dealt with first in this report.'

Bishop A. K. Warren (Chairman of the Committee) explained the careful procedures of consultation and scrutiny by which the proposals concerning the General Budget had been prepared and examined and, in presenting the following section of the report, read in full paragraphs 3-10.

(*a*) *General Budget of the World Council of Churches*

'2. The Finance Committee examined the report on the operations under General Budget from 1954 to 1960 (*Evanston to New Delhi*, pages 167-8), the Financial Report for 1960, and the proposals in the report on Programme and Finance (paragraphs 83-86), bearing in mind that in giving general approval to Sections II, III and IV of that report, the Assembly had accepted the proposals in Section III concerning the organizational pattern for the period following the Assembly.

3. The contributions by member churches to the General Budget rose from $265,770 in 1949 to $314,720 in 1954 and $516,942 in 1960 and are expected to rise to approximately $530,000 in 1961. Throughout the period since the Evanston Assembly in 1954, operations have been so conducted that expenses have been kept within the level of available resources and the planned annual allocations of $20,000 have been made in each year both to the General Reserve and to the Reserve for the expenses of the Third Assembly.

4. The report on Programme and Finance proposes a model General Budget for the period following the Third Assembly totalling $751,200 per annum. This implies the need for an increase of approximately 47 per cent in member church contributions to the General Budget. Member churches were advised by the Central Committee of the probability that such an increase would be requested and were asked to take the necessary action to enable a response in 1962 if such a request should be made by the Assembly.

5. The response of the member churches has been encouraging. The report on Programme and Finance implied a need for total contributions of $727,200 as compared with $516,942 received in 1960 and approximately $530,000 expected in 1961. On the basis of reports already received from member churches, it can be forecast that contributions will, if an increase of 47 per cent is requested by the Assembly, rise to about $695,000 in 1962 and to about $710,000 in 1963. Those estimates will be exceeded to the extent that (*a*) member churches which have not yet notified action on this question may increase their contributions, and (*b*) new member churches contribute.

6. The Finance Committee reviewed the expenditure side of the General Budget proposed in the report on Programme and Finance for the period following the Third Assembly (Annexe I). After studying the proposed expenditure budget item by item, the Finance Committee concluded that it represents a sound and justified expression of the probable cost of the approved programme and structure. It was, however, noted with concern that rising costs had already absorbed a large part of the suggested provision of $25,000 in the model budget for contingencies, whereas continuing increases in costs must be foreseen as probable in the light of experience in the past period. Experience in many Western countries suggests

an inflationary rise of 2-3 per cent per annum in prices and expenses.

7. The Finance Committee received the following recommendations from the Policy Reference Committee which would imply additions to the model General Budget:

(*a*) the addition of an Associate to the Executive Secretary of the New York Office of the World Council (estimated cost $9,000 per annum on the General Budget, plus an equal amount to be covered from the budget of the US Conference for the World Council of Churches); and

(*b*) the addition of a second Assistant General Secretary to give particular attention, under the direction of the General Secretary, to the participation of the Orthodox churches in the life and programme of the World Council (estimated cost $14,000 per annum).

Thus, there seems to be a reasonable prospect that the income indicated as needed in the report on Programme and Finance may be realized but the proposed model annual Budget of $751,200 needs to be increased by $23,000 to cover the above items and its adequacy for the suggested programme is already endangered by rising costs.

8. The Finance Committee recalled the request by the Central Committee to each member church to give serious consideration to the adequacy of its present contribution to the General Budget in relation to its size and economic strength and to the giving of other member churches. The conviction was strongly expressed by several members of the Finance Committee representing member churches in Europe and other continents that the contributions of member churches in areas other than North America should be substantially increased with a view both to providing needed additional income and to achieving the oft expressed objective of securing a better relationship between the total contributions of the member churches in North America and those in other areas. The Finance Committee urges all the member churches concerned seriously to consider this question in the light of Section IV of the Report on Programme and Finance (paragraphs 62-70) and believes that the additional income which should result, plus that which will be received from new member churches, may raise the total revenue to the level needed to cover the proposed programme of operations.

9. The Finance Committee calls the attention of the Assembly to

the fact that the General Budget proposed in the Report on Programme and Finance for the period following the Third Assembly (Annexe I) is to be regarded as a model intended to show average costs and general relationships and not as an actual budget for any given year; it is the responsibility of the Central Committee to establish the annual budget for each year. The Finance Committee recognized the validity of the statement in the Report on Programme and Finance 'that the Assembly, meeting but once in six years, cannot fix a realistic budget for the whole period between Assemblies and that the Central Committee must be trusted to recommend such changes as economic conditions may require and as may be acceptable to the member churches'.

10. The Finance Committee recommends:

(*a*) that the Assembly approve the expenditure side of the model General Budget for the period following the Third Assembly totalling $751,200 proposed in the Report on Programme and Finance (Annexe I), with the addition of $23,000 for the two items indicated in paragraph 7 above;

(*b*) that the Assembly request all member churches to make an increase of at least 47 per cent in contributions to the General Budget, beginning in 1962;

(*c*) that the Assembly, recognizing that an increase of 47 per cent in contributions will not be adequate to cover the total proposed expenditure budget, call upon each member church to give serious consideration to the adequacy of its present contribution in relation to its size and economic strength and to the giving of other member churches and, where appropriate, to make an increase greater than the 47 per cent increase requested of all member churches; and

(*d*) that the revenue side of the model General Budget for the period following the Third Assembly (page 366) be raised by $23,000 to match the revised expenditure level, by increasing the item for contributions from member churches from $727,200 to $750,200, in anticipation of additional income in response to the request under (*c*) above and also from contributions from new member churches.'

Bishop Warren moved the recommendations in paragraphs 10 above and called upon each delegate to take the appeals in recommendations (*b*) and (*c*) personally and seriously, to see how much his own church was contributing and to consider whether that contribution represented a fair share. He expressed the conviction that many delegates would recognize that the World Council had been leaning too much and for too long on the churches of North America and that the churches of other areas had not done enough. He expressed the hope that all who reached that conclusion would go home with the determination to secure action to make an adequate increase in the contributions of their churches.

Canon H. L. Puxley (Anglican, Canada) asked whether the large increase in the budget for the Division of Studies resulted mainly from integration. Bishop Warren and Mr Northam replied explaining that this was not the case. In reply to a further question from Canon Puxley, Mr Northam explained at some length the reasons for the increased budget for the Division of Studies, giving details of the increase in programme and staff involved and recalling that the increase resulted from the agreed programme and structure as set out in Section III of the Report on Programme and Finance, which had been submitted to the Assembly at an earlier session and had already been adopted by the Assembly.

The Assembly voted to adopt the recommendations in paragraph 10.

In introducing the next section of the report, which is set out below, Bishop Warren commented that he was sure that the magnitude and significance of the operations of the Division of Inter-Church Aid and Service to Refugees would be of considerable interest to the Assembly and might be a revelation to some delegates.

(*b*) *Authorized budgets raised and administered separately:*

Division of Inter-Church Aid and Service to Refugees

'11. The Finance Committee examined the report on the operations under the Service Programme Budget from 1954 to 1960 (*Evanston to New Delhi*, pages 169-71), the Financial Report for 1960, and the proposals in the Report on Programme and Finance (paragraphs 87-9 and Annexe II).

12. Support for the Service Programme has risen from $636,058

in 1952 to $723,179 in 1954 and to $928,735 in 1960. The budget for 1962 has been established at $1,200,000. Operations between 1954 and 1960 were conducted within the limits of available resources. The report of the Committee on the Division will reveal the highly significant work which has been accomplished under this budget, which covers the salaries of the divisional staff and the cost of administration, travel, etc., and such items of programme as the churches desire to carry out co-operatively through the Division, e.g. refugee service, scholarships and fraternal workers, health programme, ecumenical youth services programme, etc.

13. The largest item within the Service Programme is the Service to Refugees which, during the period 1954-60, received annual allocations from the Service Programme budget varying from $425,000 to $525,229 and was able, on the basis of these resources, to secure additional grants from other sources enabling it to conduct an operation the total cost of which has varied between $1,800,000 and $3,160,000 per annum. Here, again, operations over the seven years have been conducted within the level of available resources, though there was a period in 1954-6 when the operation ran into heavy temporary deficit, by reason of the delayed receipt of anticipated income. In addition to the normal activities, valuable additional help to refugees has been and will be made possible by receipts under the World Refugee Year campaign, totalling nearly $5,000,000.

14. Apart from the foregoing activities under the Service Programme budget, the Division conducts other substantial operations. Resources handled by the Division for normal inter-church aid activities have varied in annual total from $800,000 to $2,750,000. The total inter-church aid activities of which the Division is advised, including help in cash and in kind and gifts sent through the Division and direct, were in 1960 of the order of $83,000,000.

15. The Finance Committee felt that the growth in, and the present magnitude of, the financial operations of the Division would be a source of interest and gratification to the Assembly. The policy reported to and approved by the Evanston Assembly in 1954, under which the Central Committee depends in the first instance upon the Administrative Committee of the Division of Inter-Church Aid and Service to Refugees for detailed examination and administrative control of the Service Programme, has been continued throughout the period under review.

Commission and Division of World Mission and Evangelism

16. The Finance Committee received a report on the operations of the International Missionary Council during the past years (IMC Report, pages 44-7) and examined the proposals in the report on Programme and Finance (paragraph 90 and Annexe III) concerning the budget for the Commission and Division for the period following the Third Assembly. The support for this budget is provided primarily by councils affiliated to or in consultation with the Commission. The tentative budget printed in the *Work Book* amounts in total to $201,150; the 1962 budget recommended by the IMC Assembly, at its meeting immediately prior to the Assembly, is slightly higher at $207,900.

17. An IMC Project Fund was initiated in July 1959 to give a broader base and greater flexibility to the operation and to permit councils with special interest in projects consonant with the general programme and policy, to provide special resources for the realization of such projects. In the first two years additional resources totalling about $90,000 were received under the Projects Fund.

Commission of the Churches on International Affairs

18. The Finance Committee examined a report on the operations of the CCIA from 1955-60 (*Evanston to New Delhi*, pages 172-3) and the proposals in the Report on Programme and Finance (paragraph 91 and Annexe IV). Until 1961, the CCIA has been supported by grants from the International Missionary Council and the World Council, the latter grants coming both from the General Budget and from the Service Programme Budget of the Division of Inter-Church Aid and Service to Refugees. The operations of the CCIA have been conducted within the level of available resources. Total expenses rose from nearly $80,000 in 1955 to nearly $88,000 in 1960 and will amount to about $98,000 in 1961. Following integration, support will come from the three World Council Budgets—the General Budget and the budgets for the Service Programme and for the Commission and Division of World Mission and Evangelism, and the total level is expected to be about $110,000 per annum.

19. The Finance Committee recommends:

that the Assembly approve the proposal in the Report on Programme and Finance that the budgets of the Division of Inter-Church Aid and Service to Refugees, of the Commission and

Division of World Mission and Evangelism and of the Commission of the Churches on International Affairs be raised and administered separately, in accordance with Rule VIII(2) of the revised Rules of the World Council of Churches.'

Bishop Warren then moved and *the Assembly voted to adopt the recommendation in paragraph* 19 *above.*

In presenting the next three sections of the report, Bishop Warren read paragraphs 20 and 21 and summarized the information in paragraphs 22-6.

II. Programme Project Activities Related to General Budget

'20. The Finance Committee reviewed the principles established by the Central Committee to control appeals for special support for activities related to the General Budget but not financed within that budget (paragraphs 71-8 of the Report on Programme and Finance), and also the record of projects financed under those principles during the period since 1954 (*Evanston to New Delhi,* pages 168-9). The Finance Committee was in agreement both with the principles and with the reasoning underlying the procedures which have been developed and noted that those principles have already been reaffirmed by the action of the Assembly in receiving and giving general approval to Sections II, III and IV of the Report on Programme and Finance.

21. The Finance Committee was informed of the programme project items which had been submitted by Assembly committees to the Policy Reference Committee and approved by the latter, subject to the observance of the above-mentioned principles governing appeals for support and subject to assurance of adequate support before commitments are entered into, and was in agreement with the actions taken.'

III. Reserves

'22. The General Reserve of the World Council of Churches has been raised from about $5,000 in 1948 to nearly $128,000 in 1954 and to nearly $268,000 in 1961, by annual allocations of $20,000 from current income, as directed by the Amsterdam Assembly in 1948 and reaffirmed by the Evanston Assembly in 1954. The Finance

Committee felt that, although the position has clearly been strengthened considerably since 1948, the reserve remains modest and the maintenance of an annual allocation of $20,000 in the period until the Fourth Assembly as proposed in the Report on Programme and Finance is clearly reasonable.

23. The Programme and Finance Report proposes that, whereas the annual allocations to the expenses of the next Assembly have been at the rate of $20,000 during the first two inter-Assembly periods, the amount should be raised to $30,000 per annum in the period between the Third and Fourth Assemblies. This increase in annual allocations would create a larger reserve towards the expenses of the Fourth Assembly than was available for the Second and Third Assemblies, but the reserve is not expected to be adequate to cover the total cost of the Fourth Assembly and some special fund-raising effort will therefore again be necessary.

24. The implementation of the proposals in the two preceding paragraphs is implicit in the adoption, recommended earlier in this report, of the model General Budget for the period following the Third Assembly.

25. The Finance Committee reviewed the other reserves of the World Council such as the reserves for repairs to properties at Malagnou and Bossey and the Investment Fluctuation Fund.'

IV. Investment Portfolios

'26. The Finance Committee reviewed the investment portfolios maintained by the World Council and was in agreement with the principles adopted governing their administration. The portfolios are for the investment of the credits held in the General Reserve, in the reserve for the expenses of the next Assembly and in the Headquarters Properties Fund and there is also a Revolving Portfolio for the investment of current liquid resources.'

Bishop Warren then presented the following section of the report and paragraph 29, which records the action taken by the host churches in India, was received with loud applause.

V. Revenue and Expenditure on the New Delhi Assembly Budget

'27. The budget for the expenses of the New Delhi Assembly totals $325,000. The annual allocations of $20,000 from current income towards this budget have provided a sum of $140,000. The further resources needed were sought by an appeal to member churches to take an offering in connection with the use of the pre-Assembly study booklet. Some member churches found it possible to take action in accordance with that suggestion and others made a special contribution from central church resources. Special thanks are due to all member churches which, in one way or another, responded to the appeal. In addition, the sales of the pre-Assembly study booklet, of which about 600,000 copies have now been published in thirty-three languages, will result in a substantial profit. Total income of $325,000 is now virtually assured.

28. The expenditure budget included a provision for contingencies and unforeseen expenses which, in the light of experience, may prove to have been inadequate, but it is hoped that total final expenses may none the less be within the limits of available income and that the accounts may be closed without deficit. Final accounts will, of course, be presented to the Central Committee.

29. Our host churches in India have raised a significant sum—at present over Rp. 40,000—for the expenses of the local arrangements Committee and for various kindly acts of hospitality. The gratitude of the Assembly will certainly be expressed at a later point in these sessions for the many ways in which we have been welcomed and cared for by our host churches, but this financial aspect calls for comment in this report.'

Bishop Warren then read in full the following section of the report:

VI. Headquarters Properties

'30. The progress made in raising the Headquarters Properties Fund has been reported separately to the Assembly. The Finance Committee briefly reviewed the position in respect of receipts, probable further contributions, the progress of construction plans and estimated costs.

31. The Finance Committee wishes to draw the attention of the Assembly to one particular and generous gift and recommends:

that the Assembly express its special appreciation of the generous gift of the family of the late *Mr Thomas J. Watson* to provide a library in his memory at the new headquarters building of the Council in Geneva. Mr Watson was an elder of the Brick Presbyterian Church in New York. He had shown his interest in the international association of the churches in many ways, including his donation of the use of simultaneous translation equipment for the First and Second Assemblies of the World Council. He had visited the First Assembly at Amsterdam in 1948, seen the usefulness of his gift, and had taken satisfaction in it.

32. The Finance Committee noted that the estimated costs exceed gifts received or assured up to the opening of the Assembly by from $400,000-$600,000. The Central Committee had decided to withhold approval of the commencement of construction work on one of the three wings of office buildings, since resources adequate to cover the full costs were not assured. This matter will be reviewed and decided by the new Central Committee in the light of any new information available at the close of the Assembly. The Finance Committee recommends:

(*a*) that the Assembly urge any member churches which have not yet made or secured a contribution to the headquarters buildings to seek to do so, in order that the new headquarters may represent the fruits of an effort by all member churches and the countries in which they are placed; and

(*b*) that participants in the Assembly seek to assist by giving or securing further contributions—from individuals or from foundations or from commerce and industry—so that the building project and the equipment of the new headquarters may be completed.'

The recommendation in paragraph 31 *expressing thanks to the family of the late Mr Thomas J. Watson was adopted with prolonged applause.*

Before moving the recommendations in paragraph 32, Bishop Warren moved the following two additional resolutions:

(i) that the Assembly express gratitude for all contributions to the Headquarters Properties Fund which have been received or promised from churches. individuals, foundations and commerce and industry, and to those in all countries who have assisted in securing those gifts; and

(ii) that the Assembly express its heart-felt appreciation of the devoted service given by Bishop Sherrill as Chairman of the International Committee for the Headquarters Properties Fund, recognizing that the encouraging progress made towards raising the total sum needed is due to his enthusiastic efforts.

The Assembly voted to adopt recommendation (i) *and voted enthusiastically and with prolonged applause to adopt recommendation* (ii).

Bishop Warren then moved and *the Assembly voted to adopt the two recommendations in paragraph* 32.

Bishop Warren then presented the final section of the report, explaining that this section was presented for information and required no action.

VII. Salaries and Retirement Fund

'33. The Finance Committee received a report in some detail on salary scales and allowances and on the principles which are basic to a revised scheme, which is to be recommended from the old Central Committee to the new Central Committee. The Finance Committee wishes to advise the Assembly that it is satisfied that the revised scheme, developed after careful and extended study, represents a justified but modest improvement in terms of remuneration.

34. A scheme for pensions for retired staff and for widows and orphans is at an advanced stage of development and will be presented for approval to the Central Committee when finalized. It is a scheme designed to meet as well as possible the needs of the international staff of the World Council, many of whom serve the World Council only for a limited period of time. Provision for the financing of the scheme has been made from current income since July 1957 at the level provisionally indicated as necessary by the actuarial advisers.'

Bishop Warren paid a tribute to Mr Northam and his lay advisers and reported that the Finance Committee wished the member churches to know what a debt of gratitude the World Council owes to them.

Bishop Warren then moved and *the Assembly voted to adopt the report as a whole.*

The Chairman, Dr Payne, spoke in the name of the whole Assembly to express thanks to Dr E. C. Blake for the devoted work and leadership which he had given over the past seven years as

Chairman of the Finance Committee and of the Committee on Programme and Finance, pointing out that the progress made and the present sound financial position are in important measure due to his devoted service. The Assembly expressed its agreement with this tribute by applause.

18 · REPORT OF THE COMMITTEE ON THE DEPARTMENT OF INFORMATION

The following Report of the Committee on the Information Department was received by the Assembly in Business Session, generally approved, and transmitted to the Central Committee.

Introduction

1. The Department of Information was established by the action of the Evanston Assembly. It is directly responsible to the General Secretariat. It works in close co-operation with all departments and divisions of the World Council of Churches. In the seven years since Evanston a sound basis for future development has been laid. In some parts of its work, especially in photography and the design of publications, it has become an acknowledged pace-setter. The Committee wishes to pay a warm tribute to the work of the first Director, the Rev. John Garrett.

2. In the years after New Delhi, the Information Department, like the whole WCC, will face a new situation. The accession of new member churches, especially in Africa and Eastern Europe, the integration of the IMC with the WCC, and the developing life of the regional conferences in East Asia and Africa, will increase the need for ecumenical information in parts of the world where hitherto the Department has been relatively inactive. The 600,000 circulation of the pre-Assembly booklet *Jesus Christ, the Light of the World* and the unprecedented volume of world-wide coverage of the Assembly in press, radio and television mean both that the WCC's audience in the churches has been widened, and also that there is much increased interest on the part of the world at large.

3. The WCC thus finds itself no longer addressing an audience that is mainly of the informed and the keenly interested. We now have effective access, perhaps for the first time, to the local church. But if the man in the pew and the man in the street are to hear what the WCC says, all WCC agencies which communicate with the church or general public will need to pay renewed and far-reaching attention to the Evanston Assembly's request that 'it

should be the aim of the Department to render theological and other technical vocabularies intelligible without dilution and distortion'.

II. General Policy

The nature of ecumenical information

4. The primary need and demand of the member churches is for factual information about the activities and policies of the WCC and of the member churches themselves. The simpler and shorter such news items are the more likely they are to secure a wide and undistorted coverage all over the world. But factual information of this kind which is the principal content of any issue of the *Ecumenical Press Service* is only a beginning in the task of 'promoting the growth of ecumenical consciousness in the members of all churches' (WCC Constitution). More complete interpretative material of wide variety is also needed. If information is to be truly Christian it must tell of both the failures and the achievements of church life. If it is to be truly ecumenical it must help churches and their members to meet one another and help one another in mutual service, inspiration and correction. WCC information must be sufficiently diverse and adaptable to reach and be of value to *all* parts of the Church and the world. The word 'information' in the title of the Department describes only a part of its work. The inclusive task of the Department is to try to communicate to the world and to the churches what the life and mission of the Church are in the middle of the twentieth century.

The clientèle of the Department

5. The Department seeks to communicate with many different clientèle. Distinctions need to be drawn

—between larger churches with well-developed information services and smaller (often minority, or younger) churches without them; the needs of the latter may often be unexpressed.

—within the church public, between those who are theologically equipped; those who are informed about and committed to the ecumenical movement; and committed Christians who have hardly been touched by the ecumenical movement. (Those in ministerial training represent a constituency of particular importance.)

—between the secular press and broadcasting agencies on the

one hand and the religious press and broadcasting agencies on the other.

The Department has also to deal with specialized agencies in government and social service.

The task of the Department of Information

6. (*a*) To distribute news about the life of the churches and of the WCC and to interpret this life and work to the churches. This activity must be conducted as dialogue between churches rather than monologue about ecumenism. Such a conversation should issue not only in understanding but in intercession and thanksgiving. The long and honourable history of the missionary movement includes a deep experience of fostering in sending churches this spiritual partnership with younger churches which can transcend the barriers of distance and culture. This partnership needs to be widened and made many-sided.

(*b*) To help churches to develop the relevant type of information service that each requires; and to train and assist their specialists.

(*c*) To study the mass media of communication (press, film, radio, television, etc.) and stimulate churches and other departments and divisions of the WCC to make effective and responsible use of these powerful means of shaping men and society.

(*d*) To advise the WCC about its strategy and programme of publications from the point of view of their adaptation to the needs both of the churches' members and of the general public, and in co-operation with the WCC publications office to promote the circulation of all WCC publications.

Forms of action

7. Two elements define what the Department can do. One is a matter of principle; the other is arbitrary. Principle requires that nothing should be done by the Department which can be done more economically or relevantly by some other body of professional competence. The limitations imposed by finance on the other hand on what the staff can undertake are arbitrary, and are severe.

The forms of action of the Department are therefore:

Production, where this is an obvious responsibility of the WCC.

Stimulation of the work of the churches by the example of high standards, by technical advice and by the experience of the Department.

Co-operation and co-ordination of existing work where this will be of value.

Assistance to national and regional councils and churches in carrying on their own information programmes.

Assistance to the WCC and its divisions and departments in ensuring suitable press and broadcasting coverage at conferences and other meetings.

Themes

8. In recent years the Department has concentrated on news and interpretation of the WCC in general, on the work of DICARWS, and on the Third Assembly. There is now need:

(*a*) to give more attention to interpreting churches to each other, seeking to ensure that attention is drawn not only to the creative 'signs of renewal' of the small minority, but also to what is typical of the life of the churches.

(*b*) to develop the field of ecumenical missionary information in collaboration with the newly formed Division of World Mission and Evangelism.

(*c*) to consider how the work of other Divisions than DICARWS and DWME can be presented and interpreted effectively in the churches.

(*d*) to produce material on special subjects on which the member churches request help. Noted in the discussion as possibilities were:

(i) simple statistical information about the churches, especially for the ordinary layman who commonly has access only to information about his own church and possibly its missionary work, and has no idea how these relate to the whole;

(ii) the churches and the race problem;

(iii) the churches and international affairs;

(iv) relations of member churches with the Church of Rome and modern developments within the Church of Rome.

III. Press and Publications

Needs of the various regions and churches

9. The most significant demand now comes from Asia, Africa

and Latin America, and is for simple material in the local languages. Material produced in Geneva is too often in a form and style unsuitable for a particular country. The assistance of the Department is most wisely invested in measures which enable churches to produce their own publications, aided by the stimulus and example of Geneva.

10. The question of the WCC's official languages now calls for reconsideration. Many of the WCC's materials are available only in English. The provision of many more of them in French and German is very desirable. The addition of Spanish and Russian to the official languages would immensely increase the areas and populations covered.

11. It is to be noted that the Department's 'language' of design and photography is acceptable everywhere, and is readily intelligible to local congregations of uneducated people. It is also to be noted that some of the Department's services are not very well known and need more active promotion.

The Ecumenical Press Service

12. EPS is issued in three separate editions in English, French and German. It is widely appreciated and used, particularly in Europe and North America. A beginning has been made in Spanish. There is need, however, (*a*) of more short and simple news items which can be easily reprinted in translation without distortion and (*b*) of important documents being made available *in extenso* and (*c*) longer articles from time to time on particular churches, or problems of the Church. Above all, the Department needs to be able to get the news from the churches. Closer co-operation with national or regional bodies such as the East Asia Christian Conference would help to solve the problem, but there is probably no final solution short of a network of trained journalists acting as local correspondents and receiving a modest fee for their expenditure of time and energy as well as their expenses. Serious attention needs to be given in the Department and in the churches to increasing its circulation.

Releases and features

13. The Department should continue to publish news releases on WCC activities to be distributed free to the press; and to develop the feature articles along the lines of the series of articles written in preparation for the Assembly. Because of understaffing in the De-

partment, this service is very inadequate in French and German. It is to be noted that French is the lingua franca of large parts of Africa.

Relation with the press

14. Neither the WCC nor the member churches should ever lose sight of the secular press, which in many countries represents the principal means by which the churches and the WCC may hope to be heard by the people at large.

It is important therefore

(*a*) that periodical conferences between journalists working for the secular and religious press continue;

(*b*) that at ecumenical and church meetings every co-operation should be given to the press, radio and TV to enable them to present these meetings with understanding and discernment;

(*c*) that churches gain an understanding of how the press works; how the church can support those who work in the press in maintaining high professional standards; and how its services can be secured for church purposes.

Publications policy

15. Because of the striking increase of interest in the ecumenical movement the WCC needs to pay more serious attention than ever before to the language in which its publications are written. It is undeniable that there is much criticism of the 'jargon' of the ecumenical movement in general and the WCC in particular. Criticism of 'ecumenical jargon' is in part misconceived. A form of English developed for international and interconfessional theological discussion is unlikely to possess the vitality and grace of a mother tongue. It may none the less serve the processes of theological discussion. The real difficulties arise when the results of such discussion are presented in the language of the discussion to people who have had no part in it. They must be communicated in a form which does not irritate the scholar or bewilder the layman. People who have newly become open to ecumenical news and views will close their minds again if they cannot understand what we say.

16. The Committee would warmly welcome the appointment of an Editorial Secretary of the WCC, and assure him of the wholehearted co-operation of the Information Department. It also be-

lieves that the WCC as a whole needs to develop a greatly increased sensitivity to the needs of its varied audiences.

17. The Committee is also impressed with the range of publications which emanate from the WCC, to which must be added the books which are published for it by publishing houses in various countries. The Committee understands that difficulties arise from time to time in securing adequate circulation, in connection with problems of costing and pricing, and in relations between the WCC and its publishers.

18. The Committee therefore recommends that the Department of Information and the Publications Section of the Department of Finance and Administration, in co-operation with other departments of the WCC and representatives of national councils and the official WCC publishers, set up a working party to consider carefully

(*a*) ways in which the style of WCC publications, including those in the field of study, may be rendered more attractive to the users of the various languages in which they are published;

(*b*) the best means of publishing and circulating the various categories of WCC publications;

(*c*) the proper costing and pricing of the publications of which the WCC is itself the publisher.

The Committee is aware that the Department of Information is not itself responsible for many of the WCC's publications. But one of its functions is 'to work out a general policy concerning the regular publications of the WCC, to co-ordinate such and to give guidance to those who are responsible for their preparation and presentation' (*Evanston Report,* page 207).

IV. The Role of the WCC in Broadcasting and Film

19. Since the Evanston Assembly the WCC has been seeking to get to grips with its own proper role in the expanding field of Christian broadcasting. The Committee has had before it the results of the detailed enquiry undertaken by Dr James W. Kennedy, to whose tireless energy in this cause the WCC is greatly indebted. It has also received a report on the recent conference of the World Committee on Christian Broadcasting. It has been able during the Assembly to have a joint meeting with a sub-committee of the Committee of the Division of World Mission and Evangelism.

20. The WCC should be concerned with broadcasting because it offers an effective means of carrying out the tasks laid upon the WCC by its constitution of supporting the churches in their task of evangelism and promoting ecumenical consciousness. Broadcasting is an effective means of evangelism and education, especially if attention is given to securing a response from the audience. Many member churches will welcome help in the use of these media. Broadcasting is also a potentially dangerous force, of disastrous effect when incompetently or evilly used. The WCC should assist churches in facing together the immense possibilities of action which are offered.

21. On the basis of the enquiry carried out by Dr Kennedy and the advice received, it appears that the WCC must in any case assume responsibility for:

(*a*) Ecumenical information and interpretation, especially by

(i) the production of broadcasting materials of information and interpretation on the life of the churches and the ecumenical movement, and the stimulation of the interest of broadcasters in them;

(ii) the establishment of channels of exchange for TV programmes, films, etc., of ecumenical value.

(*b*) Ecumenical study of broadcasting problems, especially by

(i) the arrangement of meetings of broadcasters to study together their professional problems and responsibilities; and meetings of broadcasters with theologians, evangelists and educators to study the impact of broadcasting on the churches and the world, and the consequent ministry of the Church;

(ii) attention to technical developments in broadcasting, and in particular the way in which television is becoming steadily more international.

With regard to other aspects of Christian broadcasting, it may well be that the World Association of Christian Broadcasting now in process of formation will prove a satisfactory ecumenical instrument. But no decision can yet be made.

22. The training of Christian broadcasters and the planning and production of programmes should be undertaken locally or regionally wherever possible and not centralized in a world office. Help

should be given to national and especially regional councils to enable them to strengthen their broadcasting work.

23. The Committee warmly welcomes the proposal advanced by the Division of World Mission and Evangelism 'that a person be appointed for a limited period, to be attached to the General Secretariat of the WCC and to give part of his time to the Department of Information and part to liaison and co-operation with the World Association of Christian Broadcasting 'in process of formation' and agrees that the appointment should be 'strictly of a provisional nature'.

24. Since Evanston, film work has constantly increased, especially in the last two years. The Department has produced films on subjects relating to the work of the WCC: its latest film, *As the Nightingale Waits for the Summer,* on the resettlement of Old Believers in Brazil, has been shown at four international film festivals.

The main emphasis, however, should lie as it has lain in the past, on co-operation with member churches, national councils and others in joint production or advice; and in the discovery of good examples of films and their exchange between member churches and national groups. This activity is especially appreciated by churches and television organizations with modest facilities for production. The Department should continue to sponsor a number of conferences on the Church and the film. The Committee believes that this work should be expanded as far as staff time and energy allow.

V. Co-operation with the Division of Inter-Church Aid, Refugee and World Service

25. The Division of Inter-Church Aid, Refugee and World Service expressed appreciation of the full co-operation it had received from the Department of Information and would happily continue the pattern of liaison between itself and the Department established since Evanston. DICARWS recognized that new responsibilities will inevitably devolve on the Department of Information in the next few years because of the expansion of its work resulting from integration of the IMC with the WCC, the needs of member churches in the new nations for information services, participation in the Freedom from Hunger Campaign of the Food and Agriculture Organization of the United Nations, and new programmes developed out of the studies on Rapid Social Change. The Division assured the

Department of Information that it would continue to stand ready to provide resources as these become available to enable the Department to respond to these new demands.

VI. The Structure and Finance of the Department

26. The Department needs the advice and support of a well-attended Working Committee meeting each year. It has been a grave disadvantage that in the period since Evanston so few members have been able to attend. The Committee hopes that in making appointments the Central Committee will give high priority to probable availability. It hopes further that the new Working Committee will include both trusted church leaders with interest in and a feel for this work, and also people who are expert in one or other of the fields with which the Department is concerned.

27. The Committee has considered the financial proposals of the Committee on Programme and Finance set out on pages 52-3 of the *Work Book,* and the provision for staff and other expenditure implied. (The General Budget provides for a director and three secretaries, plus one secretary for inter-church aid work financed by DICARWS, and the time of one secretary in the New York office.)

The Committee believes that the work of the Department will be seriously hampered by its inability under these provisions to meet the following urgent needs:

(*a*) the further development of the Spanish edition of EPS.
(*b*) the recruiting and payment of local correspondents for EPS.
(*c*) the active promotion of the distribution of materials published and produced by the various divisions and departments of the WCC.
(*d*) a provision for staff travel without which it will not be possible adequately to develop ecumenical information services in the areas where they are most lacking.
(*e*) the expansion of the existing photographic service.
(*f*) a comprehensive filing service for the use of the Department: it would require both space and staff for effective functioning.

The Committee urges the Central Committee to give consideration from time to time to these needs with a view to seeing if they can be met before the next Assembly.

VII. Re-definition of Aim and Functions

28. The Committee proposes the following definitions:

The *aim* of the Department shall be to make the policies of the WCC known and understood, to provide and disseminate news of its activities, and to inform the churches about each other's life.

The *functions* of the Department, under the supervision of the General Secretary shall be:

(i) to issue general publicity material about the WCC and the ecumenical movement, and to supervise, or when invited prepare, departmental publicity;

(ii) to represent the WCC in relation to the secular and religious press and broadcasting agencies; and to issue all press releases in the name of the WCC and its divisions and departments;

(iii) to provide such services as will help the churches to understand each other's life and the ecumenical movement as a whole;

(iv) to assist the divisions and departments of the WCC to appreciate and meet the linguistic needs and desires of its varied audience;

(v) to work out a general policy concerning the regular publications of the WCC; to co-ordinate such publications; and to give guidance to those who are responsible for their preparation and presentation;

(vi) to co-operate with other agencies in the fields of the press, radio, television and film, and of the arts; to help to ensure their intelligent use; and to study the problems intrinsic to them.

VIII. Summary of Principal Recommendations

29. (i) The active development of information work in languages other than English and areas other than Western Europe and North America (paragraphs 9-11).

(ii) The presentation of ecumenical documents in language understandable and attractive to the expanding audience of the WCC (paragraphs 15-16).

(iii) A thorough study of the publications policy of the WCC (paragraphs 17-18).

(iv) Increased activity in broadcasting and films (paragraphs 19-24).

(v) A Working Committee capable of attending regularly and made up of interested church leaders and experts in some aspects of the Department's work (paragraph 26).

(vi) Careful consideration by the Central Committee at appropriate intervals before the next Assembly of the unmet needs of the WCC in this field (paragraph 27).

In the discussion the following points were made:

Dr Gerald O. McCulloh (Methodist, USA) emphasized the importance of the reference in paragraph 5 of the report to the need to inform men in theological training about the work of the World Council and the ecumenical movement.

Dr John Marsh (Congregational, England) emphasized the importance of paragraph 23. He spoke as a representative of the World Committee on Christian Broadcasting. There would be a tremendous development in radio and television in the next years. He felt that the proposal limited the WCC unhappily.

Bishop J. A. do Amaral (Methodist, Brazil), referring to paragraph 27a, pointed out that the largest portion of South America was Portuguese-speaking.

V

CLOSING ACTIONS OF THE ASSEMBLY

1 · REPORT OF THE COMMITTEE ON THE MESSAGE OF THE ASSEMBLY TO THE CHURCHES

First Session, 4 p.m., December 3, 1961. Dr Payne presided.

The Message was presented by Dr Kathleen Bliss, Chairman of the Committee. The Committee was representative of various churches and regions. It had met four times. It had unanimously decided that the Message should be addressed to the members of local congregations in such a way as to indicate that the World Council does not stand apart from them. It was not intended to talk about their domestic life but about their conversation with the world around them. It was designed to be brief enough to be read in the course of congregational worship. This approach was a response to the preparation in Bible study and prayer that had taken place in so many congregations around the world.

The Committee had noted: (1) the meeting of the Assembly in India and the reception of many new churches into membership. This had underlined the fact that the centre of Christendom is not in the West but that Christianity has a home everywhere. The collapse of the centrality of the West had not led to a disintegration of the Church but had inspired a drive towards unity in faith and experience between various regions of the world. (2) The Evanston Assembly had spoken about Hope in rather sombre terms, but New Delhi had revealed a grateful confidence among Christians who were discovering that they had a witness to bear in relation to contemporary man's search for life, and, although the world had its dark side, Christians were feeling a new sense of oneness with the common man. (3) A new sense of the uniqueness of Christ had been given, not in elevating ourselves by treading down others but by a greater sensitivity to God's work in the world and a greater emphasis on the one Saviour as the inspiration of our service, witness and unity. Therefore the Committee had included 'affirmations' for use in the final act of worship of the Assembly and invited the congregations to use them in their worship.

Some might feel that the message lacked the note of prophecy, but the Committee felt that there was everything to be said for speaking to the congregations quietly.

Dr Robert S. Barbour (Church of Scotland) read the Message. Dr Bliss moved the adoption of the Message and the Affirmations. This was seconded.

Fr L. E. Gauthier (Old Catholic, Switzerland) pointed out that the delegates represented churches not parishes. The Assembly should not by-pass the churches but address the parishes through them. Dr Bliss accepted this suggestion.

Metropolitan Justin (Rumanian Orthodox) thought that the Message should refer to some of the great achievements of the Assembly, notably Integration, the reception of new churches and the new Basis.

The Rev. A. E. A. Sulston (Church of England) thought that the closing words of the original draft of paragraph 1* were unscriptural. He suggested changing 'in the world for which he died' to 'for all men everywhere for whom he died', and in the first sentence of the third paragraph he suggested 'everywhere on earth' for 'everywhere in the world'.

Bishop N. Beste (Evangelical Church in Germany) suggested that the phrase in paragraph 1 'Christianity now has a home' should be replaced by 'in all parts of the world the Gospel has been preached'. The idea that Christianity had a home in the world was contrary to John 15 and Phil. 3.

In paragraph 3 *Commissioner R. Woods* (Salvation Army, UK) missed any reference to the social evils caused by alcoholism, sexual immorality, etc.

Bishop H. J. A. Meyer (Evangelical Church in Germany) questioned the substance of paragraph 3. He missed any affirmation that Jesus Christ is the light even if God permitted an atomic holocaust to overtake the world.

Dr Bliss commented on Bishop Meyer's speech that if this thought were not carefully worked out it would give the impression, which was already too common, that Christians were only concerned

* The references are to the paragraphs as numbered in the final version reproduced below.

about the other life. An adequate exposition of the eschatological truth would call for a longer message. *Bishop Meyer* replied that without its inclusion the Message would be cheaply optimistic leaving out the promise of the Gospel which would be fulfilled however desperate the situation became. He subsequently proposed the words: 'but our strongest hope is the fact that Christ is and will remain our eternal life whether God will permit mankind to develop new possibilities of life on earth or whether in his judgment he will permit an atomic holocaust and ultimate destruction to overtake us'.

Archpriest V. Borovoy (Patriarchate of Moscow) said that Christians by virtue of their faith are optimists. Bishop Meyer's suggestion might be misunderstood as permitting the possibility of atomic destruction and covering it with the name of Christ. Christ is in truth the Lord of all men, but his name must not be associated with any suggestion of atomic warfare.

Bishop Barbieri (Methodist, Argentina) said that paragraph 3 referred to members of congregations but not to the ministry. He hoped that the message would convey a word of challenge and encouragement to the ministry also.

Sir Kenneth Grubb (Church of England) proposed an amendment to add 'inspiration' at the end of paragraph 3 with reference to the Holy Spirit. *Dr Bliss* said that the words used were biblical and she questioned whether 'inspiration' was the right word to add. *Dr S. M. Paterson* (United Presbyterian, USA) said that to add the word 'inspiration' in relation to the Holy Spirit was tautologous.

The amendment was put to the vote and lost.

Dr Christian Baeta (Presbyterian, Ghana) asked what was the meaning of the last sentence of paragraph 4? What was the relation of the messenger to Christ?

Mr M. M. Thomas (Mar Thoma, India) suggested adding 'and are addressed by him' at the end of paragraph 4, and of substituting 'indifference or hostility' for 'indifference or hatred' in paragraph 5. He wanted the phrase 'community of nations' to be included in the third sentence of paragraph 6.

The Rev. S. B. Coles (Presbyterian, Canada) suggested that to the words 'only one way to the Father' in paragraph 4, there should be added 'He has purchased our peace by the blood of his cross'. In paragraph 5 he questioned the words 'give to them the living Christ' in the third sentence of the draft. He proposed the addition of the sentence 'These are the theatre of God's action' after the words 'secular agencies' in paragraph 6.

The Chairman asked the Assembly for guidance regarding the length of the message. There was a fervent negative to his question whether it should be lengthened. The debate was then closed. Individuals were asked to send their suggestions in writing to the Committee on the Message.

Second session, 4.00 p.m., Tuesday, December 5. Dr Fry presided.

Dr Bliss presented the message as amended by the Committee in the light of the previous debate. Some suggestions had been incorporated but others cancelled one another out.

Synodal Praeses K. Gottschald (Lutheran, Brazil) proposed to amend the second sentence. Fellowship in the WCC was 'wider' than before, but it was difficult to say whether it was 'deeper'. *Dr Bliss accepted the amendment which was moved and carried.*

Dr Noth (Evangelical Church in Germany) asked for the German and English versions to be aligned.

Bishop Gulin (Lutheran, Finland) challenged the statement in paragraph 3 that 'man is not paralysed by these threats'. He suggested 'Mankind is in danger of being paralysed, nevertheless the momentum of change is not reduced'. After *Dr Bliss* had stated that the amendment reversed the sense of the sentence, *it was put to the vote and lost.*

Dr R. M. Clark (United Church of Canada) said he was still uneasy about this sentence. *Dr Bliss* resisted further change and no proposal was brought before the Assembly for a vote.

Bishop K. Støylen (Lutheran, Norway) proposed to substitute 'on that one way we have to walk together witnessing to him and serving all men' for the second sentence of paragraph 4. *Dr Bliss* said that the sentence had been much discussed in the Committee, which had deliberately turned aside from a reference to other religions and concentrated on the thought of Christ seeking lost sheep.

The amendment was put to the vote and lost.

Bishop Gulin (Lutheran, Finland) proposed to substitute 'God has already sought for him' for 'Christ has already sought him' in paragraph 4. *Archbishop John* (Moscow Patriarchate) opposed the amendment.

It was put to the vote and lost.

Professor R. Hartford (Church of Ireland) moved to amend the first sentence of paragraph 7 to read 'We must together seek the fullness of Christian unity'.

The amendment was approved.

Professor R. Mehl (Reformed, France) wanted the reference to unity in the latter part of paragraph 7 to be strengthened. *Dr Bliss* suggested that the fourth sentence might be amended to read '. . . but we have made progress in giving content to the unity we seek'.

The amendment was approved.

Dr Joseph Hromadka (Czech Brethren) expressed heartfelt thanks for the Message. On behalf of the Czechoslovakian and Hungarian delegation he wanted this Message to be a basis for further encounter and fellowship. Some had criticized the representatives of these countries on the grounds that their engagement in the Prague Peace Conference movement indicated that they were not fully engaged in the ecumenical movement. He rejected this view. He hoped that the Message would be triumphantly adopted.

It was moved that the Assembly adopt the Message and the affirmations. The Message was adopted nem. con. *as follows:*

The Message of the Assembly to the Churches

1. The Third Assembly of the World Council of Churches, meeting in New Delhi, addresses this letter to the member churches and their congregations. We rejoice and thank God that we experience here a fellowship as deep as before and wider. New member churches coming in considerable numbers and strength both from the ancient Orthodox tradition of Eastern Christendom and from Africa, Asia, Latin America and other parts of the world visibly demonstrate that Christianity now has a home in every part of the world. In this fellowship we are able to speak and act freely, for we are all partakers together with Christ. Together we have sought to understand our common calling to witness, service and unity.

2. We are deeply grateful for the prayers of countless Christian people and for the study of our theme 'Jesus Christ the Light of the World' by which many of you have shared in our work. Now we return to our churches to do, with you, the things that have been shown to us here.

3. All over the world new possibilities of life, freedom and prosperity are being actively, even passionately, pursued. In some lands

there is disillusionment with the benefits that a technically expert society can produce; and over all there hangs the shadow of vast destruction through war. Nevertheless mankind is not paralysed by these threats. The momentum of change is not reduced. We Christians share men's eager quest for life, for freedom from poverty, oppression and disease. God is at work in the opening possibilities for mankind in our day. He is at work even when the powers of evil rebel against him and call down his judgment. We do not know by what ways God will lead us: but our trust is in Jesus Christ who is now and always our eternal life.

4. When we speak to men as Christians we must speak the truth of our faith: that there is only one way to the Father, namely, Jesus Christ his Son. On that one way we are bound to meet our brother. We meet our brother Christian. We meet also our brother man; and before we speak to him of Christ, Christ has already sought him.

5. Christ is the way and therefore we have to walk together witnessing to him and serving all men. This is his commandment. There is no greater service to men than to tell them of the living Christ and no more effective witness than a life offered in service. The indifference or hostility of men may check our open speaking but God is not silenced. He speaks through the worship and the sufferings of his Church. Her prayers and patience are, by his gracious acceptance of them, made part of the witness he bears to Christ.

6. We need to think out together in concrete terms the forms of Christian service for today and together act upon them. In no field has Christian co-operation been more massive and effective than in service to people in every kind of distress. There is no more urgent task for Christians than to work together for community within nations and for peace with justice and freedom among them, so that the causes of much contemporary misery may be rooted out. We have to take our stand against injustice caused to any race, or to any man on account of his race. We have to learn to make a Christian contribution to the service of men through secular agencies. Christian love requires not only the sharing of worldly goods but costly personal service. All over the world young people are giving an example in their spontaneous offering of themselves.

7. We must together seek the fullness of Christian unity. We need for this purpose every member of the Christian family, of Eastern and Western tradition, ancient churches and younger churches, men

and women, young and old, of every race and every nation. Our brethren in Christ are given to us, not chosen by us. In some things our convictions do not yet permit us to act together, but we have made progress in giving content to the unity we seek. Let us therefore find out the things which in each place we can do together now; and faithfully do them, praying and working always for that fuller unity which Christ wills for his Church.

8. This letter is written from the World Council of Churches' Assembly. But the real letter written to the world today does not consist of words. We Christian people, wherever we are, are a letter from Christ to his world 'written not with ink but with the spirit of the living God, not on tablets of stone but on tablets of human hearts'. The message is that God in Christ has reconciled the world to himself. Let us speak it and live it with joy and confidence, 'for it is the God who said "Let light shine out of darkness" who has shone in our hearts to give the light of the knowledge of the glory of God in the face of Jesus Christ'.

1st Sunday in Advent 1961

The Assembly decided that the following affirmations, which were said by all in its closing service, should be sent to the churches with the message, so that they can be used in congregational worship and especially in united services.

We confess Jesus Christ, Saviour of men and the light of the world;
Together we accept his command;
We commit ourselves anew to bear witness to him among men;
We offer ourselves to serve all men in love, that love which he alone imparts;
We accept afresh our calling to make visible our unity in him;
We pray for the gift of the Holy Spirit for our task.

2 · MESSAGE TO CHRISTIANS IN SOUTH AFRICA

On the proposal of the Business Committee, the following Message to Christians in South Africa was adopted without dissenting vote by the Assembly in Business Session on Monday, December 4.

The members of the Third Assembly of the World Council of

Churches, meeting in New Delhi, have been aware of the developments within the past eighteen months in the relationships between Christians and churches in South Africa and the World Council of Churches, and wish to send fraternal greetings to you in the name of Jesus Christ, our Lord.

Our concern at this Assembly has been to testify to Jesus Christ as the Light of the World, and to seek God's guidance for our witness to him, our service in his name and our unity in him. In our worship together, in corporate study of the Bible and in all our discussions, we have become increasingly and vividly conscious of the power of the Spirit to lead his Church amid our troubled times, and of his bringing us into deepened fellowship with one another and with him. We have rejoiced as twenty-three churches have joined our fellowship at this Assembly, eleven of them from the Continent of Africa. Nor have those churches which to our regret have felt bound to leave our fellowship been forgotten in our prayers.

During the Assembly, our convictions concerning the unity of the Church have grown. A year ago, our representatives shared with South African Christians at Cottesloe in declaring: 'The Church as the Body of Christ is a unity and within this unity the natural diversity among men is not annulled but sanctified. No one who believes in Jesus Christ may be excluded from any church on the grounds of his colour or race. The spiritual unity among all men who are in Christ must find visible expression in acts of common worship and witness, and in fellowship and consultation on matters of common concern.' We subscribe to this principle to the full, and we stretch out our hands to all our fellow Christians to encourage them to manifest such unity in Christ.

Gathered here at New Delhi from all parts of the world, we have heard again God's clear call to us to fulfil the mission of the Church, both in its unfinished evangelistic task and in the submission of the world in which we live to the Spirit of Christ. Specially heavy obligation for both types of mission rests upon Christians in countries where the Church is strong. Those at Cottesloe said: 'We give thanks to Almighty God for bringing us together for fellowship and prayer and consultation; we resolve to continue in this fellowship, and we have therefore made specific plans to enable us to join in common witness in our country.' To all of you who preach Christ to the unbelieving and to all who manifest the Spirit of Christ to their neighbours, we offer our encouragement and fellowship, and assure you of our prayers.

The contrast between the light of Christ and the darkness of our present-day world has been deeply on our minds and consciences. Fear of war, injustice and the suffering of people have challenged our obedience to the servant-Lord. Racial strife is a world problem, and we stand behind the convictions on this matter expressed by the Evanston Assembly in 1954. Christians everywhere are involved in the struggle for the elimination of segregation or discrimination on the grounds of race or colour.

We know that in the name of Christ, many in South Africa are engaged in this struggle. May all who thus serve, and all who suffer, be strengthened. May dignity and unity among men be established through the righteousness of God, in your land as well as in those from which we come. We pray that as the peoples of Africa move into their new day the Church of Christ will play an ever-increasing creative role in promoting understanding, justice, faith, hope and love.

May we share with you our dominant conviction? It is simply stated in the theme of our meeting. Jesus Christ is the Light of the World!

In his name, we send you this message of greetings.

In discussion, the following points were made:

Dr Fry introduced the Message on behalf of the Business Committee. Dr Fry referred to the Cottesloe Consultation of December 1960, at which 10 members from each of the then member churches in South Africa and 6 representatives of the WCC had conferred concerning major problems confronting the churches, especially race relations. In view of this consultation and the opposition it had aroused, it had seemed impossible to those here who had also been at Cottesloe to remain quiet. Therefore Dr Fry moved the adoption of the Message, which he then read.

The Rev. Basil Browne (Congregational Union of South Africa) spoke in support of the Message. There are many Christians in South Africa who struggle, who feel alone and isolated in their witness. The echo of their cry has reached us here in New Delhi. As President of the Christian Council of South Africa and on behalf of the member churches, Mr Browne expressed warm appreciation of the action of the WCC which led to Cottesloe and of the proposed Message.

The Rev. Gabriel Setiloane (Methodist Church of South Africa, Youth Participant) asked whether it was right to single out individual Christians for such a message. He also urged that we ask directly for greater contact and dialogue among the churches in South Africa.

Dr Fry replied that there are many individuals in churches which have withdrawn who await to hear from us. We have been informed that the member churches are planning means of further contact. We also know of ecumenical discussion groups.

3 · MESSAGE TO CHRISTIANS IN EAST GERMANY

The Archbishop of York (Church of England) moved and *it was voted that the following message be sent to the absent delegates from East Germany* mentioned in the Report of the Credentials Committee, and also to Bishop Krummacher and Präses Kreyssig:

> This Assembly sends a message to the people from East Germany who were refused permission to leave their country to attend this Assembly.
>
> The message assures its recipients of the sorrow of members of the Assembly because of their absence, of their constant prayer for them, and of their joy that we are united across all barriers in him who is the Light of the World.

4 · INVITATIONS TO THE FOURTH ASSEMBLY

The *Abuna Theophilos* (Church of Ethiopia) presented an invitation on behalf of His Holiness Abuna Bassilios, the Patriarch of Ethiopia and the Holy Synod, to hold the Fourth Assembly in Addis Ababa.

The *Archbishop of Melbourne* (Church of England in Australia) speaking for himself, but after consultation with his colleagues, indicated that if Australia could be considered for the Fourth Assembly he and others would be glad to have it there and would welcome an initiative from the Central Committee.

The Chairman, Dr Fry, indicated that usually the Central Committee decides three to four years before the Assembly as to its location after full consultation between the World Council and the member churches concerned. He expressed appreciation for both invitations.

5 · CHAIRMAN'S CLOSING REMARKS

Dr Fry, Chairman, addressed the Assembly as follows:

One of the favourite illusions of all men is that they live in times of great importance in history. I suppose there has never been an age in which those then alive did not think they were standing on some kind of eminence from which they could survey both the past and the future; and very frequently they have been deceived and confounded by what they thought they saw. Everyone who has been here is convinced that we have been present on an occasion that will go down in history as one of the decisive moments in the history of the ecumenical movement. This Assembly has been one of fruition, and one also of new beginnings. Our eyes have looked out on horizons that have been broadened by accretions to our membership and by the fusion of the two main streams of the ecumenical movement, one with a primary emphasis on the unity of the Church and the other which has devoted itself with zeal and devotion to the Church's mission.

Seeing these days humanly, which is always the first impulse of everyone, I believe you will join me in saying that these two and one-half weeks of the Third Assembly of the World Council of Churches have been studded with friendships which will shine like jewels in our memory as long as we live. We have been impressed by the breadth of the community of faith in which the Lord Jesus Christ is gathering us together as brothers, who belong to one another. Our divergencies, which no one has attempted to conceal, have rather accentuated our unity, which spreads over most of the spectrum of our belief more and more as we pray and talk with those who are our brothers in Jesus Christ, and we are deeply grateful for what the Spirit has imparted to each of us through our Master's other servants. We cannot escape from a feeling of restlessness deep in our being; everyone feels more stirring within himself than can possibly come to utterance in an Assembly like this, leading to dissatisfaction first with ourselves and then with what we have been able to achieve. We small men today are confronted by events of such magnitude that they almost stun our spirits and certainly make us humble. We pray to God that he may take even the poor offerings of these days in word and in deed, and may magnify them far beyond any content that we now find in what has been done.

We have experienced some heart-searchings about the nature of the Assembly itself. Most of us came here in an attitude which was half one of anticipation and half one of apprehension, knowing that the obligation upon us not to fail is intensified by the fact that we represent an increasing proportion of the total number of Christians in this world. I presume we part from each other with a feeling half of satiety and half of incompleteness. We have lived through such strenuous days in this Assembly that everyone must be depleted at the end of them. We have confronted such deep issues, first of our faith and then in the world of today, that everyone must feel in his inmost soul that we have not made sufficient impact on them in what we have said and done. Nevertheless, with one voice we are wholly grateful for the experience, marvelling that the Lord has raised up such as us in such days of peril and of opportunity, when he might have chosen others far more gifted or more receptive to his Spirit. We leave here determined to be interpreters and advocates—of the ecumenical movement, yes, but far above that and far beneath it: interpreters and advocates of the Gospel of Jesus Christ and of the whole cause of God our Saviour.

We have essayed a bold experiment in conducting a thoroughly democratic Assembly into which all the concerns of the World Council of Churches and most of the concerns of our day have been crammed in one way or another. The attempt to come to something approaching decision on such an immense variety of issues in so few days as these in which we have met has been a bold one. Every detail of the operations of the ecumenical movement as represented in the World Council and also in the International Missionary Council has been sieved through the Committees of this Assembly, and has been subject to debate on the floor of the plenary meetings, with every delegate given the privilege of speech until the Assembly itself decided to call a halt. Is this practical any longer? Your presiding officers strongly hope that as you reflect on the experience we have had together, you will believe that the assets of this procedure, this democratic sounding of the mind of the Church, have outweighed the obvious liabilities of throwing open discussion to so many with such disparate viewpoints.

In any event, the Central Committee will undoubtedly give serious and prolonged attention to the exact procedures and even to the structure of the next Assembly of the World Council, striving for improvement, learning from our failings, in a spirit of appreciation of the unity of spirit which has enabled us to come so far and of the unity of conviction which has often often found a voice.

The Chairman concluded by expressing the thanks of the Assembly (see Appendix 8).

APPENDICES

Appendix 1

THE PLAN OF THE ASSEMBLY

by Dr Robert S. Bilheimer

I. *Preparation*

1. The process of planning the Third Assembly began at the meeting of the Central Committee which took place immediately after the adjournment of the Evanston Assembly. A distinctive element in the preparatory process lay in the fact that, with two exceptions only, the work was done by the normal committees of the WCC. For previous Assemblies, extensive sets of preparatory commissions had been created, but the New Delhi Assembly was planned by the Central Committee and the divisional and departmental working committees. The Central Committee developed the general plan, there being discussion of the Third Assembly at each of its meetings between 1954 and 1960, with the major work being done at the meetings of 1957, '58, '59, and '60. Divisional and departmental working committees of the WCC were used to prepare the sections, with the exception that some additional consultants were invited to meetings in 1959 and 1960. Preparatory work for the Assembly committees was done either by the Central Committee or by the divisional and departmental committees. A Commission on the General Theme was specially appointed by the Central Committee.

2. Changes were made in both the date and place originally proposed for the Third Assembly. It had been envisaged that 1960 would be the appropriate date, thus keeping a six-year schedule between assemblies. The requirements of the process of integrating the International Missionary Council and the WCC, however, made a further year desirable, and in 1958 the Central Committee decided that the date of the Third Assembly should be at the close of 1961. An invitation from the churches and National Christian Council of Ceylon to hold the Assembly there had been accepted, but the consequences in Ceylon of the change of date made it necessary, with the full support of those who had issued the invitation, to accept, in 1959, an invitation from the churches and National Christian Council of India to hold the Assembly in New Delhi. The dates of November 18-December 6, 1961, were fixed in consultation with the hosts in India.

3. The *General Theme* of the Assembly, 'Jesus Christ—the Light of the World', was chosen after consultation with many in the member churches by the Central Committee in 1958. It was agreed that, in contrast to the Evanston Assembly, the theme should not be a subject in itself for discussion at the Assembly, but should serve as a guide and focus for the consideration of related topics. Accordingly, a Commission was created to prepare Biblical studies which would be used in the member churches generally and among those intending to come to New Delhi, as a foundation for the consideration of the other major Assembly topics.

4. In 1959, this plan was further developed, and it was decided to publish a *booklet for wide distribution in the churches* bearing the title 'Jesus Christ

—the Light of the World', which would include the Biblical studies on the theme, a description of the subjects of the sections of the Assembly, and a description of the WCC. The request to the member churches to send this booklet with an explanatory letter to each parish minister, with the request that a group or groups be established in the parish to study the material, met with widespread response. The booklet was translated into thirty-two languages, the English, French and German editions alone running into a total distribution of about half a million copies. No WCC document had ever before reached so large a number of people in the parishes. The preface contained an invitation 'to come to New Delhi'; not to come physically, but to come in spirit and in participation. It was readily accepted.

5. From 1957, when the decision was taken to proceed if possible with the plan to integrate the International Missionary Council and the WCC, *Integration* was a dominant part of the Assembly planning. All plans were carefully discussed with representatives of the IMC, and, as we shall indicate below, the basic structure of the Assembly was given point by the fact of Integration. One of the factors which made the general theme so readily acceptable was its essentially missionary character.

6. Another part of the continuing work of the Central Committee had a direct bearing upon plans for the Assembly. The Report on *Programme and Finance* submitted by the Central Committee to the Assembly did not call, as had been the case at Evanston, for a reorganization of the Council. It was, rather, a careful assessment of the demands of a rapidly growing organization and programme. Its recommendations concerning the development of the structure, programme and budget gave a sound and realistic basis for Assembly actions concerning the future work of the Council.

7. As already indicated, the *preparation for the sections* at New Delhi was done by existing WCC committees. Even the first suggestions concerning the sections envisaged three only, as contrasted with six at Evanston. In 1958, it was decided that these should be on Unity, Witness and Service. Furthermore, it was decided that the issues to be treated under these headings should be those which appeared to be the most urgent ones arising out of the work of the churches together in the ecumenical movement. The committees most intimately in touch with these concerns were precisely the working committees of the various divisions and departments of the WCC. Accordingly, in 1959 and again in 1960, three 'Commissions' were formed, made up of members of the many working committees of the departments and divisions of the WCC. Thus, each division and department participated in the preparation for each of the three sections, bringing its own distinctive contribution to the subjects of Witness, Service and Unity. It was also decided that the basic document should differ from those prepared for either Amsterdam or Evanston, and should be in the form of an extended or annotated agenda. At New Delhi, therefore, each section met with an agenda which set forth the most urgent issues which had appeared in the course of a two-year discussion carried on by those most thoroughly in touch with the problems which the churches face in their work together in the ecumenical movement.

8. The Central Committee and the Working Committees were also responsible for the preparation of the *committees* at the Assembly. The general report of the work of the WCC for the period 1954-61, entitled *Evanston-New Delhi,* 1954-61, *The Report of the Central Committee to the Third Assembly of the WCC,* was prepared by the general secretariat, the divisions and departments under the authority and review of the Central Committee. Proposals for the work of the Council as a whole were drawn up by the general secretariat, the various units of the Council, and the International

Missionary Council, and were put together in the Assembly *Work Book*. These two documents formed the basic preparatory material for the committees, with, in some cases, supplementary memoranda in cyclo-styled form.

9. *Documentation* for the Assembly therefore consisted of:

Jesus Christ—the Light of the World—the pre-Assembly booklet
Evanston-New Delhi, 1954-61
The Report of the International Missionary Council
The Assembly *Work Book*
Annotated Agendas for the sections
Supplementary memoranda for committees.

10. An important part of the *preparatory work* for the Assembly took place *in India*. There were essentially two aspects to this. The first was the task of public relations. All were convinced that it was necessary to take special measures, as had indeed been the case in the USA prior to Evanston, to ensure that those responsible for the media of public opinion, particularly the Indian and the English language newspapers and the radio, understood the basic facts concerning the WCC, the Assembly and its work. Furthermore, it was necessary that the membership of the churches in India should also have a knowledge of these matters. Throughout the planning stages, all were deeply concerned that the Assembly make a positive impression upon general public opinion in India, not only for the sake of the ecumenical movement, but far more for the sake of the churches in India. Questions of a religious or a political nature were certain to arise, and it was deemed to be of the utmost importance that there be careful preparation for the way in which the Assembly would approach these matters. Beyond this was the organizational task of making arrangements for the Assembly in New Delhi. Questions of housing, relations with many government departments involving visas, import permissions, customs, use of buildings and the like, needed the most careful attention.

11. For both the public relations side of the work and the organizational aspects of it, many people set aside large amounts of time, energy and money. The churches and the National Christian Council of India devoted their energies to interpreting the Assembly to their constituencies and to raising a fund of over 40,000 rupees towards the expenses of the Assembly. A Delhi Arrangements Committee was organized under the leadership of Rajkumari Amrit Kaur as President, and Mr Samuel Mathai as Vice-President. The most decisive single contribution was that made by the National Christian Council in seconding Mr Korula Jacob for eight months, during which period Mr Jacob carried the burden of the work with the most highly effective results for both aspects of the total task.

II. *The Structure of the Assembly*

12. The Assembly constituted itself as planned and proposed by the Central Committee. A Business Committee, Credentials Committee and Nominations Committee were appointed, and the basic structure of the Assembly confirmed.

13. The first element of the Assembly was *worship and Bible study*. This is described in detail in the narrative account, but two points should be noted here. First, the provisions for Holy Communion followed the pattern suggested by the Lund Conference on Faith and Order, and used in WCC meetings since that time. These were printed in the Assembly Handbook, as follows:

Communion Services. The recommendations of the Lund Conference regarding communion services at ecumenical gatherings were as follows:

1. There should always be a united Service of Preparation for Holy Communion, with special emphasis on the note of penitence for our separation from each other.
2. There should be opportunity for communion services at such times as will make it possible for every member of the conference to receive communion somewhere without violation of his own conscience or disloyalty to his church tradition. These should be held at different times.
3. Though on the grounds already indicated there are some who object to open communion services, yet we believe there should be an opportunity of this kind for the many who desire such services and are free to partake. Such services should, where possible, be held on the invitation of the local church or churches which sanction such services. (Usually a very large proportion of the members of a conference will partake. Notable examples of this were the communion services held in the Nieuwe Kerk of Amsterdam, in 1948; in Lund Cathedral, in 1952; in the First Methodist Church in Evanston, in 1954, and many regard such memorable occasions as of historic importance. At the IMC Conference at Tambaram in 1938 two open communion services were held, one of which was Anglican.) . . .
5. It is important that those who cannot partake at a particular communion service should be invited to attend the service as worshippers, though they cannot receive communion. This has been found by many to be a means of real blessing of spiritual communion, and of deeper understanding and fellowship.

In accordance with these recommendations a united Service of Preparation for Holy Communion will be held in the Shamiana on Saturday, November 25, at 6.30 p.m.

Intimations concerning the Communion Services in the following week have been given by those in the churches listed below who have been responsible for arranging these services:

The Church of India, Pakistan, Burma and Ceylon (Anglican), Sunday, November 26, at 9.30 a.m., in the Shamiana.

The Syrian Orthodox Church of Malabar, Tuesday, November 28, at 7.30 a.m., in the Shamiana.

The Lutheran Churches of India, Thursday, November 30, at 8.00 a.m., in the Shamiana.

The Greek Orthodox Church, Friday, December 1, at 7.30 a.m., in the Shamiana.

The authorities of the respective churches desired that the following statements be printed in the Handbook concerning the Communion Services:

From the Church of India, Pakistan, Burma and Ceylon (Anglican): The service of the Lord's Supper according to the use of the Church of India, Pakistan, Burma and Ceylon will be open to all present who are baptized communicant members of their Churches.

From the Syrian Orthodox Church of Malabar: The Orthodox Syrian Church of Malabar extends a cordial invitation to all the participants of the Third Assembly of the World Council of Churches to attend the Holy Qurbana (Eucharist) of St James, which will be celebrated by the Orthodox Syrian Church delegates.

From the Lutheran Churches in India: The Federation of Evangelical Lutheran Churches in India invites all Lutheran communicant members and other baptized communicant members of the member churches of the World Council of Churches to participate in the Holy Communion Service, to be held according to the Lutheran Order of Holy Communion.

From the Greek Orthodox Church: The delegates of the Eastern Orthodox Patriarchates and Churches, gathered from all around the world in order to attend the Third Assembly of the World Council of Churches, invite with great pleasure all the participants of the New Delhi Third Assembly to attend the Divine Liturgy of St John Chrysostom and join their prayers in Christ with them.

In addition to the Opening Service of Worship, the Morning and Evening Services, the Service of Preparation for Holy Communion, and the Closing Service of Worship, the Assembly engaged for eight mornings in *Bible study*. This was an innovation for corporate Bible study had not been planned for previous Assemblies. The method used is described on p. 17.

14. For eight sessions, involving sixteen hours, the Assembly met in the *sections on Witness, Service and Unity*. Over three hundred people attended each section, and it was necessary for sub-sections to be formed, and for drafting committees to be appointed for these sub-sections. Their work was brought together by the drafting committee of each section, and a draft report submitted to the section as a whole, for amendment, revision and forwarding to the Assembly. The officers of the sections met together in a co-ordinating group during the time in the programme when the sections were meeting.

15. The *committees* met for a similar period of time. There were nineteen committees in all, eighteen as listed under Chapter IV and the Committee on the Message.

The committees were not uniform in size, some being as small as 25 and others as large as 150. Drafting procedures were similar to those employed in the sections, although on a smaller scale. The officers of the committees met together during the time in the programme when the committees were in session for purposes of co-ordination.

16. *Addresses* given to the Assembly consisted of two types. The addresses during the first three days dealt with the scope and task of the newly integrated WCC, with the General Theme, and with each of the three sections. Thereafter addresses in the evenings dealt with the work and concerns of different WCC departments and divisions (see Appendix 5).

17. The Third Assembly, following the initial discussion concerning it which took place at the Evanston (1954) Central Committee and detailed work thereafter, followed a new set of *Rules of Debate and Procedure* which considerably affected its structure and facilitated its work. These Rules provided for three types of session in which the Assembly might meet, and specified the type of business which could be dealt with in each.

General Session. For ceremonial occasions, public acts of witness, formal addresses, etc.

Deliberative Session. For resolutions or reports of such a theological or general policy nature that they ought not to be amended in so large a body as the Assembly; specifically for reports of sections. The only recommendation in order in a Deliberative Session was that the Assembly approve the substance of the document, and commend it to the churches for study and appropriate action. The only motions from the floor in order were to refer back to the committee or section reporting, or to request a hearing on the report before it was again brought to the Assembly.

Business Session. For the adoption of agenda, nominations, elections, proposals with reference to the structure, organization, budget or programme of the WCC, or other business except that for General or Deliberative Sessions.

In accordance with these procedures the reports of all sections and committees were submitted to general discussion and decision by the Assembly in plenary session.

18. The *Press and Public Relations Committee* formed a particularly important part of the Assembly structure. It was the general task of this Committee to serve the 350 press, radio and TV representatives which had been accredited. Daily press and briefing conferences, releases, provision of Assembly documents, services in providing contacts with Assembly participants were the chief means of carrying out this task. It is to be noted that television played a far larger role in the reporting of the Third Assembly than hitherto, and was perhaps the medium through which the largest number of people was reached. A dinner for accredited representatives of press, radio and TV on November 18 served as both reception and initial briefing.

19. The *Assembly staff* numbered 297, 187 of these being co-opted and 110 being staff of the WCC. The co-opted staff served voluntarily. This total staff was organized into the general administration including the finance, office, translators and stewards and aides staff; the sections staff; the committees staff; and the press and public relations staff.

Appendix 2

REPORT OF THE CHAIRMAN OF THE CENTRAL COMMITTEE

Dr Franklin Clark Fry

Anyone who presumes to report for the Central Committee of the World Council of Churches is undertaking a formidable task. The dimensions are big no matter how one measures them. As the responsible organ of the Council between assemblies, the committee's duties are exceedingly broad in scope, ranging over the whole gamut of our common life and activities. In its composition, it is made up of a galaxy of personalities, representative of all of the confessions in the Council's membership, Orthodox and Protestant, Anglican and Old Catholic, spread over all the inhabited earth, ecumenical as much in diversity of their convictions and of disparate Christian points of view as in their geographical spread in today's world; coming from Asia to the Atlantic community, from the East in the customary special meaning of the word nowadays and from the West; from ancient churches with a long and valiant past which have witnessed to the Lordship of Christ over many centuries; from churches in the vigour, if one may use the analogy, of younger adulthood which are consequently likely to be present-minded; and from still others which have only recently achieved full autonomy, for which the most important tense inevitably is the future.

It is hardly necessary to say, it is inherent in the nature of the case, that the fellowship of such a group, such a kaleidoscopic cross-section of the Council, has been exhilarating. You will be gratified to hear that it has equally been congenial, effective, marked by a marvellous unity, the kind of oneness of spirit that can spring only from faith in one Lord and Master of us all. Beyond that it has been a token, and in itself an adumbration, of unity also in the church. Confronting our joint task, all have been united in diligence and in loyalty to the ecumenical cause. One evidence has been that attendance at the annual meetings has been good, commendably so when seen in the light of the demands laid on men and women who were already fully occupied in their churches and in other vocations at home; in addition, participation of those who have been present has consistently been wholehearted and excellent. Of its personnel and its dedication to its assignment, this, as a preface, is a composite portrait of your Central Committee.

The report proper of the committee, in the formal and strict sense of the word, it should be made clear at once, is really to be found in the paper-back book, *Evanston to New Delhi*, which is already in the hands of all official participants in the Assembly and which, it is safe to predict, will increasingly come to be seen by everybody as a basic and utterly indispensable document for the days that lie ahead of us. Nothing—it cannot be stressed too firmly—nothing being said now is designed to replace a single paragraph of the book or to reduce anybody's obligation to read it thoroughly. At most and at best, all the present statement even pretends to be is a kind of oral introduction to it and, in a limited sense, a commentary on it. Scarcely a single hour will be required to read *Evanston to New Delhi* for every year of ecumenical activity compressed (a still more accurate verb would be crammed) into it. Could there be a better bargain? It is just that skilful a piece of condensation. Some parts of the book—revealingly, they will be different parts for different people—may strike you as prosaic; however, take the word of the chairman of the committee, not one of them is superfluous. Granted that not every detail is momentous; yet there is hardly one that could not become so before this Assembly adjourns. Furthermore, there is no telling ahead of time which it may turn out to be.

One feature all the way through that should not fail to impress every reader is the utter candour with which the accounting of the past seven years is given. You will not find a tinge of special pleading or of conscious salesmanship in the book, nothing that can be described by that much maligned word 'promotion' from its introduction to its index; no attempt to colour facts, to put an artificially good face on what has occurred for the sake of concealing imperfections and inadequacies. Above all, this is not a subtle device to make up the Assembly's mind for it in advance. Here the report stands; it is an honest and full disclosure. All that we ask is that you read it as carefully as it has been prepared.

Two general observations dominate the past seven years in memory and go far toward summarizing all that has taken place. The first is that the tempo, the pace of life, for the World Council of Churches, as well as and as much as for the rest of human society, has been intense. The winds of history, which we know behind history belong to the Lord whom we serve, have blown increasingly and with gale force, here and there twisting into actual cyclones. The acceleration of events, without and within the Council, has been relentless, often frightening, until all of us have been tempted to exclaim: Who is sufficient for these things?

The World Council by now ought to be used to it. It is certainly no new experience. The Council has never known anything different in its whole life—and more. Who was it remarked that even before 1948, the date of its birth, the World Council was the liveliest—and one might add the busiest—embryo that anyone had ever seen? And from the very moment that it was born it has been expected to be an adult, girded like a man to run a race. Unlike many of our churches, and perhaps accounting in large part for the difference in attitudes that seldom but occasionally can be detected here or there, the World Council has never experienced a really calm day since it came into existence, not a single twenty-four hours on which it could be phlegmatic or relaxed or introverted. God has simultaneously called it into life and to strenuous action. For the World Council of Churches, it is more than merely a matter of being swept along by the rushing stream of history, it has momentum in itself.

Deeper than that, the fact that the tumult of these hectic days has conscripted, compelled common efforts of Christians through the ecumenical movement ought to occasion no surprise. It has not been optional, not at all. Neither the World Council nor the separate churches could ignore that demand or insulate themselves against it, without going far toward vitiating the very reason why God brought them into being. Actually, our Council, acting in the churches' behalf, sees itself called not only into the tide of events but to be ahead of them—and that is where it has earnestly striven to be. The Christian community, acting together, needs to feel an obligation nowadays to be the pathfinder. It will never again be enough for us to assume what has sometimes been called our customary role in the past, that of being simply critics after the fact. We need to guide or at least to contribute to guiding.

In that spirit the World Council since 1954 has not only been panting to keep up with life; it has pioneered in a far-sweeping series of inquiries as to how Christians in widely differing environments can help their nations to cope with rapid social change. It has commendably been in the van, through the Commission of the Churches on International Affairs and by the Central Committee's own actions, in dealing with emergent issues affecting war and peace by a living enunciation of principle while decisions are still in the balance and by skilful liaison at the places where they are being made. The World Council has striven for a Christian consensus in the face of the population explosion; it has interested itself constructively in the emerging status of women; it has been alert in advance to the need for constitutional safeguards of religious liberty in nations new and old. Even with that, the list is only partial.

A second and balancing general observation is that, with all this, the World Council during these same seven years has remained very much itself. In negative terms, its activities have not been characterized by discontinuity; it has not worked in spasms. Positively, the Council has become more deeply confirmed than ever in the personality which it has had from the beginning which is indeed implicit in its own nature. The entire period has been one of congruous development; no temptation at all has been felt to deviate from it and, to the credit of everybody, there has been little or no pressure from inside our own membership to distort it. Despite the fact that precedents in an organization as young as ours are few, procedures have been consistent. Neither the basic principles nor the habits of thought and action which have been deduced from them have been in question. They have been under constant examination, yes; but in dispute, no.

Numerous illustrations readily come to mind, including, as one thinks about it, practically all the recommendations which are coming from the Central Committee to this Assembly. Look at the elaboration of the Basis, for instance. It simply and solely, consciously and deliberately, makes explicit what has been implied from the beginning; it could not adhere more strictly to the Christological accent stipulated at Amsterdam. The fuller staffing and the enhanced scope to be given to Faith and Order, many others I am sure will be quick to point out without my having to say a word, actually do no more than return, than come closer to the original intent. What will look like—and what deserves to look like—the important new definition of 'Christian Witness, Proselytism and Religious Liberty', if you will examine it more closely, you will find is deeply rooted in and in a true sense really only the natural flowering of the 1950 statement on 'The Church, the Churches and the World

Council of Churches' that was sent out for study and comment eleven years ago. On still another front some of the noteworthy accessions to membership that we have welcomed, that have been accepted here at New Delhi, are the fruitage of hopes that go back long before that. Even the financial measures that are being proposed are a logical, almost inevitable, extension of what has gone before, only a conservative evolution from the past. And so on.

All this ought not to be interpreted to mean that your council and those who have been at its helm since Evanston have been lacking in ingenuity and creativity. New applications of the tested principles can be numbered in the scores, with adaptations, flexibility, guided development all along the line as there ought to be in any organism as vividly alive as ours is. No symptoms are to be found that there has been stagnation; anything but that! Nor, even less, has there been any settling down, any subsiding into institutional rigidity. What it all does mean, the gratifying lesson of this second inter-assembly period as we read it, is that the wisdom of the builders of the council has been vindicated by the test of the thronging events of these years; the grand design with which they—and, we devoutly believe, the Holy Spirit—endowed it has proved to be sound.

Turning now to look inside, you are entitled to an intimate glimpse of how the Central Committee itself has operated. It may help you to evaluate better what has been achieved and to get in clearer perspective the papers and recommendations that have been prepared for presentation to this Assembly if you have first seen what our annual meetings are like, how they have been conducted and what has happened at them. A very human element, whether we like it or not, is involved in all our judgments and, for the sake of a true perspective, you deserve to have that pictured clearly too.

Perhaps the most distinctive single feature is that in every meeting of the Central Committee there is a conscious balance. A study or thought component is introduced to match the action component. Just as the World Council as a whole has its Study Division and would find it inconceivable to be without it, equally its ad interim administrative organ, the Central Committee, keeps scholarship and reflection based on research in something like equipoise with the oversight that it has to give the council's far-flung and accelerating programme. This is not done only to whet interest nor, as some might suspect, as a sop to the theologians in our number to compensate them for the hours that they will be asked to spend later on practical affairs; certainly not only for appearance's sake. It is because one and all have been resolved that our meetings must never be allowed to deteriorate—if one who is himself a church executive may use the disparaging words—into mere management of affairs. In short, it is because ecumenicity is never at its best without basic, penetrating thought.

It would be a blunder, of course, to press the dichotomy too far. Theory and actuality, thought and action are not rigid antitheses, not by any means, in the World Council of Churches. Each is a large ingredient of the other and we know it. Ideas stream into functional activities and the tide flows back. Faith and Order is a strongly marked example. It has not consisted only of intellectual pursuits during these seven years, but has gone far toward colouring, if not yet saturating, the whole outlook of everything else. Or consider the Division of Studies. While a few of its projects have soared into the abstract, others could hardly have been more concrete, right down on the solid and sometimes harsh earth on which men live.

The contributions of our essayists have no less uniformly had a ring of reality in them, but we have valued them most for the updraft that they have given to our minds. It would be invidious to mention the name of anyone without calling the complete roll, but here is a generous sampling. It is a list of distinction.

1955
Implications of Christian Unity for Inter-Church Aid and for Assistance to Underdeveloped Countries: the Rev. Canon (now Bishop) Chandu Ray and Dr Robert C. Mackie.
The Various Meanings of Unity and the Unity Which the World Council of Churches Seeks to Promote: General Secretary, W. A. Visser 't Hooft.

1956
The Churches and the Building of a Responsible International Society: Sir Kenneth Grubb.

1957
The Calling of the Church to Witness and to Serve: Professor Henrik Berkhof and Professor Russell Chandran.

1958
Religious Liberty: Professor Niels H. Søe.

1959
The Significance of the Eastern and Western Traditions Within Christendom: Professor C. E. Konstantinides (now Metropolitan of Myra) and Professor Edmund Schlink.

1960
The Role of the World Council of Churches in Regard to Unity: Professor Henri d'Espine.
Responsible Parenthood and the Population Problem: the Rt Rev. Stephen F. Bayne, jr., and Professor Egbert de Vries.

Happily the mental stimulus from these papers, the deposit of good that they left behind, have extended far beyond even the circle of the Central Committee. They have reached out into hundreds, running into thousands, of your own homes since so many of them have been reprinted in the *Ecumenical Review*. Here is a salute of appreciation in the name of us all.

As for the other side, the action component, perhaps the best way to say it is that it stretches as far as the eye can see. It covers almost literally the whole spectrum of what the World Council, under the broad mandate given by the churches, undertakes to do. If this sounds like a vague definition, it is because defining means limiting, and practically nothing occurs in the Council's life between Assemblies that lies outside the portfolio of the Central Committee. The exceptions that there are—or, more accurately, that there seem to be—are few and are quickly enumerated; and even they are subject to qualification.

The Faith and Order Commission is frequently and fairly looked upon as having something of an independent stance, even though the constitution does explicitly put it under the general supervision of the Central Committee, because everyone agrees that powers of initiative exist within its all-important area of interest that are distinctively its own. The CCIA, as a jointly sponsored agency with the International Missionary Council, has even more properly and inevitably enjoyed substantial autonomy to the obvious benefit of all parties concerned. And, by grace, the Administrative Committee of the

)ivision of Interchurch Aid and Service to Refugees has in the nature of the ase had to have left to it detailed administration of the immense and gushing rogramme in its field simply because of the tempo with which it has to act nd the volume of work that flows through its hands.

Aside from these three, there are no other exceptions, either apparent or eal. In case anyone should ask, yes, this answer includes the Executive Com-iittee too. Since Evanston it has confined itself with a new strictness to iterim or housekeeping functions and has stayed far from even the appear-nce of encroaching on the prerogatives of the Central Committee. No voice, o the best of our knowledge, has even made any accusation of that in these even years. The Central Committee, in sum, carries ultimate inter-Assembly esponsibility and does so alone.

Proximately—which is another matter and one almost equally important—ur committee, like the World Council itself, regularly puts heavy reliance on he divisional and departmental committees in dealing with the wide, func-onal segments of the work that have been under their continuous oversight. Jo healthier or livelier spectacle occurs each year than the veritable congress f the members of such committees who stream together at a central point in ne year: hundreds of earnest people brimming with ideas and keen to ex-ress them, coming out of all continents and confessions but alike in being glow with intense interest, which reveals a gratifying depth of ecumenical onviction. It strengthens one's own faith in the World Council of Churches ıst to be among them. For the week or more that they are together, the staff as to have the dexterity of jugglers to keep everything in order and going imultaneously but, no doubt about it, it does lay a broad and democratic ase for all that we plan and do. The one thing surest is that the ecumenical novement is no longer, if it ever was, the affair of a coterie of specialists. 'he policies of the World Council of Churches of today grow out of the col-ective wisdom, they represent the consensus of a swelling multitude of the rusted leaders of the churches all over the world.

The Central Committee takes all this very seriously, as it should. When-ver a recommendation of a divisional committee comes before us, the pre-umption is invariably in favour of it. The burden of proof, to turn it around, s on those who disagree. This does not imply that there is automatic ap-roval; far from it. The Central Committee takes its own responsibility far oo conscientiously for that. What it does is to listen to and depend on the roposals of its co-workers. The judgment of the divisional and departmental ommittees powerfully counts.

Those committees speak for themselves, effectively and clearly, in *Evan-ton to New Delhi*, and it would be an unprofitable exercise indeed for any-ne, including this one, to try to reduce to capsule form the able reports that hey are submitting in their own names to this Assembly. All that is required s to transmit them. Every self-respecting speaker half resents a chairman's aking it on himself to explain after an address what he (the speaker) had ttempted to say, which is a tacit form of literary criticism which nobody ppreciates; it would be doubly bad (and in this case entirely gratuitous) to ndertake to do so in advance.

A goodly number of other duties rest directly on the Central Committee. ·xternal relationships—and who can overestimate their cruciality in the preading ecumenical mood of these days?—are in that class and applications or membership are also. Twenty new member churches in sixteen nations in ve continents have been admitted into membership of the World Council of 'hurches by the Central Committee between the years 1955 and 1960, and, as ou already know, others, including notable ones, have been screened for

recommendation to this Assembly. Vast tracts of time have been consumed i
thorough and earnest and sometimes plodding attention to the details of inte
gration with the International Missionary Council, which has come in thes
days at last to such a triumphant result. Not the least nor the lightest of th
preoccupations of the Central Committee have been the preparations for th
Assembly itself; the choice of its locale here at New Delhi, handsome capita
symbol of the new India, one of the foci of Asia and the world; its theme
whose wealth of Biblical content has dawned and will shine with a memor
able radiance in our Bible study and lastingly, let us hope, in our hearts; th
intricacies of the network of sections and business committees; preparator
publications; even physical arrangements.

Statements have been developed like the one, to mention it again, on 'Chris
tian Witness, Proselytism and Religious Liberty'. Reflection, sober study, no
only second thoughts but third or fourth thoughts, have been given to th
amplification of the Basis. In what may prove to be the most solid legac
from this period to the future, funds have been raised to a monumental sun
through the all but indefatigable efforts of one of our presidents to provid
a new headquarters building to house the Council and so to give it a secur
base in the years to come. All six of our weeklong yearly meetings of th
Central Committee have been strenuous; every day of them, indeed ever
hour has been fully occupied and eventful.

A special paragraph should be included about finances; you expect it, an
the subject deserves it. The novelty will be its length; it will be only six sen
tences long. The basic fact is this: from the standpoint of its cost, the Counci
is far, very far from being the behemoth that it is sometimes pictured to be
The truth, seen in fair perspective, really is the exact opposite; the Council i
a notably frugal operation, so much so that numerous parts of its pro
gramme suffer from both acute and chronic fiscal anaemia. Year by year i
requires little less than a *tour de force* to balance the slender resources tha
the member churches are able to make available to the Council with even th
ecumenical imperatives, let alone the massive opportunities of our day. Ever
rupee, franc, crown, pound that is given sacrificially to the World Council o
Churches is carefully husbanded and cautiously disbursed; it receives th
diligent attention of some of the Council's most capable leaders. The marve
is that so little in the way of means has been made to go so far. The spend
ing, no less than the giving, exhibits stewardship of a high order.

One misconception, if anyone holds it, needs to be dispelled forthwith. Th
World Council does not exist primarily to receive from the churches; it exist
to do for them and to give to them. The whole predisposition of the Worl
Council of Churches is to search for avenues through which it can enrich, no
drain, the churches; to find ways to become an instrument, which it hope
will be increasingly valuable and effective but always wholly in their hands
One simple, mundane proof of it is to be found right in the high percentag
of its budgets that is devoted to common counsel, to Assemblies like this, t
consultations of every kind.

The Central Committee, to look back to it, is perhaps the most graphi
example of all. It has seen itself as the voice, a kind of miniature parliamen
of the churches; it has been a representative democracy in which every indi
vidual is honoured and his contribution is welcomed and cultivated, just be
cause he does personify a church. If even one individual is detected lapsin
into silence, seemingly because he underestimates the contribution he or hi
church can make, he has been actively encouraged to speak up. Not only fo
reasons of courtesy but for this deeper reason, nobody has ever been slighte
or rebuffed. No matter how earnestly we have been seeking consensus on an

issue, if the authentic voice of even a single church is raised in the minority, it has been respected and listened to. Furthermore, let me assure you, this has been true not only of certain churches but of everyone and anyone. Churches are esteemed in the World Council not only for their numbers or their financial power or depth of history, but equally for the height of their potential and often even in proportion to the problems that confront and sometimes threaten to overwhelm them. It is the kind of spiritual mathematics that only Christians would employ; it is very foreign to the world. What is instinct in it is the feeling of the family of God.

If the question is ever asked, Are the churches in control? the answer is an emphatic yes. Nobody who has ever seen the Central Committee in action would have the slightest doubt about it. Some, with whom this reporter certainly does not agree, even profess to believe that this principle is being carried too far. Without any derogation of the fact, or the slightest lack of appreciation of the blessing, that the Holy Spirit frequently adds a dimension of insight when we act together, there is no question that the churches are the ones that determine the course of the World Council. It, under God and for his purposes, is their servant rather than the opposite. The World Council not only disavowed becoming a 'super-church' at its beginning at Amsterdam; its total development since then has been the most convincing refutation of the whole notion. We who are closest to the Council are constantly baffled how any such charge can be made or any such misconception can still exist, except in critics who are deliberately self-deceived.

Actually, the World Council is not even an 'outside force', except to the degree that a church or churches keep it outside. If there is any failure of contact, the fault usually goes back to the structures that the churches have created or have failed to create within themselves to keep in touch with the Council and give their guidance to it. The greatest need for such provision is self-evidently, in those churches, now more than half our membership, which at any one time cannot be represented personally on the Central Committee but from which we are equally eager to hear—but it applies with emphasis to all. Will it be offensive if, very simply, we express regret that the response has been so sporadic and sometimes almost casual as it has been from many churches; and that in all cases it is not fuller and more constant than it is? If any church ever harbours any doubt that its words are taken seriously, let that doubt be dissipated at once. The World Council and the Central Committee as its organ, solicit your communications and your counsel, earnestly await them, never shrug them off, attentively hear when you speak.

Behind everything that has been said to this point and indeed at every point, pervasively in the background wherever you look, stands the really admirable staff that God has given to us in the World Council during the past seven years. They, under the leadership of our superbly gifted general secretary, have not only been the human channels for the work that has been done but they come the closest to being the epitome of it all and the embodiment of the spirit that animates the Council's very life. We would be doing less than is just if we did not openly thank the Lord for them, for the calibre of their minds, the temper of their souls, their dedication to their tasks. To appraise them must be to praise. One and all they have regarded themselves as among the most privileged of men and women, but we in the Central Committee, on our side, have more than once been a little conscience-stricken and have asked ourselves if we have not made them, or at least permitted them, to pay too high a forfeit in comfort and in the security of their families for that privilege.

One unobtrusive little word in *Evanston to New Delhi* which I would not have you overlook—it appears on page 28—is so typical that it is reassuringl revealing of the spirit of the staff. It is the remark that the very terms of th service of the staff *protect* them from becoming a bureaucracy. Mind you, i does not read *rebuff* them in any such attempt or even *stand in the way* of natural drift in that direction! It has been their own mood to be servants o the Spirit, working for the churches, for Christ's sake. Although they hav supplied, as they ought, many of the initial impulses, have suggested most o our courses of action, they have never resisted when their recommendation have been sifted, refined, altered; more than once we have seen them tak open satisfaction when we, the direct representatives of the churches, hav made up our minds in quite contrary directions. This all of us in the Centra Committee can and do testify.

All that remains is valedictory; to speak a word of sincere gratitude to ou wise and helpful and unfailingly faithful vice-chairman; for each to salute hi colleagues in thankfulness for the comradeship we have had in the Lord an for the deep draughts of time and of energy of body and spirit that so man have given to the discharge of our common responsibility; to return to yo with humility that matches our appreciation the commission laid upon us a Evanston; and to invoke our successors not to go and do likewise but to g and do far better, more diligently, more worthily, in the years ahead. Ou homage is to God who rules and overrules.

Appendix 3

PRESENTATION OF THE CENTRAL COMMIT TEE'S REPORT ON PROGRAMME AND FINANCE

Dr Eugene Carson Blake

This report is neither the most interesting nor the most important report tha is to come before this Assembly. You may ask why it is presented on thi first day of business of this Assembly, and why the Agenda provides for suc prolonged and full attention to it.

The answer is simple. This report is the most comprehensive report havin to do with the organization and programme of the World Council of Churche with which this Assembly must deal. Again and again during this Assembl you will be confronted with specific decisions about the organization or pro gramme for the next years. These will be interrelated decisions. It is the hop of the Central Committee that you will make your specific decisions in th light of your thoughtful response to this comprehensive report on Programm and Finance.

First, I call to your attention that this Report, by its very name, is designe to help us in this Assembly to make our programme decisions and our finan cial decisions together and *not* separately. The final judgment on any pro gramme question must include our judgment as to whether there will b money available to do this or that *good thing*. Similarly, all financial decision ought to be made finally in the light of what we believe the World Council o Churches should be and should do.

Let me then ask you now to note the major parts of this Report. Para graphs 1-5 are the introduction, which gives the history of the report. Thi you may easily skip, provided you have confidence that your Central Committee has made an effort to give careful attention to the programme and organization of the World Council of Churches for the next period in the life of the World Council of Churches.

Paragraphs 6-48 are, in my judgment, the crucial section of this Report, and if they are not carefully studied by the members of this Assembly you will not be in a position to make your programme decisions on the assumptions which the Central Committee believe are vital to the health and to the proper controlled growth of the World Council of Churches. Here is set forth in precise terms an analysis of the *task* of the World Council of Churches, its method of operation and a history of its growth so far, including programmes proposed, but not undertaken. Also, you will find an analysis of the reasons why some of you will feel it has grown too big and why others of you will feel it has been confined too much.

I would read to you the general conclusion of the Central Committee in these matters with which we hope that you will agree:

> 46. The World Council is still a young organization, which is in the process of discovering and defining its task. In that early period it must avoid on the one hand the danger of an expansion which would be out of proportion to the spiritual, human and financial resources available, and on the other hand the danger of failing to respond to real needs in the life of the churches or in the world and real opportunities for serving the cause of the Kingdom.
>
> 47. It must at all cost avoid becoming an institution which just grows because that seems to be the inherent law of institutions. But it must be ready to go forward when to go forward means obedience to the call of the Lord of the Church.
>
> 48. The fear of bigness must not make us blind to those signs of the times which indicate that we live in an age of world forces and of decisions to be taken at the international level. At such a time the Christian churches must be present on the world scene, and for this they need a common instrument of action, of witness. At such a time the Christian churches must demonstrate clearly that there is in the midst of the great confusion a coherent people of God, conscious of its unity and ready to bring the light of the Gospel into the human situation.

Section III of the Report (paragraphs 49-61) is the recommendation of the Central Committee as to the structure and organization of the World Council of Churches for the next period in its life. Each programme or organizational decision made by this Assembly must fit into or modify this section of this Report.

Section IV is financial (paragraphs 62-78). But please note that it is a philosophy of the World Council of Churches' finance, or, if you will, a theology of the World Council of Churches' finance, and is not written for accountants only. Next to Section II, this Section IV is the most important for you to read and to understand.

Section V (paragraphs 79-91) is straight finance and can well be skipped by those members who do not like finance. But, everyone should read paragraph 5, which is a quick summary of the increases in programme that are recommended to you by the Central Committee.

Finally, I call to your attention Section VI (paragraphs 93-94), which outlines how we hope this Assembly will deal with this Report.

Paragraph 93 provides for this presentation which I am now concluding. Second, it provides, if you desire it, that there be a hearing scheduled early in the docket on Tuesday at 11.15 in this Hall.

Third, that on Thursday you are dealing with the recommendation that the Assembly receives and gives general approval to Sections II, III and IV of this Report, i.e. paragraphs 6-78, and that at the same time you refer Section V, the budget section, to your own Assembly Committee on Finance so that all the interrelated financial decisions supporting the programme you finally approve, may be considered together, after careful financial scrutiny and at a time when you as a responsible Assembly can take your decisions, not piecemeal, but in the light of the whole of the problems and opportunities which we now together face.

May God, our Father, enable us to do his will with this Report as revealed by Jesus Christ and illumined by the Holy Spirit.

Report on Programme and Finance from the Central Committee to the Third Assembly

I. Introduction

1. A Programme and Finance Committee was authorized at the 1956 meeting of the Central Committee at Galyatetö. In 1957, at New Haven, the Central Committee heard a first report of the work of the Committee and further developed its terms of reference. This action defines the task of the Committee:

'that a special committee of seven be appointed by the Officers of the Central Committee with representatives of the Finance Committee, the programme divisions and the Joint Committee, to examine the programme and budget of the World Council of Churches and the nature and scope of the programme which the World Council should carry on in the light of its declared principles, the expressed needs and desires of the churches and their ability to support the programme; and to consider in particular:

(i) the preparation of a General Budget which would carry the basic programme of the World Council and which could be supported on a fairly shared basis by the whole constituency of the World Council; and

(ii) the provisions under which churches and other givers might support such projects and additions to the basic budget as might prove feasible and advance the programme of the World Council.'

2. The Committee appointed by the Officers of the Central Committee was composed of:

Dr Eugene C. Blake—*Chairman*	*Staff Consultants*
Dr Hanfried Krüger	Dr W. A. Visser 't Hooft
Mr Francis P. Miller	Dr R. S. Bilheimer
Dr Ernest A. Payne	Dr L. E. Cooke
Rev. Kenneth Slack	Rev. Francis H. House
Dr Eugene Smith	Mr. Frank Northam
Count S. van Randwijck	

3. The Committee held four meetings, each of two or three days. It reported on its work to the Central Committee in 1957 and 1958. It prepared an Interim Report in 1959, which was examined in August 1959 by the Administrative Committee of the IMC, the Joint Committee and the Divisional and Departmental Committees, before being presented to the Central Committee. The Interim Report was included as an appendix to the minutes of the 1959 Central Committee meeting and the General Secretary's letter to the member churches dated October 5, 1959, asked for their comments and criticisms on it by March 15, 1960; not many member churches were in fact able to respond to this request before April 1960. The Programme and Finance Committee prepared a final report in April 1960 in the light of such reactions as were received through all those processes.

4. The Central Committee received that final report in August 1960 and reviewed it, taking account of comments received from the Administrative Committee of the IMC, the Joint Committee and the Divisional and Departmental Committees. After adopting a number of modifications, which are incorporated in the following text, the Central Committee agreed to adopt the report as its own report to the Third Assembly.

5. In the light of present probabilities, this final report has been prepared on the supposition that the integration of the WCC and the IMC will take place at the end of 1961. It will therefore require re-examination if integration does not take place.

II. The Scope of the WCC Programme

(a) The Task of the World Council

6. The *nature* of the WCC has been defined in the 'Toronto' statement on 'The Church, the Churches and the World Council of Churches'. We do not have a comparable statement on the *task* of the World Council. But various official documents contain affirmations about the task of the WCC. The most important of these documents are: the Constitution, the report of Committee II of the Amsterdam Assembly, the Toronto statement, the report on 'The Calling of the Church to Mission and Unity' of 1951, the report on 'Structure and Function' of the Evanston Assembly and the Draft Plan of Integration between the WCC and the IMC of 1957.

7. On the basis of these various formulations the following general statement can be made:

M

The task of the WCC is to serve the churches in the fulfilment of their common God-given calling in the whole world.

In this formula three words need special emphasis. The WCC exists in order to *serve* the churches; in the words of its Constitution 'it offers counsel and provides opportunities of united action', but it does not legislate for the churches. The WCC has to perform tasks which belong to the *common* calling of the churches; it is concerned with those aspects of the Church's life and mission which can be performed more adequately or fully by the churches acting or speaking together. The WCC helps the churches to see their task as part of the task of the Church in *the whole world*, that is to bring the Gospel to all men and healing to all nations.

8. It is the conviction of the churches in the WCC that unity grows as the churches learn to fulfil their mission together, that is to say when they 'receive correction from each other' (Amsterdam message), when they share with one another experiences of renewal of church-life by the Holy Spirit (see Toronto statement IV 8), when they speak out together, when 'vital issues concerning all churches and the whole world are at stake' (Committee II, Amsterdam Assembly), when they render assistance to each other in case of need, when they support each other in the task of evangelism and mission. The WCC seeks to promote this co-operation and mutual service, not merely with a view to realizing the objectives of the particular activities themselves, not merely for the sake of organizational effectiveness, but also for the sake of the deeper unity for which they prepare the churches.

9. The World Council is concerned with the full manifestation of the unity of the Church of Christ. The task of its Commission on Faith and Order 'to proclaim the essential oneness of the Church of Christ and to keep prominently before the World Council and the churches the obligation to manifest that unity and its urgency for the work of evangelism' (Faith and Order Constitution) is also the task of the whole World Council. The World Council promotes conversation between churches which, recognizing that differences in faith and order exist, seek to explore these differences in mutual respect, trusting that they may thus be led by the Holy Spirit to manifest more fully their unity in Christ (see Toronto statement).

10. In the life of the World Council this concern for unity has to be understood in the context of the total calling of the Church. Thus from the outset it has been affirmed that unity must be seen in connection with the renewal and with the evangelistic-missionary task of the Church.

11. Thus it is natural that the Assembly and the Central Committee in their decisions concerning the programme of the WCC have given the Council tasks in each of the main areas of the common calling of the churches. While the Assembly and Central Committee have implicitly stated that the WCC is concerned with the wholeness of the Church, the Draft Plan of Integration makes this explicit. 'They (the IMC and WCC) exist to witness to the wholeness of the Gospel, and must, therefore, seek to express that wholeness in their own life.'

(*b*) *The Method of Operation of the World Council*

12. The method of operation of the World Council is defined in the sections of the Constitution dealing with 'Functions' and 'Authority'. The fundamental points are that the Council shall not legislate for the churches, but shall offer counsel and provide opportunities of united action in matters of common interest and that it may take action on behalf of constituent churches in such matters as one or more of them may commit to it. The Constitution mentions further the following specific functions: to carry on the work of

the two world movements for Faith and Order and for Life and Work, to facilitate common action by the churches, to promote co-operation in study, to promote the growth of ecumenical consciousness in the members of all churches, to support the churches in their task of evangelism, to establish relationships with denominational federations and with other ecumenical movements and to call world conferences.

13. In other official documents adopted by the first or second Assembly specific mention is also made of the tasks to draw the churches out of isolation into conference about questions of Faith and Order, to express Christian solidarity, to help in the relief of human need, to speak out when vital issues concerning all the churches and the whole world are at stake, to work for the renewal of the churches through active ecumenical encounter, to achieve the purpose that the churches in the WCC and the councils in the IMC promote unitedly the world mission of the Church.

14. From these various formulations the following conclusions can be drawn with regard to the method of operation of the Council as an instrument of the churches in their ministry in the world:

(i) The World Council acts as a link between the member churches and seeks to establish relations of active fellowship between them.

(ii) The World Council renders service to the churches.

(iii) The World Council promotes ecumenical study of issues of common concern to the churches.

(iv) The World Council facilitates common action by the churches.

(v) The World Council acts and speaks on behalf of the churches in matters of common interest which the churches have committed to it.

(*c*) *The Growth of the World Council's Programme*

15. It is important to remember that the period in which the programme of the World Council grew most rapidly was that of the years just before the first Assembly of 1948. Since that time only few new activities have been added. Decisions concerning the creation of new departments or the undertaking of new activities are made by the Assembly or the Central Committee. It may be useful to identify the origin of the present activities of the Council:

16. Heritage of Faith and Order and Life and Work. The World Council continued the activities of the Faith and Order and Life and Work movements. Faith and Order had its Theological Secretariat which is continued in the present Department on Faith and Order. Life and Work had its Research Department which became the Department of Church and Society. Similarly the present Youth Department, the Service to Refugees and the Ecumenical Press Service grew out of corresponding activities of the Life and Work Movement.

17. During the second world war a beginning was made with the work for the reconstruction of the churches in Europe. This was adopted as part of the WCC programme in 1946 and became later the Division of Inter-Church Aid and Service to Refugees.

18. The creation of the Commission of the Churches on International Affairs (a joint creation of IMC and WCC) and of the Ecumenical Institute was first approved in 1946. The latter was financed during the first years by a special gift.

19. The first Assembly at Amsterdam in 1948, representing the member churches, examined and approved the programme which had developed prior to the official constitution of the Council and added two further activities: the Department of Evangelism and the Department on the Life and Work of Women in the Church (later: Co-operation of Men and Women in Church

and Society). It also laid the foundations for the Department of the Laity.

20. The East Asia Secretariat (of the WCC and the IMC) was set up by action of the Central Committee in 1951.

21. The Central Committee in 1951 set up a committee to examine the structure and functioning of the World Council; that Committee reported through the Central Committee to the Evanston Assembly which gave approval to the proposed structure and definition of the functions of the various divisions and departments. The Evanston Assembly took at the same time the initiative to propose the setting up of a Department on Inter-Group Relations and approved the setting up of the Secretariat of the Joint Committee of IMC and WCC.

22. The Secretariat for the study of Religious Liberty was proposed by the Central Committee in 1958 and organized in 1959.

23. In a number of cases proposals concerning new activities have originally come from one or more member churches. Thus the origin of the Department on the Co-operation of Men and Women in Church and Society was the request of the French Reformed Church to put this matter on the agenda of the first Assembly. The East Asia Secretariat was set up in response to the requests of the member churches in Asia.

24. The proposed integration of the World Council of Churches and the International Missionary Council will, if adopted, represent an important further stage of the growth of the World Council.

(*d*) *Activities proposed but not undertaken*

25. The Assembly and Central Committee have not always found it possible to provide adequate funds for the programme which they have adopted. The Evanston Assembly recognized this fact in relation to the Division of Studies when it adopted the recommendation that 'additional resources and personnel be sought' (Report, p. 225).

26. When proposals are made concerning new activities, two questions arise; should this activity receive higher priority than some of those now on the regular budget? Should additional funds be sought? In some cases this problem had been solved by the raising of funds for special projects (see section IV (*b*) of this report which deals specifically with this subject).

27. In other cases it has not been found possible either to include an approved new activity in the budget or to raise special project money for it.

28. With regard to the Study of Religious Liberty, funds have been raised outside the budget to cover the expenses for the initial period.

29. For the study of the role of the WCC with regard to radio and television (approved in 1957), the study of education (1954), the strengthening of the translation section (1957) and the study on theological education (Central Committee 1956 and Executive Committee 1957) it has not yet been found possible to raise sufficient funds.

30. At the same time a number of proposals which have been made at various times in various WCC meetings have never reached the stage of consideration by the Assembly or Central Committee. Among these may be mentioned: the study of rural work and rural problems, stewardship, Christian social work, the family, organization of historical archives of the ecumenical movement, documentation service.

(*e*) *Controlling factors in the development of the WCC Programme*

31. *Varying expectations.* Different churches expect different types of services from the WCC. Some are specially concerned with the 'theological', others with the 'practical' aspects of our work. At the same time different

parts of the membership in the churches have different preoccupations. There are the concerns of youth, of the laity, of women, of the pastoral ministry, of theological faculties, of the church press, of those specially concerned about mission and evangelism and of those interested in social and international affairs. The World Council has to keep all major sectors and concerns of its member churches in mind.

32. *Varying needs of the churches.* Churches with limited resources need help in aspects of their life in which they are not able to render the service expected from them. On the other hand, strongly organized churches need ecumenical contacts which will help them to see their task in the context of the world-wide mission of the Church and to operate effectively on a world level.

33. *Varying conceptions of the role of the World Council.* There is considerable difference of opinion concerning the function of a World Council of Churches. Some fearing the growth of 'bureaucracy' desire to restrict its programme to a few essential activities. Others feel that the ecumenical development does not move forward sufficiently rapidly and would like to see the WCC intensify its activities and widen their scope.

34. *Varying conceptions of size.* From the perspective of small and financially weak churches the World Council is a large organization. From the perspective of large and financially strong churches it is a small organization. There are local congregations and local councils of churches which have a budget larger than the General Budget of the World Council of Churches.

35. *Varying readiness of the churches.* The churches differ also in their readiness and (or) their capacity to respond and co-operate in an ecumenical programme or in their willingness and ability to use the results of the WCC programme. For some the amount of time and energy demanded is a burden, because the number of persons available for ecumenical work is too small or there are no adequate channels to relate ecumenical activity to the normal life of the church.

36. *The dynamic factor in the ecumenical fellowship.* There is a dynamic factor in the growth of ecumenical fellowship which finds expression in the growth of the World Council. As the churches discover increasingly their common calling and their need of each other, as they see more clearly the tasks which in the present international and interdependent world must be performed by the churches together, the World Council's programme is bound to grow.

(f) Responsible Growth

37. The World Council in its whole life and programme is responsible to the churches which constitute it. Its work must therefore reflect the convictions of the churches concerning their common tasks.

38. The work and programme of the Council is however not the only index to the development of ecumenical consciousness and solidarity in the churches. The attitudes prevailing in the churches themselves and the direct contacts which the churches maintain with their sister churches are fully as important factors in the development of Christian unity.

39. Responsible growth is a growth which is not merely a response to incidental pressures, however justifiable in themselves. Growth is responsible when it represents a common act of response to the calling addressed to the churches together and when it is the result of a serious consideration of the tasks which the churches must perform in the present world situation.

40. Responsible growth must therefore take account of the spiritual resources which are available. The expansion of the programme must not mean

the watering down of the quality of the programme. The growth of the staff must also depend on the availability of men and women who have the depth and breadth of insight without which an ecumenical movement ceases to be a challenge to the churches and to the world.

41. Responsible growth is also conditioned by two basic principles concerning financial support:

that the main funds must come from the member churches so that they are truly in control of the situation;

that all churches should share in the support of the programme on an equitable footing.

42. Responsible growth implies choice between the many possible tasks which an ecumenical body representing 178 churches with their manifold concerns and interests could undertake. First things must come first. To decide, on the basis of a clear conception of the mission of the Church and the historical situation in which we find ourselves, which are the first things is one of the most difficult, but also most rewarding, duties of the Assembly and the Central Committee.

43. Responsible growth also presupposes pruning. Activities which may have represented priorities in one period may have to make place for other activities in another period.

44. The World Council should never undertake tasks which can equally well or better be undertaken by the churches themselves, by national councils of churches, by regional bodies or by functional groups which collaborate in and with the ecumenical movement.

45. In selecting the activities which the Council should undertake the following criteria should therefore be applied:

whether the activity proposed has to do with a real need in the life of the Church or of the world;

whether the activity proposed is a necessary expression of the declared purposes of the WCC;

whether the activity proposed represents a concern shared by a considerable number of the member churches;

whether a sufficient number of member churches will participate in the proposed activity;

whether the activity proposed can best be undertaken on a world scale or whether it can equally well or better be undertaken on a national or regional scale;

whether it can find a place in a budget without violating the principles that the main funds must come from the churches and that there must be a fair sharing of the total financial responsibility.

(g) *Conclusion*

46. The World Council is still a young organization, which is in the process of discovering and defining its task. In that early period it must avoid on the one hand the danger of an expansion which would be out of proportion to the spiritual, human and financial resources available, and on the other hand the danger of failing to respond to real needs in the life of the churches or in the world and of real opportunities for serving the cause of the Kingdom.

47. It must at all cost avoid becoming an institution which just grows because that seems to be the inherent law of institutions. But it must be ready to go forward when to go forward means obedience to the call of the Lord of the Church.

48. The fear of bigness must not make us blind to those signs of the times which indicate that we live in an age of world forces and of decisions to be

taken at the international level. At such a time the Christian churches must be present on the world scene and for this they need a common instrument of action, of witness. At such a time the Christian churches must demonstrate clearly that there is in the midst of the great confusion a coherent people of God, conscious of its unity and ready to bring the light of the Gospel into the human situation.

III. Organization of the World Council of Churches

49. The Committee recognizes that the next period will require a certain flexibility in regard to organizational matters. This will be particularly true in the period between the Third and Fourth Assemblies if integration takes place, especially in regard to the problem of relationships between the new Division of World Mission and Evangelism and the other divisions. In preparing this report, the Committee has taken account of the changes which would follow from integration. The Committee has also examined the Report on the Future of Faith and Order and the discussions which have so far taken place on that subject and recommends below certain steps which might be taken in that connection. At a deeper level, however, certain questions concerning the nature and task of the WCC and the way in which these may be best expressed in organizational terms need further discussion over a considerable period of time. This is due primarily to the fact that the WCC is new and is finding its life and form of organization amid a dynamic situation within the churches and upon the world scene. The Committee hopes that these fundamental issues will in the future be a matter of discussion in the Central Committee and the member churches, to the end that the structure of the WCC may be more adequate to its true, and unfolding, task. The Committee therefore recommends that, while it is clear that the Assembly establishes the main lines of policy and programme and the general organizational pattern, it be recognized that modifications in the organization need not necessarily wait for a decision of an Assembly, but can be made between Assemblies by the Central Committee. The Committee recommends that the Third Assembly request the new Central Committee to give full attention to this question and to set up the necessary machinery for the re-examination of the organizational pattern as soon as experience indicates that this is needed.

50. The draft plan of integration proposes the creation of a new Commission and Division of World Mission and Evangelism. The Joint Committee proposed, and the Central Committee agreed, at the meetings in the summer of 1959, the following arrangements regarding responsibility for work in the area of *Missionary Studies*:

(*a*) There shall be a Working Committee for the Department of Missionary Studies within the Division of Studies.

(*b*) This Committee shall be appointed by the Central Committee on the nomination of the Divisional Committee of the Division of World Mission and Evangelism, after consultation with the Divisional Committee of the Division of Studies.

(*c*) This Committee shall report annually to both Divisions, and shall report to the Central Committee through the Division of Studies.

(*d*) Necessary staff, including the Executive Secretary for the Department of Missionary Studies, shall be made available to the Division of Studies by the Division of World Mission and Evangelism.

The Joint Committee further proposed and the Central Committee agreed, at the meetings in August 1960, the following arrangements regarding responsibility for work in the area of *Evangelism*: that the work of the Division of World Mission and Evangelism which is concerned with assisting the churches and councils in their work of evangelism, other than long-range study, shall be carried on by one or more of the portfolios of the Division of World Mission and Evangelism; and that the present WCC Department on Evangelism shall become the Department on Studies in Evangelism, and that the following provisions shall govern its structure, work and staff:

(*a*) The Department on Studies in Evangelism shall be located within the Division of Studies.

(*b*) There shall be a Working Committee of the Department, to be appointed by the Central Committee on the nomination of the Divisional Committee of the Division of Studies, after consultation with the Divisional Committee of the Division of World Mission and Evangelism.

(i) The Working Committee of the Department shall report to the Commission or Committee of the Division of World Mission and Evangelism for advice and comment.

(ii) The Working Committee of the Department shall report to the Central Committee through the Division of Studies, transmitting to the Central Committee such comments on its report as may have been made by the Commission or Committee of the Division of World Mission and Evangelism.

(*c*) The responsibility of the Department on Studies in Evangelism shall be to undertake long-range studies concerning evangelism. In addition, the Department may undertake such short-range studies as the Commission or Committee of the Division of World Mission and Evangelism may request. This would mean that the DWME would be free to regard the Department on Studies in Evangelism as its instrument for conducting such studies as may be required under this head. This would, however, not prohibit the DWME from conducting short-range studies directly within its own framework.

(*d*) The Department on Studies in Evangelism shall have an Executive Secretary. In addition, the Secretary in charge of the portfolio of evangelism in the DWME shall participate in the meetings of the Committee, and shall, in the event of the Committee being requested by the DWME to undertake short-range studies as indicated in (*c*), be available to give staff assistance in respect of these studies.

(*e*) It is important to note that summer meetings schedules should provide that the Working Committee of the Department meet so that it may be able to make its report to the Commission of the DWME.

51. The draft plan of integration also proposes that, in the committee structure after integration, there shall be a *Committee on National Council Relationships* with responsibility for giving continuous attention to the development of relationships of mutual helpfulness between the World Council of Churches and national and regional councils of churches and Christian councils. The proposals for amendment of the Rules of the World Council of Churches after integration include an amendment to the Rules to create this Committee and define its functions. The Committee will be appointed by the Central Committee and will be related directly to the General Secretary' office.

52. Problems concerning the structure and organization of the Commission and Secretariat on *Faith and Order* were examined in the period 1957-60 by the Working Committee and the Commission on Faith and Order and by the Committee on Programme and Finance. The Central Committee adopted the recommendation of the Committee on Programme and Finance, in which the Commission on Faith and Order concurs, that at the present stage, in the ligh

of the total situation in WCC and in view of the importance of study in the programme of Faith and Order, the Commission or its Working Committee should continue to be represented on the Committee of the Division of Studies and the Secretariat should continue to work, as at present, under the authority of the Constitution of Faith and Order and within the Division of Studies. It is, however, considered that the position and programme of Faith and Order should be further strengthened and therefore recommended that the following steps should be put into effect not later than the Third Assembly, and sooner if possible:

(*a*) that the Commission on Faith and Order in future meet every two years, rather than (as provided by its own present constitution) every three years or that the Working Committee which meets annually be made larger and more representative or that other arrangements to strengthen the regular operation of the Commission be developed;

(*b*) that time be afforded by the Central Committee for a report each year by Faith and Order on general developments or specific issues in the realm of unity;

(*c*) that the Secretary (or Director) of the Commission be a member of the Staff Executive Group; and

(*d*) that the budget of Faith and Order be increased from the 1960 level of $18,460 to $42,000 p.a., which would support a Secretarial Staff of three.

53. The proposed *titles for the divisions of the WCC and the units within them* would be as follows:

Division of Studies: Commission and Secretariat on Faith and Order; Department on Church and Society; Secretariat on Racial and Ethnic Relations; Secretariat on Religious Liberty; Department of Missionary Studies; Department on Studies in Evangelism. (In accordance with the proposals of the Joint Committee IMC-WCC, these last two units are shown as being related to both the Division of World Mission and Evangelism and the Division of Studies.)

Division of Ecumenical Action: Youth Department; Department on the Laity; Department on Co-operation of Men and Women in Church, Family and Society; and the Ecumenical Institute.

Division of Inter-Church Aid, Refugee and World Service.

Division of World Mission and Evangelism: Theological Education Fund Committee; Standing Committee on the Ministry; Committee on the Church and the Jewish People. (The Department of Missionary Studies and the Department on Studies in Evangelism of the Division of Studies are also related to this Division—see paragraph 50.) Proposals for the structure for the Division are being developed for action by the Third Assembly.

Units related directly to the General Secretariat: Information Department; Finance and Administration Department; and the Commission of the Churches on International Affairs.

54. Thus within the *Division of Studies,* the following units would be grouped. The organization of each of these units is different from the others, and the relationship of each to the Division and to the WCC as a whole is also different from the others. Faith and Order has been described in paragraph 52. The Department on Church and Society would continue as at present, except for the addition to it of the Secretariat on Racial and Ethnic Relations. The Department on Studies in Evangelism is related to both the Division of Studies and the Division of World Mission and Evangelism, as is the Department of Missionary Studies. The Secretariat on Religious Liberty is not related to any unit in the Division of Studies, and, while functioning in

that Division, has a direct relationship to the General Secretary. Representatives from the Committees of Faith and Order, Church and Society, Evangelism and Missionary Studies are on the Committee of the Division of Studies.

55. Within the Division of *Ecumenical Action*, the Ecumenical Institute will continue to function as an experimental centre for study and education, being linked with the Division of Studies, the Division of Ecumenical Action and the Division of World Mission and Evangelism with regard to programme, and being related administratively to the Division of Ecumenical Action. The Youth Department will continue to work on established lines, having as one of its principal functions the relation of the entire programme of the World Council to the youth constituency. The Department on the Laity will continue to work in close association with the Department on Co-operation of Men and Women in Church, Family and Society. The Department on Co-operation of Men and Women in Church, Family and Society will have a special relation to the Division of World Mission and Evangelism as described in the following agreement:

(*a*) The Co-operation Department shall be renamed 'The Department on Co-operation of Men and Women in Church, Family and Society';

(*b*) The functions of the Department shall include the following new clause:

'To assist churches and Christian councils to discover and express the significance of the Christian faith in the realms of marriage and family life particularly in the context of other religions and secularism';

(*c*) The Division of Ecumenical Action will consult the officers of the Division of World Mission and Evangelism before submitting to the Central Committee names for appointment to the Working Committee of the Department;

(*d*) In line with procedures to be adopted in relation to concerns of other departments of the integrated World Council of Churches and International Missionary Council the Division of World Mission and Evangelism will refer requests from national and regional councils for assistance in the field of Christian Home and Family Life to the Department on Co-operation of Men and Women in Church, Family and Society. The Division of World Mission and Evangelism will be expected to make any recommendations it sees fit regarding these requests, and there will be reciprocal consultation between the Department and the DWME whenever necessary on requests for assistance in this field received directly by the Department. Responsibility for formulating, approving and carrying out actual projects for work in this field shall rest in the first instance with the Department:

(*e*) The Division of World Mission and Evangelism will offer and the Co-operation Department will welcome assistance in securing funds and personnel for carrying out projects approved by the Department and, where appropriate, the Division of World Mission and Evangelism will make available part-time service of its own staff for these purposes;

(*f*) In the event that the Department is unable to carry out the supervision of an approved project to which the Division of World Mission and Evangelism attaches great importance, the Division of World Mission and Evangelism may undertake direct responsibility for the promotion and supervision of such a project, in consultation with the Department.

56. The *Division of Inter-Church Aid, Refugee and World Service* exists to help the churches fulfil their obligation to aid one another and to co-operate in ministering to people in need through ecumenical service. It carries respon-

sibility for the work of the World Council of Churches in these fields. The Committee is informed that the Administrative Committee of the Division is reviewing its programme and organization in the light of the steps so far taken in fulfilment of the world-wide mandate given to the Division at Evanston, the increasing co-operation with the IMC and the anticipated development of that co-operation with the Division of World Mission and Evangelism, the results of the Rapid Social Change study, the theological re-thinking in the whole realm of Christian service, and the growing world-wide awareness of the needs of the homeless, the hungry and the underprivileged. The churches themselves both individually and through their national, regional or confessional organizations or their agencies of inter-church aid and relief, are seeking through the Division or under its guidance and co-ordination to widen and develop the range of their service. In response to these new needs and opportunities the Division proposes to develop its internal organization on the principle that the approach to the churches and people should be on the basis of areas. The staff of the Division would then be constituted of area secretaries who would carry responsibility for the Division's work in the main regions of the world, and functional secretaries who would provide the specific competences for service rendered in those areas in the strategy of world-wide programmes in refugee work, material aid, scholarships and fraternal workers, health, ECLOF, etc.

57. The *Commission and the Division of World Mission and Evangelism* will seek to carry forward and develop, within the integrated World Council of Churches, the work hitherto carried on by the International Missionary Council and the Department on Evangelism. Their aim is defined as 'to further the proclamation to the whole world of the Gospel of Jesus Christ, to the end that all men may believe in Him and be saved'. They will seek to foster the sense of responsibility for the outreach of evangelism by the local church; to assist the churches in every part of the world to bring the Gospel to bear upon situations where there is no effective witness to Christ; and to make the best use of the urgent opportunities for evangelism which call for combined action by several churches or other missionary agencies. To this end, the Division will engage in study, survey, consultation, and the establishment of contacts designed to secure a more effective deployment of resources, co-ordination of missionary effort, encouragement of experiments in 'multilateral action', and in joint action where appropriate. The Commission and Division will continue to carry the present responsibilities of the International Missionary Council in respect of the Theological Education Fund, World Christian Books and other ecumenical projects at present in progress, and will initiate new projects as may be expedient from time to time. They will carry certain responsibilities for the Committee on the Church and the Jewish People. Through study and research the Commission and Division will seek to explore the meaning in contemporary circumstances of the world-wide missionary and evangelistic task, and by the publication of the International Review of Missions, research pamphlets and other materials, to provide information and illumination to the churches on this subject. The Commission and Division will seek to bring into all parts of the life of the World Council of Churches an awareness of the missionary dimension of the Church's life and to deepen the concern for evangelism in the whole life of the Council. They will seek to establish contacts with evangelistic groups and movements which are still unrelated to the ecumenical movement. The Commission will maintain offices in New York and London as well as in Geneva. It will be financed by special sources outside the General Budget apart from the budget for work in the field of Evangelism.

58. The *Departments of Information* and *Finance and Administration* will remain, as at present, directly related to the General Secretariat.

59. The *Commission of the Churches on International Affairs*, which was set up by the WCC and the IMC, continues as a specialized agency of the WCC, with the mandate to express the convictions of the WCC and the churches in the realm of international affairs. In view of its specific function, it has a special status and is directly related to the General Secretariat of the WCC. The CCIA has the power to act and speak within its field of work subject to the provisions of the Regulations of CCIA and provided that when questions arise on which the governing bodies of the WCC have not specifically expressed themselves, it consults with the officers of the WCC. When the Commission speaks, it indicates clearly whether it speaks in its own name or in the name of the WCC or on behalf of one or more of the member churches at their request. In its specific field of work, the CCIA serves the interests of all divisions of the WCC. In view both of the historical and of the functional relationships, it entertains special relations with the Division of World Mission and Evangelism. There is also a close link with the Division of Inter-Church Aid, Refugee and World Service. These relationships find their expression in cross-representation at the Committee level, co-operation at the staff level and financial support of CCIA from the divisions concerned.

60. The Committee proposes an addition to the *General Secretariat*. The present General Secretariat, composed of the General Secretary and the Associate General Secretaries, is unduly burdened with detailed administration and co-ordination which distract from the principal tasks of the General Secretariat. To correct this situation, it is proposed that the General Secretary's office be strengthened by the addition of a person of sufficient seniority to undertake certain delegated tasks of administration and co-ordination. His duties would consist in representing the General Secretary with regard to such matters as need the attention of the General Secretariat but do not necessarily require the attention of the General Secretary himself. His duties would also include those of Secretary to the Committee on National Council Relationships (see paragraph 51). The budget which is set forth below provides for such a person.

61. The Committee has considered an analysis presented by the Division of Studies of the role and nature of ecumenical study as carried out in the WCC as a whole, and makes two recommendations which grow out of that analysis. Both concern the problem of *the co-ordination of studies* and arise from the fact that many studies are carried on by units of the Council which are outside the Division of Studies, and from the fact that present arrangements for this work of co-ordination need to be augmented. It is proposed:

(*a*) that there be a 'Staff Co-ordinating and Advisory Committee on Studies' of which the General Secretary would be the chairman and the Director of the Division of Studies would be the secretary. The Committee would be composed of the Staff of the Division of Studies, the Directors of the other Divisions and staff representatives of such other units as are engaged in studies. The Director of the Division of Studies would need to give considerable time to the work of this Committee. The functions of the Committee are indicated generally in its name. It would meet normally twice a year. This arrangement should be reviewed by the Central Committee after having been in operation for two or three years.

(*b*) that the Committee of the Division of Studies be authorized to convene at its discretion meetings of representatives of the Committees of other units in the Council which are conducting studies. It would be the purpose of these meetings to review the total study programme of the WCC and to present the results of its review following each meeting to the Central Committee. These meetings, though purely advisory, would provide an opportunity for the various units of the Council and for the Central Committee periodically to secure an overall view of the study work of the WCC.

Neither of the above Committees would affect the existing relationships between the Divisions, Departments, and the Central Committee. Divisions and Departments would receive authorization from the Central Committee and would report to the Central Committee as heretofore.

IV. Principles of Financial Support for WCC General Budget

(a) Support from the member churches

62. The ecumenical movement, because of its very nature, is not only a fellowship of churches of widely different ecclesiastical traditions, confessions and church orders. Its member churches also live in different political and social environments; they are set amidst different nations, races and cultures. It is therefore natural that there should also exist great differences in financial strength among the member churches of the WCC and, consequently, in their contributing capacity to the Council. Moreover, their methods of financing their own operations differ widely. Some have developed among their members a far greater sense of personal responsibility and the stewardship of money and possessions than have others. There are even churches which have as yet little or no machinery for the making of grants to bodies like the World Council.

63. When facing such long-range policy questions as are related to programme and finance, the WCC will have to take a stand in regard to the problems arising from these differences. The Council will have to face the fact that some of its member churches are found in the wealthiest countries of the world and others in 'low-income countries'; that some count their members by millions and others by thousands; that some live in societies where the influence of the churches and the percentage of church membership are growing, whereas elsewhere these are on the decline or at best static; that some churches live in 'pre-Christian' and others in 'post-Christian' societies; that some are national churches and others small minority churches; that some receive considerable state help, and that others have no resources but their own or have to rely upon other churches' financial assistance; that some have a long tradition of generous personal giving whether to central funds or to special appeals, whereas others are accustomed to rely on church taxes or on endowments of various kinds. These differences will remain even if there be agreement as to the task of the WCC and the immediate programme which it should undertake.

64. The immediate pressing problems are two: (i) that created by the difference in respect of financial support which exists between the churches in the USA, which carry at present far more than half the cost of the ecumenical movement, and most other churches in the world, and (ii) that created by the differences in church contributions whatever area of the world is considered, differences which are the result of quite other factors than varying economic standards.

65. The difference between the financial contributions available for the WCC from the American and the non-American churches is apt to create some uneasiness both within and without the ecumenical movement. It was discussed at length both at Amsterdam and at Evanston. It may all too easily

lead, in regard to the financial decisions which have to be taken, to a frustrating feeling of superfluity and irresponsibility among those churches whose contributions to the WCC, however generous in proportion to their contributing capacity, cannot by far match the North American churches' share in terms of size. Any decision by the WCC entailing financial consequences tends therefore to be looked upon by the non-American majority of churches as a proceeding which is not basically their responsibility; they know that its implementation very largely depends upon the North American minority of member churches. Moreover, the North American financial preponderance in the WCC is likely to be interpreted by outsiders as implying decisive USA influence in any ecumenical decision touching on international affairs.

66. There are good reasons for taking these considerations seriously. They should not, however, be too hastily or uncritically accepted. First of all it should be noted that with few exceptions all member churches contribute to the WCC budget and that small contributions from financially weak churches may represent a larger percentage of their total income than large contributions from financially strong churches. But there is more to be said. We must challenge the tacit assumption which is so often made that in an ecumenical organization the influence wielded by any member church is, or should be, at least partly proportionate to its financial contribution. This assumption, however, is of an essentially worldly character. The contributions which the WCC hopes to receive from its member churches are not primarily of a financial nature and there are responsibilities and burdens to be borne in the ecumenical movement which, not appearing in financial accounts, are none the less real.

67. The World Council of Churches was established by the churches to enable them to bear a more effective witness to Christ in the world. The most important obligation of each church in this association is, therefore, to be faithful in its witness and to strengthen the others in their witness. The nature of the burdens to be borne by the several churches varies according to the situations in which they find themselves. For some, in the midst of a hostile political or social environment, the burden involves especially difficult decisions and courageous action. For others—small minorities in nations where another religion is predominant—the burden is to bear witness with few institutions and trained leaders. Still others may be called to bear a disproportionate share of the financial support of the ecumenical fellowship and its agencies. The burdens which the churches bear for one another in their total witness are thus of a wide variety.

68. The only valid authority in this fellowship of churches is that of Holy Scripture and of the Holy Spirit. The only valid influence is that of the faith, understanding, obedience, witness and service of those who participate in it. No inequality in size, culture, history or financial strength of its member churches could ever justify an unequal influence of their representatives. There is no evidence in the history of the ecumenical movement that the financially stronger member churches have acted upon the false worldly assumption. On the contrary, precisely because these member churches rightly reject any undue influence based upon considerations incompatible with the WCC's character, there is every reason for other member churches in financial decisions so to exercise their full responsibilities that the invalidity of these considerations is apparent. If the right principles for an ecumenical fellowship are practised in its daily life, there is moreover no more reason for the WCC to fear outside criticism based upon decisive USA influence than there is to fear the analogous criticism caused by the membership of churches in communist countries.

69. But when all this has been said, there are good reasons for insisting that, whatever the difficulties, the financial contributions from the non-American churches should be not only maintained, but their relative size increased, even if—as some anticipate—outward circumstances exert pressure the other way. Just as it is unwise and unhealthy for individual churches to depend too much upon endowments or upon a few generous individuals, so it is with a body like the WCC. The wider the constituency the sounder the enterprise. It will then be less likely to be suddenly embarrassed by changes in world conditions, and more likely to command the full co-operation at all points of all the member churches. Any further concentration of the financial resources of the WCC in one area of the world should be agreed to only with the greatest reluctance and if all other means of spreading support fail.

70. The second problem—that created by the difference in church contributions resulting from differences in church structure, finance and tradition in these matters—has two facets: (*a*) it has been quite impossible to achieve a standard or develop machinery equitably to compare or evaluate the contributions of the various churches, and (*b*) it is clear that the WCC has neither the right nor the responsibility to urge better stewardship upon Christians or churches merely to increase WCC support. Although it seems unsatisfactory to allow each member church to decide wholly for itself its reasonable or equitable contribution, it would appear that the WCC must continue to correspond with church authorities about the adequacy of their financial contributions and to continue to depend upon the interest and efforts of representatives of the churches to persuade their church authorities to increase their interest in and contributions to the support of the Council's programme.

(*b*) *Support from sources other than member church contributions*

71. Since 1954, the Central Committee has authorized a number of 'programme projects' which have, in essence, been distinguished by the fact that they are financed outside the general budget of the WCC. Substantial additions to the programme especially of the Division of Studies and the Division of Ecumenical Action have been made possible by this means. This development has been under the constant scrutiny of the Finance, Executive and Central Committees. In the opinion of the Programme and Finance Committee it is a policy which should be continued for the following reasons.

72. A first reason for programme projects is the need for flexibility. It is difficult to make quick adjustments in the general budget of the WCC, so that for the periods between the Assemblies at least, the financial structure of the WCC is relatively inflexible. Experience, however, indicates that it is important for the WCC to have some means to ensure flexibility in its financing of programme, especially in order that emerging needs, properly recognized by the Assembly or the Central Committee, may be met.

73. A second reason lies in the need to provide services in the form of *ad hoc* programmes which are specialized. They may be specialized in their subject matter, or they may be specialized in that they refer primarily to a group of member churches within the total constituency. Indeed, a case can be made that the general work of a Department is made more significant in so far as it can provide more specialized and highly competent programmes within its overall task. But this specialization is, in comparison with the funds available for the general budget, expensive. The 'programme project' is a way to meet these demands, which appear to be growing rather than to be diminishing.

74. Thirdly, the programme project is a means of experiment. By setting up an *ad hoc* project, the WCC can determine whether a new area of work, or a new emphasis of programme, is of real value without committing its general

budget. The programme project thus becomes a means of securing flexibility, not only in financing, but in programme as well, providing that kind of pioneering effort which may well result in the enrichment of the WCC as a whole.

75. If experience has indicated reasons for continuing and regularizing 'programme projects', it has also pointed to *certain points where control* should be constantly exercised.

76. First, it is important to ensure that the development of 'programme projects' does not proceed in such a way that 'the tail wags the dog'. It is easier to get money from foundations and individuals for some causes than for others. There are also special groups within the member churches which are glad to contribute to further their particular concerns ecumenically. Care must be exercised to ensure that the total balance of the WCC programme is maintained.

77. Second, financial proportions must be maintained, so that it is always true that the WCC depends upon the member churches for its financial life and not upon special sources of income. This point is so widely recognized as not to need development, but it must be mentioned and constantly be the subject of review in order that responsibility is felt by the churches for the finances of the WCC and that special sources of income be regarded as only supplementary to the main financial structure.

78. Thirdly, it is important to control the appeals which are made so that there is no competition between them or between special appeals and the income for the general budget. This has been provided for since the inception in 1955 of procedures for special appeals and it is of crucial importance that administrative measures be maintained which will assure the proper clearance so that both objectives are secured. This will be of particular importance in the event of integration of the IMC-WCC. With these factors in mind, the Committee proposes that the following points which have been adopted by the Executive Committee be reaffirmed:

(i) *Definition*

A WCC Programme Project is an activity, proposed for a limited period of time, which grows out of and is in line with the established programme and policy of the WCC, which is not financed from the General Budget and which is carried on under the direction of a Division or a Department, or directly under the General Secretariat of the WCC, under the general control of the Central Committee.

(ii) *Authorization*

A WCC Programme Project shall be a programme item which has been properly approved and authorized by the Assembly but for which, by reason of the inadequacy of resources, financial provision has not been included within the General Budget, or shall be a programme item which has been authorized by the Central or Executive Committee on recommendation from the General Secretariat or from the appropriate Divisional or Departmental Committee and after reference to the Committee or Sub-Committee.

(iii) *Sources of support*

The main sources of support for WCC Programme Projects shall be individuals, foundations and church agencies. In order to avoid competition between appeals or with income for any WCC budget, appeals to such sources may be made only after authorization by the General

Secretary and the Chairman of the Finance Committee and, if the appeal is to be presented to a church agency, only after clearance with the appropriate officers of the church concerned. Contributions may be accepted from member churches for the support of a WCC Programme Project, provided that such designated gifts shall not be accepted if the effect would be to reduce income otherwise available for the General Budget.

V. The Budgets of the World Council of Churches

79. The World Council of Churches operates upon two budgets, and if integration takes place, it is proposed that it should operate upon three budgets. The two present budgets are the General Budget and the Service Programme Budget of the Division of Inter-Church Aid and Service to Refugees. The third budget, in the event of integration, would be the budget of the Commission and Division on World Mission and Evangelism.

80. The basic reason for these three separate budgets lies in the fact of different sources of income. The General Budget is supported chiefly by contributions from the central agencies of member churches. The Service Programme Budget of DICASR is supported by the various agencies of the member churches which raise money for relief, inter-church aid and refugee work. The budget of the proposed Commission and Division of World Mission and Evangelism would be supported by those agencies now supporting the International Missionary Council, namely, its constituent councils and their member bodies (whether missionary societies, boards or churches) and individuals. Giving by individuals is a major factor in the present IMC budget and therefore in the support of the proposed Commission; there is some individual giving to the present WCC budgets.

81. The procedures required now, and in the future, for the administration of these separate budgets differ. The Central Committee, through its Finance Committee, controls and administers the General Budget. The Service Programme Budget of DICASR is prepared, raised and administered as a separate budget for which the Administrative Committee of DICASR is responsible, under the control of the Central Committee in accordance with procedures which have been developed and which it is proposed to incorporate in the provisions of the proposed new Rule VIII (2) of the WCC. The Joint Committee's Sub-Committee on the financial aspects of integration has made proposals concerning the procedures to be followed, if integration takes place, for the preparation and administration of the budget of the new Commission and Division of World Mission and Evangelism; those proposals will come forward through the Administrative Committee of IMC and the Joint Committee.

82. Mention must also be made of a fourth budget—that of CCIA. CCIA has, until now, been an agency related to both WCC and IMC and supported by grants from both organizations. Suggestions are made below for the future operation of the CCIA budget (see paragraph 91).

(a) *General Budget of the World Council*

83. At the outset of its work, the Committee on Programme and Finance foresaw the need for a substantial increase in the General Budget, reporting to the Central Committee in 1957 that 'a study of the financial needs to permit the present programme to be adequately maintained without increase in the period following the Third Assembly indicated the clear conclusion that substantial increase in the budget would be necessary'. In 1958, the Com-

mittee reported to the Central Committee some fifteen points at which in its judgment increase in the budget might be required for this period. In 1959, the Committee presented to the Central Committee a suggested budget for the post-Assembly period which implied need for an increase of about 47 per cent in member church contributions from the forecast 1960 level. The suggested budget was circulated to all member churches as an Appendix to the Interim Report. In that report the Committee recognized that an increase of about 47 per cent in contributions raises a very substantial problem and asked whether the member churches would be willing and able to provide the resources needed for such a General Budget. The Committee also pointed out that it had reached the conclusion that no substantial reduction in the proposed budget could be made without drastically curtailing the programme of the World Council in a manner which does not appear to correspond to the desires of the member churches.

84. The discussion in the Central Committee and the comments received from member churches appear to indicate that there is a recognition of the need for such an increase in budget and a willingness to provide the necessary resources. The Committee on Programme and Finance therefore re-examined the budget in April 1960 and, in the light of more recent information and subsequent developments, revised it at some points. The budget proposed by this report totals $751,200 (see Annex I) and implies a need for member church contributions totalling $727,200. This latter figure must be compared with estimated total member church contributions in 1960 of $495,000 (after deducting from estimated 1960 revenue certain extraordinary receipts). The needed average increase in member church contributions thus remains equivalent to approximately 47 per cent.

85. The major increases proposed fall in the following categories:

(i) to implement authorizations already given, namely for work on racial and ethnic relations (to be carried out within the Division of Studies, under the Department on Church and Society) and on religious liberty (to be carried out within the Division of Studies). The provision for these items is $28,000;

(ii) to provide for possible new regional developments—$15,000;

(iii) to increase the annual allocation to the reserve for the expenses of the next Assembly by $10,000 from $20,000 to $30,000. The Committee does not foresee that this increased provision will cover the full cost of the Fourth Assembly and therefore notes that a special appeal will be necessary for that meeting;

(iv) maintenance and services in the new building will be more expensive than in the present accommodation. Provision for the increased expense is included in the suggested budgets for the divisions, departments, etc., and amounts in total to about $20,000;

(v) the Committee considers that it is unwise to prepare a budget for a period several years in advance, without making provision for contingencies. $25,000 is included for this purpose. If there should be continuing inflation, the resultant increases in costs, particularly in relation to staff salaries, will be a first charge against this item;

(vi) the remainder of the increase, namely $144,860, represents provision for the strengthening of departments or other units to enable them more adequately to carry the responsibilities which have been placed upon them. The Evanston Assembly recognized that the efficient operation of a department requires that there be two Secretaries, whereas in most departments it has been possible only to provide for one Secretary up to the present time; the proposed new budget would ensure that no department is served by only one Secretary. Provision is made for a fourth member of the professorial staff at Bossey (as approved by the Evanston Assembly), for strengthening the General Secretary's office, the Information Department, the Department of Finance and Administration and the CCIA and for improving the library and translation services.

Even these increases provide only a modest operation in the departments and divisions. The only provision for new developments is the small item of $15,000 for new regional developments. Accordingly, as has been indicated above, the Committee considers it necessary to recognize that special 'project funds' will be required for any new programme items which may be authorized by the Assembly or the Central Committee and which are not included in the proposed General Budget.

86. The proposed budget cannot be more than a model to show average costs and general relationships. It is quite impossible at this date to forecast the economic conditions in the years that lie ahead. Steady inflation or rapid deflation would, of course, present severe problems. It is therefore clear that the Assembly, meeting but once in six years, cannot fix a realistic budget for the whole period between Assemblies and that the Central Committee must be trusted to recommend such changes as economic conditions may require and as may be acceptable to the member churches.

(*b*) *Other Budgets*

(i) *Division of Inter-Church Aid, Refugee and World Service*

87. The Service Programme budget of this Division provides for the salaries of all divisional staff, including the Director, the costs of administration, travel, etc., and such items of programme as the churches desire to carry out co-operatively through the Division, e.g. refugee service, scholarships and fraternal workers, health programme, ecumenical youth services programme, etc. The Service Programme budget for 1961 totals $1,106,000 and is attached as Annex II to this report.

88. In the Division, the churches and their national, regional and confessional agencies provide themselves with facilities for the initiating and sustaining of certain ecumenical undertakings which call for regular financial support over a period of years. Examples of such items at the present time include the maintenance of the office and the secretary of the Relief Committee of the Near East Christian Council, the office of the secretary of the Hong Kong Christian Welfare and Relief Council, the service of ecumenical teams and contributions to the EACC and the AACC secretaries. Such items as these are selected by the Administrative Committee and will be included in the future in a special Ecumenical Responsibilities Programme only when the support for them is assured. For these items neither the Division nor the World Council of Churches accepts financial liability.

89. In addition the Division carries responsibility for presenting requests from the churches for ecumenical help through project lists compiled by the staff and commended to the churches by the Administrative Committee for support. The Division also carries responsibility for alerting the churches to emergency needs and for seeking and channelling funds in response to appeals for resources to meet those needs.

(ii) *Commission and Division of World Mission and Evangelism*

90. If integration takes place, the budget of the Commission and Division of World Mission and Evangelism will be administered as a separate budget under the proposed new rule VIII (2) and will be supported by those agencies

now supporting the IMC. A tentative budget for the period following the Third Assembly totalling $201,150 is set out in Annex III.

(iii) *Commission of the Churches on International Affairs*

91. Following integration, CCIA will become an agency of the WCC, whereas it has, until now, been related to both WCC and IMC. Whereas separate bodies have provided financial support until now, the main sources of its income after integration will be grants from the WCC from the General Budget and from the budgets of the Divisions of World Mission and Evangelism and of Inter-Church Aid, Refugee and World Service. The Committee considers that the special nature of CCIA as originally conceived and as it has developed over the years warrants the maintenance of a separate budget for its operations. The administration of that budget under the proposed new Rule VIII (2) would represent little change from past procedures, since it has been the practice for CCIA to submit its budget to WCC and the audited annual accounts of CCIA have been presented regularly to the Finance Committee of the Central Committee. A tentative budget for the period following the Third Assembly, totalling $110,000 is set out in Annex IV.

(c) *Summarized listing of Budgets*

92. The totals of the Budgets foreseen by this report are thus as follows:

(i)	General Budget Proposed level for period following the Third Assembly	$751,200
(ii)	Service Programme Budget of the Division of Inter-Church Aid, Refugee and World Service 1961 level ... ... plus any increase that may be authorized	$1,106,000
(iii)	Commission and Division of World Mission and Evangelism Tentative budget for period following Third Assembly	$201,150
(iv)	Commission of the Churches on International Affairs— tentative budget for period following Third Assembly ...	$110,000

VI. Proposed procedure for action by Assembly on this report

93. The Committee recommends the following procedure for the presentation of this report at the Assembly and for action upon it by the Assembly:

(*a*) that the report be presented to the Assembly on the morning of the second day (Monday, November 20, 1961);

(*b*) that, if desired, a hearing be held at some convenient time on the third or fourth day (Tuesday or Wednesday, November 21 or 22, 1961); and

(*c*) that the following two actions be proposed on the afternoon of the fifth day (Thursday, November 23, 1961):

(i) that the Assembly receives and gives general approval to Sections II, III and IV of the report of the Central Committee on Programme and Finance; and

(ii) that the Assembly refers Section V of the report of the Central Committee on Programme and Finance to the Finance Committee of the Assembly.

94. It is most desirable that proposals for the enlargement of any item of the programme or for additions to the programme should be considered at the time at which the Assembly debates the whole programme and should not be considered piecemeal; any other procedure can lead to distortion of the programme as a result of a desire to perform an adequate task in one particular field of work, without due consideration of the claims of other pro-

grammes. The Assembly can only exercise its sovereign right of decision as to priorities if all proposals regarding programme and finance are before it. Without in any way seeking to limit the right of Assembly Committees to challenge the content of this report, the Committee recommends, with a view to meeting this problem:

(*a*) that the Committee on Programme and Finance be authorized to address a communication to the Chairman of each Assembly Committee setting out in some detail the financial implications and limitations implied in this report for the organizational unit with which that Committee is concerned;

(*b*) that the Central Committee make provision for procedures whereby any proposals which may arise in Assembly Committees which would imply additions to or increases in programme or budget can be discussed with representatives of all Assembly Committees, including the Finance Committee, within the framework of the total programme and budget; and

(*c*) that any such proposals from Assembly Committees be considered by the Assembly not piecemeal at the time at which each Committee reports but at the time at which the total programme and budget are considered on the basis of this report, of the report of the Finance Committee on it and of any recommendations resulting from the discussions under the procedures proposed under (*b*) above.

ANNEXE I

PROPOSED GENERAL BUDGET
for period following Third Assembly

Expenditure	1960 Approved Level $	Proposed Budget for Period after Third Assembly $
General Secretary's Office, Geneva	46,545	66,000
General Units:		
New York Office	55,000	60,000
Far East Office	10,000	10,000
Joint Committee	4,250	—
CCIA	58,000	70,000
Information	25,730	34,200
Finance and Administration	29,500	34,500
Library	7,735	22,000
Translation	2,800	11,000
Division of Studies:		
Divisional Staff	27,000	26,000
Faith and Order	18,460	42,000
Church and Society	14,310	28,000
Racial and Ethnic Relations	—	14,000
Studies in Evangelism	3,570	28,000[1]
Missionary Studies	—	—[1]
Religious Liberty	—	14,000
	(63,340)	(152,000)
Division of Ecumenical Action:		
Divisional Staff	16,825	26,000
Youth	40,515	39,500
Laity	15,105	28,000

	1960 Approved Level $	Proposed Budget for Period after Third Assembly $
Expenditure		
Co-operation of Men and Women in Church, Family and Society	13,650	28,000
	(86,095)	(121,500)
Ecumenical Institute	63,830	75,000
	(149,925)	(196,500)
Division of Inter-Church Aid, Refugee and World Service	10,515	—
Contribution to Ecumenical Press Service ...	5,000	5,000
Allocation to Reserves:		
General Reserve	20,000	20,000
Assembly Reserve	20,000	30,000
Provision for:		
New Developments	—	15,000
Contingencies	24,000	25,000
Total Expenditure	532,340	751,200

[1] The proposed arrangements regarding responsibility for work in the area of evangelism and missionary studies in the integrated WCC-IMC (see paragraph 50 of this report) include provision that 'necessary staff, including the Executive Secretary for the Department of Missionary Studies, shall be made available to the Division of Studies by the Division of World Mission and Evangelism' and assume that the expenses of the Department on Studies in Evangelism and of the portfolio on evangelism in the DWME shall be carried by the General Budget of the WCC.

	1960 Approved Level $	Proposed Budget for Period after Third Assembly $
Revenue		
Member Churches	511,500	727,200
Interest	10,325	10,000
Division of Inter-Church Aid, Refugee and World Service for Divisional Staff	10,515	—
Special contributions to Department on Co-operation of Men and Women in Church, Family and Society	—	14,000
Total Revenue	532,340	751,200

ANNEXE II

DIVISION OF INTER-CHURCH AID AND SERVICE TO REFUGEES

1961 Service Programme Budget

I. Service of the Churches through the Division:

	$	$
1. Service to Refugees:		
(*a*) Supervision of the Programme ...	30,000	

	$	$
(*b*) Resettlement Headquarters ...	39,000	
(*c*) Maintenance pastoral services other countries	21,000	
(*d*) Resettlement offices and welfare services in Europe, Asia, Latin America	350,000	
(*e*) Field Staff Services	85,000	
		525,000
2. Fraternal Workers and Exchanges ...		10,000
3. Scholarships		60,000
4. Material Relief		3,000
5. Literature		10,000
6. Health and medicaments		30,000
7. Casa Locarno		20,000
8. Fidelity Insurance		4,000
9. Ecumenical Staff Services:		
(*a*) Ten senior staff, including travel and administration	209,500	
(*b*) Provision for proposed additional staff	28,000	237,500
		899,500
II. Co-operative Services:		
1. Ecumenical Youth Services:		
(*a*) Work Camps	37,000	
(*b*) World Youth Projects	8,000	45,000
2. CCIA		25,000
3. Division of Studies		1,500
4. Department of Information		20,000
5. East Asia Christian Conference, ICA Secretariat		10,000
6. All Africa Church Conference ...		8,000
		(109,500)
III. National Co-operation and Initiative in Asia, Africa and Latin America:		
1. Asia: Near East	10,000	
Hong Kong	8,000	
Vietnam	5,000	
Burma	4,000	
others	5,000	
2. Africa: Kenya	5,000	
others	5,000	
3. Latin America: Pilot Projects ...	5,000	47,000
IV. Special Emphases:		
1. Migration Conference and Secretariat (1961)	25,000	
2. Subsidy for Orthodox in the West ...	25,000	50,000
Grand total		1,106,000

ANNEXE III

COMMISSION AND DIVISION OF WORLD MISSION AND EVANGELISM

Tentative Budget for period following Third Assembly

Revenue	$
Contributions from affiliated councils	159,650
Canada—special gift	3,500
Grant from WCC General Budget for evangelism	14,000
Contributions from special sources	22,000
Deficit	2,000
Total Revenue	201,150
Expenditure	
Salaries, allowances, accountancy, rent, office expenses and equipment:	
Geneva[1]	40,500
London	29,200
New York	73,950
East Asia Secretariat	10,000
Staff travel	19,000
Promotion and Printing	2,500
Contribution to:	
Commission of the Churches on International Affairs	15,000
Ecumenical Press Service	500
International Review of Missions	500
Reserve for meetings	10,000
Total Expenditure	201,150

[1] Includes also staff travel.

ANNEXE IV

COMMISSION OF THE CHURCHES ON INTERNATIONAL AFFAIRS

Tentative Budget for period following Third Assembly

Revenue	$
World Council of Churches General Budget	70,000
Commission of World Mission and Evangelism	15,000
Division of Inter-Church Aid and Service to Refugees	25,000
Total Revenue	110,000
Expenditure	
Geneva office	18,000
London office	23,500
New York office	63,500
Extended services—part-time assistance (Asia, Africa, Latin America), travel, UNESCO (Paris)	5,000
Total Expenditure	110,000

Appendix 4

LISTS OF THOSE PRESENT AT THE ASSEMBLY

The following lists were presented by the Credentials Committee

A. DELEGATES FROM MEMBER CHURCHES

NOTE: * Not present.
° Delegates appointed according to the plans of integration between WCC and IMC.
† See note under United Kingdom, Church of England

Presidents:
Barbieri, Bishop S. U., *Methodist Church USA* (*also delegate*)
Dibelius, Bishop Otto, *Evangelical Church in Germany* (*United*)
Iakovos, Most Reverend, Archbishop of North and South America, *Ecumenical Patriarchate*
Juhanon, Metropolitan, Mar Thoma, *Mar Thoma Syrian Church of Malabar*
Sherrill, Bishop Henry Knox, *Protestant Episcopal Church, USA*

ARGENTINA
Evangelical German Synod of Rio de la Plata
*Hoppe, Propst Friedrich
Obermüller, Rev. Prof. Rodolfo

AUSTRALASIA
Methodist Church of Australasia
Hambly, Rev. W. F.
Lade, Rev. Principal Norman
Trigge, Rev. Prof. H. H.
Wyllie, Mrs M. G.

AUSTRALIA
Church of England in Australia and Tasmania
Church, Rev. Canon Ivor F.
Coaldrake, Rev. Canon F. W.
Garnsey, Rt Rev. D. A., Bishop of Gippsland
Gough, Most Rev. H. R., Archbishop of Sydney
Kerle, Rt Rev. R. C.
Webb, Prof. Leicester
Woods, Most Rev. Frank, Archbishop of Melbourne
Congregational Union of Australia
Merry, Rev. Isabelle
Rees-Thomas, Rev. Thomas
Federal Conference of Churches of Christ in Australia
Williams, Rev. Principal E. L.
Wright, Rev. Charles H. J.

AUSTRALIA—continued

Presbyterian Church of Australia

Cumming-Thom, Rev. Dr W.
°Engel, Rev. Frank
Ritchie, Principal Catherine
Walker, Rt Rev. A. Trafford
Wilson, Mr R. D.

AUSTRIA

Evangelische Kirche A.u.H.B. in Österreich

May, Rt Rev. Bishop Gerhard
Zerbst, Rev. Prof. Fritz

BELGIUM

Eglise Chrétienne Missionnaire Belge

Lacocque, Rev. Prof. A. M. L.

Eglise Evangélique Protestante de Belgique

Pichal, Rev. E. A. D.

BRAZIL

Synodal Federation, Evangelical

Gottschald, Rev. Karl

Church Luther. Confession in Brazil

Schlieper, Präses Ernesto Th.

Methodist Church of Brazil

Amaral, Bishop Joao A. do

BULGARIA

Bulgarian Orthodox Church

*Jossif, Most Rev., Metropolitan of Varna and Preslaw
Nikodim, Most Rev., Metropolitan of Sliven

BURMA

Burma Baptist Convention

°Chain, Mrs Ba Maung
Hmyin, Rev. U Ba
Kyaw, Rev. S'Aye Mya

CAMEROUN

Eglise Evangélique du Cameroun

Kotto, Rev. Jean

Union des Eglises Baptistes du Cameroun

Mbende, Rev. Paul

CANADA

The Anglican Church of Canada

Brewin, Mr F. A.
†Davis, Rev. Canon A. H.
Puxley, Rev. Canon H. L.
Rendell, Miss M. D.
Wright, Most Rev. W. L., Archbishop of Algoma

Churches of Christ (Disciples)

McCully, Rev. Oliver W.

CANADA—continued
Presbyterian Church in Canada
Coles, Rev. Stuart B.
Johnson, Rev. Dr Edward H.
United Church of Canada
Chalmers, Rev. Prof. R. C.
Clark, Rev. Robert M.
Cragg, Prof. Laurence H.
°Honey, Rev. T. E. F.
Long, Rev. Dr Ernest E.
McLeod, Rt Rev. Hugh A.
Young, Miss Dorothy M.
Yearly Meeting of the Society of Friends
Abbott, Dr Edwin V.

CENTRAL AFRICA
Church of Province of Central Africa
Lee, Rev. F. W. M.
Sillet, Rev. Frederick T.

CEYLON
Church of India, Pakistan, Burma and Ceylon
De Soysa, The Ven. Archdeacon Charles H. W.
Methodist Church in Ceylon
Silva, Rev. F. S. de

CHILE
Pentecostal Church of Chile
Campos, Rev. E. Chavez
Pentecostal Mission Church
Ortiz, Rev. V. Pavez

CYPRUS
Church of Cyprus
Mitsides, Mr Andreas N.

CZECHOSLOVAKIA
Evangelical Church of Czech Brethren
Hajek, Very Rev. Dr Victor
Hromadka, Rev. Prof. J. L.
Evangelical Church in Slovakia, Augsburg Confession
*Chabada, Rt Rev. Bishop Jan
*Michalko, Prof. Jan
Ziak, Prof. Andrej
Reformed Christian Church in Slovakia
Varga, Bishop Emerich
Evangelical Church of the Augsburg Confession, Silesia
*Cymorek, Rt Rev. Bishop Georg

DENMARK
Baptist Union of Denmark
Nørgaard, Rev. Dr Johannes
Church of Denmark
Bender, Miss Edith O.

DENMARK—continued

Church of Denmark—continued

Engberg, Mr Paul M. T.
Høgsbro, Rt Rev. Bishop H. R.
Westergaard-Madsen, Rt Rev. Bishop W.
Søe, Rev. Prof. N. H.

EAST AFRICA

Church of the Province of East Africa

Beecher, Most Rev. Leonard J., Archbishop of East Africa
†Kalume, Mr T. J.

Presbyterian Church of East Africa

Kareri, Rev. Charles M.

EGYPT

Coptic Orthodox Church

Assabghy, Rev. I.
Tadros, Mr Mikhail
Makary el Souriany, Rev. Fr
Yoannis, Most Rev., Metropolitan of Khartoum and Uganda
Abdou, Rev. Fr Yousaf

Greek Orthodox Patriarchate of Alexandria

Galiatsatos, Rev. N.
Parthenios-Aris, Most Rev. C., Metropolitan of Carthage

ETHIOPIA

Ethiopian Orthodox Church

Kebede, Rev. H. W. Ermias
Petros, Abba
Samuel-Terefe, Rev. Dr W. M.
Theophilos, His Beatitude, Archbishop of Harrar
Workineh, Abba Habte Mariam
Yohannes-Gabre, Dr E. W.

FINLAND

Evangelical Lutheran Church of Finland

Castrén, Miss Inga-Brita
Gulin, Rt Rev. Bishop E. G.
Nikolainen, Rev. Prof. A. T.
Teinonen, Rev. Dr Seppo A.
Vuorela, Rev. Olavi

FORMOSA

Presbyterian Church in Formosa

*Hwang, Rev. Dr C. H.

FRANCE

Eglise de la Confession d'Augsburg d'Alsace et de Lorraine

Appel, Rev. Dr André
Jung, President Etienne

Eglise Evangélique Luthérienne de France

Sweeting, Rev. Maurice

Eglise Réformée d'Alsace et de Lorraine

Mehl, Rev. Prof. Roger

FRANCE—continued

Eglise Réformée de France

Burgelin, Prof. A. H.
Gaillard, Rev. Albert
Westphal, Rev. Charles

GABON

Eglise Evangélique du Gabon

Amvame, Rev. President B. Ndong

GERMANY

Altkatholische Kirche in Deutschland

Küppers, Pfarrer Prof. W. F. A.

Evangelische Brüder-Unität

Motel, Pfarrer Dr Heinz

Evangelische Kirche in Deutschland

Lutherisch

Becker, Schwester Elisabeth
Beste, Landesbischof Dr N.
Düll, Dekan Hanns
Glombitza, Superintendent Otto
Harms, Hauptpastor, Dr H.
*°Hoffmann, Dr Gerhard
Hübner, Oberkirchenrat Dr F.
Lllje, Landesbischof Dr Hanns
*Mager, Präsident Reimek
Metzger, Prälat Dr Wolfgang
Meyer, Bischof H. J. A.
Nold, Mrs Liselotte
Noth, Landesbischof Gottfried
Peters, Landessuperintendent H. H.
°Pörksen, Missionsdirektor Pfarrer Dr M.
Scheffbuch, Pfarrer Rolf
Vicedom, Prof. Dr Georg F.
Wischmann, Präsident Adolf
Thomä, Mrs Hedwig M. L.

Reformiert

Niesel, Prof. Dr Wilhelm
Smidt, Landessuperintendent Udo

Uniert

*Becker, Frau Pfarrvikarin Ingeborg
Beckmann, Präses D. Joachim
Bismarck, Dr Klaus von
Brennecke, Missionsdirektor Dr G.
Dietze, Prof. Dr C. Von
Heinemann, Dr Gustav
*Hornig, Bischof D.
*Jacob, Dr Gunter K. A.
Kloppenburg, Oberkirchenrat Heinz
Krüger, Oberkirchenrat Dr H.
Locher, Pfarrer Benjamin
Müller, Pfarrer Dr Martin
Niemöller, Pfarrer Dr Martin

GERMANY—continued

Scharf, Präses K. F. W.
Schlink, Prof. Dr Edmund
Thadden-Trieglaff, Dr R. von
Thimme, Vizepräsident Dr H.

GHANA

Methodist Church

Amissah, Mr Samuel H.

Presbyterian Church of Ghana

°Baëta, Rev. Dr C. G.
Richter, Rev. Philip C.

GREECE

Church of Greece

Alivisatos, Prof. Hamilcar
Barnabas, Most Rev., Metropolitan of Kitrous
Bonis, Prof. Konstantinos
Dionysius, Most Rev., Metropolitan of Edessa and Pella
*Dionysius, Most Rev., Metropolitan of Servia and Kozani
Iakovos, Most Rev., Metropolitan of Mytilene
Ioannidis, Prof. Basil
Kalogiru, Prof. Ioannis
Konidaris, Prof. Gerassimos
Kotsonis, Very Rev. Prof. Jerome
*Meletios, Most Rev., Metropolitan of Kithiron
*Moraitis, Prof. Dimitrios
Panteleimon, Rt Rev., Bishop of Achaia
Philippos, Most Rev., Metropolitan of Drama
Phytrakis, Prof. Andreas
Siotis, Prof. Markos
Trakas, Prof. Ioannis

Greek Evangelical Church

Kaloterakis, Rev. Stelios

HUNGARY

Lutheran Church of Hungary

Káldy, Rt Rev. Bishop Zoltán
Ottlyk, Rev. Prof. Ernö

Reformed Church of Hungary

Bartha, Bishop Dr Tibor
Szamosközi, Bishop István
Varga, Prof. Dr Zsigmond

ICELAND

Lutheran Church of Iceland

*Einarsson, Rt Rev. Bishop S.

INDIA

Church of India, Pakistan, Burma and Ceylon

De Mel, Rt Rev. Lakdasa, Bishop of Kurunagala
Sadiq, Rt Rev. John W., Bishop of Nagpur

INDIA—continued

Church of South India

Chandran, Rev. J. R.
Daniel, Sister Beatrice
Jebaraj, Rt Rev. A. G.
Paul, Mr R. D.
Sahayam, Rev. V. D.
Sumitra, Most Rev. H.

Federation of Evangelical Lutheran Churches

Devadoss, Rev. President K.
Kandavalli, Rev. President K.
Kondpan, Rev. A. C.
Manikam, Rt Rev. Bishop Rajah
Pichai, Dr Robert I.
Raman, Rev. President Emmanuel

Mar Thoma Syrian Church of Malabar

John, Rev. C. V.
Mathew, Prof. C. P.
Thomas, Rt Rev. Bishop, Mar Athanasius
Thomas, Mr M. M.

Orthodox Syrian Church of the East

Abraham, Most Rev. Metropolitan, Mar Clemis
Cherian, Mr K. M.
Dionysius, Most Rev., Mar Thoma
Philipos, Rev. Fr Korah
Samuel, Rev. Prof. V. C.
Thomas, Mr A. M.

United Church of Northern India and Pakistan

Bhatty, Dr Emmanuel C.
Moses, Rev. Dr David G.
Massey, Mr Nathaniel
Yohan-Masih, Rev. Dr Kenneth
Ud-Din, Very Rev. Dr S. N. Talib

INDONESIA

Christian Church of East Java

Tasdik, Rev.

Christian Church of Mid Java

Probowinoto, Rev. B.

Christian Church of Mid-Sulawesi

Sidjabat, Dr Walter B.

Christian Evangelical Church of Minahassa

Wenas, Rev. A. Z. R.

Christian Evangelical Church of Timor

Radjahaba, Rev. L.

Evangelical Church of Kalimantan

Saloh, Rev. Ethelbert

Protestant Christian Batak Church

Pardede, Mr Tumpal D.
Rahantoknam, Rev. B. A.
Siagian, Mr M. L.
Sihombing, Rev. T.

Protestant Church in Indonesia

Rompas, Rev. Paul

INDONESIA—continued

Reformed Church in Indonesia

Abineno, Dr J. L. Ch.

Sudanese Christian Church of West Java

Tjakraatmadja, Rev. M. K.

ITALY

Evangelical Methodist Church of Italy

Sbaffi, Rev. Mario

Waldensian Church

Rostan, Rev. Ermanno

IRAN

Synod Evangelical Church of North Iran

Yusefzadeh, Mr Habib

JAPAN

Anglican Church in Japan

Nishimura, Rev. K. (until November 24, 1961)

Kan, Rev. Prof. W. E. (after November 24, 1961)

United Church of Christ

Abe, Mr Shiro

Germany, Dr Charles H.

°Muto, Rev. T.

Niwa, Rev. Iwao

Shirai, Rev. Keikichi

KOREA

Korean Methodist Church

°Kim, Dr Helen

Kim, Rev. Kwang Woo

Presbyterian Church in the Republic of Korea

Yong, Rev. Kang Won

LEBANON (SEE ALSO UNDER SYRIA)

Union of the Armenian Evangelical Churches in the Near East

Aharonian, Rev. Prof. Hovhannes P.

MADAGASCAR

Eglise Evangélique de Madagascar

*Ralambomahay, Rev. Jean B.

L.M.S. Synod in Madagascar

Rasendrahasina, Rev. Titus

MEXICO

Methodist Church of Mexico

Ruiz Munoz, Rev. A.

NETHERLANDS

Arminian Church (Remonstrant Brotherhood)

Hoenderdaal, Rev. Dr G. J.

Niewenhuijzen, Rev. J. A.

Dutch Reformed Church

Berkhof, Rev. Prof. H.

NETHERLANDS—continued

Dutch Reformed Church—continued

Emmen, Rev. Dr Egbert
Holsteijn, Miss S. M.
Randwijck, Count S. C. van
Vries, Prof. E. de

Evangelical Lutheran Church

Gramberg, Rev. Th. W. B. G.

General Mennonite Society

Oosterbaan, Rev. Prof. J. A.

Old Catholic Church

*Jans, Bishop P. J.

NEW CALEDONIA

Eglise Evangélique en Nouvelle-Calédonie et aux Iles Loyauté

Madine, Rev. Xowie

NEW ZEALAND

Associated Churches of Christ in New Zealand

Haddon, Rev. Dr A. L.

Baptist Union of New Zealand

Crozier, Rev. J. T.

Church of the Province of New Zealand

Buchanan, Mr Neal H.
Cameron, Rev. Canon M.
Gray, Rev. A. A. W.
Lesser, Most Rev. Norman, Archbishop of New Zealand
Warren, Rt Rev. A. K., Bishop of Christchurch

Congregational Union of New Zealand

Cocks, Rev. N. H. F.

Methodist Church of New Zealand

Leadley, Rev. E. C.
Peterson, Rev. G. R. H.

Presbyterian Church of New Zealand

Bates, Rev. J. M.
Perry, Mr D. N.
Rogers, Rev. R. M.

NIGERIA

Presbyterian Church of Nigeria

Ibiam, Sir Francis

NORWAY

Church of Norway

Spilling, Director Gunnar
*Stensaker, Mrs A. B.
Støylen, Rt Rev. Bishop K.
Strønstad, Rev. A. E.
Tidemann Strand, Rev. Ch.

PAKISTAN

Church of India, Pakistan, Burma and Ceylon

Ray, Rt Rev. Bishop Chandu

United Presbyterian Church of Pakistan

Nasir, Rt Rev. K. L.

PHILIPPINES

Philippine Independent Catholic Church

*Canlas, Rt Rev. N. F.
Diel, Rt Rev. C. C.
Ga, Rt Rev. M. V.
Lagasca, Rt Rev. M.
*Lorenzo, Rt Rev. F.
Villanueva, Rt Rev. D. O.

United Church of Christ in the Philippines

Evangelista, Bishop M.
Montes, Mr V. G.

POLAND

Evangelical Church of the Augsburgian Confession

Wantula, Rt Rev. Bishop A.

Catholic Church of Poland

Rode, Rt. Rev. Bishop M.

Orthodox Church of Poland

Znosko, Rev. Aleksy

RHODESIA

United Church of Central Africa in Rhodesia

Mwenda, Rev. Kingsley

RUMANIA

Hungarian Lutheran Church in Rumania

Tiberiu, Prof. Kozma

Protestant Evangelical Church of the Augsburgian Confession

Binder, Rev. Dr H.

Rumanian Orthodox Church

Ionesco, Pater Alexandrev
Justin, Most Rev. Metropolitan

Transylvanian Reformed Church

Büthi, Rev. A.

SAMOA

Congregational Christian Church in Samoa (Samoan Church, L.M.S. Synod)

Toma, Mr Vavae

SOUTH AFRICA

Bantu Congregational Church in South Africa

Ngcobo, Rev. N. G.

Bantu Presbyterian Church of South Africa

Sikutshwa, Rev. D. V.

Church of the Province of South Africa

Burnett, Rt Rev. B. B., Bishop of Bloemfontein
Knapp-Fisher, Rt Rev. E., Bishop of Pretoria
†Zulu, Rt Rev. A. H.

Congregational Union of South Africa

Brown, Rev. B. H. M.

Methodist Church of South Africa

Mahabane, Rev. E. E.
Wilkinson, Rev. C. E.

SOUTH AFRICA—continued

Moravian Church in the Western Cape Province

Krüger, Rev. Bernhard

Presbyterian Church of South Africa

*Mitchell, Rt Rev. R. B.

SPAIN

Spanish Evangelical Church

Gutiérrez-Marin, Rev. Prof. M.

SWEDEN

Church of Sweden

Boethius, Mr C. G.
Diehl, Rev. Dr C. G.
Hassler, Rev. Dr Ove
Hultgren, Most Rev. Archbishop G. A. E.
Ljungberg, Rt Rev. Bishop H. D.
Karlström, Dean Nils
Thunberg, Mrs Anne-Marie
Weman, Rev. Gunnar

Mission Covenant Church of Sweden

Hedberg, Rev. A. Gosta
Stenström, Rev. A.

SWITZERLAND

Old Catholic Church

Gauthier, Rev. Léon

Swiss Protestant Church Federation

Bührig, Dr Margarete
Döbeli, Dr A.
Reymond, Rev. Eugène
d'Espine, Rev. Prof. H.
Schnyder, Rev. C.

SYRIA

Evangelical Synod of Syria and Lebanon

Howly, Rev. Showky

Greek Orthodox Patriarchate of Antioch

Hazim, Very Rev. Ignatius

Patriarchate of Antioch and All the East

Athanasius, Most Rev. Archbishop Samuel Mar
Simon, Rev. Dr K. M.

TANGANYIKA

Evangelical Church of North Western Tanganyika

Sundkler, Rt Rev. Bishop B.

Usambara-Digo Lutheran Church

*Waltenberg, Rt Rev. Bishop H.

THAILAND

Church of Christ

Chailangkarn, Mr M.

TOGO

Eglise Evangélique du Togo

Nomenyo, Rev. S.

TURKEY

Ecumenical Patriarchate of Constantinople

*Amaryllios, Rt Rev. Archimandrite
*Anagnostopoulos, Prof. Basil
Athenagoras, Most Rev., Metropolitan of Elaia (Canada)
Athenagoras, Most Rev., Archbishop of Thyateira (UK)
Bacopulos, Rev. Fr G. (USA)
Chrysostomos, Rt Rev., Metropolitan of Myra
*Chrysostomos, Rt. Rev., Metropolitan of Neo Cesarea
Eirinaios, Rt Rev., Bishop of Kissamos and Selinos (Greece)
Emilianos, Rt Rev., Bishop of Meloa (Geneva)
Florovsky, Rev. Prof. G. (USA)
Iakovos, Most Rev., Metropolitan of Philadelphia
Kirkinen, Mr H. (Finland)
Kourides, Mr P. (USA)
*Maximos, Rt Rev., Metropolitan of Stauropolis
Meliton, Rt Rev., Metropolitan of Imros and Tenedos
Raphael, Mr C. G. (USA)
Spyridon, Most Rev., Metropolitan of Rhodes

UGANDA

Church of the Province of Uganda and Ruanda Urundi

Brown, Most Rev. L. W., Archbishop of Uganda
Lwanga, The Ven. Archdeacon B. K.
†Wakiro, Mr C. P.

UNITED KINGDOM

Baptist Union of Great Britain and Ireland

Barker, Mr C. C.
Barker, Mrs M. F.
Champion, Rev. Principal L. G.
Madge, Rev. E. G. T.
Payne, Rev. Dr E. A.

Churches of Christ in Great Britain and Ireland

Gray, Mr James

Church of England

Allison, Rt Rev. S. F., Bishop of Winchester
Batten, Miss E. M.
Bliss, Dr Kathleen
Clark, Mr O. W. H.
Coggan, Most Rev. F. D., Archbishop of York
Cooper, Rev. Henry
Dalby, Rev. Fr F. B., S.S.J.E.
Dillistone, Very Rev. F. W., Dean of Liverpool
†Eley, Rt Rev. S. A., Bishop of Gibraltar
Grubb, Sir Kenneth
°Houghton, Rev. A. T.
Howard, Miss Christian
Kirk, Mr Peter
Lawrence, Mr John

UNITED KINGDOM—continued

Church of England—continued

†MacInnes, Most Rev. A. C., Archbishop in Jerusalem (Jordan)
Ramsey, Most Rev. A. M., Archbishop of Canterbury
Richardson, Rev. Canon Alan
Roxburgh, Rev. J. W.
†Sansbury, Rt Rev. C. K., Bishop of Singapore
†Satterthwaite, Rev. J .R.
*Say, Rt Rev. R. D., Bishop of Rochester
°Sulston, Rev. A. E. A.
°Taylor, Rev. J. V.
Tomkins, Rt Rev. O. S., Bishop of Bristol

† The Churches of the Anglican Communion were allocated an additional twelve places, of which eleven were used. The delegates so appointed are included in their respective delegations.

Church of Ireland

Hartford, Rev. Dr R. R.
Herdman, Commander C. A.

Church of Scotland

Barbour, Rev. Dr R. A. S.
Graham, Rev. Dr J. M.
Hay, Mrs W. G.
Longmuir, Rev. J. B.
Munn, Rev. James
Shillinglaw, Rev. A. R.
Tindal, Rev. Prof. W. S.
°Walls, Miss E. A. C.
Wemyss, Rt Hon. the Earl of

Church in Wales

Jacob, The Ven. W. U. Archdeacon of Carmarthen
Richards, Rt Rev. J. Richards, Bishop of St Davids

Congregational Union of England and Wales

Follett, Rev. C. T.
Janes, Rev. M. O.
Marsh, Rev. Dr John
Stanley, Rev. H. S.

Congregational Union of Scotland

George, Rev. J. T.

Episcopal Church in Scotland

Easson, Rt Rev. E. F., Bishop of Aberdeen

Methodist Church

Baker, Rev. Dr Eric
Bingle, Mrs L. R. M.
Coulson, Prof. C. A.
Edwards, Rev. M. L.
Greet, Rev. B. A.
Pande, Rev. C. C. (India)[1]
Roberts, Rev. Dr Harold
Rogers, Rev. Edward
Sherlock, Rev. Hugh (Jamaica)[1]
Thompson, Rev. D. W.

[1] The Methodist delegation is eight from United Kingdom, plus two from overseas (total ten).

UNITED KINGDOM—continued

Methodist Church in Ireland
Ranson, Rev. Dr C. W.
Moravian Church in Great Britain and Ireland
Vittoz, Rev. P.
Presbyterian Church of England
MacLeod, Rev. Prof. A. G.
Presbyterian Church in Ireland
Fulton, Very Rev. Dr A. A.
Patterson, Rev. T. C.
Presbyterian Church of Wales
Roberts, Miss G. R.
Salvation Army International (not listed under countries)
Benjamin, Lieut-Col. B. (Pakistan)
Cook, Col. A. B. (New Zealand)
Corputty, Major J. A. (Indonesia)
Dahya, Lt Comm. (India)
Marshall, Commissioner N. S. (USA)
Munyi, Sen. Maj. J. (Kenya)
Sanjivi, Col. D. A. (India)
Woods, Comm. Reginald (United Kingdom)
Yamamuro, Lieut-Col. T. (Japan)

USA

African Methodist Episcopal Church
Baber, Bishop George
Bright, Bishop John D. (Southern Rhodesia)[1]
Gomez, Bishop Joseph
Wright, Bishop R. R.
African Methodist Episcopal Zion Church
Eichelberger, Dr J. W.
Shaw, Bishop H. B.
Walls, Bishop W. J.
American Baptist Convention
Bonell, Rev. Harold
Dahlberg, Rev. Dr E. T.
Gallup, Mr Stanton
Gezork, Rev. Dr Herbert
°Jones, Dr Irene
Martin, Mrs Mabel B.
Miller, Mr James C.
Morikawa, Rev. J.
McBain, Rev. Dr L. D.
Skoglund, Rev. Dr John E.
Tuller, Rev. Edwin H.
°Willingham, Rev. Dr E. B.
American Evangelical Lutheran Church
Riber, Rev. H.
The American Lutheran Church
Miottel, Dr R. W.
Schuh, Rev. Dr H. F.
Schiotz, Rev. Dr F. A.

[1] The African Methodist Episcopal delegation is three from USA, plus one from Africa.

U S A—continued

The American Lutheran Church—continued

Rogness, Rev. Dr A. N.
Haas, Dr Dorothy
Fendt, Rev. Dr E. C.
Falde, Rev. Dr G.
Brown, Rev. L. D.
Larsen, Rev. Dr W.

Augustana Evangelical Lutheran Church

Sorensen, Dean C. W.
Bersell, Rev. Dr P.
Lundeen, Rev. Dr M. H.

Christian Methodist Episcopal Church

Graves, Rev. William
*Smith, Bishop B. Julian

Church of the Brethren

Baugher, Rev. Dr N. J.
Ziegler, Rev. Dr E. K.

The Church of the East (Assyrian)

Shimun, Patriarch Catholicos Mar Eshai

Evangelical United Brethren Church

Baker, Miss M. L.
*Church, Rev. Dr P. V.
Eller, Rev. Dr P. H.
Milhouse, Bishop P. W.
Mueller, Bishop R. H.
Roberts, Rev. Dr W. N.

Hungarian Reformed Church in America

Beky, Bishop Zoltan

International Convention of Christian Churches (Disciples of Christ)

Beazley, Rev. George
Blakemore, Rev. Dr William B.
Cook, Rev. Dr Gaines M.
Fiers, Rev. Dr A. D.
Miller, Mr J. Irwin
Pennybacker, Rev. A. M.
Sikes, Rev. Prof. Walter
°Sly, Rev. Dr Virgil
Ward, Rev. Dr Mae Y.
West, Rev. Dr William G.

The Methodist Church, USA

Amstutz, Bishop H. B. (Singapore)
Barbieri, Bishop S. U. (Argentina)
Booth, Bishop Newell S.
Bosley, Rev. Dr Harold
Brown, Mrs P.
Cannon, Rev. Dr W. R.
*Chou, Dr Ivy (Sarawak)
Chow, Rev. Timothy Y. H. (Hong Kong)
Christdas, Miss Chanda (India)
Corson, Bishop F. P.
Crutchfield, Rev. F. A.
Denman, Mr Harry
Ensley, Bishop F. G.

U S A—continued

The Methodist Church, USA—continued

Griffith, Dr E. S.
Ho Seng Ong, Rev. Dr (Malaya)
Jones, Mr Edwin L.
McCulloh, Rev. Dr Gerald
Martin, Bishop William C.
°Mathews, Bishop James K.
Mayfield, Dr Robert G.
°Miguez-Bonino, Rev. Prof. J. (Argentina)
Mondol, Bishop Shot K. (India)
Moreira, Principal Neliya (Malaya)
Moreland, Dr J. Earl
Morrison, Rev. Dr Paul
Muelder, Dean Walter G.
Nelson, Rev. Prof. J. Robert
Outler, Rev. Prof. A. C.
Parlin, Mr Charles
Potts, Rev. J. Manning
Ragsdale, Rev. Dr Ray W.
Richardson, Rev. Dr Harry V.
Raines, Bishop Richard C.
Ram, Miss Sarah Kashi (India)
Sahai, Rev. Dr George S. (India)
Saunders, Rev. Dr Ernest W.
Shain, U San (Burma)
Short, Bishop Roy H.
Shungu, Rev. John W. (Congo)
Sigg, Bishop Ferdinand (Switzerland)
Smith, Rev. Dr Eugene L.
Sundaram, Bishop Gabriel (India)
Tillman, Mrs Sadie
Valencia, Bishop José (Philippines)
°Wakatama, Principal Matthew (Southern Rhodesia)
Wunderlich, Bishop Friedrich (Germany)

NOTE: The Methodist delegation is 27 from USA, plus 16 from overseas—total 43.

National Baptist Convention, USA, Inc.

Davis, Dr A. L.
Freeman, Rev. E. A.
Hampton, Dr C. H.
Jackson, President Joseph H.
Jackson, Mrs Maude T.

Presbyterian Church in the US

Caldwell, Rev. Dr F. H.
Green, Miss Evelyn L.
Millard, Rev. Dr James
Stell, Rev. Dr Lawrence I.

Protestant Episcopal Church

Bayne, Rt Rev. Stephen
Burgess, The Ven. Archdeacon John M.
†Cabanban, Rt Rev. Benito (Philippines)
Johnson, Mrs Jean
Kennedy, Rev. Dr James

U S A—continued

Protestant Episcopal Church—continued

Lichtenberger, Rt Rev. A.
Morehouse, Dr Clifford P.
Mosley, Rt Rev. J. B.
Pusey, Dr Nathan M.
Scaife, Rt Rev. Lauriston
†Simoes, Rt Rev. P. L. (Brazil)
Wedel, Dr Cynthia
Wilmer, Very Rev. R. H.

Reformed Church in America

Jenks, Rev. David W.
TePaske, President Henry J.

The Religious Society of Friends

Five Years Meeting of Friends

Levering, Mr Samuel

Friends General Conference

Wilson, Dr E. Raymond

Rumanian Orthodox Episcopate of America

*Trifa, Rt. Rev. Bishop Valerian

Russian Orthodox Greek Catholic Church of America

Czap, Mr Ivan M.
Kunett, Mr R.
Meyendorff,[1] Rev. Prof. Jean
John, Most Rev., Archbishop of San Francisco

Seventh Day Baptist General Conference

Hansen, Rev. Clifford

Syrian Antiochian Orthodox Church (Archdiocese of New York and all North America)

Represented by Meyendorff,[2] Rev. Prof. Jean

United Church of Christ

Anderson, President Stuart
Bladen, Mr Ashby E.
°Carleton, Rev. Dr Alford
Dearborn, Dr Donald C.
Douglass, Rev. Dr Truman B.
Hargraves, Rev. Archie
Hazelton, Rev. Dr Roger
Herbster, Rev. Dr Ben M.
Hoskins, Rev. Dr Fred
Kapitzky, President Frances H.
Manthei, Rev. Dr Edward F.
Moss, President Robert V.
Owen, Mrs Frances
Smith, Miss Helen
Wagner, Rev. Dr James E.

United Lutheran Church in America

Bracher, Mrs Marjory L.
Cooper, President Charles M.
Erb, Rev. Dr Earl S.
Fry, President Franklin C.
Menges, Mr R. J.

[1] See also Syrian Antiochian Orthodox Church.
[2] See also Russian Orthodox Greek Catholic Church of America.

U S A—continued

United Lutheran Church in America—continued

Rhoads, Mr Paul H.
Sittler, Rev. Prof. Joseph
Stackel, Rev. Dr Robert W.
Tabor, Rev. Dr L. R.
Weber, Mr Carl N.

United Presbyterian Church in the USA

Blake, Rev. Dr Eugene C.
Brown, Rev. James D.
Colston, Dr J.
Cort, Mr David A.
°Dorman, Rev. Dr H. G.
Kearns, Jr, Rev. Dr R. V.
Little, Rev. Dr Ganse
McCord, President James I.
McKelvey, Mr Paul D.
Paterson, Rev. Stuart
Piper, Mrs Julia
Rodriguez, President Alfonso A.
Tunnell, Mr J. M.
Shannon, Miss Margaret
Smith, Rev. Dr J. Coventry
°Van Dusen, President H. P.
Zimmerman, Mrs D.

USSR

Russian Orthodox Church

Alexis, Rt Rev., Bishop of Tallinn and Estonia
Anthony, Rt Rev., Bishop of Sergievo (London)
Borovoy, Very Rev. Archpriest V.
Buevsky, Mr A.
Dzvonchik, Very Rev. Archpriest J. (New York)
Ioann, Most Rev. Archbishop (Berlin)
Juvenaly, Rev. Hieromonk
Kotliarov, Rev. Priest V.
Kudinkin, Mr B.
Leonty, Very Rev. Archimandrite
Nicolas, Rt Rev., Bishop of Mukachevo and Uzhgorod
Nikodim, Most Rev., Archbishop of Yaroslav and Rostov
Pitirim, Very Rev. Archimandrite
Sergius, Most Rev., Archbishop of Perm and Solikamsk
Shishkin, Mr A.
Varlamov, Mr I.

WEST AFRICA

The Church of the Province of West Africa

Howells, Rt Rev. A. W., Bishop of Lagos

WEST INDIES

Anglican Church of the West Indies

Swaby, Rt Rev. J. C., Bishop of Kingston

The Presbyterian Church of Jamaica

Miller, Rev. D. R.

WEST INDIES—continued
Presbyterian Church in Trinidad
Samaroo, Mr B.

YUGOSLAVIA
Reformed Christian Church of Yugoslavia
Csete, Bishop Istvan

OTHER CHURCHES
Esthonian Evangelical Lutheran Church in Exile
Pöhl, Propst Hjalmar (Sweden)

B. LISTS OF PARTICIPANTS OTHER THAN DELEGATES

1. Advisers

Alter, Rev. James P., *United Church of N. India and Pakistan* (*India*)
Ambrosio, Mrs J. P., *United Church of Christ in the Philippines*
Arbuthnot, Rev. Dr C. W., *United Presbyterian Church in the USA*
Arrowsmith, Ven. H. M., *Church of England in Australia and Tasmania*
Assaad, Mr A. A., *Coptic Evangelical Church* (*Egypt*)
Bahamonde, Rev. W. O., *Methodist Church* (*Peru*)
Bennett, Rev. Prof. J. C., *United Church of Christ* (*USA*)
Berg, Rev. Christian, *Evangelical Church in Germany* (*Lutheran*)
Boulos, Rev. A., *Syrian Orthodox Patriarchate of Antioch*
Brevik, Rev. K. H., *American Lutheran Church*
Buckner, Rev. Dr G. W., *International Convention of Christian Churches* (*USA*)
Buma, Rev. Kentaro, *United Church of Christ* (*Japan*)
Busia, Dr K. A., *Methodist Church* (*Ghana*)
Byatt, Rev. F. F., *Methodist Church* (*Australia*)
Carlson, Dr C. E., *Southern Baptist Convention* (*USA*)
Castro, Rev. E. E., *Methodist Church* (*Uruguay*)
Chiu, Rev. Ban It, *Church of England in Australia and Tasmania* (*UK/Malaya*)
Cho, Mrs. K. T., *United Church of Christ* (*Japan*)
Cox, Rev. H. G., *American Baptist Convention*
Cragg, Rev. Canon A. K., *Church of England*
Dedman, Mr J. J., *Presbyterian Church of Australia*
Derby, Miss M., *Methodist Church* (*USA*)
Devadutt, Rev. Dr V. E., *Baptist Union of India, Pakistan, Burma and Ceylon* (*India*)
Devanandan, Rev. Dr P. D., *Church of South India*
Endo, Rev. J. Y., *Anglican Church in Japan*
Evans, Miss M. T., *Baptist Union of Great Britain and Ireland*
Farley, Mrs M. L., *Protestant Episcopal Church* (*USA*)
Fleming, Rev. J. R., *Church of Scotland* (*Singapore*)
Fransz, Miss A. L., *Protestant Church in Indonesia*
Galanis, Rev. Dr E., *Ecumenical Patriarchate of Constantinople* (*Turkey*)
Havea, Dr J. A., *Methodist Church of Australasia* (*Tonga*)
Helfferich, Rev. Dr R. H., *United Church of Christ* (*USA*)
Hellstern, Rev. H., *Swiss Protestant Church Federation*
Horton, Rev. Dr Douglas, *United Church of Christ* (*USA*)
Horton, Mrs M. M., *United Church of Christ* (*USA*)

Hsiao, Mr A., *Evangelical Lutheran Church of Hong Kong*
Hunt, Rt. Rev. H. R., *Anglican Church of Canada*
Istavridis, Prof. V. T., *Ecumenical Patriarchate of Constantinople (Turkey)*
Jacob, Mr Korula, *Church of South India*
Johnston, Rev. Dr G., *United Church of Canada*
Jong, Rev. Dr J. M. de, *Dutch Reformed Church*
Kiano, Dr J. G., *Church of the Province of East Africa (Anglican)*
Kim, Rev. K. C., *Presbyterian Church (Korea)*
Kinder, Prof. Dr E., *Evangelical Church in Germany*
Kishi, Rev. Dr C., *Evangelical Lutheran Church (Japan)*
Knoff, Rev. Dr G. E., *Methodist Church (USA)*
Kozaki, Rev. Dr M., *United Church of Christ (Japan)*
Kylstra, Mr R. W., *General Mennonite Society (Netherlands)*
Lacey, Miss Janet, *Church of England*
Laham, Mr A., *Greek Orthodox Patriarchate of Antioch (Lebanon)*
Lansdale, Dr H. P., *United Presbyterian Church (USA)*
Lawson, Rev. J. M., *Methodist Church (USA)*
Lawson, Rev. J. S., *Protestant Methodist Church (Togo)*
Lerrigo, Miss E. M., *United Church of Christ (USA)*
Letts, Dr H. C., *United Lutheran Church (USA)*
Lloyd, Rev. Dr R. W., *United Presbyterian Church (USA)*
Lombard, Mr G., *Swiss Protestant Church Federation*
Lopez, Prof. M. A., *Plymouth Brethren (Argentine)*
Mackie, Rev. Dr R. C., *Church of Scotland*
McCaughey, Rev. Prof. J. D., *Presbyterian Church of Australia*
MacLeod, Mrs M., *Presbyterian Church in the US*
Malonzo, Mr C. C., *United Church of Christ (Philippines)*
Mance, Dr R. W., *African Methodist Episcopal Church (USA)*
Marais, Rev. Prof. B. J., *Dutch Reformed Church of South Africa*
Mathai, Mr S., *Mar Thoma Syrian Church of Malabar (India)*
Mathew, Mr E. V., *Mar Thoma Syrian Church of Malabar (India)*
Matson, Rev. Dr T. E., *Augustana Lutheran Church (USA)*
M'Timkulu, Dr D. G. S., *Methodist Church of South Africa*
Mukerji, Miss R., *Church of South India*
Nasir, Rev. E. S., *Church of India, Pakistan, Burma and Ceylon (Anglican)*
Naylor, Rev. Dr K. F., *Church of the Brethren (USA)*
Nielsen, Rev. Erik W., *Church of Denmark*
Norgren, Rev. W. A., *Protestant Episcopal Church (USA)*
Paton, Rev. D. M., *Church of England*
Patijn, Dr C. L., *Dutch Reformed Church*
Pe, Mr J. Maung, *Church of India, Pakistan, Burma and Ceylon (Anglican)*
Pepper, Rev. Canon A. R., *Protestant Episcopal Church (USA)*
Peter, Rev. Prof. M. Elia, *Methodist Church (India)*
Potter, Rev. Philip, *Methodist Church (West Indies)*
Renkewitz, Rev. Dr H. G., *Evangelical Church in Germany*
Roberts, Miss Helen, *Church of England*
Samuel, Mr Henry, *Church of India, Pakistan, Burma and Ceylon (Anglican)*
Scheuner, Prof. U., *Evangelical Church in Germany*
Schomer, Dr H., *United Church of Christ (USA)*
Shacklock, Rev. Dr F., *Methodist Church (USA)*
Simatupang, Mr T. B., *Indonesian Christian Church*
Sobrepena, Rt Rev. E. C., *United Church of Christ (Philippines)*
Stewart, Rev. Dr W., *United Church of Northern India and Pakistan (UK)*
Stowe, Rev. Dr D. M., *United Church of Christ (USA)*

Street, Rev. Dr T. W., *Presbyterian Church in the US*
Subhan, Rt Rev. J. A., *Methodist Church in Southern Asia* (*India*)
Swain, Mrs S. C., *American Baptist Convention*
Swart, Dr G. J., *Dutch Reformed Church* (*S. Africa*)
Taft, Mr C. P., *Protestant Episcopal Church* (*USA*)
Takenaka, Prof. M., *United Church of Christ* (*Japan*)
Taylor, Rev. Dr T. M., *United Presbyterian Church of USA*
Thetgyi, Rev. J., *Burma Baptist Convention*
Thurian, Rev. M., *Reformed Church of France*
Van Wyk, Mr F. J., *Dutch Reformed Church, Transvaal*
Verghese, Rev. T. P., *Orthodox Syrian Church of Malabar* (*India*)
Wagoner, Rev. Dr W. D., *United Church of Christ* (*USA*)
Walker, Rev. Dr A., *Methodist Church of Australasia*
Walz, Dr H. H., *Evangelical Church in Germany*
Wedel, Rev. Canon T. O., *Protestant Episcopal Church* (*USA*)
Williams, Rev. Prof. C. W., *Methodist Church of Australasia*
Wilson, Dr M. H., *Church of the Province of South Africa* (*Anglican*)
Witschi, Rev. H., *Swiss Protestant Church Federation*
Zigler, Dr M. R., *Church of the Brethren* (*USA*)

2. Youth Participants

AFRICA

Adegbola, Rev. E. A. Adeolu, *The Methodist Church* (*Nigeria*)
Carr, Rev. Burgess, *Protestant Episcopal Church* (*Liberia*)
Fummey, Mr Archie G., *Presbyterian Church of Ghana*
Kebede, Rev. Ermias, *Ethiopian Orthodox Church*
Maraisane, Mr Julius, *Church of Basutoland* (*Presbyterian*)
Mwenda, Rev. Kingsley, *United Church of the Province of Central Africa in Rhodesia*
Ntogota, Rev. Adonia, *Church of Uganda* (*Anglican*)
Okere, Rev. Robinson Obasi, *The Church of the Province of West Africa* (*Anglican*) (*Nigeria*)
Otieno, Mr Zadok, *The Church of the Province of East Africa* (*Anglican*) (*Kenya*)
Rajoelisolo, Rev. Raymond Laikera, *Evangelical Church of Madagascar*
Setiloane, Rev. Gabriel, *Methodist Church of South Africa*
Sone Ajangson, Rev. Daniel, *Evangelical Church of Cameroon*

ASIA

Abraham, Rev. M. V., *Mar Thoma Syrian Church of Malabar*
Adhikari, Mr Sushil Kumar, *Baptist* (*Pakistan*)
Castro, Mr George Feliciano, *IEMELIF* (*Philippine Independent Evangelical Church*)
Gouw, Rev. Kim Hok, *Chinese Church in West Java*
Hla Gyaw, Miss Esther, *Church of India, Pakistan, Burma and Ceylon* (*Anglican*)
Ikenaga, Miss Masuyo, *United Church of Christ in Japan*
Jacob, Rev. Ernest Peter, *Baptist Church* (*English*) (*India*)
James, Mr Emmanuel E., *Methodist Church in Southern Asia*
Jesuthasan, Rev. Samuel Sebenesan, *Diocese of Singapore* (*Anglican*)
Lai, Rev. James Ko Yee, *Church of Christ in China*
Mangunsong, Mr Mangara, *Batak Church* (*Indonesia*)
Murata, Rev. B. Toyotsume, *United Church of Christ in Japan*

ASIA—continued

Ninan, Mr A. George, *Church of South India*
Oh, Mr Jae Shik, *Presbyterian Church (Korea)*
Park, Mr Sang Jung, *Holiness Church (Korea)*
Perera, Mr Darrell George, *Methodist Church in Ceylon*
Santram, Rev. P. B., *Church of India, Pakistan, Burma and Ceylon (India)*
Seneviratne, Mr Nissanka, *Church of India, Pakistan, Burma and Ceylon*
Sobrepena, Rev. David A., *United Church of Christ in the Philippines*
Srisang, Mr Koson, *Church of Christ in Thailand*
Supit, Mr Elly Anak, *Methodist (Sarawak)*
Tin, Mr Win, *Burma Baptist Convention*
Varghese, Rev. C., *Syrian Orthodox (India)*

AUSTRALASIA

Challen, Rev. Michael Boyd, *Church of England in Australia and Tasmania*
Cocks, Miss Ruth M. F., *Congregational Union of Australia*
Gamel, Mr William George, *The Methodist Church (Australia)*
Hayman, Mr John Malcolm, *Methodist Church of New Zealand*
Lock, Miss Dorothy, *Church of the Province of New Zealand*
Moore, Miss Margaret Myra Moore, *Presbyterian Church (New Zealand)*
Phillips, Mr Garth, *Presbyterian Church of Australia*

EUROPE

Aitken, Rev. E. Douglas, *Church of Scotland*
Van Andel, Rev. Hendrik, *Dutch Reformed Church*
Beggs, Miss Kathleen Mary, *Presbyterian Church of Ireland*
Bellardi, Miss Eva-Maria, *Evangelical Church in Germany (Lutheran)*
Chambron, Rev. Marc, *Reformed Church of France (Belgium)*
Coe, Miss Ann, *Church of England*
Duckworth, Rev. Brian, *Methodist Church (UK)*
Gutsch, Mr Wolf-Dietrich, *Evangelical Church in Germany (Lutheran)*
Hallencreutz, Mr Carl, *Church of Sweden (Lutheran)*
Henricson, Mr Carl Gustav, *Ev. Luth. Church in Finland*
Holmes, Mr Gordon Wilson, *Baptist Union of Great Britain and Ireland*
Juvenaly, Rev. Heiromonk Pojarkov, *Russian Orthodox Church*
Killinger, Rev. Walter, *Evangelical Church in Germany (Lutheran)*
Kirkinen, Mr Heikki, *Ecumenical Patriarchate of Constantinople (Finland)*
Leveelathi, Mr Seppo, *Evangelical Lutheran Church of Finland*
Lewis, Rev. Donald Edward, *Church in Wales (Anglican)*
Morales Matthey, Mr Carlos, *Spanish Evangelical Church (Spain, Italy and Portugal)*
Nielsen, Mr Aksel, *Church of Denmark (India)*
Opocensky, Mr Milan, *Evangelical Church of Czech Brethren*
Rein, Mr Gerhard, *Evangelical Church in Germany (Lutheran)*
Ritter, Mr Walter, *Swiss Protestant Federation*
Roux, Miss Danièle, *Swiss Protestant Federation (Reformed)*
Schulze, Mr Klaus Henning, *Evangelical Church in Germany (Lutheran)*
Tsiropoulos, Mr Constantinos, *Church of Greece (Orthodox)*
Wikstrom, Mr Jan-Eric, *Mission Covenant Church of Sweden*
Uhl, Dr Harald, *Evangelical Church of the Augsburg and Helvetic Confession (Lutheran)*

LATIN AMERICA

Dominguez-Perez, Miss A. E., *Methodist Church of Mexico*

LATIN AMERICA—continued
Gonzales Ramirez, Rev. Daniel, *Methodist Church of Mexico*
Lopes, Rev. Sergio Marcus Pinto, *Methodist Church of Brazil*
Lopez Mendoza, Mr Hugh, *Methodist Church* (*Chile*)

NEAR EAST
Ayad, Mr Mikhail, *Coptic Orthodox Church* (*Egypt*)
Domian, Mr John, *Evangelical Synod of Syria and Lebanon* (*Lebanon*)
Mottahedeh, Rev. Iraj, *Episcopal Church in Iran* (*Anglican*)
Rizk, Mr Raymond, *Greek Orthodox Patriarchate of Antioch* (*Lebanon*)

NORTH AMERICA
Baumer, Miss Martha Ann, *United Church of Christ* (*USA*)
Brown, Miss Rita Diane, *United Presbyterian Church in the USA*
Bush, Mr Walker Adams, *Methodist Church* (*USA*)
Cooley, Mr John Hay, *Presbyterian Church in USA*
Daniels, Mr William Roy, *International Convention of Christian Churches* (*Disciples of Christ*) (*USA*)
Demakis, Mr D. John, *Greek Orthodox Archdiocese of North and South America*
Dickerson, Miss Carolyn Louise, *Methodist Church* (*USA*)
Fields, Mr Wayne, *American Baptist Convention*
Graves, Mr William, *Christian Meth. Episc. Church* (*USA*)
Hanna, Miss Patricia, *Presbyterian Church of Canada*
Lathrop, Mr Gordon, *American Lutheran Church*
Ledger, Miss Joan, *Churches of Christ* (*Disciples*) (*Canada*)
Macdonald, Rev. David, *United Church of Canada*
Pavlik, Mr Philip M., *Protestant Episcopal Church in USA*
Pool, Mr Larry Howard, *American Baptist Convention*
Rathbone, Mr Bruce, *Anglican Church of Canada*
Rigdon, Mr V. Bruce, *The United Presbyterian Church of the USA*
Rochester, Mr Enoch Benjamin, *African Meth. Episc. Zion Church* (*USA*)
Wood, Rev. John S., *Methodist Church* (*USA*)

YMCA
Joseph, Mr George N., *Church of South India*
Tollin, Mr Björn-Fredrik, *Church of Sweden*

YWCA
John, Miss Joyce Shiela, *Patna Union Church* (*Baptist*) (*India*)
Moffat, Miss Carol, *United Church of Canada* (*India*)
Ranosiarimanana, Miss Pénélope, *Protestant Reformed* (*Madagascar*)

WSCF
Adler, Miss Elisabeth, *Evangelical Church in Germany* (*Lutheran*)
Cardoso, Mr Edir, *Presbyterian Church of Brazil*

WCCESSA
Buma, Rev. Kyoji, *United Presbyterian Church in USA*
Castro, Miss Eppie, *United Church of Christ in the Philippines*
Kirkpatrick, Dr Lawrence, *International Convention of Christian Churches* (*Disciples of Christ*)

THE SALVATION ARMY
Sanjivi, Miss Evelyn Prema, *The Salvation Army* (*India*)

3. Fraternal Delegates

Alvez, Rev. Ewaldo, *Evangelical Federation of Brazil*
Artus, Rev. Wilfrido, *Confederation of Evangelical Churches of the River Plate*
Bader, Dr Jesse M., *World Convention of the Churches of Christ* (*Disciples*)
Baroi, Rev. R. N., *East Pakistan Christian Council*
Benignus, Rev. Pierre, *Société des Missions Evangéliques de Paris*
Bennett, Rev. R. M., *Canadian Council of Churches*
Blauw, Dr J., *Nederlandsche Zendings-Raad*
Carral, Rev. Anselmo, *Concilio Cubano de Iglesias Evangelicas*
Chappel, Dr Nelson, *World Council of Christian Education*
Chetsingh, Mr Ranjit M., *Friends World Committee for Consultation*
*Cook, Colonel A. Bramwell, *Commission on Overseas Missions and Inter-Church Aid, NCC, New Zealand*
Dankbaar, Prof. W. F., *Oecumenische Raad van Kerken in Nederland*
Dillner, Miss H. Maria, *Swedish Missionary Council*
Espy, Mr R. H. Edwin, *National Council of the Churches of Christ in the USA*
*Frederick, Rev. A. E. D., *National Christian Council of India*
Gallagher, Rev. Dr W. J., *Canadian Council of Churches*
Galland, Rev. Valdo, *World's Student Christian Federation*
Gotwald, Dr Luther E., *Division of Foreign Missions, NCCC/USA*
Grais, Rev. Girgis, *Near East Christian Council*
Gribble, Rev. Cecil F., *National Missionary Council of Australia*
Hall, Rt Rev. R. O., Bishop of Hong Kong, *Anglican Communion*
Hart, Rev. Roland, *National Council of Churches in New Zealand*
Hastings, Rt Rev. Selwyn U., *Jamaica Christian Council*
Hirai, Rev. Kiyoshi, *National Christian Council of Japan*
Hla-Bu, Dr, *Burma Christian Council*
Inbanathan, Rev. Dr A. E., *United Bible Societies*
Johansson, Dr Harry, *Swedish Ecumenical Council*
Kenéz, Dr Ferenc, *Ecumenical Council of Churches of Hungary*
Kiel, Rev. G. C., *National Christian Council of Korea*
Koh, Rt Rev. Roland, *Malayan Christian Council*
Kretser, Rev. B. de, *National Christian Council of Ceylon*
Küppers, Prof. Werner, F. A. (*Arbeitsgemeinschaft christlicher Kirchen in Deutschland*)
Lehtonen, Mr R. R. F., *Ecumenical Council of Finland*
Leung, Dr S. C., *Hong Kong Christian Council*
Limbert, Dr Paul H., *World Alliance of YMCAs*
Martin, Rev. Milton, *Christian Council of South Africa*
Marantika, Rev. Simon, *National Council of Churches in Indonesia*
Masih, Rev. Inayat, *West Pakistan Christian Council*
Mathews, Rev. E. J. Peter, *Christian Council of Northern Rhodesia*
Niewieczerzal, Dr Jan, *Polish Ecumenical Council*
Nordenhaug, Dr Josef, *Baptist World Alliance*
Ondra, Dr Jaroslav N., *Ecumenical Council of Churches in Czechoslovakia*
Palmer, Miss Elizabeth, *World Alliance of YWCAs*
*Pande, Rev. C. C., *National Christian Council of India*
Perkins, Rev. Harvey L., *Australian Council of Churches*

Pradervand, Rev. Dr Marcel, *World Presbyterian Alliance*
Rajosefa-Rakotovao, Rev., *Conseil des Eglises Protestantes de Madagascar*
*Richter, Rev. P. C., *Christian Council of Ghana*
Rossel, Rev. Jacques, *Conseil Suisse des Missions Evangéliques*
Saenz, Dr Michael, *Puerto Rico Christian Council*
Schmidt-Clausen, Dr Kurt, *Lutheran World Federation*
Short, Rev. Frank, *Conference of British Missionary Societies*
Slack, Rev. Kenneth, *British Council of Churches*
Sundström, Rev. Erland, *International Congregational Council*
Tuttle, Dr Lee F., *World Methodist Council*
Wichiadist, Rev. Charoon, *National Christian Council of Thailand*
Williams, Rev. P. A. J., *Sierra Leone United Christian Council*
Wilson, Miss Doris M., *National Christian Council of India*
Yap, Rev. José, *Philippine Federation of Evangelical Churches*

* Also delegate.

4. Observers

Observers from non-member Churches

Andrianarijaona, Rev. Rakoto, *Lutheran Church of Madagascar*
Bartling, Rev. Prof. V., *Missouri Synod*
Berkhouwer, Dr G. C., *Gereformeerde Kerken, Netherlands*
Borges dos Santos, Rev. Dr J., *Presbyterian Church of Brazil*
Crouse, Dr M. C., *Advent Christian Church, USA*
Duff, Rev. Edward, *Roman Catholic Church*
Edamaran, Rev. Dr T., *Roman Catholic Church*
Extross, Rev. I., *Roman Catholic Church*
Groot, Rev. Prof. J. C. de, *Roman Catholic Church*
Guillou, Rev. Prof. M. le, *Roman Catholic Church*
Kenwar, Miss Anandi, *Council of Baptist Churches in North-East India*
Kerhuo, Mr Kenneth, *Council of Baptist Churches in North-East India*
Lang, Rev. Samuel, *Missouri Synod*
Löken, Rev. A., *Evangelical Lutheran Church of South Africa*
Malagar, Bishop P. J., *Mennonite Church in India*
Marak, Mr Pramkumar, *Garo Baptist Union, East Pakistan*
Mattison, Rev. O. O., *Seventh-Day Adventists, USA*
Molina, Bishop S. M., *Reformed Episcopal Church of Spain*
Moore, Rev. Lazarus, *Russian Orthodox Church outside Russia*
Novak, Bishop M., *Czechoslovak Church*
Pereira, Bishop L. C. R., *Lusitanian Church, Portugal*
Poladian, Bishop T., *Armenian Orthodox Church*
Pouw, Rev. Dr B. G., *Chinese Church of Indonesia*
Roxas, Mr Jose, *Philippine Independent Evangelical Church (Indigenous)*
Royster, Rev. J. E., *Church of God*
Rumainum, Rev. F. J. S., *Evangelical Christian Church of Dutch New Guinea*
Sarkissian, Very Rev. K., *Armenian Orthodox Church of Lebanon*
Schmidt, Rev. C. G., *United Evangelical Lutheran Church in Australia*
Shaidi, Mr A., *Lutheran Church of Northern Tanganyika*
Teutscher, Rev. H. J., *Evangelical Christian Church of Dutch New Guinea*
Tobing, Mr R. S. L., *Huria Kristen, Indonesia*
Visarion, Bishop Kostic, *Serbian Orthodox Church*
Wickramasinghe, Rev. W. G., *Baptist Union, Ceylon*
Wilson, Mrs M. L., *Society of Friends, Gt Britain*
Yona, Rev. Manase, *Lutheran Church of Central Tanganyika*

Observers personally invited

Du Plessis, Rev. D. J., *Pentecostal Churches, USA*
Graham, Rev. Dr Billy, *Southern Baptist Convention*
Metzler, Rev. A. J., *Mennonite Church General Conference*
Pannabecker, Dr S. F., *Mennonite Church General Conference*
Rees, Dr Paul, *World Vision Inc.*

Observers from National Councils of Churches

Ademola, Dr G. A., *Christian Council of Nigeria*
Chipenda, Rev. J. B., *Angola Christian Council*
Grant, Mrs I. M., *Southern Rhodesia Christian Conference*
Munyi, Brigadier J., *Kenya Christian Council*

Observers from organizations

Faber, Rev. Dr H., *International Association for Liberal Christianity and Religious Freedom*
Ondra, Rev. J. N., *Prague Peace Conference*

Appendix 5

GENERAL SESSIONS OF THE ASSEMBLY

At the Opening Session of the Assembly at 3.00 p.m. on Sunday, November 19, Bishop Otto Dibelius, President, presiding, addresses were given by the General Secretaries of the IMC and the WCC as follows:

The missionary dimension of the Ecumenical Movement, Bishop Lesslie Newbigin.

The calling of the World Council of Churches, Dr W. A. Visser 't Hooft.

The discussions of the general theme 'Jesus Christ the Light of the World' in the three sections on Witness, Service and Unity, were introduced by four addresses delivered in general sessions and followed by brief discussion as follows:

Sunday, November 19, 6.20 p.m., Metropolitan Juhanon Mar Thoma presiding.

Jesus Christ the Light of the World, Bishop Gottfried Noth.

Monday, November 20, 4.30 p.m., Bishop S. U. Barbieri presiding.

Called to Witness, Dr Paul Devanandan.

Monday, November 20, 6.30 p.m., Bishop Henry Knox Sherrill presiding.

Called to Service: The Service of the Church in the Changing World Today, Prof. Masao Takenaka.

Tuesday, November 21, 9.45 a.m., Archbishop Iakovos presiding.

Called to Unity, Professor Joseph Sittler.

Addresses were delivered at other general sessions of the Assembly as follows:

Wednesday, November 22, 6.30 p.m., Bishop Dibelius presiding.

The Laity: The Church in the World.

Speakers: Dr Klaus von Bismarck, Mr E. V. Mathew, Miss Mollie Batten.

Thursday, November 23, 6.30 p.m., Metropolitan Juhanon Mar Thoma presiding.

The Future is Now, Dr O. Frederick Nolde.

What about Africa?, Sir Francis Ibiam.

Friday, November 24, 6.30 p.m., Bishop S. U. Barbieri presiding.

Unity, Truth and Holiness, the Archbishop of Canterbury (The Most Rev. Michael Ramsey).

The Witness and Service of Eastern Orthodoxy to the One, Undivided Church. Dr Nikos Nissiotis.
Going Forward together into Manifest Unity, the Rev. Philip Potter.

Sunday, November 26, Bishop Dibelius presiding.
'God is our refuge and strength', a biblically based presentation in word and pictures of the churches' world-wide ministries of inter-church aid and service to refugees, introduced by Dr Eugene C. Blake, with the participation of Mr Max Robertson (interviewer), the Rev. Kentaro Buma, Mr James Atkinson, Dr Donald M'Timkulu, Mr P. C. Joseph, the Rev. Alan Brash, Miss A. Fransz and The Most Rev. Leonard J. Beecher, Archbishop of East Africa.

Tuesday, November 28, 6.30 p.m., Metropolitan Juhanon Mar Thoma presiding.
The Challenge of Social Change, introduced by the Rev. Emilio Castro.
The Churches of the West in a Dynamic Society, Dr Egbert de Vries.
The Challenge to the Churches in the New Nations in Africa and Asia, Mr M. M. Thomas.

Thursday, November 30, 6.30 p.m., Dr Christian Baeta presiding.
Why We Must Speak, panel discussion led by the Rev. Dr D. T. Niles. The panel included: the Rev. Emilio Castro, Father Ignatius Hazim, Mr J. Irwin Miller, Dr Mary Moore, Dr Constant Patijn, the Rev. Ezechiel Mahabane.

Friday, December 1, 6.30 p.m., Bishop Barbieri presiding.
The Bible and the Churches' Task, the Archbishop of York (The Most Rev. Donald F. Coggan).
The use of the Bible, the Rev. E. H. Robertson.
The Bible and Evangelism, the Rev. Dr A. E. Inbanathan.

Appendix 6

LIST OF OFFICERS AND STAFF OF THE SECTIONS AND COMMITTEES OF THE ASSEMBLY

A. THE OFFICERS OF THE SECTIONS

Witness:	Co-Chairmen:	Mrs Mildred Horton
		Dr Gerhard Brennecke
	Co-Secretaries:	Dr José Miguez-Bonino
		Bishop A. H. Zulu
Service:	Co-Chairmen:	Sir Kenneth Grubb
		Dr Egbert de Vries
	Co-Secretaries:	Dr Masao Takenaka
		Dr Virgil Sly
Unity:	Co-Chairmen:	Dr David Moses
		The Bishop of Bristol, Dr Oliver Tomkins
	Co-Secretaries:	Dr Joseph Sittler
		Dr Jean Meyendorff

B. THE OFFICERS OF THE COMMITTEES

The Business Committee of the Assembly
Chairman: Dr Franklin Clark Fry

The Worship Committee of the Assembly
Chairman: Principal J. R. Chandran

The Nominations Committee
Chairman: Dr W. S. Tindal
Secretary: Dr H. H. Harms
The Policy Reference Committee
Chairman: Archbishop Iakovos
Secretary: Dr Robert C. Mackie
The Credentials Committee
Chairman: Rev. F. G. A. Stenström
The Press and Public Relations Committee
Chairman: Bishop Lakdasa de Mel
Vice-Chairman: Mr Charles C. Parlin
Committee on the Division of Studies
Chairman: Dr James I. McCord
Secretary: Dr Davis McCaughey
Committee on the Department on Faith and Order
Chairman: Bishop Hanns Lilje
Secretary: Principal John Marsh
Committee on the Department on Church and Society
Chairman: Mr M. M. Thomas
Secretary: Dr John C. Bennett
Committee on the Department of Missionary Studies
Chairman: Bishop H. Sumitra
Secretary: Rev. Eric Nielson
Committee on the Department on Evangelism
Chairman: Dr Eric Baker
Secretary: Canon Chu Ban It
Committee on the Division of Ecumenical Action
Chairman: Dr H. Thimme
Secretary: Dr Reuben Mueller
Committee on the Department on the Laity
Chairman: Dr Klaus von Bismarck
Secretary: Dr B. Istavridis
Committee on the Department on Co-operation between Men and Women in Church and Society
Chairman: Bishop John Sadiq
Secretary: Dr George Johnston
Committee on the Youth Department
Chairman: Rev. U Ba Hmyin
Secretary: Dr Colin Williams
Committee on the Ecumenical Institute
Chairman: Dr Victor Hajek
Secretary: Miss Molly Batten
Committee on the Division of Inter-Church Aid and Service to Refugees
Chairman· Sir Francis Ibiam
Secretary: Bishop H. R. Hunt
Committee on the Division of World Mission and Evangelism
Chairman: Bishop Rajah Manikam
Secretary: Bishop James K. Mathews
Committee on the Commission of the Churches on International Affairs
Chairman: Dr Nathan Pusey
Secretary: Dr Ulrich Scheuner
Committee on the Department of Information
Chairman: Bishop R. C. Raines
Secretary: Rev. David Paton

Committee on Finance
Chairman: Bishop A. K. Warren
Vice-Chairman: Bishop Westergaard-Madsen
Secretary: Mr J. Irwin Miller

C. Assembly Staff Assignments

1. General Administration

Dr W. A. Visser 't Hooft, General Secretary
Dr Robert S. Bilheimer, Secretary, Business Committee
Mr Jens Thomsen, Secretary, Assembly Organization
Mr Korula Jacob, Secretary, Local Arrangements Committee
Mr Andreas Schneider, Mr Frank Northam } Finance

2. Sections

Sections Co-ordinator: Miss Leila Anderson

Witness: Rev. Gwenyth Hubble
Rev. Harry Morton
Rev. Robbins Strong
Also present:
Rev. Victor Hayward
Dr H. J. Margull
Bishop Lesslie Newbigin

Service: Rev. Henry Makulu
Rev. Alan Brash
Rev. Alan Booth
Also present:
Rev. Paul Abrecht
Dr O. Frederick Nolde
Dr Leslie E. Cooke

Unity: Dr N. A. Nissiotis
Dr D. T. Niles
Dr Lukas Vischer
Also present:
Dr Paul S. Minear
Rev. P. C. Rodger
Rev. Francis H. House

3. Committees

Committees Co-ordinator: Dr Edgar Chandler

Policy Reference Committee: Dr Roswell P. Barnes
Dr Norman Goodall
Dr A. Carrillo de Albornoz
Dr Lewis S. Mudge

Credentials Committee: Rev. Jens Thomsen

Nominations Committee: Dr W. A. Visser 't Hooft

Divisional Committee, Studies:
Dr Robert S. Bilheimer

Faith and Order: Dr Paul S. Minear
Dr Lukas Vischer
Rev. P. C. Rodger

Church and Society: Rev. Paul Abrecht
Rev. Daisuke Kitagawa

Missionary Studies: Rev. Victor Hayward

Evangelism: Dr H. J. Margull

Divisional Committee, Ecumenical Action:
Rev. Francis H. House
Miss Dorothea Woods

Youth: Rev. Roderick French
Rev. C. I. Itty
Rev. Ralph Weltge
Miss Anita Diehl

Laity: Rev. H. R. Weber
Rev. Ralph Young

Ecumenical Institute: Dr H. H. Wolf
Dr N. A. Nissiotis
Rev. Henry Makulu

Co-operation: Dr Madeleine Barot
Miss Helen Morton

Division of Inter-Church Aid and Service to Refugees:
Dr Leslie E. Cooke
Rev. Raymond E. Maxwell
Mr Walter Kilpatrick
Rev. Harry Morton
Dr Garfield C. Williams
Dr H. Puffert
Dr Laszlo Ledermann
Rev. H. C. Shorrock
Mr B. Sjollema
Rev. T. Tschuy
Propst J. Krohn

Division of World Mission and Evangelism:
Bishop Lesslie Newbigin
Dr George Carpenter
Dr Paul Lœffler
Rev. Gwenyth Hubble
Dr Hans Gensichen
Rev. A. Gjerding

Commission of the Churches on International Affairs:
Dr O. Frederick Nolde
Dr Richard Fagley
Rev. Alan Booth
Rev. Dominique Micheli
Rev. Elfan Rees
U Kyaw Than

Information: Mr Philippe Maury, and other members of the staff of the Department

Finance: Mr Frank Northam
Mr Andreas Schneider

4. Worship Committee:
Rev. Raymond E. Maxwell

5. Press and Broadcasting Office:
Mr Philippe Maury
Mr John Taylor
Miss Nancy Lawrence
Miss Betty Thompson
Mr Geoffrey Murray
Mr P. Carlson

6. Typists-Cyclostyle Office:

Mrs Gwendoline Bæhr

7. Translators-Interpreters Office:

Rev. A. Boyens
Miss M. Evans
Mme E. Lauber
Miss I. Soltau

8. Steward-Aides Office:

Mr A. M. Z. Rolston
Rev. A. van den Heuvel

9. Assembly Report:

Dr Samuel McCrea Cavert
Mrs Blanche Britton

10. Assembly Notices:

Miss Frances Maeda

11. Information Office:

Rev. K. C. Thomas
Miss Eleanor Kent Browne

12. Special Assignments:

Miss A. Guittart, Secretary to Dr Visser 't Hooft
Miss S. Morden, *Who's Who*
Miss M. Williams, Finance Office
Miss P. Morison, WCC Bookstand
Miss T. Yamaguchi, Committee Room Assignments

Appendix 7

REPORT OF THE NOMINATIONS COMMITTEE

The Nominations Committee is pleased to make the following proposals for:

PRESIDIUM

Honorary President: Oldham, Dr J. H., *United Kingdom*

The Presidium: Canterbury, Most Rev. Arthur Michael Ramsey, Lord Archbishop of, *Church of England*
Iakovos, Most Rev., Archbishop of North and South America, *Ecumenical Patriarchate of Constantinople* (*USA*)
Ibiam, Sir Francis, *Presbyterian Church of Nigeria*
Moses, The Rev. Dr David G., *United Church of Northern India and Pakistan* (*India*)
Niemöller, The Rev. Dr Martin, *Evangelical Church in Germany* (*United*)
Parlin, Mr Charles, *The Methodist Church* (*USA*)

CENTRAL COMMITTEE

Abe, Mr Shiro, *United Church of Christ in Japan*
Alexis, Rt Rev. Bishop, of Tallinn and Estonia, *Russian Orthodox Church*
Alivisatos, Prof. Hamilcar, *Church of Greece*
Allison, Rt Rev. S. F., Bishop of Chelmsford, *Church of England*
Athenagoras, Most Rev., Metropolitan of Elaia and Canada, *Ecumenical Patriarchate of Constantinople* (*Canada*)
Baëta, Rev. Dr Chr. G., *Presbyterian Church of Ghana*
Baker, Rev. Dr Eric, *The Methodist Church* (*United Kingdom*)
Barbieri, Bishop S. U., *The Methodist Church, USA* (*Argentina*)
Bartha, Bishop Tibor, *Reformed Church of Hungary*
Baugher, Rev. Dr Norman J., *Church of the Brethren* (*USA*)
Beecher, Archbishop L. J., *Church of the Province of East Africa* (*Kenya*)
Berkhof, Rev. Prof. H., *Dutch Reformed Church*
Binder, Rev. Dr. F., *Protestant Evangelical Church, Augsberg Confession* (*Rumania*)
Bismarck, Dr Klaus von, *Evangelical Church of Germany* (*United*)
Blake, Rev. Dr Eugene C., *United Presbyterian Church in the USA*
Bliss, Dr Kathleen, *Church of England*
Borovoy, Very Rev. Vitaly, *Russian Orthodox Church*
Brennecke, Rev. Dr G., *Evangelical Church of Germany* (*United*)
Burnett, Rt Rev. B. B., Bishop of Bloemfontein, *Church of the Province of South Africa*
Carleton, Rev. Dr Alford, *United Church of Christ* (*USA*)
Chandran, Rev. J. R., *Church of South India*
Chou, Dr Ivy, *The Methodist Church of the USA* (*Sarawak*)
Chrysostomos Konstantinidis, Most Rev., Metropolitan of Myria, *Ecumenical Patriarchate of Constantinople*
Cocks, Rev. Norman H. F., *Congregational Union of Australia*
Coulson, Prof. C. A., *The Methodist Church* (*United Kingdom*)
Engel, Rev. Frank, *Presbyterian Church of Australia*
Ensley, Bishop F. G., *The Methodist Church* (*USA*)
d'Espine, Rev. Prof. H., *Swiss Protestant Church Federation*
Fry, Rev. Dr Franklin C., *United Lutheran Church in America*
Fulton, Rev. Dr A. A., *Presbyterian Church in Ireland*
Ga, Rt Rev. M. V., *Philippine Independent Church*
Harms, Rev. Dr Hans H., *Evangelical Church in Germany* (*Lutheran*)
Hazim, Very Rev. Ignatius, *Greek Orthodox Patriarchate of Antioch* (*Lebanon*)
Hromadka, Rev. Prof. J. L., *Evangelical Church of Czech Brethren*
Hultgren, Rt Rev. Archbishop G., *Church of Sweden*
Iakovos, Most Rev., Metropolitan of Philadelphia, *Ecumenical Patriarchate of Constantinople*
Ioann, Most Rev. Archbishop, *Russian Orthodox Church* (*Berlin*)
Ioannidis, Prof. Basil, *Church of Greece*
Jackson, Rev. Dr Joseph H., *National Baptist Convention, USA, Inc.*
Jans, Bishop P. J., *Old Catholic Church, Netherlands*
John, Archbishop, of San Francisco, *Russian Orthodox Greek Catholic Church of North America*
Justin, Most Rev., Metropolitan of Jassy, *Orthodox Church of Rumania*
Káldy, Rt Rev. Bishop Zoltán, *Evangelical Lutheran Church of Hungary*
Kapitzky, Miss Frances H., *United Church of Christ* (*USA*)
Kotsonis, Very Rev. Prof. J., *Church of Greece*

Kotto, Rev. Jean, *Evangelical Church of Cameroun*
Kyaw, Rev. S'Aye Mya, *Burma Baptist Convention*
Lichtenberger, Rt Rev. A., *Protestant Episcopal Church* (*USA*)
Lilje, Bishop Hanns, *Evangelical Church in Germany* (*Lutheran*)
Long, Rev. Dr Ernest E., *United Church of Canada*
Mahabane, Rev. E. E., *Methodist Church of South Africa*
Makary el Souriany, Father, *Coptic Orthodox Church* (*Egypt*)
Manikam, Rt Rev. Bishop Rajah, *Federation of Evangelical Lutheran Churches* (*India*)
Marsh, Rev. Dr John, *Congregational Union of England and Wales*
Mathews, Bishop James K., *The Methodist Church* (*USA*)
Mathew, Prof. C. P., *Mar Thoma Syrian Church of Malabar* (*India*)
Mbende, Rev. Paul, *Union of Baptist Churches* (*Cameroun*)
Meliton, Most Rev., Metropolitan of Imros and Tenedos, *Ecumenical Patriarchate of Constantinople* (*Turkey*)
Millard, Rev. Dr James A., *Presbyterian Church in the US*
Miller, Mr J. Irwin, *International Convention of Christian Churches* (*Disciples of Christ* (*USA*)
Montes, Mr V. G., *United Church of Christ in the Philippines*
Mueller, Bishop R. H., *Evangelical United Brethren Church* (*USA*)
Niesel, Rev. Prof. W., *Evangelical Church in Germany* (*Reformed*)
Nikodim, Most Rev., Archbishop of Yaroslav and Rostov, *Russian Orthodox Church*
Nikolainen, Rev. Prof. A. T., *Evangelical Lutheran Church of Finland*
Noth, Bishop G., *Evangelical Church in Germany* (*Lutheran*)
Obermüller, Rev. Prof. R., *Evangelical German Synod of Rio de la Plata* (*Argentina*)
Panteleimon, Rt Rev., Bishop of Achaia, *Church of Greece*
Parthenios-Aris, Most Rev. C., Metropolitan of Carthage, *Greek Orthodox Patriarchate of Alexandria* (*Egypt*)
Payne, Rev. Dr E. A., *Baptist Union of Great Britain and Ireland*
Philipos, Rev. Dr Korah, *Orthodox Syrian Church of the East* (*India*)
Pusey, Dr Nathan, *Protestant Episcopal Church* (*USA*)
Probowinoto, Rev. B., *Christian Church of Mid-Java* (*Indonesia*)
Rasendrahasina, Rev. Titus, *LMS Synod in Madagascar*
Ray, Rt Rev. Chandu, *Church of India, Pakistan, Burma and Ceylon* (*Pakistan*)
Say, Rt Rev. R. David, Bishop of Rochester, *Church of England*
Sadiq, Rt Rev. John W., Bishop of Nagpur, *Church of India, Pakistan, Burma and Ceylon* (*India*)
Schiotz, Rev. Dr F. A., *The American Lutheran Church*
Schlieper, Präses E. T., *Synodal Federation Evangelical Church Lutheran Confession in Brazil*
Shishkin, Mr Alexander, *Russian Orthodox Church*
Short, Bishop Roy H., *The Methodist Church* (*USA*)
Sihombing, Rev. T., *Protestant Christian Batak Church* (*Indonesia*)
Simon, Rev. Dr K. M., *Syrian Orthodox Patriarchate of Antioch and all the East* (*USA*)
Smith, Bishop B. Julian, *Christian Methodist Episcopal Church* (*USA*)
Smith, Rev. Dr John Coventry, *United Presbyterian Church in the USA*
Stenström, Rev. F. G. A., *Mission Covenant Church of Sweden*
Støylen, Rt Rev. Bishop K., *Church of Norway*
Sundkler, Rt Rev. Bishop B., *Evangelical Church of North Western Tanganyika*

Theophilos, Archbishop, *Ethiopian Orthodox Church*
Tillman, Mrs Sadie, *The Methodist Church (USA)*
Tindal, Rev. Prof. W. S., *Church of Scotland*
Tuller, Rev. Dr Edwin H., *American Baptist Convention*
Warren, Rt Rev. A. K., Bishop of Christchurch, *Church of the Province of New Zealand*
Wemyss, Rt Hon. Earl of, *Church of Scotland*
Westergaard-Madsen, Rt Rev. Bishop W., *Church of Denmark*
Westphal, Rev. Charles, *Reformed Church of France*
Woods, Most Rev. Frank, Archbishop of Melbourne, *Church of England in Australia and Tasmania*
Woods, Commander Reginald, *Salvation Army International (UK)*
Wright, Most Rev. W. L., Archbishop of Algoma, *The Anglican Church of Canada*
Wyllie, Mrs M. G., *Methodist Church of Australasia*

NOTE: One of the representatives of the Ecumenical Patriarchate will be also the representative of the Greek Orthodox Patriarchate of Jerusalem.

COMMISSION ON FAITH AND ORDER

* Signifies a member of the Working Committee.

AFRICA

Ghana

King, The Rev. Prof. N. Q., *Church of the Province of West Africa (Anglican)*

Kenya

Gatu, The Rev. J., *Presbyterian Church of East Africa*

Madagascar

Ralambomahay, The Rev. J., *Evangelical Church of Madagascar*

Nigeria

Adegbola, Mr E., *Methodist Church in Nigeria*

Sierra Leone

*Sawyerr, The Rev. Prof. H., *Church of the Province of West Africa (Anglican)*

South Africa

Zulu, The Rt Rev. A. H., *Church of the Province of South Africa (Anglican)*
one place for a person from the Dutch Reformed churches
one place for a person from the independent African churches

Tanganyika

Kibira, The Rev. J., *Evangelical Lutheran Church of North-Western Tanganyika*

Togo

Nomenyo, The Rev. S., *Evangelical Church of Togo*

LATIN AMERICA

Argentina

*Miguez-Bonino, The Rev. J., *Methodist Church in Argentina*
Dr Belà Lesko, *Iglesia Evangelica Lutherana Unida*

Brazil

Beato, Dr J., *Presbyterian Church of Brazil*

Cuba

Rodriguez, The Rev. Dr A. A., *United Presbyterian Church (USA)*

Jamaica

Farris, The Rev. W. J. S., *Presbyterian Church in Canada*

LATIN AMERICA—continued

Puerto Rico

Gonzales, Dr J., *Methodist Church*

Uruguay

Fernandez Arlt, Dr A. E., *Lutheran Church in Uruguay*
Artus, The Rev. W., *Waldensian Church*

NORTH AMERICA

Canada

*Fairweather, The Rev. Prof. E. R., *Anglican Church of Canada*
Aldwinckle, The Rev. R. F., *Baptist Federation of Canada*
*Hay, The Rev. Prof. D. W., *Presbyterian Church in Canada*
Chalmers, The Rev. Dr R. C., *United Church of Canada*

USA

Handy, The Rev. Prof. R. T., *American Baptist Convention*
*Skoglund, The Rev. Prof. J. E., *American Baptist Convention*
Liefeld, Prof. T. S., *The American Evangelical Lutheran Church*
Bridston, The Rev. Dr K. R., *The American Lutheran Church*
Groff, Prof. W. F., *Church of the Brethren*
Beazley, The Rev. George G., *Disciples of Christ*
*Florovsky, The Rev. Prof. G., *Ecumenical Patriarchate* (*Greek Orthodox*)
Ensley, Bishop F. G., *The Methodist Church*
Muelder, Dean W. G., *The Methodist Church*
*Nelson, The Rev. Dr J. R., *The Methodist Church*
*Outler, The Rev. Prof. A. C., *The Methodist Church*
Thomas, The Rev. Prof. J. N., *Presbyterian Church* (*US*)
Coburn, The Very Rev. J., *Protestant Episcopal Church* (*USA*)
Hardy, The Rev. Prof. E. R., *Protestant Episcopal Church* (*USA*)
Stringfellow, Mr W., *Protestant Episcopal Church* (*USA*)
Meyendorff, The Rev. Prof. J., *Russian Orthodox Greek Catholic Church of North America*
Pelikan, Prof. J. J., *Slovak Evangelical Lutheran Church*
Moody, Prof. D., *Southern Baptist Convention*
Arndt, Dr E. J. F., *United Church of Christ*
Calhoun, Prof. R. L., *United Church of Christ*
Lazareth, Prof. W. H., *United Lutheran Church of America*
*Sittler, Prof. J. A., *United Lutheran Church of America*
Hendry, The Rev. Dr G., *United Presbyterian Church* (*USA*)
McCord, Pres. J. I., *United Presbyterian Church* (*USA*)
Taylor, The Rev. Prof. T. M., *United Presbyterian Church* (*USA*)

ASIA

Ceylon

Wickramasinghe, The Rev. W. G., *Baptist Union of Ceylon*
de Soysa, The Ven. H., *Church of India, Pakistan, Burma and Ceylon* (*Anglican*)

Formosa

Chow, Dr L. H., *Taiwan Baptist Convention*

India

*Chandran, The Rev. Princ. J. R., *Church of South India*
Minz, Dr N., *Federation of Evangelical Lutheran Churches in India*
Athanasius, The Rt Rev. T. Mar, *Mar Thoma Syrian Church of Malabar*
Krishnan, Dr J. Radha, *Methodist Church of Southern Asia*
Samuel, The Rev. Prof. V. C., *Orthodox Syrian Church of the East*

ASIA—continued

India—continued

Stewart, The Rev. Dr W., *United Church of Northern India and Pakistan*

Indonesia

Tobing, Dr A., *Protestant Christian Batak Church (Lutheran)*

Abineno, Dr J. L. Ch., *Protestant Church in Indonesia (Reformed)*

Japan

Kishi, The Rev. Dr C., *Lutheran Church in Japan*

Mayeda, Prof. G., *Non-Church Movement*

Kitamori, Dr K., *United Church of Christ in Japan*

Korea

One place reserved for a representative of the Korean churches

Pakistan

Nasir, The Rev. Prof. K. L., *United Presbyterian Church of Pakistan*

NEAR EAST

Jordan

Basilious, The Most Rev. A., *Ethiopian Coptic Church*

Lebanon

Sarkissian, The Very Rev. K., *Armenian Orthodox Church*

Hazim, The Very Rev. I., *Orthodox Patriarchate, See of Antioch*

Markarian, Pres. J., *Union of Armenian Evangelical Churches*

Turkey

*Konstantinidis. The Most Rev. C. E., Metropolitan of Myra, *Ecumenical Patriarchate of Constantinople*

Anagnostopoulos, Prof. V., *Ecumenical Patriarchate of Constantinople*

AUSTRALASIA

Australia

Woods, The Most Rev. F., Archbishop of Melbourne, *Church of England in Australia and Tasmania*

Williams, The Rev. Prof. C. W., *Methodist Church of Australasia*

Hambly, The Rev. W. F., *Methodist Church of Australasia*

*McCaughey, The Rev. Prof. J. D., *Presbyterian Church of Australia*

New Zealand

Bates, The Rev. J. M., *Presbyterian Church of New Zealand*

EUROPE

Bulgaria

Jossif, The Most Rev. Mgr, Metropolitan of Varna and Preslav, *Church of Bulgaria (Orthodox)*

Czechoslovakia

Smolik, The Rev. Dr J., *Church of the Brethren*

Denmark

*Skydsgaard, Prof. Dr K. E., *Church of Denmark (Lutheran)*

Finland

Teinonen, Dr S. A., *Evangelical Lutheran Church of Finland*

France

Guerrier, The Rev. F., *Evangelical Church of the Augsburg Confession in Alsace and Lorraine*

Mehl, Prof. R., *Reformed Church of Alsace and Lorraine*

Bobrinskoy, The Rev. Prof. B., *Russian Exarchate in Western Europe (Ecumenical Patriarchate)*

EUROPE—continued

Germany

Harms, The Rev. Dr H.-H., *EKiD* (*Lutheran*)
Kinder, Prof. Dr E., *EKiD* (*Lutheran*)
Krusche, Dr W., *EKiD* (*Lutheran*)
*Schlink, Prof. Dr E., *EKiD* (*Lutheran*)
Niesel, Prof. Dr W., *EKiD* (*Reformed*)
Hamel, The Rev. Dr J., *EKiD* (*United*)
*Jacob, Dr G., *EKiD* (*United*)
Winterhager, Prof. Dr J. W., *EKiD* (*United*)
Renkewitz, Dr H. G., *Moravian Church*

Greece

Alivisatos, Prof. H. S., *Church of Greece* (*Orthodox*)
Konidaris, Prof. G., *Church of Greece* (*Orthodox*)

Hungary

Vetö, Dr L., *Lutheran Church of Hungary*

Netherlands

Berkhof, Prof. Dr H., *Dutch Reformed Church*
Jans, The Rt Rev. P. J., *Old Catholic Church*

Norway

Flottorp, Prof. Dr H., *Church of Norway* (*Lutheran*)
Molland, Prof. Dr E., *Church of Norway* (*Lutheran*)

Rumania

*Chitescu, The Rev. Prof. N., *Church of Rumania* (*Orthodox*)

Sweden

Edwall, The Very Rev. P., *Church of Sweden* (*Lutheran*)
Nygren, The Rt Rev. A., *Church of Sweden* (*Lutheran*)
*Wingren, Prof. Dr G. F., *Church of Sweden* (*Lutheran*)

Switzerland

Sigg, Bishop F., *Methodist Church, Central and Southern Europe*
*D'Espine, Prof. H., *Swiss Protestant Church Federation*

United Kingdom

Champion, The Rev. Princ. L., *Baptist Union of Great Britain and Ireland*
*Payne, The Rev. Dr E. A., *Baptist Union of Great Britain and Ireland*
Chadwick, The Rev. Dr W. O., *Church of England* (*Anglican*)
Greenslade, The Rev. Prof. S. L., *Church of England* (*Anglican*)
Howard, Miss Christian, *Church of England* (*Anglican*)
*Tomkins, The Rt. Rev. O. S., Bishop of Bristol, *Church of England* (*Anglican*)
*Hartford, The Rev. Prof. R. R., *Church of Ireland* (*Anglican*)
Cairns, The Rev. Prof. D., *Church of Scotland* (*Presbyterian*)
Reid, The Rev. Prof. J. K. S., *Church of Scotland* (*Presbyterian*)
Lee-Woolf, The Rev. P., *Congregational Union of England and Wales*
George, The Rev. Princ. A. R., *Methodist Church*
*Roberts, The Rev. Princ. H., *Methodist Church*
Rupp, The Rev. Prof. G., *Methodist Church*
Ross, Mr J. M., *Presbyterian Church of England*
Creasey, M. A., *Society of Friends*

USSR

Alexis, The Rt Rev., Bishop of Tallinn, *Church of Russia* (*Orthodox*)
*Borovoy, Archpriest V., *Church of Russia* (*Orthodox*)

Appendix 8

EXPRESSIONS OF THANKS

In his closing speech Dr Fry expressed the thanks of the Assembly:

I. *To the member churches of the WCC in India and of the National Christian Council of India;*
—for the invitation to hold the Assembly in India;
—for contributions (also from individuals and institutions) to the expenses of the Assembly, towards local expenses, the Shamiana, the Indian choir, the souvenir and the lyric book;
—for seconding the Secretary of the NCC (Mr Korula Jacob) for eight months of service in making local arrangements;
to Mr Korula Jacob personally for outstanding services to the WCC and its Assembly.

II. *To the President, Vice-President, Prime Minister and Government of India;*
—for the reception at the residence of the President;
—for Mr Nehru's visit;
—for services and help provided by the Ministries of External Affairs; Home Affairs; Communications; Commerce and Industry; Information and Broadcasting; Works, Housing and Supplies;
also to the police of Delhi for assistance in regulating traffic;
also to the staff of the Vigyan Bhavan (a government unit) for co-operation at many points.

III. *To the Delhi Committee for the Third Assembly,* especially its chairman, Rajkumari Amrit Kaur; its vice-chairman, Mr Samuel Mathai, and other members for many services, including:
—the visitors' programme in the Shamiana;
—the programme for the wives of delegates;
—the excellent medical services;
—special gratitude to Dr Mrs D. D. Chacko and her colleagues for these services.

IV. To those in Delhi who have facilitated our worship; the English and Indian choirs and their leaders; those who prepared and provided the book of Indian Christian lyrics.

V. *To the management of the Baptist Mission,* Gange Higher Secondary School, especially Miss A. R. Lewis for accommodating and helping to run the Youth Camp.

VI. *To the members of the Commission on the General Theme,* which prepared the biblical study material in the pre-Assembly booklet, 'Jesus Christ—the Light of the World', and to its chairman, Dr Paul Minear.

VII. *To the Officers of sections and committees* and those on drafting committees; the *Bible Study leaders,* Dr Minear, Dr Niemöller, Father Paul Verghese; *those who have led our worship* at general sessions.

VIII. *To the Press and broadcasting representatives.*
The press and broadcasting (radio and television) coverage of the Third Assembly was more extensive and of higher quality than anyone had dared to expect.
Accreditations were issued to over 350, of which 125 were to the Indian press and broadcasting. The fine coverage and reporting in the Indian press has made an important contribution to the success of the Assembly.

It is estimated that over 250,000 words have gone out from New Delhi over the cables. All of the major wire services have been represented. No meeting in India has ever had such extensive coverage. Television coverage has exceeded that of the Evanston Assembly. Camera teams have been here from India, from Holland, from Germany, two teams from the UK and two from the USA. Through exchange arrangements, film has been sent throughout the world. Reports are not yet in, but the scope is indicated by the estimate from New York services that the procession on the first Sunday was viewed by 34 million Americans. Throughout the world more than 100 millions have seen the Assembly.

Press briefings have been held every morning at 8.15, and press conferences with programme participants at 3.15 each afternoon under the chairmanship of Bishop De Mel. His frankness and cheerful personality kept the press in a cheerful and co-operative mood, and the press has been lavish in their praise of his help and leadership.

IX. *To the staff of the Assembly.*

The total staff of the Assembly numbers 297. Of these, 187 were coopted staff, which means that they have come to New Delhi at their own expense and have worked in our sections, committees, press room, finance bureau, and as stewards and aides group without stint, for long hours and with great effectiveness.

The remainder, 110, are staff of the WCC.

For special mention: Pastor Jens Thomsen, who organized the publication of the pre-Assembly booklet in thirty-two languages, and was responsible for essential administration ranging from charter plane to credentials to hard work in a difficult hotel situation—for a two-year job exceedingly well done.

Certain groups to whom we owe a special debt:

Stewards and aides: Mr Rolston (India) and Mr Albert van den Heuvel, leaders.

They sorted mail and distributed it to the hotels, collated documents, distributed documents with the accuracy of clockwork, arranged meeting rooms, ran errands for many Assembly officers. In these and many other ways they have been the link between the Assembly administration and the membership of the Assembly.

Office Staff (Mrs Baehr in charge).

Translators—Interpreters (Mr Boyens in charge).

Press Staff—Press, TV Photo:

Releases, interviews, press conferences. Mr P. Maury and Department of Information Staff responsible. Special mention of Mr Taylor, who created the Exhibition.

The staff of the Information desk: Father Thomas, Miss Browne and others.

Staff of Jeena and Co. For months they laboured on our behalf in closest collaboration, amid a difficult hotel situation, which, if not solved to everyone's satisfaction, could have been met to no one's satisfaction without them.

Appendix 9

LIST OF MEMBER CHURCHES

(*and of addresses to which correspondence should be directed*)

ARGENTINA

Sinodo Evangelico Aleman Del Rio De La Plata
Propst Friedrich Hoppe, Esmeralda 162, Buenos Aires

AUSTRALASIA

Methodist Church of Australasia
Sec. Gen.: Rev. Prof. H. H. Trigge, King's College, Upland Rd, St Lucia, Brisbane SW6, Queensland, Australia

AUSTRALIA

Church of England in Australia and Tasmania
Primate: The Most Rev. Hugh R. Gough, Archbishop of Sydney, Bishopscourt, Edgecliff, NSW
Congregational Union of Australia
President: Mr Maynard Davies, 92 Chapman Ave, Beecroft, NSW
Federal Conference of Churches of Christ in Australia
Principal: E. L. Williams, College of the Bible, Elm Road, Glen Iris, SE6, Melbourne
Presbyterian Church of Australia
The Clerk of the Gen. Assembly: The Rev. G. Ross Williams, 156 Collins Street, Melbourne

AUSTRIA

Evangelische Kirche A.u.H.B. in Oesterreich (Evangelical Church of the Augsburg and Helvetic Confession)
Evangelischer Oberkirchenrat, Schellinggasse 12, Vienna I

BELGIUM

Eglise Chretienne Missionnaire Belge (Belgian Christian Mission Church)
M. le Pasteur D. Zorn, 76 Boul. Pierre Mayence, Charleroi
Eglise Evangelique Protestante de Belgique (Evangelical Protestant Church of Belgium)
Président: M. le Pasteur E. Pichal, 80 Bd. L. Schmidt, Bruxelles

BRAZIL

Igreja Metodista do Brasil (Methodist Church of Brazil)
Bishop J. A. Do Amaral, Caixa Postal 1101, Petropolis, Estado de Rio de Janeiro
Federacao Sinodal, Igreja Evangelica de Confisao Lutherana do Brasil (Synodal Federation, Evangelical Church of Lutheran Confession in Brazil)
Präses D. Ernst Schlieper, Caixa Postal 14, Sao Leopoldo

BULGARIA

Bulgarian Orthodox Church
His Holiness Kyrille, Patriarch of Bulgaria, Sofia

BURMA
Burma Baptist Convention
143 St John's Road, Rangoon

CAMEROUN
Eglise Evangelique du Cameroun (Evangelical Church of Cameroun)
M. le Pasteur Jean Kotto, BP 89, Douala
Union des Eglises Baptistes du Cameroun (Union of Baptist Churches of Cameroun)
Rev. Paul Mbende, BP 7, New-Bell-Douala
Presbyterian Church in West Cameroon
Rev. A. Su, Buea, Western Cameroons

CANADA
The Anglican Church of Canada
Gen. Sec.: The Ven. Archdeacon E. H. Maddocks, The Church House, 600 Jarvis St, Toronto 5, Ontario
Churches of Christ (Disciples)
Gen. Sec.: Rev. O. W. McCully, 695 A, St Clair Ave W, Toronto 10, Ontario
Presbyterian Church in Canada
Secretary: Rev. E. A. Thomson, DD, 63 St George St, Toronto 5, Ontario
United Church of Canada
Secretary: Dr Ernest E. Long, 85 St Clair Avenue East, Toronto 7, Ontario
Yearly Meeting of the Society of Friends
Mr Fred Haslam, 60 Lowther Ave, Toronto 5, Ontario

CENTRAL AFRICA (see also Rhodesia)
The Church of the Province of Central Africa
The Rt Rev. W. J. Hughes, Archbishop, Bishop's House, Park Road, Bulawayo, Southern Rhodesia
United Church of Central Africa in Rhodesia
Rev. Eric A. Read, Clerk of Synod, PO Box 1777, Kitwe, Northern Rhodesia

CEYLON (see also India)
Methodist Church in Ceylon
Rev. F. S. de Silva, Methodist Headquarters, Colombo 3

CHILE
Iglesia Pentecostal de Chile (Pentecostal Church of Chile)
Rev. Enrique Chavez Campos, Casilla No 2, Curico
Mision Iglesia Pentecostal (Chile)
Rev. Victor Pavez Ortiz, Casilla 7033, Santiago de Chile

CHINA
China Baptist Council, 169 Yuen Ming Yuen Road, Shanghai
Chung-hua Chi-tu Chiio-hui (Church of Christ in China)
128 Museum Road, Shanghai
Chung Hua Sheng Kung Hui (Church in China)
169 Yuen Ming Yuen Road, Shanghai
Hua Pei Kung Li Hui (North China Congregational Church)
29 Teng Shih Kou, Peking

CONGO

Eglise Evangelique Manianga Matadi (Manianga Matadi Evangelical Church)
President Dan. Luyindu, Kibunzi, Luozi

CYPRUS

Church of Cyprus
His Beatitude Makarios III, Archbishop of Cyprus, Nicosia

CZECHOSLOVAKIA

Ceskobratska Cirkev Evangelicka (Evangelical Church of Czech Brethren)
Synodical Senior: Dr Victor Hajek, Jungmannova 9, Prague II
Evangelicka Cirkev A.V. Na Slovensku (Evangelical Church in Slovakia, Augsburg Confession)
Generalbischof Jan Chabada, Kuzmanyho 5/11, Bratislava
Ref. Cirkev Na Slovensku (Reformed Christian Church in Slovakia)
Bishof Emerich Varga, Druzby 41, Rimavska Sobota
Slezska Cirkev Evangelicka A.V. (Evangelical Church of the Augsburg Confession in Silesia)
Na nivach 7, Cesky Tesin

DENMARK

Baptist Union of Denmark
The Rev. Johs. Nørgaard, Praedikantskolen, Tølløse
Den Evangelisklutherske Folkekirke I Danmark (Church of Denmark)
The Rt Rev. Bishop W. Westergaard Madsen, Nørregade 11, Copenhagen

EAST AFRICA

Church of the Province of East Africa (Anglican)
J. K. Buku, Esq., Lay Secretary of the Provincial Synod, Box 30422, Nairobi, Kenya
Presbyterian Church of East Africa
Church Office, PO Box 8268, Nairobi, Kenya

EGYPT

Coptic Orthodox Church
His Holiness Patriarch Anba Kyrillos VI, Cairo
Greek Orthodox Patriarchate of Alexandria
His Holiness the Pope and Patriarch of Alexandria, Mgr Christophorus II, Alexandria

ETHIOPIA

Ethiopian Orthodox Church
His Holiness Abuna Basilios, Patriarch, Addis Ababa

FINLAND

Suomen Evankelis-Luterilainen Kirkko (Evangelical Lutheran Church of Finland)
The Most Rev. Archbishop I. Salomies, Agricolankatu 2, Turku

FORMOSA

Tai-oan Ki-tok Tiu-lo Kau-hoe (Presbyterian Church in Formosa)
Gen. Sec.: The Rev. W. T. Hwang, 94 Section 2, Chung Shan North Road, Taipei, Taiwan

FRANCE

Eglise de la Confession D'Augsbourg D'Alsace et de Lorraine (Evangelical Church of the Augsburg Confession in Alsace and Lorraine)
Président du Directoire: M. E. Jung, 1 Quai St Thomas, Strasbourg
Eglise Evangelique Lutherienne de France (Evangelical Lutheran Church of France)
Président: M. Etienne Meyer, 83 Boul. Arago, Paris 14
Eglise Reformee D'Alsace et de Lorraine (Reformed Church of Alsace and Lorraine)
Commission Synodale: 2 rue de Bouclier, Strasbourg
Eglise Reformee de France (Reformed Church of France)
Président: M. le Pasteur P. Bourguet, 47 rue de Clichy, Paris 9e

GABON

Eglise Evangelique du Gabon (Evangelical Church of Gabon)
Rev. Basile Ndong Amvame, BP 80, Libreville, Gab

GERMANY

Altkatholische Kirche in Deutschland (Old Catholic Church in Germany)
The Rt Rev. Bishop J. J. Demmel, Gregor Mendelstr. 25, Bonn/Rhein
Evangelische Brueder-Unitaet (Moravian Church)
Herrnhuter Brüdergemeine, Bad Boll (Württ.)
Evangelische Kirche in Deutschland (Evangelical Church in Germany)
Kirchliches Aussenamt der Evangelischen Kirche in Deutschland, Bockenheimer Landstr. 109, Schliessfach 4025, Frankfurt/Main-Süd 10

- Evangelische Kirche in Berlin-Brandenburg
- Pommersche Evangelische Kirche
- Evangelische Kirche von Schlesien
- Evangelische Kirche der Kirchenprovinz Sachsen
- Evangelische Kirche von Westfalen
- Evangelische Kirche im Rheinland
- Evangelisch-Lutherische Landeskirche Sachsens[1]
- Evangelisch-Lutherische Landeskirche Hannovers[1]
- Evangelisch-Lutherische Kirche in Bayern[1]
- Evangelisch-Lutherische Kirche in Thueringen[1]
- Evangelisch-Lutherische Landeskirche Schleswig-Holsteins[1]
- Evangelisch-Lutherische Landeskirche im Hamburgischen Staate[1]
- Evangelisch-Lutherische Landeskirche Mecklenburgs[1]
- Braunschweigische Evangelisch-Lutherische Landeskirche[1]
- Evangelisch-Lutherische Kirche in Luebeck[1]
- Evangelisch-Lutherische Landeskirche in Schaumburg-Lippe[1]

[1] This Church is directly a member of the World Council of Churches in accordance with the resolution of the General Synod of the United Evangelical Lutheran Church of Germany, dated January 27, 1949, which recommended that the member churches of the United Evangelical Lutheran Church should make the following declaration to the Council of the Evangelical Church in Germany concerning their relation to the World Council of Churches:

'The Evangelical Church in Germany has made it clear through its constitution that it is a federation (Bund) of confessionally determined churches. Moreover, the conditions of membership of the World Council of Churches have been determined at the Assembly at Amsterdam. Therefore, this Evangelical Lutheran Church declares concerning its membership in the World Council of Churches:

GERMANY—continued

Evangelische Landeskirche in Wuerttemberg
Evangelisch-Lutherische Kirche in Oldenburg
Evangelisch-Lutherische Landeskirche Eutin
Evangelische Kirche in Hessen und Nassau
Evangelische Landeskirche in Kurhessen-Waldeck
Evangelische Landeskirche in Baden
Vereinigte Protestantische Kirche der Pfalz
Evangelische Landeskirche Anhalts
Bremische Evangelische Kirche
Evangelisch-Reformierte Kirche in Nordwestdeutschland
Lippische Landeskirche

Vereinigung der Deutschen Mennonitengemeinden (Mennonite Church)
Pastor Dr Heinold Fast, Brückstr. 74, Emden/Ostfr.

GHANA (see also West Africa)

Presbyterian Church of Ghana
Rev. Collin Forrester Paton, Sec., Comm. on Inter-Church and Ecumenical Relations, PO Box 1800, Accra
The Methodist Church
Rev. F. C. F. Grant, PO Box 403, Accra

GREECE

Ekklesia tes Ellados (Church of Greece)
His Beatitude the Archbishop of Athens and Primate of All Greece, Archbishopric, Athens
Greek Evangelical Church
Moderator: The Rev. Michael Kyriakakis, 50 Amalias Ave, Athens

HUNGARY

A Magyarorszagi Evangelikus Egyhaz (Lutheran Church of Hungary)
Ulloi utca 24, Budapest VIII
A Magyarorszagi Reformatus Egyhaz (Reformed Church of Hungary)
General Convent, Abonyi u. 21, Budapest XIV
Baptist Church of Hungary
Aradi utca 48, Budapest VI

ICELAND

Evangelical Lutheran Church of Iceland
The Rt Rev. Bishop Sigurbjorn Einarsson, Reykjavik

INDIA

Church of India, Pakistan, Burma and Ceylon
The Most Rev. the Metropolitan of India, Bishop's House, 51 Chowringhee, Calcutta 16
Church of South India

(i) It is represented in the World Council as a church of the Evangelical Lutheran confession.
(ii) Representatives which it sends to the World Council are to be identified as Evangelical Lutherans.
(iii) Within the limits of the competence of the Evangelical Church of Germany it is represented in the World Council through the intermediary of the Council of the Evangelical Church of Germany.'

INDIA—continued

Sri A. R. Rajaratnam, IAS (Retd.), The Synod Office, Cathedral PO, Madras 6
Federation of Evangelical Lutheran Churches in India
President: Rev. E. Raman, Saugor, MP
Mar Thoma Syrian Church of Malabar
Sabha Office, Tiruvalla, Kerala, Travancore
Orthodox Syrian Church of the East
The Rev. Father Korah Philipos, Orthodox Seminary, Kottayam, Travancore
United Church of Northern India and Pakistan
Stated Clerk: The Rev. Kenneth Yohan Masih, Church House, Mhow, MB

INDONESIA

Geredja Geredja Kristen di Djawa Tengah (Christian Churches in Mid Java)
Secretary: Rev. B. Probowinoto, Djl Gadean Lor 6, Salatiga
Geredja Gereformeerd di Indonesia (Reformed Church in Indonesia)
Kwitang 28, Djakarta
Geredja Kalimantan Evangelis (Evangelical Church in Kalimantan)
6 Djalan Tugu, Bandjarmasin, Kalimantan
Geredja Kristen Djawa Wetan (Christian Church in East Java)
Chairman: Rev. Mardoo Sir, Sukun 18, Malang, Java
Geredja Kristen Pasundan (Sundanese Christian Church of West Java)
The Rev. M. K. Tjakraatmadja, Djl Pasirkaliki 93, Bandung
Geredja Kristen Sulawesi Tengah (Christian Church in Mid Sulawesi)
Poso, Mid Sulawesi
Geredja Masehi Indjili di Minahasa (Christian Evangelical Church in the Minahassa)
Secretary: Rev. J. F. Parengkuan, Tomohon, Sul-Utara
Geredja Masehi Indjili Timor (Christian Evangelical Church in Timor)
Secretary: Rev. L. Radjahaba, Kupang, Timor
Geredja Protestan di Indonesia (Protestant Church in Indonesia)
Medan Merdeka Timur No 10, PB 2057, Djakarta
Geredja Protestan Maluku (Protestant Church in the Moluccas)
Kantor Pusat GPM, Batugantung, Amboina
Huria Kristen Batak Protestan (Protestant Christian Batak Church)
Gen. Sec.: Rev. T. S. Sihombing, Pearadja-Tarutung, Sumatra

IRAN

Synod of the Evangelical Churches of North Iran
Moderator: Rev. Habib Yusefzaden, PO Box 1505, Teheran

ITALY

Chiesa Evangelica Metodista D'Italia (Evangelical Methodist Church of Italy)
Chairman and General Superintendent: Pastore Mario Sbaffi, Via Firenze 38, Rome
Chiesa Evangelica Valdese (Waldensian Church)
Pastore Ermanno Rostan, 107 Via IV Novembre, Rome

JAPAN

Nippon Kirisuto Kyodan (United Church of Christ in Japan)

JAPAN—continued

Gen. Sec.: Mr Iwao Niwa, 2-4 chome Ginza, Khuo-Ku, Tokyo
Nippon Sei Ko Kwai (Anglican Church in Japan)
Presiding Bishop: The Most Rev. M. H. Yashiro, 5 Nakayamate-dori, 3 chome, Ikuta-ku, Kobe-Shi, Honshu

JORDAN

Greek Orthodox Patriarchate of Jerusalem
His Holiness the Patriarch of Jerusalem, Benedictus, PO Box 4074, Jerusalem, Via Amman

KOREA

Korean Methodist Church
Rev. C. A. Sauer, 34 Chung Dong, Methodist Mission, Seoul
Presbyterian Church in the Republic of Korea
Rev. Greenfield C. Kiel, Moderator, Room 401-402 KCLS Building, 91 Chongro, 2-ka, Seoul
Presbyterian Church of Korea
Gen. Sec.: Rev. Sang Kwon Kim, 91-2 Street Chongno, Seoul

LEBANON

Evangelical Synod of Syria and Lebanon (see under Syria)
Union of the Armenian Evangelical Churches in the Near East
Moderator: Prof. Hov. P. Aharonian, PO Box 235, Beirut

MADAGASCAR

Eglise Evangelique de Madagascar (Evangelical Church of Madagascar)
Président: M. le Pasteur J. B. Ralabomahay, 18 avenue Labourdonnais, Antananarivo
Church of Christ in Madagascar (formally LMS Synod in Madagascar)
Secretary: Prof. J. Ramambasoa, Collège Théologique Ambohipotsy, rue Webert, Tananarive

MEXICO

Iglesia Metodista de Mejico (Methodist Church in Mexico)
Bishop Rolando Zapata Olivares, Gante 5, Mexico DF

NETHERLANDS

Algemene Doopsgezinde Societeit (General Mennonite Society)
Mr H. Craandijk, Keizersgracht 726, Amsterdam C
Bond van Vrije Evangelische Gemeenten in Nederland (Union of Free Evangelical Congregations)
The Rev. P. van Vliet, Oldebroak, Prov. Gelderland
Evangelisch Lutherse Kerk (Evangelical Lutheran Church)
Secretary: The Rev. C. Pel, Erasmusgracht 28, Amsterdam W
Nederlands Hervormde Kerk (Dutch Reformed Church)
Gen. Sec.: Dr E. Emmen, Carnegielaan 9, The Hague
Oud-Katholieke Kerk (Old Catholic Church)
The Rt Rev. Bishop P. J. Jans, Kon. Wilhelminalaan 3, Amersfoort
Remonstrantse Broederschap (Arminian Church)
Mathenesserlaan 3, Rotterdam C2
Unie van Baptisten Gemeenten in Nederland (Union of Baptist Congregations)
Rev. J. Jansma, Dalweg 77, Arnhem

NEW CALEDONIA

Eglise Evangelique en Nouvelle-Caledonie et aux Iles Loyaute (Ev. Church in New Caledonia and the Loyalty Isles)
Rev. Elia Thidjine, BP 277, Noumea, New Caledonia

NEW HEBRIDES

Presbyterian Church of the New Hebrides
Rev. A. G. Howell, Via Vila, Lamenu Island

NEW ZEALAND

Associated Churches of Christ in New Zealand
The Secretary, PO Box 1354, Wellington
Baptist Union of New Zealand
Secretary: Rev. Lawrence A. North, PO Box 1773, Wellington C1
Church of the Province of New Zealand (Church of England)
Provincial Secretary: Mr L. H. Wilson, PO Box 800, Christchurch C1
Congregational Union of New Zealand
Secretary: Mr G. G. Ennor, PO Box 374, Auckland C1
Methodist Church of New Zealand
Secretary, Rev. Athol R. Penn, 17 Pukehana Ave, Auckland SE3
Presbyterian Church of New Zealand
Rev. R. M. Rogers, 16 Armagh St, Christchurch C1

NIGERIA (see also West Africa)

Presbyterian Church of Nigeria
Rev. R. M. Macdonald, The Leper Colony, Itu, E. Nigeria

NORWAY

Norske Kirke (Church of Norway)
3 S. Halvards Plass, Oslo

PAKISTAN (see also India)

United Presbyterian Church of Pakistan
Rev. K. L. Nasir, Theological Seminary, Gujranwala, W. Pakistan

PHILIPPINE ISLANDS

Iglesia Catolica Filipina Independiente (Philippine Independent Church)
The Rt Rev. Bishop Isabelo de los Reyes Jr, 1320 V. Concepcion, Santa Cruz, Manila
United Church of Christ in the Philippines
Gen. Sec.: Bishop Enrique L. Sobrepena, PO Box 718, Manila

POLAND

Eglise Autoceph. Orthodoxe en Pologne (Orthodox Church of Poland)
The Most Rev. Metropolitan of Warsaw and All Poland, Warsaw
Kosciol Ewangelicko-Augsburski W Polsce (Evangelical Church of the Augsburg Confession)
Kredytowa 2/4m. 11, Warsaw
Polski Narodoway Kosciol Katolicki (Catholic Church of Poland)
ul. Wilcza 31, Warsaw

RHODESIA (see also Central Africa)

The United Church of Central Africa in Rhodesia
Rev. Eric A. Read, Clerk of Synod, PO Box 212, Bancroft, N. Rhodesia

RUMANIA

Biserica Lutherana Ungara din Romania (Hungarian Lutheran Church in Rumania)
Superintendent Georg Argay, Str. Kossuth Lajos 1, Cluj
Biserica Evangelica Dupa Confesiunea Dela Augsburg (Evangelical Church Augsburg Confession)
The Rt Rev. Bishop D. Friedrich Müller, Piata Grivita 1, Hermannstadt-Sibiu
Biserica Ortodoxa Romanie (Rumanian Orthodox Church)
His Holiness Patriarch Justinian, Palatul Patriarhiei, Bucarest
Biserica Reformata Din Romania (Transylvanian Reformed Church)
Strada 23, August 51, Cluj

SAMOA

Samoan Church, LMS Synod
Secretary, PO Box 468, Apia, W. Samoa

SOUTH AFRICA

Bantu Congregational Church in South Africa
Rev. M. E. Mdluli, Infume Mission, Illovo Beach, Natal
Bantu Presbyterian Church of South Africa
Senior Clerk: The Rev. D. V. Sikutshwa, Somerville Mission, Tsolo, Transkei
Church of the Province of South Africa (Anglican)
The Most Rev. Archbishop of Cape Town, Bishopscourt, Claremont, Cape Province
Congregational Union of South Africa
The Rev. Vernon E. Miller, 34 Palmyra Road, Claremont, Cape Province
Methodist Church of South Africa
Sec. of the Conference: Mr M. H. Eddy, PO Box 3297, Johannesburg, Transvaal
Moravian Church in the Western Cape Province
The Rt Rev. P. W. Schaberg, 84 Lympleigh Road, Plumstead, Cape Province
Presbyterian Church of South Africa
Rev. J. Paterson Ehyte, PO Box 11347, Johannesburg, Transvaal

SPAIN

Iglesia Evangelica Espanola (Spanish Evangelical Church)
Secretary: Pastor Humberto Capo, A. L. Salvador 182, Palma de Mallorca, Baleares

SWEDEN

Svenska Kyrkan (Church of Sweden)
The Most Rev. Archbishop Gunnar Hultgren, Uppsala
Svenska Missionsfoerbundet (Mission Covenant Church of Sweden)
Tegnérgatan 8, Stockholm Va.

SWITZERLAND

Christkatholische Kirche der Schweiz (Old Catholic Church)
The Rt Rev. Bishop Dr Urs Küry, Willadingweg 39, Bern
Schweizerischer Evangelischer Kirchenbund-Federation des Eglises Protestantes de la Suisse (Swiss Protestant Church Federation)
Pastor Arnold Mobbs, Le Presbytère, Céligny, Geneva

SYRIA

Evangelical Synod of Syria and Lebanon
The Rev. Ibrahim M. Dagher, Sec. of the Synod, PO Box 235, Beirut, Lebanon
Greek Orthodox Patriarchate of Antioch
His Holiness the Lord Theodosius, Patriarch of Antioch, Damascus, Syria
Syrian Orthodox Patriarchate of Antioch and all the East
His Holiness Mar Ignatius Yacob III, Damascus

TANGANYIKA

Evangelical Church of North-western Tanganyika
The Rt Rev. Bishop Bengt Sundkler, PO Box 98, Bukoba
Usambara-Digo Lutheran Church (Tanganyika)
The Rt Rev. Bishop H. Waltenberg, PO Box 10, Lushoto

THAILAND

Church of Christ in Thailand
Gen. Sec.: Mr Charoon Widchaidist, 14 Pramuen Road, Bangkok

TOGO

Eglise Evangelique du Togo (Evangelical Church of Togo)
BP 2, Lomé, Togo

TRINIDAD

Presbyterian Church in Trinidad
The Rt Rev. Roy G. Neehall, 4 Francis Lau Street, St James, Port-of-Spain

TURKEY

Ecumenical Patriarchate of Constantinople
His All-Holiness Athenagoras, Ecumenical Patriarch, Fener, Istanbul

UGANDA AND RUANDA URUNDI

The Church of the Province of Uganda and Ruanda Urundi (Anglican)
The Most Rev. L. W. Brown, Archbishop of Uganda, PO Box 56, Kampala

UNITED KINGDOM AND EIRE

Baptist Union of Great Britain and Ireland
Dr E. A. Payne, The Baptist Church House, 4 Southampton Row, London, WC1
Churches of Christ in Great Britain and Ireland
Secretary: Mr J. Leslie Colver, Flat B, 274 Highbury Rd, Bulwell, Nottingham
Church of England
The Secretary, Council for Ecumenical Co-operation, Church House, Dean's Yard, London, SW1
Communications should also be sent to: Senior Chaplain, Lambeth Palace, London, SW1
Church of Ireland
D. W. Pratt, Esq., Chief Officer and Sec. of Representative Body, 52 St Stephen's Green, E. Dublin, Ireland
Church of Scotland
The Principal Clerk of the Assembly, 121 George Street, Edinburgh 2
Church in Wales
Secretary: Mr Richard R. Wilson, 39 Cathedral Road, Cardiff, Glam.

UNITED KINGDOM AND EIRE—continued

Congregational Union of England and Wales
Secretary: Rev. H. S. Stanley, 205 Memorial Hall, Farringdon Street, London, EC4
Congregational Union of Scotland
Rev. John T. George, 217 W. George Street, Glasgow C2
Episcopal Church in Scotland
Mr H. J. N. Fentiman, 13 Drumsheugh Gardens, Edinburgh
Methodist Church
Secretary of the Conference: Rev. Dr Eric Baker, Methodist Church House, 1 Central Buildings, Westminster, London, SW1
Methodist Church in Ireland
Rev. R. D. E. Gallagher, Grosvenor Hall, Glengall Street, Belfast
Moravian Church in Great Britain and Ireland
Rev. J. H. Foy, 5-7 Muswell Hill, London, N10
Presbyterian Church of England
Gen. Sec.: Rev. A. L. Macarther, 86 Tavistock Place, London, WC1
Presbyterian Church in Ireland
General Secretary's Office, Church House, Belfast, N. Ireland
Presbyterian Church of Wales
Sec.: Rev. R. B. Owen, The Manse, Plas Avenue, Prestatyn, Flintshire
The Salvation Army
Salvation Army International Headquarters, Denmark Hill, London, SE5
United Free Church of Scotland
Sec.: Mrs W. Bell, 11 Newton Place, Glasgow, C3

UNITED STATES OF AMERICA

African Methodist Episcopal Church
Sec.: Bishop S. L. Greene, 1105 Fountain Drive SW Atlanta 14, Georgia
African Methodist Episcopal Zion Church
Presiding Bishop: Bishop W. J. Walls, 4736 S. Parkway, Chicago 15, Ill.
American Baptist Convention
Rev. Dr Edwin H. Tuller, Valley Forge, Pa.
American Evangelical Lutheran Church
President: Rev. A. E. Farstrup, 3112 Lawnview Drive, Des Moines 10
The American Lutheran Church
President: Dr Fredrik A. Schiotz, 422 S. Fifth St, Minneapolis 15, Minn.
Augustana Evangelical Lutheran Church
President: Dr Malvin H. Lundeen, 2445 Park Avenue, Minneapolis 4, Minn.
Christian Methodist Episcopal Church
Presiding Bishop: Bishop B. Julian Smith, 8128 South Calumet Avenue, Chicago 19, Ill.
Church of the Brethren
Sec.: Dr Norman J. Baugher, 1451 Dundee Avenue, Elgin, Ill.
The Church of the East (Assyrian)
His Holiness Mar Shimun, 750 Gonzalez Dr., San Francisco 27, Calif.
Evangelical United Brethren Church
Sec.: Bishop J. Gordon Howard, 900 East End Avenue, Pittsburgh 21, Pa.
Hungarian Reformed Church in America
The Very Rev. Bishop Zoltan Béky, 180 Home Avenue, Trenton, NJ
International Convention of Christian Churches (Disciples of Christ)
Rev. Dr Gaines M. Cook, PO Box 19136, Indianapolis 19, Ind.
The Methodist Church

UNITED STATES OF AMERICA—continued

Secretary of the Council of Bishops: Bishop Roy H. Short, 201 8th Avenue South, Nashville 3, Tenn.
Moravian Church in America (Northern Province)
Vice-Pres.: The Rt Rev. K. G. Hamilton, 69 W. Church St, Bethlehem, Pa.
Moravian Church in America (Southern Province)
The Rev. Dr Gordon Spaugh, 500 S. Church St, Winston-Salem, NC
National Baptist Convention of America
Vice-Pres.: Dr C. D. Pettaway, 714 W. 10th St, Little Rock, Ark.
National Baptist Convention, USA Inc.
President: Dr J. H. Jackson, 3101 South Parkway, Chicago, Ill.
Polish National Catholic Church of America
The Most Rev. Leon Grochowski, 529 E. Locust St, Scranton 5, Pa.
Presbyterian Church in the US
Stated Clerk: Dr James A. Millard, Jr, 341-A Ponce de Leon Ave, NE, Atlanta 5, Ga.
Protestant Episcopal Church
Presiding Bishop: The Rt Rev. Arthur Lichtenberger, 281 Fourth Avenue, New York 10, NY
Reformed Church in America
Stated Clerk: Rev. Dr Marion de Velder, 475 Riverside Drive, New York 27, NY
The Religious Society of Friends
Five Years Meeting of Friends
Sec.: Mr Glenn A. Reece, 101 Quaker Hill Drive, Richmond, Ind.
Friends General Conference
Sec.: Mr Lawrence McK. Miller, 1515 Cherry Street, Philadelphia 2, Pa.
Romanian Orthodox Episcopate of America
His Grace Valerian D. Trifa, 2522 Grey Tower Road, RFD 7, Jackson, Mich.
Russian Orthodox Greek Catholic Church of America
Metropolitan Leonty, Archbishop, 59 E. 2nd Street, New York 3, NY
Seventh Day Baptist General Conference
Mr Harley D. Bond, 510 Watchung Avenue, Plainfield, NJ
Suomi Synod—Finnish Evangelical Lutheran Church of America
Dr Raymond Wargelin, 403 Cooper Avenue, Hancock, Michigan, USA
Syrian Antiochian Orthodox Church (Archdiocese of New York and All North America)
The Most Rev. Antony Bashir, Archbishop, 239 85th Street, Brooklyn 9, NY
United Church of Christ
President: Dr Ben. M. Herbster, Room 62, 297 Park Avenue S., New York 10, NY
United Lutheran Church in America
President: Dr Franklin Clark Fry, 231 Madison Avenue, New York 16, NY
United Presbyterian Church in the United States of America
Dr Eugene Carson Blake, 510 Witherspoon Building, Philadelphia 7, Pa.

USSR

Orthodox Church of Russia, Patriarchate of Moscow
Christij Perenlok 5, Moscow 34

WEST AFRICA (see also Nigeria)

The Church of the Province of West Africa (Anglican)

WEST AFRICA—continued

Clerical Sec. of the Provincial Synod: The Ven. Archdeacon I. O. S. Okunsanya, PO Box 34, Akure, Nigeria

WEST INDIES

Anglican Church of the West Indies

The Most Rev. the Lord Bishop of Guiana and Archbishop of the West Indies, Austin House, Georgetown 1, British Guiana

The Presbyterian Church of Jamaica

Clerk of the Synod: Rev. H. G. Williams, 36 Union St, Montego Bay, Jamaica

YUGOSLAVIA

Reformed Christian Church of Yugoslavia

The Rt Rev. Bishop Csete K. Istvan, Reformovani Episkop, Reformiertes Bishofsamt, Pacir (Backa)

Other Churches

Eesti Ev. Lut. Usu Kiriku (Esthonian Evangelical Lutheran Church)

Lietuvos Ev. Reformatu Baznycia (Lithuanian Reformed Church)

Appendix to list of member churches

NATIONAL COUNCILS IN ASSOCIATION WITH THE WORLD COUNCIL OF CHURCHES

Australian Council of Churches

Rev. Harvey Perkins, 511 Kent Street, Sydney, NSW

Oekumenische Rat Der Kirchen in Oesterreich

Rev. Ferdinand Mayr, Landgutgasse 39/8, Vienna X

British Council of Churches

Rev. Kenneth Slack, 10 Eaton Gate, London, SW1

Burma Christian Council

Rev. John Thetgyi, 262 Sule Pagoda Road, Rangoon

Canadian Council of Churches

Dr W. J. Gallagher, 40 St Clair Ave East, Toronto 7, Ont.

Ecumenical Council of Churches in Czechoslovakia

Pastor J. N. Ondra, Jungmannova 9, Prague 2, Czechoslovakia

Danish Ecumenical Council

Rev. Henning Talman, Skindergade 31, III, Copenhagen K.

Ecumenical Council of Finland

Rev. Dr Seppo A. Teinonen, Ecumenical Institute, University of Helsinki, Fabianinkatu 33, Helsinki

Arbeitsgemeinschaft Christlicher Kirchen in Deutschland

Dr Hanfried Krüger, Oekumenische Centrale, Bockenheimer Landstr. 109, Schliessfach 4025, Frankfurt-am-Main

Ecumenical Council of Churches in Hungary

Rev. Dr F. Kenéz, Havas utca 6, Budapest V

National Christian Council of India

Mr Korula Jacob, Christian Council Lodge, Nagpur 1, MS

National Council of Churches in Indonesia

Rev. Simon Marantika, Djl Salemba Raya 10, Djakarta IV/3

National Christian Council of Japan

Rev. Kiyoshi Hirai, 2. 4-chome, Ginza, Cho-ku, Tokyo

Ecumenical Council of Churches in the Netherlands

Miss S. M. Holsteijn, Janskerkhof 15, Utrecht
National Council of Churches in New Zealand
Rev. Alan Brash, PO Box 297, Christchurch C1
Federation of Christian Churches in the Philippines
Rev. José A. Yap, 1648 Taft Avenue, Manila, Philippines
Polish Ecumenical Council
Dr Andrzej Wantula, U1. Swierczewskiego 76a, Warsaw
Swedish Ecumenical Council
Director Harry Johansson, Nordiska Ekumeniska Institutet, Sigtuna
National Council of the Churches of Christ in the USA
Dr Roy G. Ross, 475 Riverside Drive, New York 27, NY

Appendix 10

CONSTITUTION OF THE COMMISSION ON AND DIVISION OF WORLD MISSION AND EVANGELISM

The Commission on World Mission and Evangelism

1. There shall be a Commission on World Mission and Evangelism constituted in accordance with the Constitution of the World Council of Churches (Sec. VI, (3)).

2. *Aim*

Its aim shall be to further the proclamation to the whole world of the Gospel of Jesus Christ, to the end that all men may believe in him and be saved.

3. *Functions*

The functions of the Commission shall be:

(i) to keep before the churches their calling and privilege to engage in constant prayer for the missionary and evangelistic work of the Church;
(ii) to remind the churches of the range and character of the unfinished evangelistic task and to deepen their sense of missionary obligation;
(iii) to stimulate thought and study on the Biblical and theological bases and meaning of the Church's missionary task and on questions directly related to the spread of the Gospel in the world;
(iv) to foster among churches and among councils and other Christian bodies more effective co-operation and united action for world evangelization;
(v) to deepen evangelistic and missionary concern in the whole life and work of the World Council of Churches;
(vi) to assist in securing and safeguarding freedom of conscience and religion as formulated in declarations of the World Council of Churches on religious liberty;
(vii) to co-operate with other units of the World Council of Churches;
(viii) to take such further action in fulfilment of the declared aim of the Commission as is not otherwise provided for within the World Council of Churches.

4. *Authority*

The Commission shall have no mandatory authority over any of the councils related to it, whether in affiliated or consultative relationship, in accordance with the principles enunciated in the Constitution of the World Council of Churches.

5. *Operations*

(i) The Commission shall ordinarily meet once every five years. Special meetings may be convened at the call of the Divisional Committee with the approval of the Central Committee.

(ii) The Commission shall formulate the general lines of policy and programme to be followed by the Division of World Mission and Evangelism, for submission to the Central Committee for its approval. The Division shall be responsible for the execution of this policy and programme.

(iii) The Commission shall keep its related councils fully informed and consult them regularly on matters of policy and programme. It shall send its reports and recommendations to the councils.

(iv) The Commission shall report regularly to the Assembly and the Central Committee.

(v) The Commission shall develop appropriate organs for fulfilling its functions in the area of evangelism, including the provision of staff for this purpose.

(vi) (*a*) The Commission may sponsor—or, with the approval of the Assembly or Central Committee, co-operate with other bodies in sponsoring—agencies for specialized activities.

(*b*) In each case of a sponsored agency, the constitution and the appointment of the principal executive officer shall be subject to the approval of the Commission. Each sponsored agency shall report to the Commission from time to time on its acts and programme.

(*c*) The World Council shall not be responsible for the financing of sponsored agencies except as it may in advance explicitly accept such responsibility.

6. *Affiliation and Membership*

(i) All member councils of the International Missionary Council at the time of integration will be regarded as affiliated to the Commission.

(ii) Thereafter national or regional Christian councils and national or regional missionary organizations which accept the aim of the Commission may become councils affiliated to the Commission, on the approval of a regularly constituted meeting of the Commission by a two-thirds majority of those present and voting. Any application for affiliation between meetings of the Commission may be considered by the Divisional Committee; if the application is supported by a two-thirds majority of the members of the Committee present and voting, this action shall be communicated to the councils affiliated to the Commission, and unless objection is received from more than one-third of these councils within six months the council shall be declared affiliated.

The following criteria shall determine eligibility for affiliation:

(*a*) The council shall express its acceptance of the aim of the Commission on World Mission and Evangelism and desire to co-operate in the functions of the Commission as defined in the Constitution.

(*b*) The council shall satisfy such other criteria as may be determined by the Commission. In considering applications for affiliation, the Commission on World Mission and Evangelism will take into account the size and stability of the council concerned and the relevance of its programme to the aim and functions of the Commission.

(*c*) There shall be consultation with the member churches of the World Council of Churches in the area concerned, and with the Committee on National Council Relationships.

(iii) A council which performs functions in several fields of activity may be represented in the Commission on World Mission and Evangelism through its appropriate unit(s) or division(s).

(iv) National or regional Christian councils and national or regional missionary organizations which are not affiliated to the Commission may become councils in consultation with the Commission. If any member council of the International Missionary Council informs the International Missionary Council before integration that it cannot accept affiliation, it shall automatically become a council in consultation with the Commission under this rule. Thereafter, councils in consultation shall be councils which are not yet eligible to become affiliated councils or which do not desire affiliation, but which

(*a*) accept the aim of the Commission and desire a consultative relationship with it; and

(*b*) are accepted by the Commission as eligible for such a relationship.

Councils in consultation shall be entitled to send consultants to meetings of the Commission: they shall be entitled to speak but not to vote.

(v) In accordance with a schedule which shall be prepared before each regular meeting of the Commission by the Divisional Committee and approved by the Central Committee, the Commission shall consist of members appointed by the affiliated councils and of members appointed by the Central Committee. The members appointed by Central Committee shall include persons representative of the field of evangelism. Their number shall not exceed one half of the number of places allotted to affiliated councils.

(vi) In addition to the consultants representing councils in consultation, the Divisional Committee may provide for the attendance at meetings of the Commission of persons with special competence in the field of missions as advisers. They shall be entitled to speak but not to vote.

(vii) Each sponsored agency may appoint a representative to attend the meetings of the Commission and of the Divisional Committee. They shall be entitled to speak but not to vote.

(viii) The Divisional Committee may also invite observers to meetings of the Commission from councils and other missionary agencies which are not related to the Commission. Observers shall be entitled to speak but not to vote.

(ix) The members of the Commission shall serve until appointments have been made for the next meeting of the Commission or until their successors are appointed.

(x) An affiliated council may withdraw from the Commission, but must give at least one year's written notice to the next regularly constituted meeting of the Commission or of the Divisional Committee; withdrawal shall become effective at the close of that meeting.

7. *Officers and Secretariat*

(i) At each regular meeting the Commission shall appoint a Chairman and one or more Vice-Chairmen whose term of office shall extend from the beginning of that meeting to the beginning of the next regular meeting. The nomination of the Chairman and Vice-Chairmen shall be made by the Divisional Committee prior to the meeting of the Commission.

(ii) The same Secretariat shall serve both the Commission and the Division.

(iii) The Commission may appoint an Honorary Treasurer or Treasurers.

8. *Finance*

(i) The Commission in consultation with its affiliated and other supporting councils shall prepare a budget for submission to the Central Committee for its approval.

(ii) The Commission shall be responsible for the raising and expenditure of funds in accordance with the approved budget.

(iii) The funds formerly vested in the International Missionary Council for general or specific purposes, together with such additional funds as may from time to time be entrusted to the Commission for the discharge of its functions, shall be vested in the World Council of Churches. Such funds shall be used solely for the purposes of the Commission and, if designated, in accordance with the wishes of the donor or testator. These funds shall be administered by the Commission, subject to the approval of the Central Committee.

(iv) The Commission shall provide for the cost of its staff and offices, of the meetings of the Commission and the Division and its committees, of all operations authorized by the Commission and of all services provided for the Commission by the World Council of Churches.

(v) In their financial operations the Commission and Division shall follow the procedures prescribed in the By-Laws.

9. *Quorum*

One-third of the members of the Commission shall constitute a quorum at any given session, provided that those present at the session come from at least three continents and represent at least one-third of the affiliated councils.

10. *By-Laws*

The Commission may make, amend and repeal By-Laws for the conduct of the business of the Commission.

11. *Revision*

The Constitution of the Commission and of the Division may be amended, subject to the approval of Central Committee, by a two-thirds majority of the Commission, provided the proposed amendment shall have been reviewed by the Divisional Committee and notice of it sent to the affiliated councils not less than six months before the meeting of the Commission. The Divisional Committee as well as the affiliated councils shall have the right to propose amendments.

The Division of World Mission and Evangelism

1. The Division of World Mission and Evangelism shall consist of the Divisional Committee and staff.

2. *Function*

The Division of World Mission and Evangelism shall be responsible for carrying out the aim and functions of the Commission on World Mission and Evangelism and shall act for it between its meetings save in such matters as the Commission may have reserved to its own authority.

3. *Activities*

The activities of the Division shall include:

(i) aiding the churches in their missionary and evangelistic task and where requested by churches or councils acting on their behalf;
(ii) maintaining relationships of mutual helpfulness with councils affiliated to and in consultation with the Commission and with member churches of the World Council of Churches concerning the work of the Commission and Division;
(iii) fostering relationships with other councils;
(iv) publishing such literature as may be called for in the furtherance of the aim and functions of the Commission;
(v) convening such conferences as may be required;
(vi) responsibility for any departments which may be created within the Division, and guiding their work;
(vii) co-operating with the other divisions of the World Council to carry out the purposes and functions of the Commission and of the World Council effectively;
(viii) responsibility for the raising and administration of the funds of the Commission in accordance with clause 8 (ii) of the Constitution of the Commission.

4. *The Divisional Committee*

(i) There shall be a Divisional Committee responsible for the general conduct of the work of the Division, which shall report to the Assembly and to the Central Committee as well as to the Commission. It will also report to its related councils.
(ii) The Committee shall consist of not less than twenty or more than twenty-five members appointed annually by the Central Committee on the nomination of the Commission or, in the absence of a meeting of the Commission, of the Divisional Committee. The Chairman and one member of each departmental committee within the Division shall be included in the membership of the Committee. At least two members shall be drawn from the membership of the Central Committee. Two members of the divisional committee shall be appointed after consultation with the officers of the Division of Inter-Church Aid, Refugee and World Service. The membership of the Committee shall be as representative as possible, geographically and confessionally and of men and women. The Chairman and Vice-Chairmen of the Commission shall be *ex officio* members of the Divisional Committee.
(iii) The Divisional Committee shall ordinarily meet once a year. Special meetings may be called on the authority of the officers.
(iv) The Committee shall prepare, through such procedures as the Commission may determine, an annual budget, which shall be submitted in advance of the beginning of each year to the Finance Committee of the Central Committee, which shall forward it to the Central Committee with any comments it may wish to make. The Committee shall submit financial reports to each meeting of the Finance Committee of the Central Committee.
(v) The Divisional Committee shall nominate its Chairman for appointment by the Central Committee.

(vi) The Director of the Division shall be nominated by the Divisional Committee in consultation with the staffing committee of the Executive Committee and shall be appointed by the Central Committee as an Associate General Secretary of the World Council and Director of the Division. The Divisional Committee shall determine, subject to the approval of the Central Committee, the number of the staff of the Commission and the Division. The Secretaries shall be appointed according to the Rules of the World Council, on the nomination of the Divisional Committee.

(vii) The Divisional Committee shall determine the principal duties of the staff of the Commission and the Division.

(viii) One half of the membership of the Divisional Committee shall constitute a quorum at any ordinary meeting, provided that those present come from at least three continents and five affiliated councils.

Appendix 11

THE CONSTITUTION AND RULES OF THE WORLD COUNCIL OF CHURCHES

I. Basis

The World Council of Churches is a fellowship of churches which confess the Lord Jesus Christ as God and Saviour according to the Scriptures and therefore seek to fulfil together their common calling to the glory of the one God, Father, Son and Holy Spirit.

It is constituted for the functions set out below.

II. Membership

Those churches shall be eligible for membership in the World Council of Churches which express their agreement with the Basis upon which the Council is founded and satisfy such criteria as the Assembly or the Central Committee may prescribe. Election to membership shall be by a two-thirds vote of the member churches represented at the Assembly, each member church having one vote. Any application for membership between meetings of the Assembly may be considered by the Central Committee; if the application is supported by a two-thirds majority of the members of the Committee present and voting, this action shall be communicated to the churches that are members of the World Council of Churches, and unless objection is received from more than one-third of the member churches within six months the applicant shall be declared elected.

III. Functions

The functions of the World Council shall be:

(i) To carry on the work of the world movements for Faith and Order and Life and Work and of the International Missionary Council.

(ii) To facilitate common action by the churches.

(iii) To promote co-operation in study.

(iv) To promote the growth of ecumenical and missionary consciousness in the members of all churches.

(v) To support the churches in their world-wide missionary and evangelistic task.
(vi) To establish and maintain relations with national and regional councils, world confessional bodies and other ecumenical organizations.
(vii) To call world conferences on specific subjects as occasion may require, such conferences being empowered to publish their own findings.

IV. Authority

The World Council shall offer counsel and provide opportunity of united action in matters of common interest.

It may take action on behalf of constituent churches in such matters as one or more of them may commit to it.

It shall have authority to call regional and world conferences on specific subjects as occasion may require.

The World Council shall not legislate for the churches; nor shall it act for them in any manner except as indicated above or as may hereafter be specified by the constituent churches.

V. Organization

The World Council shall discharge its functions through the following bodies:

(i) An Assembly which shall be the principal authority in the Council, and shall ordinarily meet every five years. The Assembly shall be composed of official representatives of the churches or groups of churches adhering to it and directly appointed by them. Their term of office shall begin in the year before the Assembly meets, and they shall serve until their successors are appointed. It shall consist of members whose number shall be determined by each Assembly for the subsequent Assembly, subject to the right of the Assembly to empower the Central Committee, if it thinks fit, to increase or to diminish the said number by not more than twenty per cent. The number shall be finally determined not less than two years before the meeting of the Assembly to which it refers and shall be apportioned as is provided hereafter.

Seats in the Assembly shall be allocated to the member churches by the Central Committee, due regard being given to such factors as numerical size, adequate confessional representation and adequate geographical distribution. Suggestions for readjustment in the allocation of seats may be made to the Central Committee by member churches, or by groups of member churches, confessional, regional or national, and these readjustments shall become effective if approved by the Central Committee after consultation with the churches concerned.

The Assembly shall have power to appoint officers of the World Council and of the Assembly at its discretion.

The members of the Assembly shall be both clerical and lay persons—men and women. In order to secure that approximately one-third of the Assembly shall consist of lay persons, the Central Committee, in allocating to the member churches their places in the Assembly, shall strongly urge each church, if possible, to observe this provision.

(ii) A Central Committee which shall be a Committee of the Assembly and which shall consist of the President or Presidents of the World Council, together with not more than one hundred members chosen by the Assembly from among persons whom the churches have appointed as members of the Assembly. They shall serve until the next Assembly, unless the Assembly otherwise determines. Membership in the Central Committee shall be distributed among the member churches by the Assembly, due regard being given to such factors as numerical size, adequate confessional representation, adequate geographical distribution and the adequate representation of the major interests of the World Council.

Any vacancy occurring in the membership of the Central Committee between meetings of the Assembly shall be filled by the Central Committee upon the nomination of the church or churches concerned.

The Central Committee shall have the following powers:

(*a*) it shall, between meetings of the Assembly, carry out the Assembly's instructions and exercise its functions, except that of amending the Constitution, or modifying the allocation of its own members;
(*b*) it shall be the finance committee of the Assembly, formulating its budget and securing its financial support;
(*c*) it shall name and elect its own officers from among its members and appoint its own secretarial staff;
(*d*) the Central Committee shall meet normally once every calendar year, and shall have power to appoint its own Executive Committee.

Quorum. No business, except what is required for carrying forward the current activities of the Council, shall be transacted in either the Assembly or the Central Committee unless one-half of the total membership is present.

VI. Appointment of Commissions

(1) The World Council shall discharge part of its functions by the appointment of Commissions. These shall be established under the authority of the Assembly in accordance with the Rules of the World Council and the constitutions of the respective Commissions. The Commissions shall, between meetings of the Assembly, report annually to the Central Committee which shall exercise general supervision over them. The Commissions may add to their membership clerical and lay persons approved for the purpose by the Central Committee. The Commissions shall discharge their functions in accordance with constitutions approved by the Central Committee.

In particular, the Assembly shall make provision by means of appropriate Commissions for carrying on the activities of Faith and Order, Life and Work and the International Missionary Council.

(2) There shall be a Faith and Order Commission of which the following shall be the functions:

(i) to proclaim the essential oneness of the Church of Christ and to keep prominently before the World Council and the churches the obligation to manifest that unity and its urgency for world mission and evangelism;
(ii) to study questions of faith, order and worship with the relevant social, cultural, political, racial and other factors in their bearing on the unity of the churches;
(iii) to study the theological implications of the existence of the ecumenical movement;
(iv) to study matters in the present relationships of the churches to one another which cause difficulties and need theological clarification;

(v) to provide information concerning actual steps taken by the churches towards reunion.

The Commission shall discharge these functions in accordance with a constitution approved by the Central Committee.

In invitations to World Conferences on Faith and Order, it shall be specified that such conferences are to be composed of official delegates of churches which accept Jesus Christ as God and Saviour.

(3) There shall be a Commission on World Mission and Evangelism.

Its aim shall be to further the proclamation to the whole world of the Gospel of Jesus Christ, to the end that all men may believe in him and be saved.

The functions of the Commission shall be:

(i) to keep before the churches their calling and privilege to engage in constant prayer for the missionary and evangelistic work of the Church;
(ii) to remind the churches of the range and character of the unfinished evangelistic task and to deepen their sense of missionary obligation;
(iii) to stimulate thought and study on the Biblical and theological basis and meaning of the Church's missionary task and on questions directly related to the spread of the Gospel in the world;
(iv) to foster among churches and among councils and other Christian bodies more effective co-operation and united action for world evangelization;
(v) to deepen evangelistic and missionary concern in the whole life and work of the World Council of Churches;
(vi) to assist in securing and safeguarding freedom of conscience and religion as formulated in declarations of the World Council of Churches on religious liberty;
(vii) to co-operate with other units of the World Council of Churches;
(viii) to take such further action in fulfilment of the declared aim of the Commission as is not otherwise provided for within the World Council of Churches.

VII. Other Ecumenical Christian Organizations

(1) Such world confessional associations and such ecumenical organizations as may be designated by the Central Committee may be invited to send representatives to the sessions of the Assembly and of the Central Committee in a consultative capacity, in such numbers as the Central Committee shall determine.

(2) Such national councils of churches, other Christian councils and missionary councils as may be designated by the Central Committee may be invited to send non-voting representatives to the Assembly and to the Central Committee, in such numbers as the Central Committee shall determine.

VIII. Amendments

The Constitution may be amended by a two-thirds majority vote of the Assembly, provided that the proposed amendment shall have been reviewed by the Central Committee, and notice of it sent to the constituent churches not less than six months before the meeting of the Assembly. The Central Committee itself, as well as the individual churches, shall have the right to propose such amendment.

IX. Rules and Regulations

The Assembly or the Central Committee may make and amend Rules and Regulations concerning the conduct of the Council's business, of its Committees and Departments, and generally all matters within the discharge of its task.

Rules of the World Council of Churches

The World Council of Churches shall be governed by the following Rules which are to be interpreted in the light of its Constitution:

I. Membership of the Council

Members of the Council are those churches which have agreed together to constitute the World Council of Churches and those churches which are admitted to membership in accordance with the following rules:

(1) Churches which desire to become members of the World Council of Churches shall apply to the General Secretary in writing. Under the word churches are included such denominations as are composed of local autonomous churches.

(2) The General Secretary shall submit such applications to the Central Committee (see Article II of the Constitution) together with such information as will be sufficient to enable the Assembly or the Central Committee to make a decision on the application.

(3) The following criteria, among others, shall be applied, in addition to the primary requirement of the Constitution that churches eligible for consideration for membership shall be those 'which express their agreement with the Basis upon which the Council is formed'.

(*a*) *Autonomy*. A church which is to be admitted must give evidence of autonomy. An autonomous church is one which, while recognizing the essential interdependence of the churches, particularly those of the same confession, is responsible to no other church for the conduct of its own life, including the training, ordination and maintenance of its ministry, the enlisting, development and activity of the lay forces, the propagation of the Christian message, the determination of relationship with other churches and the use of funds at its disposal from whatever source.

(*b*) *Stability*. A church should not be admitted unless it has given sufficient evidence of stability in life and organization to become recognized as a church by its sister churches, and should have an established programme of Christian nurture and evangelism.

(*c*) *Size*. The question of size must also be taken into consideration.

(*d*) *Relationship with other churches*. Regard must also be given to the relationship of the church to other churches.

(4) Before churches which are recognized as full members of one of the confessional or denominational world alliances with which the Council co-operates are admitted, the advice of these world alliances shall be sought.

(5) Where a church is a member of a council associated with the World Council of Churches or affiliated to the Commission on World Mission and Evangelism, there shall be consultation with the council concerned.

(6) A church which desires to resign its membership in the Council can do so at any time. A church which has once resigned but desires again to join the Council, must again apply for membership.

II. The Assembly

(1) *Officers and Business Committee*

(*a*) At the first business session of the Assembly the Executive Committee shall present its proposals for the chairmanship of the Assembly and for the membership of the Business Committee of the Assembly.

(*b*) Additional names may also be proposed at the first or second business session by any group of six members of the Assembly. Such proposals must be made in writing.

(*c*) Election shall be by ballot unless the Assembly shall otherwise determine.

(2) *Composition of the Assembly*

(*a*) *Members.* Full membership of the Assembly is confined to delegates appointed by the constituent churches to represent them. In appointing their delegates churches are urged not only to bear in mind the need for lay representation mentioned in paragraph V (i) of the Constitution but also to give due regard to the major interests of the Council.

(*b*) *Alternates.* The Central Committee shall make regulations for the appointment of alternates and for their duties and functions if and when appointed.

(*c*) *Advisers.* The Executive Committee is authorized to invite persons who have a special contribution to make to the deliberations of the Assembly or who have participated in the activities of the World Council. Such advisers will be appointed after consultation with the churches to which they belong. They shall be entitled to speak on the invitation of the Chairman but not to vote.

(*d*) *Fraternal Delegates.* The Executive Committee is authorized to invite fraternal delegates from organizations with which the World Council of Churches entertains relationship. They shall be entitled to speak on the invitation of the Chairman but not to vote.

(*e*) *Observers.* The Executive Committee is authorized to invite a limited number of observers from churches which have not joined the World Council of Churches and/or from councils in consultation with the Commission on World Mission and Evangelism. Observers will not be entitled to speak or to vote.

(*f*) *Youth Delegates.* The Executive Committee is authorized to invite youth delegates who will be entitled to attend the full sessions. They shall be entitled to speak on the invitation of the Chairman but not to vote.

(3) *Agenda*

The Agenda of the Assembly shall be determined by the Executive Committee and presented by it for approval to the first business session of the Assembly. Any member may move to have included in the Agenda such items of business as he may have previously notified to the Executive Committee.

III. Presidium

(1) The maximum number of Presidents shall be six.

(2) A President who has been elected by the Assembly shall be ineligible for immediate re-election when his term of office ends.

(3) The term of office of a President shall end at the adjournment of the next Assembly following his or her appointment.

(4) The President or Presidents shall be entitled to attend the Assembly with full right of speech even if they are not appointed as delegates by their churches.

(5) The President or Presidents shall be *ex officio* members of the Central Committee and of the Executive Committee.

IV. Nominations Committee of the Assembly

(1) At an early session of the Assembly, the Assembly shall appoint a Nominations Committee, on which there shall be appropriate confessional and geographical representation of the membership of the Assembly and representation of the major interests of the World Council.

(2) The Nominations Committee in consultation with the officers of the World Council and the Executive Committee shall draft proposals concerning (*a*) the President or Presidents of the World Council of Churches, and (*b*) a list of persons proposed for membership of the Central Committee.

(3) The Nominations Committee shall present its nominations to the vote of the Assembly for its acceptance or revision. In making nominations, the Nominations Committee shall have regard to the following principles:

(*a*) the personal qualifications of the individual for the task for which he is to be nominated;
(*b*) fair and adequate confessional representation;
(*c*) fair and adequate geographical representation;
(*d*) fair and adequate representation of the major interests of the World Council.

The Nominations Committee shall endeavour to secure adequate representation of lay persons—both men and women—so far as the composition of the Assembly makes this possible. It shall also satisfy itself as to the general acceptability of the nominations to the churches to which the nominees belong.

(4) It shall be open to any six members of the Assembly acting together to put forward in writing other nominations.

(5) Election shall be by a ballot unless the Assembly shall otherwise determine.

V. Central Committee

(1) *Membership*

(*a*) The Central Committee shall consist of the President or Presidents of the World Council together with not more than one hundred members elected by the Assembly (see Constitution, paragraph V (ii)).
(*b*) Any member church, not already represented, which desires to be represented directly on the Central Committee, shall have the right to send one representative to the meetings of the Central Committee, provided it does so at its own expense. Such a representative shall be entitled to speak but not to vote.
(*c*) If a regularly elected member of the Central Committee is unable to come to the meeting, the church to which the absent member belongs shall have the right to send a substitute, provided that the substitute is ordinarily resident in the country where his church has its headquarters. Such a substitute shall be entitled to speak and to vote.
(*d*) Chairmen and vice-chairmen of divisional and departmental committees and commissions who are not members of the Central Committee have the right to attend Central Committee sessions as advisers without vote.
(*e*) Advisers for the Central Committee may be appointed by the Executive Committee after consultation with the churches of which they are members. They shall be entitled to speak but not to vote.
(*f*) Members of the staff of the World Council appointed by the Central

Committee as specified under Rule IX, 1, shall have the right to attend the sessions of the Central Committee unless on any occasion the Central Committee shall otherwise determine. When they do so attend, it shall be as advisers and without the right to vote.

(*g*) The newly appointed Central Committee shall be convened by the General Secretary during or immediately after the meeting of the Assembly.

(2) *Officers*

(*a*) The Central Committee shall elect its own Chairman and Vice-Chairman or Vice-Chairmen to serve for such periods as it shall determine. They shall be entitled to attend the Assembly as advisers, should they not be reappointed as delegates by their churches.

(*b*) The Central Committee shall appoint a Nominations Committee which shall:

(i) nominate individuals to the Central Committee for the offices of Chairman and Vice-Chairman or Vice-Chairmen of the Central Committee;

(ii) nominate individuals for election as President, if between Assemblies need arises for such appointments, under the power conferred on the Central Committee by the Constitution and Rules;

(iii) nominate members of the Executive Committee of the Central Committee;

(iv) nominate members of the divisional committees and departmental working committees.

In making nominations, the Nominations Committee of the Central Committee shall have regard to the principles set out in Rule IV, 3, and in applying principles (*b*), (*c*) and (*d*) to the nomination of members of the divisional committees and the departmental working committees, shall consider the representative character of the combined membership of all such committees. Any member of the Central Committee may make alternative proposals.

(*c*) Election shall be by ballot unless the Committee shall otherwise determine.

(*d*) The General Secretary of the World Council of Churches shall be *ex officio* secretary of the Central Committee and the Chairman of the Finance Committee of the World Council of Churches shall be *ex officio* its treasurer.

(3) *Meetings*

(*a*) The Central Committee shall meet ordinarily not less than once every year. An extraordinary session of the Central Committee shall be called, whenever one-third or more of the members requests a meeting to be called or when in the opinion of the Executive Committee that is desirable.

(*b*) A quorum of the Central Committee shall be fifty voting members. The General Secretariat shall take all possible steps to ensure that there be adequate representation from each of the main confessions and from the main geographical areas of the membership of the World Council of Churches and of the major interests of the World Council.

(*c*) The Central Committee shall have power to determine its own place of meeting and to fix the date and place for the meetings of the Assembly.

(4) *Functions*

The Central Committee shall have the following duties:

(*a*) It shall, between meetings of the Assembly, carry out the general policy laid down by the Assembly and take such actions as shall be necessary to carry out the decisions of the Assembly. It shall have authority to make decisions and take action in all matters where decision or action is required before the Assembly can meet again, provided that it shall not make any decision or take any action inconsistent with the policies laid down by the Assembly.

It shall have the following sub-committees:

(i) Finance Sub-Committee (a standing committee);
(ii) Nominations Committee (newly appointed at each meeting);
(iii) Committee on National Council Relationships (a standing committee);
(iv) Reference Committee or Committees (appointed as needed at each meeting) to advise the Central Committee on any other questions arising which call for special consideration or action by the Central Committee.

(*b*) It shall vote the Annual Budget of the Council.

(*c*) It shall deal with matters referred to it by member churches.

(*d*) It shall consider applications for membership received between meetings of the Assembly.

(*e*) It shall have the responsibility of setting up such divisions and departments and regional offices or representations as may be necessary to carry out the policy laid down by the Assembly. It shall appoint divisional and departmental committees and their chairmen and vice-men. It shall determine the general policy to be followed in the work of the divisions and departments of the World Council.

(*f*) It shall report to the Assembly on the actions it has taken during its period of office, and shall not be discharged until its report has been received.

VI. Executive Committee

(1) *Appointment*

(*a*) An Executive Committee shall be elected by the Central Committee at its first meeting after its appointment by the Assembly, and shall hold office until the next meeting of the Central Committee. Its elected members shall be eligible for re-election.

(*b*) The Executive Committee shall consist of the President or Presidents of the World Council *ex officio* and the Chairman and Vice-Chairman of the Central Committee *ex officio* and of fourteen other members of the Central Committee. Substitutes shall not be permitted to attend in place of elected members.

(*c*) The Chairman of the Central Committee shall also be the Chairman of the Executive Committee.

(*d*) The officers shall have the power to invite others to attend a meeting of the Executive Committee for consultation, always having in mind the need of preserving a due balance of the confessions and of the geographical areas and of the major interests of the World Council.

(*e*) The General Secretary of the World Council of Churches shall be *ex officio* the secretary of the Executive Committee.

(2) *Functions*

The Executive Committee is a committee of the Central Committee appointed by it and responsible to it. The Executive Committee shall, between meetings of the Central Committee, carry out the decisions of the Central Committee and implement the policy laid down by it. The Executive Committee shall have no authority to make decisions on policy except that in circumstances of special urgency it can take provisional decisions. It may only issue public statements under the circumstances laid down in Rule X, 4. It shall have power to appoint Associate General Secretaries and heads of departments provisionally, but such appointments shall be subject to confirmation by the Central Committee. It shall supervise the operation of the budget and have power to impose limitations on expenditure if necessary.

VII. Divisional, Departmental and other Standing Committees

(1) There shall be a small committee for each division whose responsibility shall be to carry out the aim of the division. It shall be responsible for the preparation and presentation to the Central Committee of the reports of the division's work.

It shall propose to the Central Committee the names of persons to fill the offices of secretary or secretaries to the division and, on the basis of proposals from the departmental working committees, of secretary or secretaries in the departments within the division.

(2) Divisional committees shall be appointed by the Central Committee as follows:

(*a*) For the Division of Studies and the Division of Ecumenical Action, the Committee shall consist of up to five persons who are not members of any departmental working committee within the division, plus the chairman and one other member of each departmental working committee within the division. One of the two representatives of each departmental working committee must be a member of the Central Committee.

(*b*) For the Division of Inter-Church Aid, Refugee and World Service, the committee shall consist of not more than seventeen members, two of whom shall be members of the Central Committee. Two members of the divisional committee shall be appointed after consultation with the officers of the Division of World Mission and Evangelism.

(*c*) For the Division of World Mission and Evangelism the Committee shall consist of not less than twenty or more than twenty-five members appointed annually by the Central Committee on the nomination of the Commission or, in the absence of a meeting of the Commission, of the Divisional Committee. The Chairman and one member of each departmental committee within the Division shall be included in the membership of the Committee. At least two members shall be drawn from the membership of the Central Committee. Two members of the divisional committee shall be appointed after consultation with the officers of the Division of Inter-Church Aid, Refugee and World Service. The membership of the committee shall be as representative as possible geographically and confessionally and of men and women.

Departmental secretaries shall normally be present at the meetings of divisional committees.

(3) There shall be a working committee for each department appointed by the Central Committee and responsible for the preparation of the depart-

mental programme for submission to the divisional committee and for the execution of the programme. It shall propose to the divisional committee the names of persons to fill the offices of secretary or secretaries in the department. The chairmen of departmental working committees shall be *ex officio* members of the appropriate divisional committees. Departmental working committees shall have power to call in *ad hoc* advisers as needed on particular problems. In the case of the Ecumenical Institute its Board shall be regarded as the working committee. Normally a working committee shall consist of fifteen members, at least one of whom shall be a member of the Central Committee.

(4) There shall be a committee on National Council Relationships which shall consist of not more than fifteen members, including persons actively engaged in the work of each of the four Divisions and persons from related councils.

The aim of the Committee shall be: to give continuous attention to the development of relationships of mutual helpfulness between the World Council of Churches and national councils of churches and other Christian councils.

The functions of the Committee shall be:

(i) to develop patterns of relationship and co-operation whereby the World Council of Churches and national councils of churches and other Christian councils can strengthen each other and best serve the needs of their constituencies;

(ii) to assist such councils in utilizing the resources of the World Council of Churches and to assist divisions of the World Council to relate their programmes to the needs of such councils;

(iii) to keep before all the divisions and departments of the World Council and its member churches the significance of such councils in the fulfilment of the purposes of the ecumenical movement;

(iv) to recommend to the Central Committee ways in which such councils can participate most effectively in the life of the World Council;

(v) to advise the Central Committee regarding recognition of councils as 'associated councils' of the World Council of Churches and to consult with the Commission on World Mission and Evangelism regarding recognition of councils as 'affiliated councils' of that Commission or 'councils in consultation' with that Commission;

(vi) to provide opportunities for fellowship and exchange of experience among the officers and staffs of national and regional councils and the World Council of Churches, and in particular to arrange for consultations of representatives of associated councils as provided in Rule XI, (4);

(vii) to provide advisory staff service to national and regional councils when requested.

VIII. Financial Provisions

(1) The draft annual general budget of the World Council of Churches shall be prepared for presentation to the Finance Committee of the Central Committee by the General Secretariat assisted by the Department of Finance and Administration, on the basis of proposals made by the divisional committees.

(2) In the case of commissions, divisions and other units of the World Council of Churches which may be authorized to raise and administer separate budgets, the responsible commission, division or unit shall prepare annual budgets for submission in advance of the beginning of each year to the

Finance Committee of the Central Committee of the World Council, which shall forward any such budgets to the Central Committee with any comments which it may wish to make. The responsible commission, division or unit shall further submit financial reports to each meeting of the Finance Committee of the Central Committee of the World Council of Churches.

(3) The Finance Committee of the Central Committee shall have the following duties:

(*a*) to present annually to the Central Committee an account of income and expenditure for the previous twelve months, and a balance sheet in respect of operations of all departments of the World Council of Churches;

(*b*) to present annually to the Central Committee in advance of the commencement of each year, budgets covering the operations of all the departments of the World Council of Churches;

(*c*) to consider and make recommendations to the Central Committee on all financial questions concerning the affairs of the World Council of Churches, such as:

aproval of budgets or increases in budgets;
approval and granting of discharge for the accounts in respect of completed periods;
accounting procedures;
investment policy;
principles governing scales of salaries and pensions and travel expenses and other such expenses;
basis of calculation of contributions of member churches;
methods of raising funds;
appointment of auditors, who shall be appointed annually by the Central Committee and shall be eligible for re-election.

The Committee shall have power to consider all matters concerning the World Council of Churches in so far as they bear upon its financial position.

(4) The items of the budget of a division may be subsequently varied by the divisional committee at its discretion provided the authorized total be not exceeded, and the policy of the division be thereby advanced.

IX. Staff of the World Council of Churches

(1) The General Secretary, the Associate General Secretaries, and the Heads of Departments shall be appointed by the Central Committee.

(2) The normal terms of appointment for an Associate General Secretary shall be five years and for a Head of Department three years. Unless some other period is stated in the resolution making the appointment, the term of office of members of the staff of the World Council shall be from the date of the appointment until three months after the end of the next meeting of the Central Committee. All appointments made for a term exceeding one year shall be reviewed one year before expiring.

(3) Retirement shall be at 65 for men and 63 for women or not later than the end of the year in which a staff member reaches the age of 68 for men and 66 for women.

(4) If the position of General Secretary becomes vacant, the Executive Committee shall appoint an acting General Secretary.

(5) The General Secretariat (i.e. General Secretary and Associate General Secretaries) is responsible for carrying out the decisions of the Assembly, the Central Committee and the Executive Committee.

(6) The General Secretariat shall be responsible for the conduct of the business of the Council, for relations with member churches and other ecumenical bodies, for the preparation and administration of the meetings of the Assembly, of the Central Committee and of the Executive Committee, for the general supervision and co-ordination of the activities and publications of the commissions and departments of the Council, for the interpretation of the work of the Council to the churches and the public, and for the carrying on of activities not otherwise assigned.

(7) The General Secretariat shall have the right to attend the meetings of departmental committees and other meetings called under the auspices of the Council.

X. Public Statements

(1) In the performance of its functions, the Council through its Assembly or through its Central Committee may publish statements upon any situation or issue with which the Council or its constituent churches may be confronted.

(2) While such statements may have great significance and influence as the expression of the judgment or concern of so widely representative a Christian body, yet their authority will consist only in the weight which they carry by their own truth and wisdom and the publishing of such statements shall not be held to imply that the World Council as such has, or can have, any constitutional authority over the constituent churches or right to speak for them.

(3) The Executive Committee or any commission of the Council may recommend statements to the Assembly or to the Central Committee for its consideration and action.

(4) No committee or commission of the Council other than the Central Committee shall publish any statement until it has been approved by the Assembly, except that in circumstances of immediate urgency statements may be published by any commission of the Council on matters within its own field of concern and action, if approved by the Chairman of the Central Committee and the General Secretary, and in these cases the committee or commission shall make it clear that the World Council of Churches is not committed by any statement set forth in this manner.

(5) In cases of exceptional emergency, statements may be issued by the Chairman of the Central Committee on his own authority after consultation with the Vice-Chairman of the Central Committee and the General Secretary provided that such statements are not contrary to the established policy of the Council.

(6) Nothing in these regulations shall contravene the special provisions of the Constitution regarding the Commission on Faith and Order and the Commission on World Mission and Evangelism.

XI. Relationships with national and regional councils

(1) The World Council, recognizing that national councils of churches or national Christian councils have been established in a number of countries for purposes of fellowship and co-operation with one another and for the promotion and support of ecumenical activities and other common interests within their own area, shall invite selected national councils to enter into working relationships as associated councils.

(2) The purpose of such working relationships shall be to help national councils in their work and to encourage them to help the World Council of Churches in the promotion of ecumenical activities in the area concerned and in the furthering of the plans and policies which the Central Committee has

laid down for the various divisions and departments of the Council.

(3) These councils shall receive invitations to send a fraternal delegate to the Assembly and may, at the discretion of the Central Committee, receive an invitation to send a representative to the Central Committee; such representatives shall have the right to speak but not to vote.

(4) Opportunity shall be provided at the time of any meeting of the Assembly or Central Committee for the representatives of national councils to meet together for mutual consultation.

(5) While the World Council retains the right to deal with its member churches directly, no action shall be taken by it which would disturb any already existing fellowship or ecumenical organization within a nation or region.

(6) Any member church which prefers to have direct relationships with the World Council in any field of work can have such direct relationships.

(7) The following criteria, among others, shall be applied by the Central Committee in selecting national councils for these working relationships:

(i) that the national council accept the Basis of the World Council of Churches or express its willingness to co-operate on that Basis;
(ii) that there be prior consultation with member churches of the World Council in the area concerned,
(iii) that there be prior consultation with the Committee on National Council Relationships;
(iv) that the membership of the national council consist wholly or to a large extent of churches which hold membership in the World Council of Churches;
(v) that the national council have an interest in the work of the World Council of Churches and be willing to work for that Council;
(vi) that the national council give evidence of stability and have a staff with time to devote to World Council concerns.

(8) The Central Committee may, in consultation with the Committee on National Council Relationships, invite councils affiliated to the Commission on World Mission and Evangelism to send a representative to meetings of the Assembly and Central Committee with the right to speak but not to vote, to a number not exceeding ten in the Assembly and five in the Central Committee.

XII. World Confessional Bodies

Such world confessional bodies as may be designated by the Central Committee shall be invited to send fraternal delegates to the Assembly, and advisers to the Central Committee.

XIII. Legal Provisions

(1) The duration of the Council is unlimited.

(2) The legal headquarters of the Council shall be at Geneva. Regional offices may be organized in different parts of the world by decision of the Central Committee.

(3) The World Council of Churches is legally represented by its Executive Committee or by such persons as may be empowered by the Executive Committee to represent it.

(4) The World Council shall be legally bound by the joint signatures of two of the following persons: the President or Presidents, the Chairman and Vice-Chairman or Vice-Chairmen of the Central Committee, and the General Secretary. Any two of the above-named persons shall have power to authorize other persons, chosen by them, to act jointly or singly on behalf of the World

Council of Churches in fields circumscribed in the power of attorney.

(5) The Council shall obtain the means necessary for the pursuance of its work from the contributions of its member churches and from donations or bequests.

(6) The Council shall not pursue commercial aims but it shall have the right to act as an agency of inter-church aid and to publish literature in connection with its aims. It is not entitled to distribute any surplus income by way of profit or bonus among its members.

(7) Members of the governing bodies of the Council or of the Assembly shall have no personal liability with regard to the obligations or commitments of the Council. The commitments entered upon by the Council are guaranteed solely by its own assets.

XIV. Rules of debate during sessions of the Assembly and the Central Committee

1. *Categories of session*

The Assembly shall sit either in general session, in business session or in deliberative session.

2. *Presiding Officers*

(*a*) The Chairman of the Assembly in general session shall be one of the presidents or the Chairman of the Central Committee, as appointed by the Executive Committee.

(*b*) The Chairman of the Assembly in business session shall be the Chairman or Vice-Chairman of the Central Committee, or some other member of the Central Committee appointed by the Executive Committee or by the Business Committee of the Assembly.

(*c*) The Chairman of the Assembly in deliberate session shall be a member of the Presidium, an Officer of the Central Committee or a delegate appointed by the Executive Committee or the Business Committee of the Assembly.

3. *Responsibilities of the Chairman*

The responsibilities of the Chairman shall be to announce the opening, suspension and adjournment of the meeting; his first action shall be to announce clearly that the Assembly is in general session, or in business session, or in deliberative session; he shall ensure the observance of the applicable Rules of Debate; he shall grant the right to speak and declare the debate closed; he shall put questions to the vote and announce the result of the voting. He shall not make a motion himself. His decision is final in all matters except as to the result of voting. If the Chairman's decision as to the result of voting is challenged, a vote shall immediately be taken on the motion: 'that the Chairman's decision be reconsidered'; and reconsideration shall be permitted, if a majority of the members present and voting vote in favour of this motion.

4. *General sessions*

When the Assembly is in general session (for ceremonial occasions, public acts of witness, formal addresses, etc.) the only business that shall be in order, except with consent, is that which is proposed by the Chairman or Secretary of the Executive or Business Committee.

5. *Business sessions*

The Assembly shall sit in business session when any of the following types of business are on the agenda: adoption of agenda presented by the Business Committee, nominations, elections, proposals with reference to the structure, organization, budget, or programme of the World Council of Churches, or any other business requiring action by the Assembly, except as provided in paragraphs 4 and 6 of this Rule.

The Special Rules of Debate for the Assembly in business session:

(*a*) If any member desires to propose a motion not on the agenda, he shall be permitted to have his motion read. A vote shall be immediately taken as to whether or not his motion shall be included in the agenda.

(*b*) All motions and amendments must be proposed and seconded, handed to the Chairman in writing, and read before a vote is taken. The Chairman has the power to rule an amendment out of order as being substantially a negative of the motion.

(*c*) Any motion or amendment may be withdrawn by leave of the Assembly.

(*d*) All speeches must be addressed to the Chair.

(*e*) No member shall speak more than once on the same motion or amendment, except that the mover shall have the right to reply.

(*f*) When an amendment has been proposed and seconded the Chairman shall allow discussion on the amendment only. An amendment to an amendment is in order, but an amendment to an amendment to an amendment shall be out of order. Discussion and voting shall be in reverse order of the motions made. When the Assembly has voted to approve or disapprove the amendments which have been proposed and seconded, and the original motion is before the Assembly (amended or not as the case may be), additional amendments are in order except those which are judged by the Chair to be substantially the same as proposals already discussed and decided. A motion to refer a resolution back to the responsible committee with or without pending amendments, is always in order. Debate on such a motion shall be limited to 3 minutes by the maker of the motion, and 3 minutes by a representative of the committee making the original proposal, and comments by the Chairman and Secretary as to the feasibility of handling the matter later in the agenda.

(*g*) During the discussion, speeches shall be limited to five minutes. A bell shall be rung one minute before a speaker's time is up. A second bell shall be rung one minute later and the speaker shall then sit down, unless the Chairman proposes and receives consent that an additional minute or minutes be allowed the speaker. If translation (other than simultaneous) is required, sufficient additional time shall be allowed by the Chairman.

(*h*) Those voting with the minority may have their names recorded. Those who abstain from voting may, if they wish, have the fact and number of abstentions recorded.

(*j*) Those who desire to speak for or against a main proposal before the Assembly must hand to the Secretary, as early as possible, cards with their names, the capacity in which they are attending the Assembly, their church connection, and whether they desire to support or oppose the motion. Those who wish to propose amendments shall follow the same rule, adding on the card precise information as to the part of the resolution they desire to amend. Those who wish to amend an amendment or to discuss an amendment already proposed shall stand in their places for recognition by the Chairman. The mover of an amendment and a representative of the committee reporting shall be allowed additional final statements in this order before the vote on each amendment is taken.

(*k*) A motion to close the debate in order to proceed immediately to vote on the pending amendments and on the main question shall be in order when admitted by the Chairman. The Secretary shall be asked to report to the Assembly the names of delegates still desiring to be heard and the names of delegates whose proposed amendments have not been heard, after which the Chairman shall ask the Assembly, 'shall the Assembly now conclude the matter before it?' The Chairman shall put the question to the Assembly, without debate, when it has been moved and seconded or when he judges that the Assembly desires to conclude the matter before it. If two-thirds of the delegates present and voting agree, the vote or votes shall be taken without further debate.

(*m*) Any member may submit a point of order or procedure to the Chairman, and may, if necessary, interrupt a speaker for the purpose.

(*n*) Voting shall be by show of hands or by standing unless otherwise decided by vote of the Assembly. The Chairman shall read the motion immediately before any vote is taken. He shall first ask those in favour of the motion to vote, and then those opposed. The Chairman may, if he thinks fit, appoint members or staff to act as tellers, and he shall do so in case of doubt as to the result of the vote. A majority of those voting shall determine the decision except as may be otherwise provided in these rules. When the Assembly is equally divided, the motion shall be regarded as defeated.

If a motion for a vote by written ballot is proposed and seconded, the Chairman shall put this motion to the vote without further debate. A simple majority of those present and voting shall decide the issue.

(*o*) The three official languages are English, French and German. A speech made in any one of these languages shall, if desired, be translated into the other two. It shall be the duty of the Secretary to make arrangements for such translation. A member may speak in a language other than English, French, or German on condition that he arrange for the translation of his speech into one of the three official languages. If the Chairman shall judge that injustice has been done to a member by the strict application of these Rules of Debate due to the business having been done too quickly for comprehension in a language other than that of the member, the Chairman may suspend the strict application of the rules to allow reconsideration, motions, amendments, or speeches that would otherwise be out of order.

6. *Deliberative sessions*

The Assembly shall sit in deliberative session when resolutions or reports are before it which are of such a theological or general policy nature that in the judgment of the Executive Committee or the Business Committee they ought not to be amended in so large a body as an Assembly. A body reporting shall indicate to the Business Committee its preference regarding procedures. The reports of sections shall be debated in deliberative session.

The Special Rules of Debate for the Assembly in deliberate session are the same as those for the Assembly in business session, except that provisions 5 (*a*), (*b*), (*f*), (*g*), and (*h*) shall not apply, and that the following additional rules shall be in effect:

(*a*) The only recommendation that shall be in order from committees or sections reporting is that the Assembly approve the substance of the document, and commend it to the churches for study and appropriate action.

(*b*) The only motions from the floor that are in order are: (i) to refer back to the committee with instructions to consider whether a new or different empasis or emphases shall be included by the committee in their report, or (ii) to instruct the committee to provide for an open hearing or an additional open hearing on the report before bringing it again to the Assembly.

(*c*) Those who desire to speak on the resolution or report before the Assembly must hand to the Secretary, as early as possible, cards with their names, the capacity in which they are attending the Assembly and their Church connection, and whether they desire to speak to the report as a whole or to a particular section or sections thereof.

(*d*) Those who desire to propose either of the motions allowed in Rule (*b*) above must add this information on their card when sent forward, or else their motion shall be out of order. The Chairman, in introducing them shall indicate that a motion is to be moved.

(*e*) Speeches shall ordinarily be limited to ten minutes. The bell shall be rung at the end of eight minutes and again two minutes later and the speaker shall then sit down unless the Chairman proposes and receives consent that an additional minute or minutes be allowed. When the number of those desiring to speak is large, the Chairman may ask the Assembly to agree to a shorter time. When translation (other than simultaneous) is required, sufficient additional time shall be allowed by the Chairman.

(*f*) Rule 5 (*k*) shall be followed so far as it applies to close the debate.

(*g*) Those voting with the minority may have their names recorded. Those who abstain from voting, may, if they wish, have the fact and number of abstentions recorded.

7. *The Central Committee*

The Central Committee shall ordinarily sit in business session and these rules shall be followed except that Rules 5 (*g*) (length of speeches) and (*j*) (handing in name cards) shall only apply when it is so decided by the Central Committee itself. If on recommendation of the Executive Committee the Central Committee shall agree to sit in a general or deliberative session, the rules for these sessions shall be the same as the rules for the Assembly in general session or deliberative session, except that Rules 6 (*c*), (*d*), (*e*), and (*f*) shall not apply.

XV. Amendments

Amendments to these Rules may be moved at any meeting of the Assembly or at any meeting of the Central Committee by any member and may be adopted by a two-thirds majority of those present and voting, except that no alteration in Rules I, V and XV shall come into effect until it has been confirmed by the Assembly. Notice of a proposal to make any such amendment shall be given in writing at least twenty-four hours before the meeting of the Assembly or Central Committee at which it is to be moved.

GENERAL INDEX